Critical Essays on John Edgar Wideman

Critical Essays on

John
Edgar Wideman

EDITED BY
BONNIE TUSMITH
AND
KEITH E. BYERMAN

The University of Tennessee Press / Knoxville

Copyright © 2006 by The University of Tennessee Press / Knoxville
All Rights Reserved. Manufactured in the United States of America.
First Edition

This book is printed on acid-free paper.

LIBRARY OF CONGRESS CATALOGING-IN-PUBLICATION DATA

Critical essays on John Edgar Wideman / edited by Bonnie TuSmith
and Keith E. Byerman. — 1st ed.
    p. cm.
Includes bibliographical references (p.   ).

ISBN 1-57233-469-X (acid-free paper)

  1. Wideman, John Edgar.
  2. Wideman, John Edgar—Criticism and interpretation.
  3. Homewood (Pittsburgh, Pa.)—In literature.
  4. African Americans in literature.
  I. TuSmith, Bonnie, 1951–
  II. Byerman, Keith Eldon, 1948–

  PS3573.I26Z64 2006
  813'.54—dc22

                              2005019801

Contents

PART 2. FICTION

Introduction

THE VALUE OF READING WIDEMAN

> . . . PLAY LEADS SOMEWHERE—SO THAT IT'S
> NOT JUST RANDOM. IT'S ALWAYS THE TENSION
> BETWEEN THOSE TWO, FREEDOM AND STRUC-
> TURE, THAT IMPROVISATION IS ALL ABOUT.
>
> WIDEMAN INTERVIEW, *ColorLines*

It is impossible not to quote John Wideman. Oscar Wilde's cynical witticisms are one thing, but Wideman's take on the human condition is something else. Here is one example. In the short story "Daddy Garbage," two black men, Lemuel Strayhorn and John French, fret over a frozen baby that the dog found in a garbage can. How to give this discarded child a proper burial? Strayhorn's shack is bitterly cold, but the men have to wait until dark to avoid getting caught while digging the grave. John French asks, "Ain't you got no wood for that fire?" Strayhorn answers, "Saving it." Given the dire straights in which these down-and-out men find themselves, the words "Saving it" seem especially poignant. With these two words, a sense of human decency is conveyed. Half-frozen themselves, stuck with a thrown-away child, and in fear of the law finding them with incriminating evidence, the situation is still not bad enough for Strayhorn to use up his precious horde of wood. "Saving it" means not giving up no matter how bad it gets—a message to be found in Wideman's writings through the years.

"Jazz riff" comes to mind when one encounters a Wideman story. Seemingly unlikely elements come together, cross paths, and momentarily coalesce through language so visceral that it can be heard when read. So when we ask, "What do basketball, music, and stories have in common?" upon reading *Hoop Roots* we would agree that improvisation—as in, "I'm making it up as I go along"—is the obvious answer. Perhaps because "all stories are true," an African folk saying that the author is fond of pondering, a Wideman story can work like a fun-house mirror, rendering images, physical activity, major and minor events in various forms and shapes: expanding, contracting—now on skinny stilts, then again humpty-dumpty wide. Partly due to this versatility in his artistic medium, his mental dexterity with the written word, Wideman's prose conveys excitement, freshness—lines to be savored and not skated over. In her first encounter with a Wideman novel a promising young writer and former student of mine said, "He blew me away! His writing gave me permission to do things that I never even dreamt of."

Virtuosity is never an end in itself, however. As the author's comment in the above epigraph makes clear, "play leads somewhere." The sense of spontaneity in Wideman's works—including shifts in time, perspective, and diction—reflects active engagement within a complex worldview. No one claims that Wideman is an easy read. On the contrary, the writer challenges his readers on every level. To those who engage his work with the passionate attention he deserves, Wideman delivers one knockout punch after another—passage after passage, book after book. The variety of his subject matter and the versatility of his language bear comparison with the best writers of our time. Wideman can certainly spin a good yarn and entertain us. ("Once you're entertaining somebody then you can also instruct them," he even pointed out in an interview [TuSmith 209].) However, he knows—and feels deeply—that these are not easy times. We don't need another entertainer. What we need, and what Wideman wholeheartedly gives us, are stories to help us survive the times. Wideman's stories are cautionary tales; they are stories that ask us to pay attention. His books alert us to all kinds of dangers, including our own passivity and laziness as readers and writers. Wideman recently said that the job of writers is "to keep the language pure . . . to save it from those who would corrupt it for profit or power . . . to keep it available to all of us so that we can understand our experience and our world."[1] Wideman has done his job so well for so long that he deserves even more accolades than those he has garnered in recent years. If "writin' is fightin'," as Ishmael Reed quips, then Wideman is the heavyweight champ.

"Novels should ask questions," Wideman once stated. "If there are any answers, the answers are examples, a witness of a given life, i.e., a story. . . . That doesn't close down the question. It just means that that's *her* story, it's *his* story. I would rather have my books end that way—testifying to the fact that, if you pay attention to this powerful witness, there's something to be learned from the way he or she approached this question" (TuSmith 207). Wideman's works, whether presented as fiction or nonfiction, explore a host of issues, such as cultural survival, fatherhood, the paradigm of race, sexuality, sexism, faith, psychic trauma, criminal justice, ancestry and family, the black community. They ask difficult questions, questions that many of us consciously avoid or do not take the time to consider. As an American of both African and European ancestry who spent his formative years in what became an urban ghetto, Wideman's familiarity with trauma—with personal devastation and collective loss—is deep and abiding. From this core knowledge come some of the most honest and truthful stories of human experience imaginable. Through the voices of his fictional characters and the thoughts and insights of his diverse narrators, Wideman provides ample "eye-witness" accounts of lived experience. And in the telling, there are always wider circles of connections. An individual may seem alone and isolated, but he or she does not operate in a vacuum. Humans cross paths, impact one another and, if lucky, gain something from their interaction. The storytellers of the clan—Aunt May, Aunt Geral, Mother Bess, and Wideman's mother—keep the family legacy alive. As an accomplished, award-winning writer, Wideman continues to honor this invaluable inheritance from the women in his family.

Make no mistake: a specific brand of literacy is helpful to connect with a Wideman text. Readers who value or are literate in only standard English are at a disadvantage. Having trained himself to be fluent in several levels of discourse—from ghetto-speak to homey black vernacular to formal eighteenth-century English—Wideman's prose calls for agile readers. In response to the charge that the novel *The Cattle Killing* "may have ventured beyond [your] readers this time out," Wideman says, "If you treat a book as an intellectual exercise, if you don't swing with the language . . . then you'll have a very abstract and intellectually alienated feeling about the book. You'll miss the . . . fun parts" (TuSmith 209). The "swing" in language reflects the artist working at his craft. The motto "It don't mean a thing if it ain't got that swing" serves as the guiding light in a Wideman text. The writer is aware, however, of the racial divide as manifested through language in our society. In a review of the critical study *The Signifying Monkey*, Wideman points out Gates's apparent discomfort with "writing himself away from his people":

> Rather than growing closer, standard English and black vernacular seem to be splitting farther apart. Blacks and whites find it increasingly difficult to understand one another. As a man in the middle, Mr. Gates asks questions all of us who write and teach should be asking ourselves. Are we part of the problem? Why is it that the more we learn, the more difficult it is to share it without retreating to arcane, specialist vocabularies? At what point do our words become an irrelevance to the people who nurtured us, whose lives we sought to touch and celebrate when we embarked on a quest for knowledge? (3)

To the extent that ethnically identified writers are mainstreamed based on their ability to write in "standard" English, writers like John Wideman and literary scholars like Henry Louis Gates Jr. must keep their readership in mind. It's painful to produce American novels or critical theory that the folks back home can't read or appreciate, especially if the works are *about* them. Wideman has confronted this problem, I believe, by creating his own brand of experimental prose. In his best writing, sensory perception is key—be it visual, auditory, olfactory, or tactile. Furthermore, by dropping artificial markers—such as quotation and question marks—Wideman has generated a prose that is memorable and unique. For example, in *Cattle Killing* a question often doubles as a thoughtful statement due to the use of a period rather than a question mark. Once we get the hang of such prose, we realize that it *works*. Rhythm, incantation, orality— these qualities are prevalent in Wideman's writing. Whether they engage our ears, our minds, or our hearts, reading works by John Edgar Wideman makes us better human beings.

BONNIE TuSMITH

WIDEMAN'S CAREER AND CRITICAL RECEPTION

John Wideman has not received the attention given to other contemporary writers, despite the quality and range of his work. There is less critical commentary on him than on a number of other black writers of the same generation—including Toni Morrison, Alice Walker, and Ernest Gaines—and other nonblack writers labeled "postmodern." In fact, it is probably his range that has led to the sense that. he is a particularly "difficult" writer. He does not fit conventional notions of the African American writer and yet, in terms of subject matter and tone, he is clearly within that tradition and thus different from white postmodernists. He engages some of the themes—violence, poverty, racism—of the critical realist writers going back to Richard Wright, but does so in a manner that is self-reflexive. Especially in his early work, he draws attention to his connections to high modernism, yet applies that discourse to the social and political realities of black America. In the fictions of his mid-career, particularly in the Homewood trilogy, he embraced folk traditions, family, and history, as did many of the black writers of the time, but again did so in a manner that called attention to itself as a literary device. Moreover, he followed the postmodern method of mixing discourses by blending elements of autobiography with the devices of fiction. In more recent work, he has increased the complexity of narrative in his short fiction, novels, and nonfiction prose. As a brief example, the story "Newborn Thrown in Trash and Dies" (*All Stories* 1993) takes its title and its "facts" from a *New York Times* article. The story is told from the point of view of the newborn as it falls down the garbage chute of the tenement. It blends realistic elements about urban poverty with allegorical commentary on the American political and racial situation.

One way to think about Wideman's position among both academic and popular audiences is to compare him to Toni Morrison. Both began their careers as writers at the height of the Black Arts movement, and both were outside that discourse in that their early works did not advance a nationalist agenda and, in fact, in many ways portrayed negative rather than positive views of black community. (Interestingly, both writers in their third novels, *The Lynchers* and *Song of Solomon*, were highly critical of nationalists.) Neither received much initial critical or commercial attention, though Morrison was beginning to be recognized by the end of the 1970s.[2]

Even in these first novels, it is easy to see the differences that would account for the later patterns of reception. Morrison's first three works emphasize storytelling, with distinctive characters and narrative techniques; moreover, despite the frequent violence—incest (*The Bluest Eye*); child killing (*Sula*); neglect, suicide, and murder (*Song of Solomon*)—there is always an experience of humane enlightenment that occurs at the end of the story to offer hope to readers. In contrast, Wideman's first three books are self-consciously modernist, with frequent allusions to or echoes of T. S. Eliot, James Joyce, and William Faulkner. With literary strategies including word play, parody, stream-of-consciousness, and self-reflexive tone, he is constantly disrupting the storytelling. Also apparent is the despair often associated with the modernist critique of modern civilization. Unlike Morrison, Wideman offers little optimism in these works. In this sense, he could be seen as the last of the high modernists, at a time when literature, and especially African American literature, had moved in very different directions.

While Morrison continues to produce distinctive work over this period, Wideman takes a break from fiction writing to explore the possibilities of a more Afrocentric art.[3] This break of several years enables him to re-engage the resources associated with the Homewood of his childhood, but it also removes him from the literary world at a crucial moment. When he re-emerges in the early 1980s with *Damballah*, *Hiding Place*, and *Sent for You Yesterday*, all of which make use of family, history, and community—the key themes in contemporary black literary production—the field has come to be dominated by the work of women writers.

Of course, with the focus of critical and popular attention in the 1980s shifting to women writers, Morrison is positioned to benefit while Wideman, though receiving positive reviews of his work, is relegated to secondary status. But even if this shift had not occurred, his writing would have been challenging for some readers and teachers of black literature. His stories often discuss storytelling, as in "Lizabeth" and "Across the Wide Missouri," and thus introduce a metafictional element. He repeatedly blurs conventional boundaries between fiction and reality. Characters in the Homewood trilogy are named after actual members of his family, and the genealogical chart that is incorporated in *Damballah* is only a slight modification of the Wideman-French family tree. Moreover, stories like "Tommy" and "Solitary" convey despair over the black community that was apparent in the earlier novels.

Later works, if anything, reinforce the "difficulty" of Wideman's writing. In *Reuben, Brothers and Keepers, Philadelphia Fire, Fever,* and *All Stories Are True,* he continually raises issues of narrative reliability, of the relationship between fiction and reality, and of the role of art in shaping our understanding of racial issues. He introduces the experiences of his brother and younger son, both of whom are incarcerated for life without parole, and revisits the MOVE bombing in Philadelphia as both history and fiction. He discusses aspects of sexuality—gay, straight, voyeuristic, cross-racial—in ways that can be uncomfortable for certain audiences.

Wideman does all of this in a style that is uncompromising, that requires readers to be attentive to the nuances of language and to the full range of allusion across Western and African frames of reference. In the process, he does not simplify the task for the reader through clarifications of those allusions or through social or political nostrums for the quandaries he poses. He is postmodern in his sensibility, but clearly morally and politically committed to certain principles. Thus, his work cannot be reduced either to the gamesmanship of certain postmodernists nor to the ideological solutions of Afrocentrists. What we have, instead, is an artist committed to the highest standards of his art, demanding hard critical work on the part of his readers.

KEITH BYERMAN

SUMMARIES OF CRITICAL ESSAYS

CRITICISM CAN BE A CREATIVE ACTIVITY IN WHICH THE CRITIC DREAMS, THE CRITIC PLAYS, THE CRITIC EXPERIENCES A WORK OF ART AND COMES BACK CHANGED OR THOUGHTFUL OR ANGRY. THOSE EMOTIONS ARE A KIND OF EVIDENCE OR WITNESS TO THE POWER OF FICTION. AND I THINK THE BEST CRITICISM MAKES US REMEMBER WHAT IT'S LIKE TO HAVE A POWERFUL EXPERIENCE WITH THIS MADE-UP STUFF, THIS IMAGINARY STUFF. AND SO THERE'S AN ORGANIC RELATIONSHIP BETWEEN GOOD WRITING AND GOOD CRITICISM. TOO OFTEN THAT

MEETING DOESN'T OCCUR. SO WE KEEP TRYING.
WE SHOULD KEEP TRYING.

WIDEMAN INTERVIEW (1989)

The sixteen essays included in this volume serve as useful guides for those coming to Wideman's works for the first time. They also contribute to the ongoing conversation of the dedicated community of longtime readers of Wideman. The different approaches taken by the literary critics and scholars here both guide readers through specific texts and exemplify the range of critical methods applicable to the author's oeuvre. Taken together, the following essays explore the full scope of Wideman's career and the major features of his fiction and nonfiction from 1967 to the present. The bibliography that follows these essays provides a comprehensive view of Wideman scholarship to date.

HEATHER ANDRADE argues that Wideman's nonfictional techniques, while breaking narrative conventions, do not resort to postmodernist indeterminacy. Instead, all of his nonfictional works address sociopolitical realities from within a black cultural aesthetic, including quilting, the African concept of Great Time, *Ashe* the Nigerian spirit force, and other ethnically specific elements. She applies Karla Holloway's term, *plurisignant*, to theorize Wideman's writing.

JACQUELINE BERBEN-MASI discusses Wideman's third work of nonfiction, *Hoop Roots*, as a "love song" to his implied audience and a paean to sport as a route to self-knowledge and cultural survival. She charts the writer's self-conscious development from his earlier nonfictional works, *Brothers and Keepers* (1984) and *Fatheralong* (1994). Articulating textual clues and artistic choices, Berben-Masi says Wideman's book puts the reader under the microscope along with its author.

GERALD BERGEVIN finds that despite its passionate sex scenes, paradisal setting, and linguistic exuberance, Wideman's 2003 travel autobiography, *The Island*: *Martinique,* is suffused with melancholy. Bergevin argues that the book voices the author's determined refusal to cease mourning, to "get over" his grief—specifically, grief over the history and legacy of slavery in the Americas. This strategy of melancholy operates creatively and politically to keep alive an engagement with the past and, thereby, to clear a space for a hoped-for personal and social renewal.

STACEY BERRY reads *Philadelphia Fire* as a critique of the connection between black individuals and the black community, which has usually been seen in African American writing as a rehabilitative one. She argues that Wideman complicates this notion by pointing to social domination and power that crosses racial lines in pursuit of control of black life.

KEITH BYERMAN proposes that queer theory can be a useful tool in understanding the relationship between modernism and sexuality. In his analysis of

Wideman's first two novels, he argues that Wideman "queers" desire and the body regardless of race, gender, or sexual preference. Desire itself becomes problematic and is primarily of value in pointing to the falsity of racialized bodies and of modernity.

STEPHEN CASMIER utilizes sense-perception theory to discuss "odor and ideology" in three Wideman novels. He builds on this foundation to illuminate Wideman's later fiction and, in particular, Wideman's interrogation of conventional ideas about the senses. Casmier argues that the novelist evokes the sense of smell in ways that counter the mind-numbing and politically pacifying effects of visual and sonic overload perpetrated through today's media technology.

JENNIFER DOUGLAS describes how the narrative technique of Wideman's historical novel, *The Cattle Killing*, exposes the failure of vision that is at the root of America's racism. Douglas shows how Wideman, unwilling to stop at documenting past or present social ills, reinvents the role of the narrator and language to suggest ways that healing can be achieved through storytelling.

TRACIE GUZZIO demonstrates that public history and intensely personal father-and-son stories combine in Wideman's work to undercut conventional notions of truth that exclude and distort human values. Citing examples from both the fiction and nonfiction, Guzzio argues that Wideman's work is an imaginative re-engagement with the past that seeks to rebuild communities and save lives.

KAREN JAHN discusses the ways Wideman makes use of jazz to construct an improvisational voice in *Hoop Roots* that not only plays the changes on the experience of basketball, but also on W. E. B. DuBois's notion of double-consciousness. In doing so, she argues, he offers a postmodern version of black masculinity.

CLAUDE JULIEN proposes the term "autofiction" as a way of explaining the connection between fiction and life story in *Fatheralong*. In support of his reading, Julien points out how Wideman makes use of many of the devices of fiction, such as unreliable narration and self-reflexivity, in relating what is putatively a series of actual events.

LESLIE LEWIS reads *Philadelphia Fire* as a rewriting of James Baldwin's *The Fire Next Time* and argues that such an approach is especially helpful in understanding the metafictional second section of the novel. She shows how, in effect, Wideman updates Baldwin's insights into black masculinity.

PHILIP PAGE, in his analysis of *Brothers and Keepers*, argues that a central tension in Wideman's body of works is the relationship between individuality and community or familial cohesion. In emphasizing the complexities of the Wideman family, he concludes that the text successfully moves from the domination of John's voice to a narrative truly shared between the two brothers.

DENISE RODRIGUEZ focuses on the linked tropes of music and invisibility in *Sent for You Yesterday*. She argues that the novel is a postmodern revision of Ellison's

Invisible Man, and that it modifies the tradition of black urban fiction by transforming black city-space into a source of communal and artistic creativity.

ASHRAF RUSHDY proposes that in *The Lynchers*, Wideman not only struggles to find a language to depict violence, but that he also uses the text as a critique of American nation-building ideas and practices. In contrast to existing commentary on the novel, he argues that the novel is not so much about the failure of a particular act of racial violence as it is an examination of the violence inherent in nationalist projects.

TYRONE SIMPSON argues that Wideman's *Two Cities* utilizes and revises the model of the European *flaneur* to confront the representational crises found in postmodern ghettoization. "*Two Cities* petitions, possibly naively, for a racial politic that seeks progressive control over the black image," he concludes. Simpson's assessment of what Wideman manages to accomplish in terms of representational control provides a helpful critique for the works of other like-minded contemporary ethnic writers.

BONNIE TUSMITH analyzes descriptive passages in several works to demonstrate how Wideman uses visual perception to explore deeply paradoxical ethical and aesthetic issues. In the narrative the writer or his fictional surrogate *looks* (scrutinizes, observes) while the perceived object "shapeshifts" and "dissolves" under his gaze. TuSmith argues that, far from a postmodernist denial of objective reality, Wideman's observer conjures a reality that is multilayered, transparent, and liminal. In this sense, Wideman is a consummate "literary trickster."

NOTES

1. John Wideman made this statement at the inaugural international conference of the John Edgar Wideman Society (October 10–12, 2003, Philadelphia).
2. The MLA Bibliography lists fifteen items published on Morrison prior to 1980, ten of which appeared in 1979; in the same period, only one item for Wideman is listed.
3. This aspect of Wideman's professional life is central to James Coleman's *Blackness and Modernism*, and is the focus of the interview that makes up the appendix to Coleman's study.

WORKS CITED

Coleman, James. *Blackness and Modernism: The Literary Career of John Edgar Wideman*. Jackson: UP of Mississippi, 1989.

TuSmith, Bonnie, ed. *Conversations with John Edgar Wideman*. Jackson: UP of Mississippi, 1998.

Wideman, John Edgar. "Playing, Not Joking, with Language," *NY Times Book Review* 14 Aug. 1988: 3.

Part1
Nonfiction

"Familiar Strangers"

THE QUEST FOR CONNECTION AND SELF-KNOWLEDGE IN *BROTHERS AND KEEPERS*

EUGENE PHILIP PAGE

Throughout his fiction and memoirs, John Edgar Wideman struggles with the tensions between individuality and independence on the one hand and community and intersubjective connections on the other hand. This internal conflict is symbolized in his representation of his two parents: his "mother's first rule was love. She refused to believe she was alone" (*Fatheralong* 51); whereas "the first rule of [his] father's world is that you stand alone. Alone, alone, alone" (50). Wideman, the product of both philosophies, felt caught between them, unable to "maintain a foot in both worlds" (52). His duty was to create himself as a new entity combining his parents' divergent outlooks: "Neither Father's son nor Mother's son, betraying them both as I became myself. My mother's open arms. My father's arms crossed on his chest" (52). Wideman's fiction and his memoirs may be seen as his continuing attempts to work through this double "betrayal," to create that separate self, to understand his (and everyone's) need for both love and independence, community and individuality. As Jacqueline Berben-Masi suggests, Wideman's essential "story is the authorial presence, with its infinite potential to create anew, with its implied roles in relation to waiting audiences" (683).

In *Brothers and Keepers*, Wideman's first full-length exploration of his dominant themes, this familial dichotomy is central to his efforts to cope with his brother Robby's incarceration and its potentially devastating effects on Robby, himself, and their birth family.[1] Discussing the difficulties of trying to write a book with his brother, Wideman tellingly represents his sense of the complex relationship between individual and family. In one sense the family was a buffer against the outside world, providing the necessary protection for each individual: "Your particular feelings were a private matter and family was a protective fence around everybody's privacy. Inside the perimeter of the fence each family member resided in his or her own quarters" (79).[2] The cooperative entity of the family is necessary to allow the individual the freedom to be him- or herself, to cultivate his or her own feelings and identity: "You were encouraged to deal with as much as you could on your own, yet you never felt alone" (79). Both close community and sufficient private space—"quarters"—are needed.

But the relationship is more complex, for interaction between the individual and the family was not merely for the individual's protection: "Privacy was a bridge between you and the rest of the family. But you had to learn to control the traffic. You had to keep it uncluttered, resist the temptation to cry wolf. Privacy in our family was a birthright, a union card granted with family membership. The card said you're one of us but also certified your separateness, your obligation to keep much of what defined your separateness to yourself" (79). Besides the need for the family as a fence allowing the individual the necessary freedom to develop an identity, the family must also be kept sufficiently at bay. Each individual is not simply an integral member of the family but at the same time is a separate entity standing apart, across a gap from the family. One needs protection both from the outside world (the fence) and from the family itself (the gap). Yet, to further complicate the relationship, Wideman asserts the presence of a bridge, across which there is "traffic"—communication, shared emotions, common concerns. Wideman's attitude about such traffic is also ambivalent, for he both desires it and knows that a crucial family duty was learning to limit it, to "control" it. Given these complex structures affecting himself and his brother in their individual identities and family roles, it is not surprising that Wideman describes his relationship with Robby with an oxymoron: "So Robby and I faced each other in the prison visiting lounge as familiar strangers" (80).

In *Brothers and Keepers*, Wideman unravels the nuances of the familiarity yet strangeness of his relationship with Robby, learning to reopen the bridge to Robby and the family, controlling the traffic on that bridge, and at the same time relaxing his control to allow the traffic to proceed in both directions. For Wideman's persona, John, the book chronicles the shift from a relatively fixed and one-dimensional perspective to a much more open and multiple one. John's initial position is focused on primary concern about himself; on his tenuous relationship to the family; on his feelings of guilt, anger, and fear; and on his anxieties about Robby's future. He implicitly assumes that he knows what Robby's imprisonment means, essentially that Robby is dead (185), is "in exile" (193), has become "a nonperson, cut off absolutely from all contact" (187). Thus, John fears and initially assumes that the effect of Robby's imprisonment is to tear asunder the intersubjective web of family connections, to force Robby entirely into their father's philosophy of aloneness, to threaten the fence that is supposed to protect the family, and to render impossible any traffic across the bridge between Robby and Wideman and possibly between Robby and any of the family.

Wideman's depiction of his mother illustrates the dangers posed to the family by Robby's imprisonment. Formerly a person who "gave people the benefit of the doubt" and who "tried on the other person's point of view" (69), she becomes locked in a self-destructive binary perspective. When she realizes that the legal system is not fair and will not "grant her son's humanity" (72), she becomes "bitter" (69) and hateful (72). Losing her sense of the relativity of things like good and evil (71) and her belief in the consoling communal values of the old Homewood (73), she retreats into a hateful monologism of us versus them, which is like "a cage as tangible as the iron bars of Robby's cell" (75).[3]

As Wideman portrays him, John is also vulnerable to this syndrome. Particularly in the early stages of the book, John is nearly overcome with anger, fear, and guilt when he thinks about Robby. He feels "sudden flashes of fear, rage, and remorse" (5), and he is bitter about the white-controlled legal system and its prison in which "what counts are the unwritten rules. The now-you-see-it-now-you-don't-sleight-of-hand rules whose function is to humiliate visitors and preserve the absolute, arbitrary power of the keepers" (43). Visiting West Pen where Robby is incarcerated brings these negative emotions to the forefront. Forced to "become an inmate" (52), John experiences "an instant of pure hatred," followed immediately by a combination of "humiliation," anger, and guilt. Much later, he realizes that "This book is part of the unlearning of my first response to my brother's imprisonment" (222). A large portion of his problems stems from his guilt, guilt for having escaped the inner city, for succeeding in the white world of academia, and for not doing more to help his brother. As a "survival mechanism" (11), he had learned to shut out "disruptive emotions" such as his "brother's predicament," allowing himself the luxury of "willed ignorance" (4, 6). Robby's incarceration brings home to Wideman the price he has had to pay for his escape and his success, for in this family crisis John realizes how alone he is, how isolated he has become from the family community. "Even at home a part of me stood outside, watching me perform" (33). This isolation is potentially destructive: "Believing I was alone made me dangerous, to myself and others." And writing a book about his brother may also be destructive, for, as Yves-Charles Grandjeat and Michel Feith point out, part of the personal effect on Wideman is the risk that in writing the book he may be exploiting Robby, with, in Grandjeat's terms, "all the trappings of an imperialist ploy" ("These" 689) and, in Feith's terms, risking the danger of "incarcerating [Robby] a second time" by "shutting up his voice together with his body" (672).

In the process of producing the book, Wideman shows how John breaks out of his initial confusion, rage, self-absorption, and isolation. He learns to set aside his own ego and to allow the book to become truly his *and* Robby's, a progress repeatedly figured in terms of John's growing ability to listen to Robby. At first, he does listen (76), but not fully, for example "slip[ping] unaware out of his story into one of my own" (77). Much later, he realizes that he "didn't listen carefully, probe deeply enough" because he "knew what [he] wanted" (195), in short because he had his predetermined sense of what *his* book would be. Gradually, however, he does "teach [him]self to listen," gains the capability of "seeing [his] brother on his terms" and therefore "of learning *his* story" (77, my italics). And as John later realizes, "the breakthrough came when I started to hear what was constant, persistent beneath the changes in his life" (199). As a result the book becomes a truly shared enterprise, a true bridging as he is able to integrate his listening self and his writing self: "When I caught on, there I was, my listening, waiting self part of the story, listening, waiting for me."[4]

That statement of John's self-discovery through the process of putting the book together is part of a series of self-reflective comments that intimate several related purposes of the book. The book is an attempt to gain individual freedom for both John and Robby, to confront the fact of Robby's imprisonment with the quest for internal freedom: "So this book. This attempt to break out, to knock down the walls" (18). In the attempt to reconnect with Robby through constructing this text—"Words may help me find you" (34)—John hopes that absorbing Robby's story will help heal them both: "His story freeing me, because it forces me to tell my own" (98). And, in a kind of summary, John asserts that "Gradually, I'm teaching myself to decompartmentalize" (222), that is, not to separate the various facets of his life, not to forget about Robby when he's away from Pittsburgh, to allow sufficient traffic across the bridge.

The form of *Brothers and Keepers* enacts this shift from John's perspective to a mutually shared perspective in which John listens as much as narrates and which makes the volume Robby's book as well as John's.[5] Wideman starts with a kind of disclaimer in which, speaking as writer rather than participant, he takes responsibility for the final text but also asserts that "the voices that speak this book" are the result of his and his brother's conversations. The first section, "Visits," begins with an italicized prelude narrated presumably by Robby and addressed presumably to John ("you know those streets" [3]), which prefigures the later passages narrated by Robby and, implicitly, listened to by John.[6] But the first word of the main part of "Visits" is "I," referring to John and figuring his preoccupation with his own problems. The story begins neither with Robby's crime nor with his plight but with John's learning the news of his brother's crime. And the rest of this first section is narrated entirely by John, recounting his impressions of Robby's visit to Laramie, his memories of Homewood and his separation from it, and his own family's visits to West Pen. Because of John's initially narrow focus, in this first section Wideman allows only John's perspective.

In the second and third sections ("Our Time" and "Doing Time"), however, the form changes dramatically. Reflecting John's newfound ability to listen to Robby and therefore to empathize with him and to understand his identity and his survival in prison, Wideman broadens the narrative form to allow Robby's voice to be heard. Often shifting without notice from paragraph to paragraph, the text oscillates among a variety of points of view. There are brief passages of John's first person narration, as in "My brother had said something about a guy named Garth during one of my visits to the prison" (66). But now there are many passages in Robby's first-person oral style, as in "Yeah. I was a stone mad militant" (114). Often in this mode Robby explicitly addresses John as listener: "Well, that's who I was. I needed to tell you that" (145). Wideman also uses a third-person narrative voice with Robby as focalizer, as in "They are riding in the dark going over their plans" (155).[7] At the beginning of "Doing Time," Wideman includes examples of the notes that Robby wrote to him during the creation of the book, which begin with "*I've decided to write notes to you: thoughts as well as stories*" (169). And at the end of the volume, Wideman gives his brother not just the last word but two last "words." First, he presents Robby's graduation speech, notable especially for its formal style in direct contrast to the streetlike conversational style of most of his previous passages. And then, to reinforce the sense that the book is a shared endeavor, Wideman concludes the volume with one of Robby's letters to him.

These shifting points of view and styles have many implications. Besides illustrating the theme of John's learning how to listen to Robby, they literally widen the role of writer to include Robby—his notes, his poems, his speech, and his letter. By alternating between John's and Robby's consciousnesses, they also enact Wideman's pervasive emphasis on the necessity of a close, supportive, intersubjective web of human relationships. That healing community—sought, often mourned, and sometimes found throughout Wideman's work in Homewood, in Wideman's family, and in countless interpersonal relationships—is called into question by Robby's imprisonment.[8] In the effort to reaffirm the existence of that community, Wideman needs to represent the process of John and Robby's movement from separateness to integration; hence he needs to commingle the roles of speaker, writer, listener, and reader. To reinforce these thematic functions of the book's form, Wideman explicitly calls attention to the form and to his concerns about it. He acknowledges that the first draft was flawed because it lacked "a whole, rounded portrait of my brother" and because he was searching for "a climactic scene," "an epiphany that would reveal Robby's character in a powerful burst of light and truth" (194).[9] In other words, he wanted it to be *his* book, dominated by *his* authorial control with the kind of dramatic conclusion that a novelist might seek. But he represents the writing of the final draft in terms of his realization that he hadn't been listening to Robby, that "no apotheosis of Robby's character could occur in the final section because none had transpired in my dealings with my brother" (194). Instead, he depicts his realization that his brother has survived and has created a viable identity through "the inner changes, his slow, internal adjustment day by day to an unbearable situation" (195). He has learned that the story is not some grand novelistic transformation of Robby but something far more subtle, something that his close listening has finally enabled him to understand: "Prison had changed my brother, not broken him, and therein lay the story" (195). In short, the form of the book had to become interactive to allow Robby's voice to be heard because John had to learn to listen to Robby. By stepping back from the microphone, Wideman allows room for Robby to reconnect to the community and allows for that process to be represented in a shared volume, and at the same time he documents the building of a new and vital connection between himself and Robby. The form of the book has to be dialogic because for Wideman only through multiple perspectives is there a possibility of getting at the truth.

And only through multiple versions. Another of Wideman's central tenets is that stories must be retold and reheard over and over for their values to be fully known, and that in that retelling and rehearing all versions are equally true, a theme made explicit by his titling one of his volumes of short stories and a story within it *All Stories Are True*. In Wideman's oeuvre this is especially the case with the story of Robby's crime and incarceration. In a short story, "Tommy," and a novel, *Hiding Place*, Wideman fictionalizes Robby's crime, replacing him with the fictional character, Tommy, and using in "Tommy" some of the same language as in *Hiding Place*. Another story, "The Beginning of Homewood," is a letter written by Wideman's persona to the imprisoned Robby; "All Stories Are True" depicts an unnamed man's visit to his unnamed brother in prison; and "Solitary" relates a mother's visit to her son in prison and the consolation she receives from her brother after the visit. Keith Byerman, noticing Wideman's repetition of his brother's story in fiction and nonfiction, surmises not only that "the crime, the imprisonment, and the effects on family members are a constant motif in the fictions" but further that "it could even be argued that a primary motivation for the writing is the quest to understand this situation" (x).

Wideman's reworking of this personal and family trauma extends to other fictions in which brothers play crucial roles. In his first novel, *A Glance Away*, the protagonist Eddie is haunted by the previous death of his brother Eugene, whom Wideman names after his father's brother who was killed in World War II. In *Reuben*, the eponymous protagonist imagines a lost twin brother, Reuben II, who "was stolen from his side" (*Reuben* 64) and whom he suspects is now in prison. Like Eddie in *A Glance Away* and Wideman in *Brothers and Keepers*, Reuben cannot allow his brother to be lost forever, needing that brother to complete himself: "Perhaps he'd lost a precious part of himself forever. A loss Reuben needed his brother to heal" (*Reuben* 68). For Reuben and Wideman, brother—real, depicted, and/or imagined—is part of the past that one grieves for and that one cannot ever lose, in Reuben's terms part of the past that "all black men have. . . . Part of you. A brother trapped there forever" (*Reuben* 93).[10]

Thus, the form of *Brothers and Keepers* can be considered both as the internal form of the volume and as an extended form that incorporates the multiple—and, by implication, unending–renditions of the same and similar stories in other volumes. By reiterating Robby's story and the related stories of lost brothers, and by doing so in fiction and memoir, thus blurring the distinctions among those genres, and further by telling the stories through multiple points of view and styles, Wideman repeatedly attempts to weave and reweave the intersubjective web that he finds so essential for survival. His memoirs and stories illustrate the need for such connections on the community, familial, and interpersonal levels; each one enacts the creation of such a web; and, collectively, all the stories about Robby, Tommy, and other brothers constitute another kind of web—an interrelated set of texts speaking to each other and engaging author, narrators, characters, and readers in an extended dialogue about the themes of all the texts.

In Wideman's work as a whole and in *Brothers and Keepers*, this sense of connectedness (his mother's perspective) is always in tension with a contrasting sense of isolation amidst the harshness of external reality (his father's perspective). Wideman's recurring image for the difficulties of dealing with the latter is that of passing through the needle's eye. For example, the narrator of "All Stories

Are True" asserts that the "skein of life" must inevitably be "dragged bead by bead through a soft needle's eye" (*All Stories* 3). But, like a real needle's eye, the metaphorical one is not usually soft, for, in *Sent for You Yesterday*, "When Junebug died, Brother [Tate] had to crawl through the needle's eye" (*Sent* 176), and, in *The Cattle Killing*, individuals must pass through the meat-grinder of life, "the people an unbroken chain of sausages fed in one end and pulled out the other" (*Cattle* 149). Wideman transforms the biblical injunction that "it is easier for a camel to go through the eye of a needle, than for a rich man to enter into the kingdom of God" (Matthew 9:24) into an image of his anxiety that the confining strictures of life often cut individuals off from life-affirming connections to others, thus forcing them into life-threatening isolation.

Even though the needle's eye is a frightening image for Wideman, the image contains a micronarrative with optimistic implications. From some less confined, and presumably more supportive and connected space, the individual is compelled by irresistible forces to move into the constricted space of the needle's eye. In that fixed and narrow space, there is no freedom, no latitude, no community, so, in order to squeeze through, the individual must reduce the self to the point of extinction in conformity to the unyielding external pressures. But the individual does get through, does move through the needle's eye, past the crisis into some third, clearly more expansive, space.

In reacting to his brother's incarceration, John initially assumes that Robby is permanently stuck in the needle's eye. West Pen is presented as a confined space like the needle's eye, dominated by unyielding stones, iron, and locks, and made up of "massive, forbidding bulwarks, crenellated parapets, watchtowers buttressing the corners of walls" (42) and confining cells within it. Entering it as a visitor is for John a stripping-down process of removing his "wallet, watch, change and belt" and metaphorically losing his free self as he is forced to "tiptoe barefoot through the needle's eye" (185–86). At first, John is panicked with the sense that Robby's physical imprisonment means that he is caught forever in the untenable isolation of the needle's eye, and the progress of the book can be seen as his gradual realization that, despite his physical confinement, his brother is not isolated from humanity and does have a viable identity. Wideman, through John, comes to realize that his initial panic was overstated, that his conception of prison was narrowly monologic, that he had underestimated his brother's resilience, and that his understanding of the complexities of the intersubjective web had to be expanded.

The image of the needle's eye is also analogous to death, for, in that moment of passing through the eye, the self endures a kind of momentary dying in which it is cut off from all human contact and in which its identity is reduced to the

fession, and punishment, like the reciprocity of their speaking and listening, is paralleled by their joint roles as witnesses and testifiers.

In the newfound life of Robby's and John's intimacy, Wideman learns to accept what had previously seemed to be nearly intolerable contingencies. He is forced to alter his initial assumption that Robby was consigned to an unmitigated death-in-life and thereby to accept, metaphorically, that human life is a matter of living alongside the presence of death. He learns to allow, and control, a profound traffic across the bridge, not just between himself and his brother, but between life and death. By the end of the book, he has also realized that silence—for example, when it occurs during his visits to Robby—is not a form of intersubjective death, but instead an opening into an even deeper interpersonal connection. Whereas those silences had previously "troubled" him (237), he "learned to anticipate" them, realizing that "Silence does not stretch between us, separating us. It joins us. A common ground, a shared realization that for the moment we've come as far as we can, said what we have to say and maybe . . . maybe there will be more, but there's nothing to say now . . . just wait now for what may . . . what must come next . . ." (237–38). As embodied by the ellipses, Wideman has learned that life is always open—that, despite such iron facts as prison walls, there is room for life and love. He has also learned that the silences mark the inseparability of his and Robby's life and death: "The silence defined our mortality. Our soft individual pasts, our memories and dreams slowly taking shape, making sense, if they ever do, because they must and will form and reform within the iron silence of time" (237). As Wideman more recently phrased it, "silence is a metaphor. A way of thinking about how it might feel to be both creature and creator" ("In Praise" 549). Grandjeat, perhaps picking up on Wideman's thought, sees in the silences in *Brothers and Keepers* "the very site where the text can be released from authorial command to let the Other in" ("These" 690). Words and the absence of words, like life and death, are of a piece—soft and open-ended, yet bound by unyielding exigencies, such as time. Being in that "iron silence of time" is like being in the needle's eye. In *Brothers and Keepers* Wideman demonstrates that, even within that eye, human connections must be found and carefully nurtured and, further, that there are many more implications of passing through the needle's eye than he—and the reader—had imagined.

Notes

1. As James W. Coleman points out, in this first of his memoirs, Wideman "reintegrates himself into the black family and community" (5).
2. Unless otherwise indicated, all subsequent page references are to Wideman's *Brothers and Keepers*.

3. In "Solitary" (*Damballah* 177–89), Wideman depicts the devastating effects on Elizabeth, a fictional representation of his mother, of the imprisonment of her fictional son, Tommy. For a discussion of *Brothers and Keepers* as a quest for a symbolic mother, see Hennessy.

4. As Grandjeat puts it, Wideman's primary purpose is "decidedly aimed at blasting the literal and figurative walls in which [his] significant other—his brother—is confined," and he does this primarily "in a determination to *give voice*" to Robby ("These" 685).

5. Michel Feith describes the book as "a new form of dual autobiography" (664).

6. Grandjeat comments on this presentational paradox: "how can a narrative which is inevitably and ultimately controlled by the writer be turned into a truly dialogic or, better still, polyphonic space?" And, even if it can, he argues further that such a transformation still doesn't solve the problem: "Isn't polyphony the sign of a masked form of imperialism, the outcome of an even more impressive and invasive authorial expansionism, of an almost omnipotent creative will displaying its ability to generate, manipulate, orchestrate and finally rule over the motley crowd of its many and many-voiced creatures?" ("These" 688).

7. Berben-Masi distinguishes three narrators: an "actant-narrator" (Wideman in the book), a "brother-narrator" (Robby), and an "author-narrator" (quoted in Grandjeat ["Division" 174] and cited by Feith [671]).

8. Speaking about *Brothers and Keepers* in an interview, Wideman articulates the primacy of this theme in his work: "Working through a non-fiction book about [Robby], . . . I've been asking myself questions that have to do with how people are connected and what's at stake in these connections. And what, after all, do they mean? That's the meat of the fiction I've been writing. That's the meat of all of it" (Bonetti 61).

9. Feith sees this initial draft as Wideman's misdirected attempt to "fictionaliz[e] Robby into a mirror of the author" (672).

10. See Grandjeat ("Brother") for a provocative analysis of the significance of brother figures in Wideman's writing, particularly in *Sent for You Yesterday* and *Reuben*.

WORKS CITED

Berben-Masi, Jacqueline. "Prodigal and Prodigy: Fathers and Sons in Wideman's Work." *Callaloo* 22 (1999): 677–84.

Bonetti, Kay. "Interview with John Edgar Wideman." *Conversations with John Edgar Wideman.* Ed. Bonnie TuSmith. Jackson: UP of Mississippi, 1998. 42–61.

Byerman, Keith. *John Edgar Wideman: A Study of the Short Fiction.* New York: Twayne, 1998.

Coleman, James W. *Blackness and Modernism: The Literary Career of John Edgar Wideman.* Jackson: UP of Mississippi, 1989.

Feith, Michel. "'The Benefit of the Doubt': Openness and Closure in *Brothers and Keepers.*" *Callaloo* 22 (1999): 665–75.

Grandjeat, Yves-Charles. "Brother Figures: The Rift and Riff in John E. Wideman's Fiction." *Callaloo* 22 (1999): 615–22.

———. "Division, dédoublement et duplicité chez J. E. Wideman." Presses de l'Université de Bordeaux, *Annales du CRAA*, no. 21, 1996.

———. "'These Strange Dizzy Pauses': Silence as Common Ground in J. E. Wideman's Texts." *Callaloo* 22 (1999): 685–94.

Hennessy, C. Margot. "Listening to the Secret Mother: Reading John Edgar Wideman's *Brothers and Keepers*." *American Women's Autobiography: Fea(s)ts of Memory*. Ed. Margo Culley. Madison: U of Wisconsin P, 1992. 295–321.

Smitherman, Geneva. *Talkin' and Testifyin': The Language of Black America*. Detroit: Wayne State UP, 1986.

Wideman, John Edgar. *All Stories Are True*. New York: Vintage, 1993.

———. "All Stories Are True." *All Stories Are True*. New York: Vintage, 1993. 3–17.

———. "The Beginning of Homewood." *Damballah*. New York: Vintage, 1981. 191–205.

———. *Brothers and Keepers*. New York: Vintage, 1984.

———. *The Cattle Killing*. Boston: Houghton Mifflin, 1996.

———. *Fatheralong: A Meditation on Fathers and Sons, Race and Society*. New York: Pantheon, 1994.

———. *A Glance Away*. New York: Harcourt, Brace, and World, 1967.

———. *Hiding Place*. New York: Vintage, 1988.

———. "In Praise of Silence." *Callaloo* 22 (1999): 547–49.

———. *Reuben*. New York: Henry Holt, 1987.

———. *Sent for You Yesterday*. New York: Vintage, 1988.

———. "Solitary." *Damballah*. New York: Vintage, 1981. 175–90.

———. "Tommy." *Damballah*. New York: Vintage, 1981. 155–74.

Figures of Life in Fatheralong

CLAUDE FERNAND YVON JULIEN

I NEVER KNOW IF I'M WRITING FICTION OR
NONFICTION.

JOHN EDGAR WIDEMAN
(TUSMITH *CONVERSATIONS*)

THIS IS THE CENTRAL EVENT. I ASSURE YOU.
WHATEVER MY ASSURANCE IS WORTH. BEING
THE FABULATOR.

JOHN EDGAR WIDEMAN,
PHILADELPHIA FIRE

I COULDN'T DEAL WITH THE PAIN IN HER VOICE
SO I MADE UP ANOTHER STORY.

JOHN EDGAR WIDEMAN,
FATHERALONG

The world creation myth that opens *Fatheralong*'s concluding section, "Father Stories," tells of a place that only exists as each individual imagines it at a given moment—which may suggest that existential reality stands at the heart of the writing as well as the reading processes: figures of life, figures of hurt that have been set in words for others to possibly grasp later from the page.

What is fiction, what is nonfiction? Here is a question that surfaces in most of the interviews John Wideman has given, proving that it intrigues readers and is important to the author who becomes a reader of and commentator on his own texts. Not distinct persons, but facets, functions or roles of the same being who evolves as part of a group. Wideman's *meditation(s)* (*Fatheralong*'s subtitle also fits *Brothers & Keepers* and *Hoop Roots*) pertain to the sphere of autofiction[1] because they nourish and feed from the permeability of the line that separates actual events and feelings from the stories they have given rise to. The author makes no secret of it when he says that fiction and invention (even *poems*, as he says) find their way into his memoirs:

> In *Brothers & Keepers* it's stated clearly that it is a nonfiction work. There may be places in it—well, there are poems in it. There are places where the author is trying to imagine what it might be like to be somebody else. It tells you that. So that the techniques and the forces of fiction enter, and are represented in, what is a nonfictional work. (TuSmith 215)

Reality is an abstraction for which there is little room when writing about oneself, as Wideman does, with full awareness of one's reader as the ballpoint pen slides across the copybook. Wideman wrote the Homewood novels as if they were letters to his brother Robby (TuSmith 59). Similarly, though not under the guise of fiction, *Fatheralong* is ostensibly a personal message to the author's *lost* son whom (although unnamed) he addresses at the end of the preface, "Common Ground": "The pieces that follow on fathers, color, roots, time, language are about me, not my 'race.' They are an attempt, among other things, to break out, displace, replace the paradigm of race. Teach me who I might be, who you might be without it" (xxv). Clearly, the book is not to be approached as the story of *one* life but as a broader existential quest—a revision of DuBois's *The Souls of Black Folk*, a book Wideman reveres. *Fatheralong*'s six sections unfold in three movements: after demonstrating on an abstract level the invalidity of a common ground (a place free from the racial paradigm), the book shifts to the personal level and then concludes that the racial factor is here to stay—a capping stone rather than an epiphanic gesture, as that basic truth informs the book from beginning to end.

My analysis proceeds as follows. After identifying *Fatheralong*'s autofictional dynamics, I look at the way the book connects to some of Wideman's fiction.

Then, moving on to the author's own restatement of his case in *Hoop Roots*, I connect his philosophical stance to our times through Gérard Genette's and Gilles Deleuze's theories on time, writing, and life.

THE DYNAMICS OF A LITERARY CONSTRUCT

Philippe Lejeune's "pacte autobiographique" calls for as much faithfulness to fact as possible on the author's part. This notion is a figment of the imagination for Wideman, who has given *Fatheralong* a deliberately nonlinear form that places it beyond the ken of traditional life stories. Indeed, the book plays with time and induces a feeling of confusion, turning the Wideman persona into a functional character and bringing the terrain—the people as well as place names—into a unified symbolic web consubstantial with its discourse.

Directly following the abstractions of "Common Ground," *Fatheralong* moves onto the personal level. Two parts, "Promised Land" and "Fatheralong," deal with the relationship between John and his father. A middle part, "Littleman," brings up the Wideman family's past in South Carolina. The last two parts, "Picking Up My Father at the Springfield Station" and "Father Stories," deal with the relationship between John and his sons. The book thus seems to lay down a firm autobiography-like temporal basis for itself. However, the "About three years ago my father . . ." that opens "Promised Land" surreptitiously becomes, twelve pages or so down, "Two years ago on the way to the airport . . . "after the reader has been told five pages earlier, "The morning three years ago blends with others, before or since . . ." (3, 15, 10). The Australian aborigines' abolition of time, which will ultimately be developed into a creation myth (177–78), is then introduced on page 21. Such statements suggest the unreliability of memory and shatter the reader's expectation of a stable linear chronology right from the start. While one may at first make allowances for some negligence or flexibility induced by the opening adverb "About," it soon becomes evident that a system is at work—a chronological manipulation that is repeated later as the narration returns to memories of the Greenwood trip while the author is driving to the Springfield railroad station, *followed* by the mental preparation for the Greenwood trip with Jamal *three years before* (145–48; 149). The manipulation begins in "Promised Land" where the reader comes across typographical breaks (materialized in the form of blank spaces on pages 3, 6, 9, 15, 20, 21, 30, 34). These blank spaces suggesting chronological disjointedness are all followed by notations taking up one or several elements of the trip to South Carolina and mentioning Wideman's father and mother, Pittsburgh, the Greater Pittsburgh Airport, the cars (the father's car that does not run too well followed by the unfamiliar rented car) that are variously redistributed in the several segments (Richard 37–39).[2] Rather than a clear-cut sequential arrangement, there emerges a convoluted circularity whose capping stone is a repetitiously involved sentence propped against the consciousness of being hemmed in by winter weather: "Some facts I recall about my father, thinking about him, thinking about writing about him on this November afternoon three years after our trip to Promised Land" (34).

We have not yet, at this point, really left for South Carolina—but here we are, three years later, already back from a trip whose relevance will keep crisscrossing the book, each time completed or looked at from another perspective. Event-shuffling and circularity can be interpreted as a metaphor for the uneasy consciousness that there exists no way out of the American racial maze. Indeed, idea and story dovetail together as the chronological fuzziness consorts with the narrator's contradictory wishes: his not being in a hurry to reach Greenwood (due to moral discomfort) simultaneously denied by his urge to reach his destination to relieve the backache provoked by the "mushy car seat constructed in the American fashion to swallow not support."[3] The reader has learned the hard way what is to be stated later, that history "is not something given, a fixed, chronological linear outline."[4]

The *son* telling the story is not a person but a character in his own right, i.e., a functional cogwheel in a story—a situation which, indeed, applies to all of Wideman's memoirs.[5] Turning to "Picking Up My Father at the Springfield Station," a section of the book whose narrator has not much in common with the considerate son/father in the other parts, will perhaps help bring this into the open.

The text invites passing tolerant judgment on the persona of the *remembered John Wideman* as a mild irritation slowly creeps upon the reader when the character's racial, social, filial, and marital self-indulgence come to the fore. This other Wideman likes to think he is in command while he is in fact the toy, or victim, of oversight, circumstances, and prurient temptation. To begin with, he is a poor organizer who has overlooked his father's need for transportation from Pittsburgh to Amherst and who, at the last minute on a busy weekend, finds a motel that turns out to be a "grubby little place" (131) to put up his sister. Next, he turns out to be the condescending possessor of a Gold MasterCard (not just *any* MasterCard) and a University of Massachusetts faculty ID—in short, a successful citizen who puts the *darker* Indian immigrant hotel owner in his place. Last, he is a narcissistic and proud father who pushes his wife, the groom's mother, back into the wings and calls himself the "master of ceremonies" (172). The wedding is perfect in spite of the organizer's oversights: it is a marriage of transatlantic continents and cultures, a superb father story, a grand success in the American style, a happy end. But the ceremony is not the book's ending, and the whole passage takes on the look of a confession—becomes an exercise in self-criticism:

A little thinly disguised self-destruction, descent into the pit, mud-wrestling. Down and dirty, indulging unreasonable appetites, not only to punish yourself, but rubbing your nose in mud because your nose enjoyed rooting around in the briar patch, the pot of smells where the body's rainbow ends. (160)

As Jean-Pierre Richard shows (59), "Picking Up My Father" does involve self-deprecation arising from the representation of a smug American middle-class he-man, a construct providing a contrast with the hurt of the coming "Father Stories" in which there is precisely no proud and joyful father story to narrate and relate to. Indeed, the "lost" son is the mother's son, conceived (so we are told) for another father—her own. Wideman himself, the anguished and sorrowful father, is deprived. The trip to Greenwood he had organized in the hope his father would pass on to him stories that would allow him to subordinate history to "Great Time" has foiled this desire. The "wall," the "shadow" (197) are unbreakable barriers cutting Wideman-father off from his offspring as well as from his own father. "Little Time" has duplicated deficiencies. Edgar deserted his family; John likes to sneak into the Springfield Mardi Gras striptease show. Can such a voyeuristic peccadillo be seen as an inherited failing? However that may be, the main point here is the ongoing probing of self (i.e., "gender politics" and ethnic assessment: "Was that a fair measure of my racism?" [162]) coupled with the lost sense of place and self, the wish to blot out hurtful events:

I remembered that Promised Land road as I walked alone down that dusty rural track outside the Arizona State Complex Prison in Tucson. My feet were on the road, my mind elsewhere, telling me there is no Arizona, no South Carolina, there are only empty roads like this one, the same road always, going nowhere. (142)

In order to explain the way the book's ending denies the "blank page theory" (95), the wish and need to invent one's own space and time, to build the new world of a nonracial America, we must look at *Fatheralong*'s discursive strategy which turns the Wideman family place, Promised Land, into a mirror that both reflects broken American promises and denies the reality of historical continuity.

The past and the present are declared to be "unhinged" (95). History (or perhaps only the hunt for history) is fraught with absurdity because the photos exhibited in the Columbia, South Carolina, history museum (that were expected to be "A time capsule, treasure trove of cultural history" [145]) are in fact speechless, meaningless objects. There is nothing meaningful about black Americans' past to discover in Columbia. The Widemans have come to tie the generational knot, but are told of a host of visitors who, as they themselves do, realize they are severed from their ancestry. "Ironically," the book says (147), and Richard adds that this blank meaningless past possibly takes on increased value from the coincidence of dates between Columbus's "discovery" in mid-October 1492 and, five hundred years later, give or take a few days, the Widemans' trip to the place of their American roots (44).

There might be a danger, as in any game, in the reader's readiness to conspire with the text and actually read more into it than the author intended. Are those symbolically matching dates a mere coincidence? Or was there an unconscious selection of the date for the trip, as the celebration of Columbus's voyage was ballyhooed long in advance? Whatever the case, *Fatheralong* provides a rich symbolic terrain for the delights of heuristic and hermeneutic plowing. First, there's "Columbia," a name that connotes the hopes for the new world, but also bears the full weight of America's racist past, as advertised by the Confederate flag flown on the state capitol. Then there's "Greenwood," a pastoral name in Shakespeare and Hardy, but also the "*green* place" in Maine that turned into a mother's nightmare (180). A town named "Promised Land" is not on any map and not much of a place when at last found. And, finally, there is cousin "Littleman" ("O, Death he a littleman, /He goes from do' to do'") whose name is passed on in *The Lynchers* to the crippled fomenter of an ineffectual rebellion, but who here helps conjure up the death of history (Richard 45), or the impassable dividing line between the generations.

Consubstantiality between *Fatheralong*'s thesis and story creates a cogent whole based on existential memories but with fictionlike mechanics. Besides, the text's own lifeline creates literary ramifications. The "giant pine tree upended by lightning" (180) metaphorically connects with the "'roots' trip to Promised Land . . . with my father" (148–49), and again with the despair spoken to the roots of the tree, the "messenger to the sky" that possibly echoes Jean Toomer's pines whispering and then shouting to Jesus in "Becky."[6] The family tragedy that crushes the Long Lake people, mother and father alike, is not related in "Father Stories" where parental trauma gives way to the drama of a childhood incident, the stealing and the hiding of all the sets of car keys in the camp.[7] The family's overbearing grief haunts the book's last segment through the metaphorical fire that takes on "the color of blood" and the oxymoronic "water burning" (180) which tell infinitely more than a merely factual account would have.

THE *FATHERALONG* CONNECTION

The personal history message sent to the "lost" son is that no one need be tied down by what people say about them, that it is best to be one's own self because the stories one tells about oneself make up one's own world. Beyond the tradition of the slave narrative—the archetypal fugitives striking out for themselves to shape their own lives, to become what they knew they were—*Fatheralong* revisits American pragmatism.

The cover of *All Stories Are True* is printed in black and gray in a way that subliminally reveals the word *liar*. "Casa Grande" begins with a ten-year-old boy's story of a fantastic extraterrestrial world that transforms into a prison story, converging with "Father Stories" while also remaining silent on the events that brought the son to jail. Included in a short story collection and appearing after an opening text relating a visit to Robby, "Casa Grande" is also a memoir. As a creative autobiographical piece, it is connected to *Fatheralong* by its emphasis on the passage of time in describing the Hobokam (literally, so we are told, "those that are gone"), a Native American culture. Their mysterious ruins are the forsaken and enigmatic remains of a prosperous society that white visitors flock to in the well-meaning hope to encounter otherness, as well as to leave behind, as their vacation ends, the burdens the conquest of the West has placed on their consciences. "Casa Grande" also coheres with "Father Stories" through its water and fire images as well as its humanlike green creatures—some tall as trees, some short and maimed on the desert floor. As far as literary affiliation goes, "Casa Grande" echoes T. S. Eliot's *Waste Land* through the "dry rain" oxymoron, the dust, and the cacti conjuring up visions of stunted men.

Fatheralong can also be described as a palimpsest for "Across the Wide Missouri" in *Damballah*. An identical memory surfaces under different forms in the two books, in a way that discloses the modulations of creation. The "film" of the father shaving at his mirror in "Picking Up My Father" (138–39) first came out under the guise of Clark Gable brushing his teeth with scotch in the story's "The white man at the mirror is my father" (134). Second, the Kaufman's restaurant episode that is described as a wholly masculine affair in "Fatheralong" (38–42) is the mother's initiative (because she needs money to pay the gas company) in *Damballah*. The short story that insists on alternatives (a posh dining room vs. a mere cafeteria—success vs. downfall) and the risk of losing one's way, or of being submerged in unfamiliar territory, must be quoted at some length because "John," the narrator, actually states this mode of the flexible where life becomes fiction and vice versa:

> I am meeting my father. I have written this story before. He is a waiter in the dining room of the twelfth floor of Kaufman's Department Store. Not the cafeteria. Be sure you don't get lost in there. He's in the nicer place where you get served at the table. The dining room. A red carpet. Ask for him up there if you get lost. Or ask for Oscar. Mr. Parker. You know Oscar. He's the head waiter up there. Oscar who later fell on hard times or rather hard times fell on him so hard he can't work anywhere anymore. . . . I wrote it that way but it didn't happen that way because

she went with me to Kaufman's. . . . If I had written it that way the first time I would be kissing her again and smelling her perfume and hearing the bells and steel pulleys of the elevators and staring apprehensively through the back of my head at the cavernous room full of white people and the black men in white coats moving silently as ghosts but none of them my father. (134–35)

So clear a statement of (could we say *demand for*?) creative leeway calls to mind other connections. Indeed, both the memoir and the story connect to *The Lynchers*, where memories of the father at his shaving mirror also surface when young Thomas Wilkerson is haunted by the urge to disclose the "plan" to Tanya, his girlfriend. In that scene, the mirror is a broken one the father brings into the kitchen (rather than shaving in the bathroom where the mother is busy with babies and diapers) (79–81). Characters and real-life people share common traits. For instance, Thomas Wilkerson's father has a good tenor voice just like John Wideman's.[8] Minimal biographical knowledge is enough to tell Edgar Lawson Wideman apart from Orin Wilkerson. But need we do that? Persons, actual or fictional, stand in their own right in the stories in which they appear. Which one of the two Kaufman's episodes is true? The one in *Damballah*, or that in *Fatheralong*? Perhaps we may ask whether any version is factually accurate at all. Maybe a better question would be: Is this obsession with actuality relevant, or merely intrusive? Do the facts of life matter? Does the nameless narrator of "All Stories Are True" who reminisces about his mother's dragging him to Sunday school (9) surface again as a reluctant churchgoing lad in "Everybody Knew Bubba Riff" (67)? If this is correct, then Wideman's voice is the one that takes over from the story's multiple speakers and takes a leap over the years to feel kinship with the revolted Bubbas, grandfather Bubba and grandson Bubba.[9] Who is Bubba, the narrator's childhood "buddy"? Is he a real person? And one now dead? Does the character owe something to Wideman himself? Do we, as readers, need to know the facts? Are the facts more important than the ideas the story's construct of life proposes: the weight of oppression, past and present?[10]

FIGURES OF LIFE

The right to blend fact and fiction is an author's privilege that Wideman insists upon repeatedly, both in private conversation and in practically each of the interviews Bonnie TuSmith has collected. This stance amounts to a personal philosophy, a visceral distaste he harbors for what might be called, for lack of a better term, literary apartheid. At work is an intellectual posture that is also social and that rejects separation:

Figures of Life in *Fatheralong*

If there's anything consistent in the body of my work I think it's that impulse to yoke together those things that other people have sundered. Not only have they sundered them, but they have set up rules that say you can't yoke them together or you shouldn't or it's best not to. Not only has *that* been a dimension of my literary life, *that's* been a dimension of my personal life. (TuSmith 164)[11]

Genre merging belongs in the realm of insistent persuasions. It is a half philosophical and half ontological matter (Who is the writer, who is the character/narrator, who is the person?). Seen from the perspective of racial protest, genre merging pertains to a vision of the world in which there is no room for the simplistic dichotomies that cripple society, for the Manichaeism that infects the minds even of those who are accepted (Should we say tolerated?) on the sidelines of mainstream America. Wideman's introduction to DuBois's *The Souls of Black Folk* is important in this respect because it speaks against "either/or distinctions,"[12] against the impulse to divide the world into us/them, good/evil, rich/poor, white/black, new world/old world, winner/loser categories. In literature, this leads to Wideman's insistence on a land of the "interface": "I like the idea that at times I get sort of in the middle ground between essay and fiction" (TuSmith 170). While this land of the in-between amounts to a literary signifying against all forms of exclusion, it also underlines Wideman's modernity. My point is not to confine the author in a "school of thought," but to suggest his relationship with and possibly interest in philosophies that stress the personal and discount transcendence.

Richard uses Gérard Genette's "figure theory" in *Figures I* as a key to the shifting ground between fact and fiction, although Genette only applies it to the role of words[13] in literary creation. Genette quotes Pascal: "Figure porte absence et présence, plaisir et déplaisir."[14] Beyond duality, Genette is interested in literature's paradox: literary creation or re-creation is an order resting on the ambiguity of signs, based on the narrow but deep interstice opening between two words with the same meaning, two meanings for the same word (221).

When translated to Wideman's artistic practice such as outlined above, "figure" could signal the moment when storytelling breaks away, takes off from factual account, transcends mere recollection to match and carry the purpose of the moment in a world where words emancipate themselves, gain the ability to induce imagination and create their own truth. Indeed, the author readily expresses his awareness of the flexibility and autonomy words and stories enjoy: "Writing lets you imagine you're outside time, freely generating rules and choices, but as you tell your story you're bound tighter and tighter, word by word, following the script you narrate" (*Hoop Roots* 12). The figure concept excludes boundary. During creation, it is the magic moment when language, beings, space, situations, symbols, and textual strategy converge and blossom into a new configuration. It is not a misappropriation of the factual. Fact and creation are not mutually exclusive because, to use Freeda's image about Carl and Brother in *Sent for You Yesterday*, they are "like two peas in a pod" (36). The figure concept also excludes permanence and turns the factual into a potential. For the reader, it is the border where communication comes into its own—which naturally brings in any number of personal and immanent factors for consideration.

While Genette argues from a linguist's perspective, Gilles Deleuze places himself at the ontological level in his essay "La Littérature et la vie." Literature as he sees it is not restrained to relating one's peregrination through real and fantasized life. It only comes into its own when it discovers a strength that transcends the personal, when a force emerges that pushes the author onto the sidelines. To be sure, characters remain perfectly individualized (as distinct as "Doot" is from *Fatheralong*'s narrator, or DaddyGene in *A Glance Away* from John French), but that individuality precisely boosts them into a world that submerges their singularity. Deleuze's preferred writers are healers, healers of themselves and of the world; not amanuenses that spin the fables of a dominant self-congratulatory group, but those restless against the tyranny of unilateralism.[15] Deleuze heads *Critique et clinique* with an epigraph from Marcel Proust's *Contre Sainte-Beuve*, "Fine books are written in a sort of foreign language." Proust did not mean "foreign" as "other" but as an offshoot of the majority language, a lifeline dangling from the dominant system. Deleuze calls this "difference" (not spelled as in Derrida) or "deterritorialization," a rhizome, horizontal thought that makes frontiers permeable.

I have no clue as to whether Wideman has ever come into direct contact with Genette's or Deleuze's writings (although the latter is much better known in the United States than in France), but that is only a half-pertinent question. Deleuze's vision of the fundamental liability of time, of the past as a concurrent creation of the present, follows in Henri Bergson's wake and is close to Wideman's insistence on poetic inflections. But what matters here, beyond theory, is the two men's neighborliness as contemporaries whose thoughts have been informed by the consciousness of disjunctive worlds around them, the world of words and that of life.

Before I conclude, I must mention a classroom reading experiment involving four graduate students. While being given the title story of *All Stories Are True*, two of them received minimal biographical information while the other two were simply given a short story and assumed it was fiction. Strangely, both groups concurred in finding the final episode of the dead leaf blowing itself out of and back within the prison premises a beautifully made-up metaphor. Only Wideman can say whether this tree leaf was brought by the wind of the text or was indeed a whirling unattached element—if his memory cares to or can reach back to the time when there was no story on paper.

         Figures of Life in *Fatheralong*

Richard's thesis is that Wideman's works have been moving out of "little time" into "great time," also called "dream time": " . . . the always present tense of narrative where every alternative is possible, where the quick and the dead meet, where all stories are true" (*Fatheralong* 62). Those very words and ideas first appeared in the preface to the 1992 edition of the Homewood trilogy, in which the use of family and relations (already components, though undisclosed, of the earlier novels) moved into the open. If anything, this essay concentrating on *Fatheralong* has brought out the "poetic" facets of an attitude to life that has consistently informed a body of work whose preferred ground is a world where there is no *either/or* choice—a middle ground where "great genre" frees itself from the yoke of "little genre."

Autofiction, perhaps better termed "creative autobiography" in Wideman's case, is not the narrative of a life but of a self,[16] which accounts for the mingling of fiction and nonfiction. As any paper person is a creation, the autobiographical pact is a sham hiding constant selection and concealment. Creative autobiography involves another very important parameter: the driving forces of the text, the inflections it imposes. It is not simply a matter of going by one's recollections, by what one is/has become at the moment of writing. Creative autobiography points out the limits of the hunt for fact because what primarily matters is the magic created by the words of a self-supporting text, a medium primarily meant to do something for the writer—without precluding social consciousness.

NOTES

1. Autofiction as a literary concept runs the gamut from a *bildungsroman* like Chester Himes's *The Third Generation* to Wideman's "Backseat" in *All Stories Are True*. The term is used loosely here as Wideman's memoirs could also be called *creative autobiography*.

2. Jean-Pierre Richard is Wideman's French translator. This essay is indebted to his insightful dissertation.

3. See *Fatheralong* 33. One might add to this critique a denial of personal development, difference, or preference.

4. See *Fatheralong* 101. Although I cannot say Wideman was consulted on the book's appearance, this reading of flexible history and chronology is supported by the cover of the English 1995 Picador edition in which the face of a black youngster is inserted in the dial of a clock without hands associated with objects harking back to Africa and bondage: keys, a nail whose tip has been hammered into a spearhead, a padlock, and a shackled slave.

5. Although James Coleman reasoned he should not include *Brothers and Keepers* in his study, he calls the "John Wideman" in *Brothers and Keepers* a *character* and places him on the same footing as "John" in *Damballah* and "Doot" in *Sent for You Yesterday* (see Coleman's introduction). Other correspondences can be added. For instance, Bubba (in

All Stories Are True) owes something to Wideman's childhood churchgoing memories, and "Doot" is also in "Backseat" in the same collection.

6. See *Fatheralong* 192. Richard discusses this point (65). The intertextual link with Jean Toomer's *Cane* (8, 13) is my own construct.

7. The author-father's hurt has to do with a sense of lost trust. See *Fatheralong* 182.

8. See *The Lynchers* (27) and *Fatheralong* (142). Instances of crisscrossing between life and fiction come to mind the moment one starts looking. The "Bee Ohh" the novel *Hurry Home* plays with (41) becomes a more literal, and not so unpleasant, B.O. (body odor) in *Hoop Roots* (69). One can also think of the magic street number *7415* on Finance in *Hoop Roots* and on Cassina in *Two Cities*.

9. The spelling of names also varies. The Charlie Rackett in *Hoop Roots* (18) is spelled Charley Rackett in *All Stories Are True* (69). Charlie the rebellious ancestor also appears in *Brothers and Keepers* (22).

10. See Julien.

11. *That* is italicized in the quotation because a simple personal pronoun would have been grammatically functional: a potentially simple subject has been turned into a *theme*. Wideman's posture is made quite explicit in *Fatheralong* through references to social issues: "all these decisions possessed an edge of awkwardness and discomfort for me because they involved exclusion, segregation" (3–4).

12. See Wideman's introduction to *The Souls of Black Folk* (xiii). The idea of an alternative "third world" may have first surfaced in print in *Brothers and Keepers* with words that are very close to those in the introduction: "Your world. The blackness that incriminated me. Easier to change the way I talked and walked, easier to be two people than to expose in either world the awkward mix of school and home I'd become. When in Rome. Different strokes for different folks. Nobody had pulled my coat and whispered the news about Third Worlds. Just two choices as far as I could tell . . ." (Wideman 27). In a way, one may regard *Souls* (especially the final essays concentrating on the psychological aspects of black culture and life) as an intellectual father story. Indeed, *Fatheralong*'s whole point is saying DuBois's hope ("Surely there shall yet dawn some mighty morning to lift the Veil and set the prisoned free" [231]) has not come true —neither for him nor for the next generation.

13. *Two Cities* confirms Wideman's stance on the question of whether remembrance precedes vision, or the contrary (228). Words are traps that Kassima compares to a "briarpatch" or a "tarbaby" pit (204).

14. "Figure encompasses absence and presence, pleasure and displeasure" (my own translation). Genette uses this quotation for an epigraph in *Figures I*.

15. "Literature only begins when a third person has been born that deprives the writer of the power to say 'I'. . . . To be sure, persons in literature are unique, neither vague nor general; but all of their individual traits boost them to a vision that takes them away into an indefinite condition that overwhelms their existence" ("La Littérature et la vie" [13]—my own translation). Deleuze and Guattari apply this stance to protest fiction in *Kafka*, chapter 3.

16. See *Fatheralong* 187 and TuSmith 123–24.

WORKS CITED

Coleman, James W. *Blackness and Modernism: The Literary Career of John Edgar Wideman.* Jackson: UP of Mississippi, 1989.

Deleuze, Gilles. "La Littérature et la vie." In *Critique et clinique.* Paris: Les Editions de Minuit, 1993.

Deleuze, Gilles, and Félix Guattari. *Kafka—Pour une littérature mineure.* Paris: Les Editions de Minuit, 1975.

DuBois, William E. B. *The Souls of Black Folk.* New York: Signet, 1969.

Genette, Gérard. *Figures I.* Paris: Seuil, 1966.

Julien, Claude. "Ecrire aux limites du dire: l'exemple de 'everybody knew bubba riff.'" Schoelcher, Martinique, CELCAA-GRELCA, 2000.

Richard, Jean-Pierre. *Du Négrier au bateau ivre: figures et rythmes du temps dans l'œuvre de John Edgar Wideman.* Unpubl. diss. Paris: Université de Paris 7, 1998.

Toomer, Jean. *Cane.* New York: Perennial, 1969.

TuSmith, Bonnie. *Conversations with John Edgar Wideman.* Jackson: UP of Mississippi, 1998.

Wideman, John E. *A Glance Away.* New York: Harcourt, 1967.

———. *All Stories Are True.* New York: Vintage, 1993.

———. *Brothers and Keepers.* 1984. London: Alison & Busby, 1985.

———. *Damballah.* London: Fontana, 1986.

———. *Fatheralong.* London: Picador, 1995.

———. *Hoop Roots.* New York: Houghton Mifflin, 2001.

———. *Hurry Home.* New York: Harcourt, 1970.

———. Introduction to *The Souls of Black Folk.* New York: Vintage, 1990.

———. *The Lynchers.* New York: Owl Books, 1986.

———. *Philadelphia Fire.* 1990. New York: Vintage, 1991.

———. *Sent for You Yesterday.* New York: Vintage, 1988.

———. *Two Cities.* Boston: Houghton Mifflin, 1998.

Of Basketball and Beads

Following the Thread of One's Origins

Jacqueline Berben-Masi

THE GAME A STRING OF BEADS, BRIGHT AND
COLORFUL. YOU DANCE THEM TO CATCH THE
LIGHT, COIL THEM, LET THEM SPILL THROUGH
YOUR FINGERS, MOUND IN YOUR CUPPED HANDS.
YOU PLAY THE BEADS, OBSERVE HOW EACH TINY
SPHERE'S A WORK OF ART IN ITSELF. TIME'S AN
INVISIBLE CORD HOLDING THEM TOGETHER,
WHAT YOU CAN'T TOUCH, CAN'T SEE, TIME CON-
NECTS GLITTERING BEAD TO BEAD, FORMS THEM
INTO SOMETHING TANGIBLE, A NECKLACE, A GIFT.

JOHN WIDEMAN, *HOOP ROOTS*

Ostensibly about playground basketball and its evolution, John Edgar Wideman's nonfictional work *Hoop Roots* is a love song to an implied primary audience and a paean to an all-encompassing sport. We are dealing with a confessional exploration of the soul of the mature artist who is conscious of who he is—where he came from and how he got here—and desperate to keep in touch with his inner self. The author shares his universe directly with us, now as if they were his thoughts, now filtered through the device of a primary reader whom we must intuit. Textual clues indicate it is not the French journalist "Catherine" to whom the book is dedicated, but an African American lover lost, recovered, and volatile. The final chapter of the book becomes epistolary in a belated letter that hints that there was always another reader intended: namely, the deceased grandmother whose presence overshadows the work. Grandmother Freed adorns the book's dust-jacket photo where she stands with a child—the author's mother—in her arms. The latter, too, is meant to "receive" the tale. Hence, the "love song" is sung with a tripartite primary audience in mind.

That love is filial and romantic in turns. In keeping with this sense of an intimate communication, Wideman maintains a predominantly first- and second-person dialogue. This artistic choice accentuates the sensation of confidentiality and passion: we readers eavesdrop on a private conversation, perhaps put ourselves into the "you" or the "I" as we participate vicariously in the unfolding of the narrative. Experiential, composed of multiple segments, the book advances the basic themes set in the subtitle of the book—"basketball, race, and love"—plus one: the experience of writing. This is a highly self-conscious work wherein how the story gets told is as important as what it has to say. The various themes occur sequentially, but also simultaneously when they overlap in memory and time. Conversations minus the tags "he said, she said"—a trademark of Wideman's style—have the effect of speeding up the exchanges and making them seem less "contrived" or written. They involve the reader by requiring a close following of the communication back and forth as each interlocutor "threads the pill," i.e., passes the ball back and forth to his or her teammate and adversary. A split-second's inattention and the identifying voice is a lost cause, like the pea in the shell game or the ace in the three-card shuffle that street hustlers ply. "Now you see me, now you don't" demands concentration beyond normal reader investment. Yet, read aloud, it makes for a more natural rendering of speech, and adds immediacy to the reader's participation in the event's unfolding.

The prefatory paragraph quoted above explicitly draws a parallel that is woven throughout the book and that we cannot avoid exploring ourselves. In short, basketball is as much a cultural ritual for the African American community as the intricate, patterned beadwork that retraces timeless symbols of the interpretation of life and the realms that constitute it among the Yoruba peoples of Africa.[1] Like beads, it has become part of Great Time: timeless, permanent, formative, defining. And like beads sewn into age-old designs of the cosmos that guide life in the here and now, the past, and the hereafter, Wideman implies that the movements on the basketball court, the apparel, the colors and textures, and the body language are all-determining for a lifetime in a black man's existence:

> If urban blight indeed a movable famine, playground ball the city's movable feast. Thesis and antithesis. Blight a sign of material decay; ball a sign of spiritual health rising from the rubble. One embodying apartheid, denial, and exclusion, the other in-your-face, finding, jacking what it needs to energize an independent space. The so-called mainstream stigmatizes the "ghetto" while it also celebrates and emulates hoop spawned in the "ghetto," discovering in playground basketball a fount of contemporary style and values. Feast and famine connected, disconnected, merging, conflicting in confounding ways, both equally, frustratingly expressive in their separate modes of the conundrum of "race." (50)

On the one hand, the basketball court is an escape valve from the ghetto conditions of life; on the other hand, it is a celebration of triumph in the creation of a counterculture adulated even by those who normally exclude the residents of the ghetto. There is a dimension that goes beyond mainstream's grasp of hoop: the basketball court is also the scene of an initiatory passage from adolescence to manhood, guided by the experts of the game. The initiates are both harassed and protected even as they are tested before being recognized and admitted to the fold. Wideman illustrates the process:

> My father . . . would have taken a prodigy like Ed Fleming under his wing, tested him, whipped on him unmercifully, protected him with hard stares if anybody got too close to actually damaging the precious talent, the fragile ego and vulnerable physique of a large, scrappy, tough kid just about but not quite ready to handle the weight and anger of adult males who used the court to certify their deepest resources of skill, determination, heart, resources they could publicly exhibit and hone few other places in a Jim Crow society. . . . More abstractly applied, the lesson reminds you to take seriously your place in time, in tradition, within the community of players. Ed Fleming and the other vets teaching me to take my time, no matter the speed I'm traveling. Teaching me to be, not to underreach or overreach myself. Either way you cheated the game, cheated your name, the name in progress, the unfolding narrative, told and retold, backward, forward, sideways, inside out, of who you would turn out to be as you played. (54–56)

On one level, battles are waged, and won or lost. The adversaries are racial and/or social discrimination: one must earn and establish a name, a reputation to be known by. The ultimate emergence and dominance of the jungle rules of playground ball in the professional domain bespeak the shift from one set of rules to another, from mainstream's monopoly over the game to begrudging acknowledgment of a different form, more improvisational, jazzlike, individualistic, calculated—and impulsive—rather than team coordinated. In parallel evolution with the author's own coming of age viewed at different periods of his life is the emergence of an alternative form of the game. The latter at last compensates for neglected homage to the long-overlooked role of the black minority in acculturating a homebred sport before its export around the world. That homage gets paid in a lyrical approximation of ghetto-speak—with rhymes, repetitions, and oppositions that suggest a musical theme, a backdrop against which to play the game, a fight song for the fans, a hymn to the heroes. On another, more personal level, this is the social finishing school whose unwritten rules convey the deeper sense of community values, of living together as a civilization. Basketball supplants the novels and films that teach the mainstream its mores and values, its "do's and don'ts," its rhythms of life, its manner of looking at itself in the mirror.

In brief, the basketball sequences are principally about the socialization of the author as youth: his ritualistic trials in the initiatory rite of becoming a black man in America, where the basketball court furnishes surrogate fathers and role models. In contrast, the episodes of the adolescent's patiently watching over his ailing grandmother define his relationship to the female element—running the gamut from male protector, respectful to the nth degree, to male predator of the desirable woman and her body. The two constitute a dual loss of innocence: learning the boundaries and limits, grasping when the latter can be bypassed to enable the necessary maturation of the author-subject. On another plane, the segments about the Aztec ruins at Chichén Itzá and the internal stories associated with this experience compose a single strand: it is the wooing of the ideal love and the struggle to hold on to her, as well as a dream of the self that does not negate the effects of time's passage on the body and mind of the adult-implied author. The preoccupation with controlling all stories told opens onto the question of art itself:

> Art is someone speaking, making a case for survival. The art in our styles of playing hoop as eloquent as our styles of playing music. Art is what we experience, how we feel about being alive. Art's a medium for expressing what's crucial and worthy of being preserved, passed on. What works and doesn't. A culture's art shouts and whispers secrets the culture couldn't exist without, unveils its reasons for being. (230)

In essence, basketball is art: it is a narrative of its own with a clear plot and development. Like jazz, it has its own rhythms and riffs. As a tradition, it preserves the culture. Ultimately, it provides the thread connecting the episodes of this book into a life, an autobiography based on relationships over time with family, game, and art. For basketball, over the centuries, over a lifetime, lets us step out of linear time and into Great Time. It inscribes itself into the cosmic sphere, where Wideman patiently tries to lead us. Basketball is a portal to another universe.

Of Basketball and Beads

In a broad sense, *Hoop Roots* picks up where *Fatheralong* leaves off. The latter work portrays the author through the prism of his male genealogy: the missed occasions for cementing ties between father and son, the tantalizingly missing links and the attempts at compensating for what never happened but should have. *Brothers and Keepers* provides the first installment of John's autobiography based on the relationship between himself and his imprisoned younger brother Robby, but also between all black brothers and their prison guards, whether those brothers are incarcerated or simply visitors. Body language between the two camps communicates the patent demarcation between those in control and those who are controlled. There, too, basketball serves as a channel of understanding between the brothers, a glimmer of hope for change—leading the transgressor back to respect for the rules, back to a place on the team and in society. Wideman is rounding out his personal history not chronologically, nor methodically, but through exploring the formative and defining links most important to his adult life. Although the spotlight shines on another subject, the one we learn the most about in these three books is John Edgar Wideman. The practice is not unique—in *L'Afrique fantôme* (1934), *L'Age d'homme* (1939), and *La Règle du jeu* (1948–1976), Michel Leiris inscribed his autobiography thematically—but it is both unusual and effective as a form. By sharing his hobby horses, the author portrays himself riding them, allowing glimpses of the self that seem more natural, more candid, more complete than if he had written a classic, chronological history. As D. Bergez points out in an article on Leiris, the result of the displacement is a less narcissistic attitude of accommodation and a renewal of the genre as such.[2] It is my conviction that Wideman accomplishes the same in these nonfictional works, making a seamless piece of the three.

Like *Brothers and Keepers* and *Fatheralong*, part of *Hoop Roots* is written in Wideman's "other voice," what he sometimes refers to as his "other language." This is the blend of black English, street talk, scraps of black folklore, family tradition, skipped copulas, noun clauses rather than full sentences—or predicates without repeated subjects—punctuated with grunted expletives like "Uh huh!" or "Huh uh." There is an alternation between the scholarly and the colloquial, creating a linguistic blend that leaves the author's indelible mark on the work. At the same time, the coexistence of two voices allows both sides of the author's being to come to the fore and impress upon the reader a complicity that runs the gamut from the intensely personal to the strictly intellectual, from the women's domain to the men's. For Wideman's agenda restores the equilibrium to the purportedly matriarchal African American family unit by showing its protagonist participating in both domains, being deeply struck by the exquisite, life-catching moments that make up the daily routines of both sexes. Animus and anima are truly complementary, no matter what differences might pit seemingly opposing philosophies.

Hoop Roots works in both directions: on the one hand, it delves into the roots of playground basketball; on the other, it clarifies basketball's role in helping a young man set down his own roots. It expands upon the book's introductory passage, underlining the need for separate interests to be shared at day's end by men and women (1). Between the lines, we intuit that this is a group history, one common to many African Americans. Indeed, setting down those roots is tantamount to claiming one's masculinity and black heritage with the encouragement of the women who surround and assist one. The women's role in John's upbringing (but also that of other young blacks in the ghetto) is germane to the love song the author sings in this book. His appreciation for the women's gifts, support, and understanding inform the intuited lover-reader, hence us as well, about the man courting her. It entices her into his world, implicates her in a social circle to which she is foreign and uninitiated—but not alien in the sense of a deliberate exclusion.

Highly diversified sequences are wound together, much like the grandmother's long braid of good hair. Arguably an African American obsession, that good hair intertwines the dark and the silver, all of it a shining mass offered to the lover like a string of multicolored beads, each hue rich in symbolic values such as virginity, fertility, and magic powers. In microcosm, the visit to Chichén Itzá with the mysterious re-found love repeats this pattern in the stories told by the lovers to mutually entertain and challenge one another, again much like the one-on-one of playground basketball. The true stories exchanged, like all nonfiction, involve the listener and invite contradiction. Between the lines the implied message reads as follows: You tell me a story that catches me by surprise; I one-up you by my own tale. If your story doesn't satisfy me, I recast it to correspond to my expectations and demands. Thus, one bare-bones account goes through four distinct versions or putative approximations of what really occurred. Here, the storytellers act as players in a simulated game of hoop: each tests the limits of the other's strategy, possessiveness, trust, and vision of life. They take on the accomplice-adversary and offer titillating episodes, but neither listener can resist intervening—challenging the teller's sincerity or objectivity. Both teller and listener reveal secrets that invite analysis and unveil deep feelings. Again, here is the indirect approach to the autobiography: we readers observe the subject interacting with others while reflecting upon his behavior and struggling to drop the mask even as he must retain a certain author persona—for the essence of truth cannot be unfiltered or unshaped, lest it lose its unity and impact.

Thus, as autobiographical treatise, *Hoop Roots* stretches the conventions of the genre: Wideman cannot resist revising the mythos of a fact to suit his own aesthetic needs, thereby fictionalizing the nonfictional and raising the text to the metafictional level. Dialogue between the teller and the listener heightens the antagonistic stance. As audience as well as artist in these sequences, Wideman can never drop his guard in the game because of his need to "score a point" on his partner. Why else invert the roles in her story about introducing a dog into an erotic scene—first assuming a macho subtext rather than a feminist reading, and then inserting a historically antiracist theme to subvert the entire anecdote? Her rejection of his interpretation signals the gulf in consciousness, each teller's take on life and time. While she can forget the past, he needs to insert all elements into an overall pattern of Great Time, because the "past is present," as Wideman reminds us time and again throughout his oeuvre. No incident is without universal significance. How a story is remembered and edited forges the links between yesterday and today and solders these links into a continuous chain. Again, as in *Brothers and Keepers*, the reader encounters a self-accusing narrator blaming his own spontaneous behavior for the consequences he has dreaded facing. Dread, guilt, and acceptance underpin the main themes in *Hoop Roots*, for love without betrayal of one kind or another requires a superhuman being. Such a creature's place is not in a realistic, nonfictional piece where the reader can challenge the text's authority, can exert his or her right to an opinion, and can exercise options as a caring agent with a stake in the tale.[3] And Wideman is not indifferent to our having a stake in his tale, as the militant tone of the final pages makes clear. His autobiographical essays are a manifest polemic designed to draw the reader into either collaboration or confrontation.

Deliberately or not, the reader unwittingly dons the garments of "the other" and gradually slips into the "you" of the text. Like twin mirrors, each reflecting the perceived image of the other, we alternate in voyeuristic turns—just like the lovers spinning their tales: "Did I ask you to tell your stories so I could watch. Imagining myself a fly on the wall. Invisible, powerless, watching. Could I bear the sight of you in some white man's arms. A black man's" (124). The lover whose story unfolds is now the grandmother whose scrutinized body reveals her stories, now the younger woman lover. The "you" being spied upon through a crack in the door is also both women—one literally, the other figuratively. Moreover, we readers meld into that "you" in both directions. The author tests us, staring back at our "reflections" of the face he has chosen to uncover, at our reactions that he controls by his "now you see me, now you don't" style. In exchange, we train our vision on the man—relating experiences that are at times his own, at times fictionalized accounts that allow him to increase the distance between teller and tale, to change the vortex from centripetal to centrifugal, from inward to outward orientation. In these exchanges, the rule is the same as in basketball: "There are no shadows on the court. No place to hide. Everybody alone. Vertical" (108).[4] Before such exposure, we each contemplate the other, searching to recognize ourselves in the image. It is hardly coincidental that a mirror motif returns again and again throughout the text—the man trying to catch a glimpse of himself, turning the mirror to catch the other's, watching us watch him, perhaps judge his portrait. But also watching him watch us, gauge our reaction, anticipate our next move. The double mirror he invokes in *Brothers* allows constant surveillance. Meanwhile, he is both vulnerable and in control by choosing the information acquiesced: love and jealousy, sexual awareness and desire, racial identity and militancy— tricks and treats of reading African American culture in its multiple forms.

Admittedly, this book is a quest for self-knowledge in process, a confession that seeks first to bare, then to claim the self in the soul laid naked. So were *Brothers* and *Fatheralong*. As seen above, two voices relate the journey to the center of the man's private universe. I would now like to show how the two collaborate in a specific example. The colloquial style of the italicized first enunciation calls attention to itself and surprises the reader, heralding more intimate communication to come. It implies the reader is part of an inner circle. The more writerly style of the second passage, closer to Wideman's fictional voice, takes successive approximations of the truth to arrive at a precise rendering:

> *One reason I'm telling all this old stuff, the hard stuff and silly kid stuff too, is because it ain't over yet.* (102; italics in text)

> Have I harbored some deep, dark secret. Do I own a face I cannot bear to behold, a mask beneath the other masks that would turn a lover's heart to stone. Nothing so melodramatic, I hope. Rather a reckoning. A slow threshing. Grain by grain I must dig and sift, lift and comb. Not to censor or reveal things I've wished away. Not to confess or beg forgiveness. To see. To name. To enter the room, then begin to find my way safely out. (103)

Note that there are inside voices and outside voices as well. In counterpoint to the adult voices tracing a pattern of proper conduct, which amounts to the internalization of other values, is the adolescent's discovery of an escape route that allows him to be simultaneously dutiful and prodigal. Creating a mental void, inner silence serves as a cosmic portal for safe entry into another dimension without abandoning his post at Grandmother Freeda's bedside. Just as the young author-would-be-ballplayer first watches and plays at a distance, wordlessly, he accompanies his grandmother for days on end in a state of suspended preoccupation:

> The quiet I carried with me from the room didn't fit in. I had to preserve a place within myself for silence, where I could steal away and be alone with it. Quiet a defense and refuge, a refusal to connect with everything it wasn't, couldn't be. . . . If I didn't let the quiet go, I could leave the house and not lose. And that was an immense relief, a freeing, even if maintaining inner silence exacted dues I've never, then or now, learned how to stop paying. (98–99)

Quiet becomes a talisman for acceding to, then hanging on to, what counts most.[5] It is a means of reducing the distance between the I and the you as long as Wideman's lover persona takes precedence over the militant black rights activist. The latter stealthily emerges in the final chapters of the book: temporarily, the context shifts from the first- and second-person dialogue to a third-person narration resembling fiction. Under the title of "Who Invented the Jump Shot, A Fable," Wideman retraces a plausible, perhaps authentic, episode of the adventures of the early traveling Harlem Globetrotters basketball team. Their hectic, one-night stands in the heart of "cracker" America are juxtaposed with the static story of an archetypal ghetto figure, a slightly retarded black man who witnesses a racist pogrom and becomes the victim of a lynching.[6] His portrait is tenderly drawn; his ostracism from the white community painfully depicted. Once the atrocity of this innocent soul's being sacrificed to white racial prejudice has been touched upon, there is no avoiding a denunciation of the general appropriation of all things black by whites trying to make a buck, to rob the blacks, to exert and reassert their dominance. Here, too, is the author assuming his burden of social responsibility, championing lost causes like that of Mumia Abu-Jamal or of Robby Wideman. Instead of saying, "I am a militant!" he demonstrates his militancy directly. The autobiographical may seem to take a back seat to the oratorical, yet the confessional mode does not disappear. In this harangue, the author vents his outrage as if forgetting momentarily that he has another agenda to honor. Yet, he has revealed a great deal of himself even as he tries to recover from this lapse. A handy transition appears to end the digression as the author tosses in an admission: he is perhaps jealous of a ballplayer he and Catherine are watching. He is called back to the present moment and steps out of Great Time to reassume his role as wooer and "confessor," after having stepped up to challenge the evils of racism and the double standards imposed by the many upon the few. Somehow, though, his inner peace seems shattered. One wonders if the explosion is the price he refers to paying for his earlier silence. Or, is it more the turn he takes with the ball, scoring points as long as he can, having at last earned his chance by seizing the rebound from the shift to third-person voice in "Jumpshot"? There is an "in-your-face" quality to the opening and closing lines in that section, mocking scholarly attempts like the present essay to pin down the ephemeral so we can analyze, dissect, and discourse over it. The implication is that the truth lies in another dimension of reality. We university critics find ourselves under the microscope, find our pitiful efforts derided as we struggle with the pregnant silence a work like *Hoop Roots* leaves in our own minds. It seems insufficient to look at questions of voice, form, and style—of social, cultural, and racial grounding. Yet, it looks equally perilous to pursue further analysis and risk breaking a butterfly on the wheel. For such is the true nature of this text: real and imaginary, solid yet evanescent, permanent but temporal, strong and fragile. The book is a true reflection of the dust-jacket photo on its cover: deep emotions that emanate from the slightly faded images which, despite the uncompromising eye of the camera, maintain an aura of mystery.

Notes

1. See Drewal and Mason's *Beads, Body, and Soul.* Wideman prefaces his novel with a quote from this source and intersperses his text with brief excerpts. Read in conjunction with *Hoop Roots*, it becomes impossible not to see the deliberate thread spun between them.
2. On Leiris, see Bergez, 2024–25.
3. Here, we are following various theories on narrativity in nonfictional works, from Northrop Frye through James Phelan, David Lehman, and Eric Heyne. An interesting overview and criticism of the issue and the critics are to be found in a dialogue of three articles published by Heyne and Lehman.
4. "No place to hide" recalls the lyrics of a favorite hymn Wideman evokes in his 1981 novel, *Hiding Place.*
5. See "In Praise of Silence": "Silence times our habits of speech and non-speech, choreographs the intricate dance of oral tradition, marks who speaks first, last, how long and with what authority. Silence indicates who is accorded respect, deference, modulates call-and-response, draws out the music in words and phrases. Silence a species of argument, logical and emotionally persuading, heightening what's at stake. Silence like Amen at the end of a prayer invokes the presence of invisible ancestors whose voices, though quiet now, permeate the stillness, quicken the ancient wisdom silence holds" (549).
6. Like the one encountered by Clement in *Hiding Place* or again in "Loon Man" in *All Stories Are True.* In a September/October 1984 National Public Radio interview, Wideman commented on the inescapable presence of such figures in every ghetto community.

Works Cited

Bergez, D. "Leiris Michel, 1901–1990." *Dictionnaire universel des littératures.* Paris: PUF, 1994.

Drewal, Henry John, and John Mason. *Beads, Body, and Soul: Art and Light in the Yoruba Universe.* Los Angeles: UCLA Fowler Museum, 1998.

Heyne, Eric. "Where Fiction Meets Nonfiction: Mapping a Rough Terrain." *Narrative* 9.3 (2001): 322–33.

———. "Mapping, Mining, Sorting." *Narrative* 9.3 (2001): 343–45.

Lehman, David. "Mining a Rough Terrain: Weighing the Implications of Nonfiction." *Narrative* 9.3 (2001): 334–42.

Wideman, John Edgar. *All Stories Are True.* New York: Pantheon, 1992.

———. *Brothers and Keepers.* New York: Holt, Rinehart and Winston, 1984.

———. *Fatheralong.* New York: Random, 1994.

———. *Hiding Place.* New York: Avon, 1981.

———. *Hoop Roots.* Boston, New York: Houghton, 2001.

———. "In Praise of Silence." *Callaloo* 22–3 (1999): 547–49.

Race, Representation, and Intersubjectivity

in the Works of John Edgar Wideman

HEATHER RUSSELL ANDRADE

YOU CAN PICK UP IN THE PLAYING IF YOU LIS-
TEN HARD, LISTEN EASY ENOUGH, THE CHORUS
SAYING, WE ARE DOING THIS TOGETHER. . . .

JOHN EDGAR WIDEMAN, *HOOP ROOTS*

TO RECONSTITUTE THE DISCOURSE OF CUL-
TURAL DIFFERENCE DEMANDS NOT SIMPLY A
CHANGE OF CULTURAL CONTENTS AND SYM-
BOLS. . . . IT REQUIRES A RADICAL REVISION OF
THE SOCIAL TEMPORALITY IN WHICH EMER-
GENT HISTORIES MAY BE WRITTEN, THE RE-
ARTICULATION OF THE SIGN IN WHICH CUL-
TURAL IDENTITIES MAY BE INSCRIBED.

HOMI BHABHA, "POSTCOLONIAL CRITICISM"

In the work of John Edgar Wideman, words ebb, spill, flow, converge, fragment. At times, there is a sense of complete fragmentation or, more accurately, complex free association. It is this seeming randomness and sometimes radical yoking of apparent opposites that have led some commentators to categorize both Wideman's authorship and his oeuvre as postmodern. The designation sometimes carries with it, I think, an implicit notion that the form of Wideman's work enables a transcendence of what is distinctive—that is, cultural and racial energies and markers conditioning Wideman's corpus. If, however, we step back from the allure of postmodernist transcendence for a moment, we can note that in African American critical discourse, as well as African American philosophical and expressive traditions, there are what Wideman himself might call clear "hoop roots" that ground his most outstanding productions.

What is the nature of these critical and philosophical currents? One might fruitfully turn to recent African American and African Caribbean feminist models to suggest alternatives to the postmodern as a way of understanding the rich variegation and hybrid combinations of Wideman's form and narrative philosophy. In her seminal work *Moorings and Metaphors* (1992), for example, Karla Holloway theorizes about "where and when" black women enter the terrain of literary convention. The answer, Holloway seems to suggest, is that black women writers self-consciously subvert conventions by creating narratives which "strain against the literal narrative structure for an opportunity to disassemble the text through their diffusive character" (59). These narratological montages "strain" against the dictum of Western hegemonic discursive form, de-centering the a priori status of the narrating subject. They are what Holloway terms "*plurisignant* . . . allowing the polyphonic texts to claim the quality of translucence as part of their methodology" (60). Holloway's critical theory provides generative material for interpreting Wideman's textual representations, which are unequivocally plurisignant. In Wideman's works, narrators, voices, stories, histories, myths, imaginations, readers, are woven together, ebbing, flowing, spilling out onto each other's textual bodies and into the body of the text.[1] I use the term "woven" very purposefully. A second culturally informed theoretical model describes the "quilting structure" of form as a reconfiguration of the privileged status accorded fragmentation in postmodernism (Davies and Fido 6).[2] A reconfiguration of "fragment" as "quilt" engenders my subsequent reading of Wideman's work. Such a redefinition fosters the re-entry of materiality: the quilt as literally "material," of course, but also the quilt as an architectonically functional object or objet d'art.[3]

Wideman's writing disassembles most formalistic conventions, but not the use of language itself. The writer tells us, "Long before I met Caliban, I experienced his ambivalence towards Prospero's tongue" (*Hoop Roots* 15). I would argue, however, that Wideman's narratives—though foregrounding the complex-

Race, Representation, and Intersubjectivity

ity of writing in a "world already wrapped up tight in somebody else's words" (*Fatheralong* 15)—resist postmodern indeterminacy. Like Holloway's plurisignance and Davies and Fido's quilt, his narratives insist upon sociopolitical functionality grounded within an endemically black cultural aesthetic. This aesthetic includes African concepts such as Great Time, *ashe,* and African New World *orisha* ideology that provide theoretical frames for understanding the cultural markers, logic, and revolutionary potential of Wideman's narrative structure. At the core of these African concepts is the belief that the imagination is vested with the power to enact social transformation.

Brothers and Keepers (1984) is, I suggest, a plurisignant African American autobiography which foregrounds the convergence of race, politics, power, and the imagination. The narrative quilts together Robert Wideman's involvement in a robbery that results in someone's death and his subsequent life sentence and incarceration. These narrated moments combine with authorial and familial reflections, multiple and unannounced shifts in time sequence, and narrative voice. Grounding all, like the firm starched backing of quilts, is a sharply ironic critique of the prison industrial complex and its impact on the African American community.[4] In *Brothers and Keepers*, personal, intimate, and revelatory tales are woven or quilted with gritty, evocative depictions of prison life—including the rules, codes, and mores governing the incarceration of black male bodies. Wideman writes:

> I wonder if the irony of a river beside the prison is intentional. The river was brown the last time I saw it. . . . Nothing pretty about it . . . but viewed from barred windows and tiered cages, the river must call to the prisoner's hearts, a natural symbol of flight and freedom. (45)

Reading this image against the backdrop of African American literary traditions, one might recall Frederick Douglass looking out at the Chesapeake Bay, at ships sailing on with a freedom he does not possess (Douglass 39).[5] Douglass's recognition of inherent contradictions between the public space of his enslavement and his own innate desire for freedom encapsulates all the discursive and regulatory perversions of the "peculiar institution" of slavery. Douglass's soliloquy is dialectical—and it is existential to the core.[6]

In like manner, the institutionalization of incarceration frames the discursive enactments of *Brothers and Keepers*:

> Although society declares to the prisoner you are no longer one of us . . . the prisoner's body continues to breathe, his mind nags and races; he must be somewhere, something. He wants to know, as we all need to know: what am I? Into the vacuum society creates when it exiles the prisoner, step the keepers. (188)

We are told of the "keepers" for whom "guarding the inmates' bodies turns out to be a license for defining what a prisoner is" (188). The imprisoned body becomes, in paradoxical fashion, the "body politic." In short, if we accept the logic of critic Donna Haraway, bodies "materialize in social interaction" in terms of "siting/ (situating)/sighting(visually marking)." As such, interactive social practice is not, according to Haraway, "disengaged discovery" or, in Robby's case, disengaged spatial configuration. Rather, the coerced and sometimes brutal duality inscribed by the phrase "brothers and keepers" is a coextensively "mutual and unequal structuring" (Haraway 208).

In *Brothers and Keepers* the siting/sighting—or visual situating—of black bodies transcends the boundaries of the cells, biological and institutional, and enters public space inhabited by visitors who also possess black bodies that reflect and reify within the broader social structures of America's public paradigm of race. Thus, nation, public discourse, and private humiliation conjoin, compelling grandmothers (i.e., Robby's) to remove their bras or "go back home" due to a metal detector's "extreme sensitivity" (185). Keepers of the cells, like keepers of the justice system, stand in hierarchical relation to the black bodies over which they exert control. Douglass may well imagine and desire to be aboard those Chesapeake ships, but his existential reality is Mr. Covey, the keeper of his body who arranges his everyday, enslaved reality—so, too, with Robby.

Wideman's subsequent plurisignant memoir is *Fatheralong* (1994). In this work, his self-consciously announced "meditation on fathers and sons," Wideman begins by announcing that "we are in the midst of a second middle passage" (xxii). As with *Brothers and Keepers*, he quilts together a family narrative of African American males who share a specific genealogical line: himself, his father, his sons. These stories are woven with profound analysis of the complexities attenuating the act of claiming "common ground" along the axes of racialized and gendered identities. In his introductory treatise on race, he suggests that even though *race* is a social construction on the one hand and a cultural code on the other— "an essentialist concept or an existential one, depending on the moment"—it signifies (xvi). Fictional or not, Wideman implies that race materializes in the forms of disenfranchisement and exclusion that have historically plagued African Americans. In other words, the materiality of race is marked by the sociopsychic space of "dislocation, violence and loss of life afflicting black communities in America today" (xxii).

It is critical to recognize that by self-consciously juxtaposing his "meditation on fathers and sons" with a framework of race and racism, Wideman invests his personal, familial stories with an inescapable sociopolitical agency. The quilted structure of the narrative is reflected by his assertion that "the *pieces* that follow on fathers, color, roots, time and language are about me, not my 'race'" (xxv, emphasis mine). Here, Wideman cautions the reader to resist reductive generalities regarding black subjectivity, especially attenuating notions of pathology or nihilism.[7] At the same time, black subjectivity is clearly circumscribed by the hegemony of racist discourse. In other words, "the pieces that follow" are located within the context of racism and dictate a reading that is already politicized, and it is the author of the text's introduction who has precisely set these terms of engagement. While the "pieces" may not be about the narrator's *race*, they are certainly intended to deconstruct the "paradigm of race." He has already told us so. The sociopolitical hope of the "pieces" of personal history, which *Fatheralong* will quilt together, inheres in Wideman's admonition that "race—the doctrine of immutable difference and inferiority, the eternal strategic positioning of white over black—can be given the lie by our life stories" (xxii). But can one, in fact, quilt so magically?

Wideman would suggest that one can. In *Imagined Communities*, Benedict Anderson contends that "communities are to be distinguished, not by their falsity/genuineness, but by the style in which they are imagined" (5). As early as his first novel, *A Glance Away* (1967), Wideman demonstrates his preoccupation with the transformative power of the imagination. In his purview, the imagination *is* "the pathway to freedom."[8] The imagination is the place where alternatives to "the doctrine of immutable difference and inferiority" posit new formulations of black subjectivity. In a 1972 interview in which the first three of his novels are discussed, Wideman declares: "the imagination plays such a powerful role in the relationship between blacks and whites in America, which is also a predominant theme in my work. It's not what we are, it's what we think we are" (TuSmith 8). More than twenty years later, Wideman's faith in the imagination is unwavering. In the preface to *Fatheralong* titled "Common Ground," he states, "Our power lies in our capacity to imagine ourselves. . . . [E]nslaved Africans in the New World found it necessary to reinvent themselves, if they were to survive as whole human beings. . . . those are the precise conditions, the awesome tasks confronting young African Americans again" (xxiii). The questions implicit in such faith are: How *can* the imagination function to give "the lie" to the "paradigm of race"? What kinds of "reconfigurations" engender African American survival? Harkening back to Anderson, we ask: What is the "style" in which the imagination can constitute African American community?

Homi Bhabha argues that "the rearticulation of the sign" of cultural identity requires "a radical revision of the social temporality in which emergent histories may be written" (437). In Wideman's writing, this rearticulation, this radical revision of social temporality, this re-inscription of emergent histories, is emblematized

through form. It is through form that Wideman imagines African American subjectivity and community. As he explains in another interview, "Writing, art, is
subversion. . . . That's its power, that's its joy . . . tell[ing] stories, is a form of artistic expression, a form of salvation." He goes on to say that the artist "causes us to
remember that there are sides to the human personality—creative, imaginative
sides—that allow us to escape, transcend, remake, transform . . ." (TuSmith 94–95).
Embedded in Wideman's form of writing are two tenets. First, time occurs cyclically, not linearly. This cyclical temporality disallows or disempowers metanarra-
tological constructs, such as race or identity, to govern discourses. Second, a
quilted form of discourse deployed by Wideman is, at least symbolically, counter-
hegemonic. These two in-forming tenets of his work do, I believe, reveal Wideman's
commitment to liberating hermeneutical processes in the representation of black
subjectivity and community. Further, I would suggest that the materiality-in-
social-action of the two in-forming tenets separate Wideman's innovations from
postmodern experimentation.

I have already argued that Wideman's structural "play" serves a key sociopolitical function that his corollary poetics of expression insist upon. In *Fatheralong*
he offers, I think, formal meditations and instances of his philosophies regarding
time, history, memory, and storytelling—each imbricated with the other:

> Sometimes I feel duration is an illusion. . . . Everything happens only once, then
> everything changes. The notion of duration, of continuity, the possibility of mak-
> ing sense, no more or less a fragile survival strategy. A hedge against chaos. . . .
> The idea that time unfolds linearly in seconds, minutes, hours, years, the terms
> we've constructed to tame it, feels utterly unconvincing. . . . Memory then isn't so
> much archival as it is a seeking of vitality/harmony, an evocation of a truer, more
> complete, saturated present tense. All of this of course relates to personality—the
> construction of a continuous narrative of self. Our stories. (186)

Time, thus, is not linear according to Wideman—it is transcendent. This conception of time resonates with what Wideman describes as "traditional [African and
African Diasporic] indigenous versions of history . . . that see time as a great sea.
Everything that has ever happened, all the people who have existed simultaneously occupy this great sea" (Miller 2). Wideman's philosophy of time reflects the
West African concept of Great Time, what John Mbiti defines as "that ocean of
time in which everything becomes absorbed in a reality that is neither after, nor
before" (22). Mbiti states, "The linear concept of time in western thought, with
an indefinite past, present and infinite future, is practically foreign to African
thinking. . . . [H]istory moves 'backward' . . . from the moment of intense experience to the period beyond which nothing can go" (17–23).

Race, Representation, and Intersubjectivity

The grand narratives of enlightenment, rationalism, and civilization are all quintessentially linear narratives—chronicling the necessary movement from an apocryphal darkness to transcendent light, from unknowingness to certain knowledge, from formlessness to perfect form. Such narratives are metaphorically phallocentric—erecting hard and fast rules—positing fixed constructs regarding Truth, History, and Justice. So, too, are the discourses surrounding "the paradigm of race." African philosophy deconstructs such linear constructions. According to the philosopher Paget Henry:

> [T]he spatial and temporal dimensions of [traditional African] spiritual ontologies are cosmogonic. Time is a durational aspect of the project of the deities. . . . The temporality of divine projects does not follow a linear path. Rather, it moves in a cyclical path. . . . Like time, the view of space is also cosmogonic. . . . Time and space are thus cosmogonic categories that help to frame the project of creation, but do not in any way limit or constrain the creator. (26)

Henry's description of African cosmogony, like Mbiti's "ocean of time," is germane to Wideman's narratological constructions.

If time and space are cyclically configured as a means by which the "universe" is ordered, then the "vitality/harmony" proposed by *Fatheralong* might indeed be achieved by an unconstrained creator like Wideman himself. Wideman's formal practice clearly illustrates how narratives that trace the genesis of an event and its causal relation to subsequent ones are "artificial." At the beginning of *Brothers and Keepers* we find the following:

> You never know exactly when something begins. The more you delve and backtrack and think, the more clear it becomes that nothing has a discrete, independent history; people and events take shape not in orderly, chronological sequence but in relation to other forces and events, tangled skeins of necessity and interdependence and chance. . . . The usual notion of time, of one thing happening first and opening the way for another and another, becomes useless pretty quickly when I try to isolate the shape of your [Robby's] life from the rest of us. . . . (19)

Here we hear distinctive echoes of the African philosophy of Great Time. If history, as Mbiti and Henry respectively assert, is "neither after nor before" but, in fact, as Wideman writes, "an evocation of a truer, more complete saturated present tense," then the discursive form of the historical enactment must adhere to such indigenous diasporic governing principles. Narrative representation itself, in its attempt to *fix* time within a traditionally "real" or "imaginary" construct—or what we familiarly call "textual representation"—cannot occur in a linear, teleological or ordered fashion. Hence, Wideman's critical imagination accounts for the cyclical and "chaotic" narratological structures of his oeuvre . . . not an adopted "postmodernism" and its enlightenment genealogy.

Wideman's narrative construct is designed to compel readers to attend to their desire for linearity and coherence, then purposely thwarts precisely their ability to produce an ordered metanarrative. In the final pages of *Fatheralong* is the assertion: "I'M REMEMBERING THINGS IN NO ORDER, WITH NO PLAN" (184). Elsewhere he has explained: "I demand that readers meet me halfway, that they participate and think and open themselves up to confronting some stuff that maybe they haven't thought about before, some feelings they're not willing to own up to" (TuSmith 144). Readers' frustrated responses to such deconstructed linear narrative schema become integral for textual engagement.

It is during such moments of calling into question expected schema that readers self-reflexively recognize their Western programming. The hegemony of Western linear, cause-and-effect discursive practice is exposed and critiqued. The frustrated reader becomes in this instant an imaginative agent, an anxious talisman toward new identities. Anticipating such creative defeats of readerly expectations, the narrator of Wideman's *The Cattle Killing* (1996) admonishes his "listeners": "no, no my tales are poor untidy things. No beginning nor ends. Orphan tales whose sole virtue is that you listen" (29). Thus, readers are asked to enter an alternative discursive space, a space that relies upon the suspension of conventional Western epistemology. Deconstructing the borders and boundaries of discourse, the imagination becomes, as it were, a writerly site of possibility. Narrative moves from individual talent to a diasporic, writerly communion in storytelling.

Throughout *Fatheralong*, Wideman proffers his belief that Great Time operates as a dimension for healing. The confluence of past, present, and future functions as a sphere where stories and their primacy, tenure, and longevity are contingent upon collective performance. The foreparents' legacies can only be kept alive via the passing on of stories. Life itself rests upon the perpetuation of "father stories." By way of example, he recalls the opening scene of Chinua Achebe's *Things Fall Apart* in which the story of Umofia's founding is told and retold.[9] Of this ritual recounting Wideman writes: "told countless times, countless ways, in each recounting the fabled bout happens again, not in the past, but alive and present in Great Time, the always present tense of narrative where every alternative is possible" (62). Achebe's ritualized creation story can only be understood within the context of African cosmogony. Time and space frame the discursive enactment of the Umofian genesis narrative, but the storyteller is unconstrained in his re-creation.

"Rules," Wideman tells us, "are the anathema as well as the bones of art" (TuSmith 94). What, then, is the function of story within this open-ended context? According to Wideman:

Race, Representation, and Intersubjectivity

> Father stories are about establishing origin and legitimizing claims of ownership, of occupancy and identity. They connect what's momentary and passing to what surpasses, materiality to ideal . . . a symbol of transfiguration, one identity dying into new hope, new life, a new name to be spoken. (*Fatheralong* 62–63)

Within this paradigm of transfiguration and transfusion, stories bleed into one another so that they might breathe life back into the "body politic." Rather than imprisoned by designated and fixed "keepers," the body politic itself is imagined as "community." The naming, renaming, and claiming of identity is participatory and have the potential to "break, displace, replace the paradigm of race."

The revolutionary potential of storytelling opens upon Wideman's wish as articulated in "Common Ground," where he declares that "the paradigm of race is the antithesis of freedom" (*Fatheralong* xxvi). Inherent in breaking, displacing, and replacing is, literally, the writerly and anxiously dislocated readerly rupturing of the "master narrative." In order to give "the lie" to "the paradigm of race," a black subjectivity must be intersubjectively re-imagined. In other words, Wideman's ateleological, achronological, and multinarrated design symbolically redresses the brutality of Western chronology: the paradigm of race which is linear, prescriptive, and predictive. Thus, "the stories must be told" (*Fatheralong* 64):

> Men's stories, women's stories. How they are about blood and roots and earth, how they must be repeated each generation or they are lost forever. If the stories dim or disappear altogether, a people's greatness diminishes, each of us becomes a solitary actor. The fighter fights alone, for riches or survival, or finds himself a puffed-up brawler, a sideshow performer of other people's stories about themselves, if there is no chorus remembering, connecting him to Great Time. (*Fatheralong* 63)

Wideman's formal refusal to create a static counternarrative—to replace linear discourse (the paradigm of race) with an alternative and merely reactive formal construction—is characteristic of his texts' plurisignance. For, as Holloway reminds us, although "the search for wholeness characterizes the critical enterprise within Western cultures" and is "a sensibility that privileges the recovery of an individual (and independent) text over its fragmented textural dimensions," within black aesthetic forms "(re)membrance cannot mean wholeness" (67). Wideman reminds us throughout his oeuvre that "solitary actors" relinquish their transformative power. Hence the critical enterprise for the black speaking subject must be choric, constituted by a necessary plurality.

The rich texture of Wideman's discursive endeavors reflects African American traditions of storytelling within which myth, history, parable, parody, folklore, fact, and fiction exist in synergy. Storytelling functions as a bridge between both past, present, and future and between history, memory, and the imagination. As stated in *Hoop Roots*, "the past presents itself fluidly, changeably, at least as much a work in progress as the present or future" (9). And meaning is only produced via active engagement in the conjuring, production, dissemination, and enacting of stories. In *Brothers and Keepers*, Wideman explains that "words are nothing and everything. If I don't speak I have no past. Except the nothing, the emptiness. My brother's memories are not mine, so I have to break into the silence with my version of the past. My words." Thus, "his story free[s] me, because it forces me to tell my own" (98). Like quilting, the recounting of stories—stories that emerge from a fluid and elemental intersubjectivity—becomes the locus of survival.

I have already argued that Wideman's challenge to the "terms we've constructed to tame" our ontological relationship to the world and to the world of the text is not mere postmodern experimentation. At the same time, scholars may be tempted to argue that the advent of postmodern theory has cleared a space for greater representation of fragmentation, multivoiced narration, self-reflexive contradiction, dreamscape, chaotic narration, and a range of stylistic innovations. While there is some merit to this claim, Wideman's writing is unequivocally informed by a self-consciously assimilated African worldview that has always privileged intersubjective, contributory, quilted modes of textual representation. I have already mentioned the author's use of Great Time. In addition, it is important to recognize and assert, as Henry Louis Gates Jr. does, that theory is not the exclusive or unique "province of the western tradition" (xx).

In *The Signifying Monkey*, Gates discusses the centrality of Esu-Elegbara, the "god of indeterminacy" who "embodies the ambiguity of figurative language" (21). Esu appears throughout New World African literature and philosophy as the *orisha*—"Legba" or "Ellegua"—"the divine linguist." Legba is the deity responsible for standing at the crossroads of discourse, balancing contradictory logics, meaning, and interpretation. As mediator, Legba facilitates communication between humans and gods. A person can only apprehend meaning as it is divined and revealed by Legba. Erik Davis describes Legba's agency in the following manner:

> Legba is always traversing that region of babble, and embodies the hope and the peril of a more open channel. . . . Eshu/Legba can transform the past into "novel utterances" because he knows that the power of ambiguity and the multiplicity of perspective can change the fixed into the free. (6)

While Paule Marshall's *Praisesong for the Widow* (1983) pays homage to Legba by explicitly weaving a Legba-like character into the narrative drama, I would argue that Wideman's narrative structure—its episteme—insinuates the crafting hand of Legba as the force within the text that metaphorizes "uncertainties of explication" and stands, finally, for "the open-endedness of every literary text" (Gates 21). Wideman, one might suggest, is the theoretical genius loci for the type of work accomplished in Marshall's novel. In a 1989 interview, Wideman discusses the "sense of play" related to his own "uncertainties of explication" as signaled by his disruption of conventional narratological structure:

> Well, it mostly means freedom. It means freedom and it means an outlet for imagination. . . . That side, that playful side, the side that says yes . . . I have to cross the *t*'s and dot the *i*'s but maybe every now and again I'll dot a *t* and cross an *i* and when I talk to you [the reader] in the writing . . . I'm doing something for you, I'm also trying to take something away from you. (TuSmith 98)

Legba is the "trickster god," a shape-shifter veiling and concealing while unveiling and revealing. As god of the crossroads, he facilitates the production of meaning through a dynamic interplay between the witness/observer/reader and the work (always in progress) of communal expression itself. The same principle can be applied to the quilt. The quilt is always already more than it appears to be. It is this art form's capacity for strategic duality that fostered its use during slavery as a subversive tool to resist white hegemonic structure by embedding the "map to freedom" within its very cloth, fibers, and cross-stitches. Wideman's "sense of play," examined within the contexts of Legba and the quilt, reifies the revolutionary potential of the canvas upon which he paints black intersubjectivity.

Yet, if a revolutionary potential is to be actualized, the "witness" must be open to the divination, to the work of figuring out what is "being done" and what, by necessity, is being "taken away." One cannot make it safely to freedom without "reading." Universes are for reading. The map is "hidden in plain view" within the quilt. How else would one identify the North Star? This is when theory becomes a freeing praxis. At the end of *Brothers and Keepers*, Wideman writes, "the book will work if the reader participates, begins to grasp what I have. I hadn't been listening closely enough so I missed the story announcing itself. When I caught on, there I was, my listening, waiting self part of the story, listening, waiting for me" (199).

Wideman's open invitation to the reader, to self-reflexively participate in the production of meaning—to read actively, to "go there" in the storytelling process— is illustrative of his commitment to liberating hermeneutic assumptions from their hierarchical configurations.[10] By de-centering the authority of the author and the overdeterminedness of the textual enterprise, he urges readers to seize discursive agency or, at least, to share the discursive terrain as enfranchised participants.

It is here, via his "politics of inclusion" signaled by his insistence upon "reader response," that Wideman imagines African American community. In *Hoop Roots*, his plurisignant narrative of "basketball, race and love," he summons readers to full participation. Basketball—namely, "playground hoop"—becomes a metonym for the active storytelling enterprise suffused with the emancipatory potential witnessed in *Brothers and Keepers* and *Fatheralong.*[11] In this regard, it is necessary to quote Wideman extensively:

> You got to go there to know there. . . . Playground hoop is doing it. Participating in the action. *Being there.* . . . You can pick up in the playing if you listen hard, listen easy enough, the chorus saying, We are doing this together. . . . The medium the message. Fragments of performance suggestive of a forever unfinished whole . . . The context that provides possibilities for the unexpected, the unknown, does not compromise or bully the moments. Playground hoop invented to offer room, become room, to bust open and disappear except as invisible frame for what's in the break. For what's next, for what no one's ever done, ever seen before. Maybe the primary reason the game exists and persists is because it reliably supplies *breaks*, moments a player dreams of seizing and making his or her own when he or she thinks *music* or thinks *basketball.* Moments when weight, the everyday dominoes collapsing one after the other of linear time, is shed. When the player's free to play. (*Hoop Roots* 46–50)

In the interstices or "breaks" in play—the breaks in form, the improvisatory cadences of narrative motion—the reader is given "room" to "dream," room to seize and make the narrative his or her own. With the row of "dominoes" toppled, the reader is "free to play" in the realm of Great Time. The reader is freed to form new configurations of time and space as the "pieces" lay askew in patterns of the reader's own making. Wideman continues: "If urban blight indeed a moveable famine, playground ball the city's movable feast. Thesis and antithesis. Blight a sign of material decay, ball a sign of spiritual health rising from the rubble" (*Hoop Roots* 50). The rising sign of hope is captured in the emancipatory potential of the narrative structure. In other words, if we (readers) can seize the ball, seize control over the production of meaning, then the enduring "paradigm of race" and its material consequences might just be given "the lie." As such, liberation from the authority of text becomes a metonym for liberation from the painful realities of black disenfranchisement, urban blight, systemic incarceration, and genocide. But this means we must pick up the ball—forget "the rules" and play our game.

The transformative power of discourse is affirmed by Robert Farris Thompson, who reminds us that Legba, according to Orisha ideology, is the repository of *ashe. Ashe* is the Nigerian spirit force which is "the power to make things happen . . . a key to futurity and self-realization"—what Wideman constructs in *Fatheralong* as the achievement of "vitality/harmony," and in *Hoop Roots* as "spiritual health." According to Thompson, "a thing, or a piece of work that has *ashe*, transcends ordinary questions about its make-up and confinements" (56). *Brothers and Keepers, Fatheralong,* and *Hoop Roots* all straddle the borders and boundaries of genres, purposely "transcend[ing] ordinary questions about [their] make-up and confinements." In these texts, Wideman strives for *ashe*, calling upon Legba to mediate the discursive enactment, so the transformative "futurity" of African American community might be assured. He only asks that we come to the crossroads of discourse, open ourselves up to the "free-play" of possibility's promise.

The concepts I have discussed in relation to Wideman's writing—plurisignance, quilting, Great Time, Legba, and *ashe*—are not in the last instance meant to stand as fixed contestations of Western hegemony. To argue thus would be to center and privilege Western discourse. Rather, such expressive critical sitings act as viable theoretical constructs whose primacy lie in their potentially emancipatory architectonics. What inheres is their centering of communal "voices": sharing, changing places, signifying, negotiating, traveling, navigating, playing, subverting, preserving, saving. This liberatory and communal necessity is captured by Wideman when he entreats us to "speak these stories to one another" (*Fatheralong* 197). *Ashe.*

Notes

1. Although Holloway is writing specifically about black women's writing, her theoretical apparatus is applicable to Wideman's work, at least in terms of the structural innovations which he employs in his writing.
2. Davies and Fido write specifically in regard to Caribbean women writers, but I would argue that marginalized groups in general often employ narratological configurations which challenge and/or signify on conventional Western discursive practice.
3. For more about the subversive nature of quilting, see Tobin and Dobard.
4. I have written more extensively on the narratological structure of *Brothers and Keepers* in a previous article ("'Mosaic Memory'").
5. This signal moment in *Narrative of the Life of Frederick Douglass* (1845) marks Douglass's moment of agnosticism and fuels his desire to reconcile the social order of the South with the moral order of American idealism.
6. Interestingly, Wideman invokes Douglass in relation to Robby's musical inclinations in *Brothers and Keepers*. See p. 197.
7. See Cornel West's *Race Matters* for further discussion of nihilism within black communities.
8. Frederick Douglass describes his newfound understanding of "literacy" as "the pathway to freedom" in his *Narrative*.
9. Umofia is the Nigerian village that serves as the fictional site of the colonial encounter described in *Things Fall Apart*.
10. According to Erik Davis, Legba is most closely associated with the pagan European deity Hermes—from whom hermeneutics is derived. See p. 4.
11. Wideman constructs "playground hoop"—over and against professional "hoop"—as a more legitimate site of improvisation, resistance, and cultural expression.

Works Cited

Achebe, Chinua. *Things Fall Apart.* 1958. New York: Anchor, 1994.

Anderson, Benedict. *Imagined Communities: Reflections on the Origin and Spread of Nationalism.* London and New York: Verso, 1991.

Andrade, Heather Russell. "'Mosaic Memory': Auto/Biographical Context(s) in John Edgar Wideman's *Brothers and Keepers.*" *The Massachusetts Review* 40:3 (1999): 342–66.

Bhabha, Homi. "Postcolonial Criticism." In *Redrawing the Boundaries.* Eds. Stephen Greenblatt and Giles Gunn. New York: MLA, 1992.

Davies, Carole Boyce, and Elaine Savory Fido, eds. *Out of the Kumbla: Caribbean Women and Literature.* Lawrenceville, NJ: Africa World Press, 1994.

Davis, Erik. "Who Is Eleggua? Trickster at the Crossroads." First published in *Gnosis,* Spring 1991. Online. Microsoft Internet Explorer. 10 Aug. 2003. <http://www.tech gnosis.com/trickster.html>.

Douglass, Frederick. *Narrative of the Life of Frederick Douglass, an American Slave.* 1845. New York, Penguin Classics, 1982.

Gates, Henry Louis, Jr. *The Signifying Monkey: A Theory of African American Literary Criticism.* New York and Oxford: Oxford UP, 1988.

Haraway, Donna. *Simians, Cyborgs, and Women: The Reinvention of Nature.* New York: Routledge, 1991.

Henry, Paget. *Caliban's Reason: Introducing Afro-Caribbean Philosophy.* New York and London: Routledge, 2000.

Holloway, Karla. *Moorings and Metaphors: Figures of Culture and Gender in Black Women's Literature.* New Brunswick, NJ: Rutgers UP, 1992

Mbiti, John. *African Religions and Philosophies.* Oxford: Heinemann, 1990.

Miller, Laura. "The Salon Interview: John Edgar Wideman." *Salon Magazine* Nov. 1996. Online. Microsoft Internet Explorer. 6 Dec. 1998. <http://www.salonmagazine.com/nov96/interview2961111.html>.

Thompson, Robert Farris. *Flash of the Spirit: African and Afro-American Art and Philosophy.* New York: Random House, 1984.

Tobin, Jacqueline, and Raymond G. Dobard. *Hidden in Plain View: A Secret Story of Quilts and the Underground Railroad.* New York: Doubleday, 1999.

TuSmith, Bonnie, ed. *Conversations with John Edgar Wideman.* Jackson: UP of Mississippi, 1998.

West, Cornel. *Race Matters.* New York: Vintage, 1994.

Wideman, John Edgar. *Brothers and Keepers.* New York: Holt, Rinehart and Wilson, 1984.

———. *Fatheralong.* New York: Pantheon Books, 1994.

———. *Hoop Roots: Basketball, Race and Love.* New York: Houghton Mifflin, 2001.

———. *The Cattle Killing.* New York: Houghton Mifflin, 1996.

Will the Circle Be Unbroken?

Jazzing Story
in *Hoop Roots*

KAREN F. JAHN

> EACH TRUE JAZZ MOMENT . . . SPRINGS FROM A
> CONTEST IN WHICH EACH ARTIST CHALLENGES
> ALL THE REST; EACH SOLO FLIGHT, OR IMPROV-
> ISATION REPRESENTS . . . A DEFINITION OF HIS
> IDENTITY: AS INDIVIDUAL, AS MEMBER OF THE
> COLLECTIVITY, AND AS A LINK IN THE CHAIN
> OF TRADITION.
>
> RALPH ELLISON, *SHADOW AND ACT*

Whether he is telling us about his imprisoned brother, the power of black fami-lies, basketball, or urban violence,[1] John Wideman weaves his biography into a postmodern fabric of history, fiction, and music. From the iconic African 'Rion in "Damballah" to the newborn baby going down the garbage chute, Wideman creates voices for his characters to sing their blues. In *Two Cities*, telling their blues story of lost love and redemption enables Kassima and Robert Jones to rally the neighborhood around Mr. Mallory's photos of their lives. Yet in his memoir *Hoop Roots*, Wideman becomes a jazz artist, like the New Orleans jazz bands who turn mourning into celebration. While the dynamic is similar—making music of one's pain to celebrate self—the process is different. Rather than give voice to myriad characters, in his memoir Wideman improvises on representative black male twentieth-century experiences, making them his own. He projects himself into the consciousness of Rastas, the Globetrotters, and Ed Fleming, sharing their perspectives with us. Rather than giving them voice, Wideman uses their experience to voice his own. Even historical events become a part of his story.

Several important essays discuss music in Wideman's writing. In "Fraternal Blues," Ashraf Rushdy explores how Wideman's narrator Doot/John develops the "epistemology of the blues mind" (333) through listening to "the other." He also discusses Wideman's portraits of musicians like Albert Wilkes in *Sent for You Yesterday* and the gospel diva in "The Songs of Reba Love Jackson" in *Damballah* (1981). Albert's art offers listeners a view of their souls, while Reba's great performance emanates from her empathy (336). Fritz Gysin cautions about stretching the jazz metaphor impressionistically in literary criticism. While jazz terms can be applied to narrative, Gysin argues that ultimately the jazz writer dramatizes a tension between words and music (278). Challenging Gayl Jones's premise that orality liberates character through voice, Gysin demonstrates how Wideman transforms the speechless Brother in *Sent* into a jazz artist (281). Using Gysin's argument that jazz writing goes beyond voice, I show in this essay how Wideman has behaved like a jazz musician in composing *Hoop Roots*. With his dedication, epigraphs, themes, improvisation, and structure, Wideman plays on DuBois's *Souls of Black Folk* as a jazz musician plays changes on popular and folk themes. In doing so, Wideman melds African, American, and European narrative into a subjective experience of double-consciousness.[2] Further, Wideman parodies racial stereotypes by improvising on them.

Finally, I would like to adapt the analogy between African American music and writing that Craig Werner develops in *Playing the Changes*. He locates these writers' source in the impulse drawn from the blues, the gospel, and the jazz traditions. Werner defines the jazz impulse as a response to postmodernism: "The jazz impulse (grounded in blues and gospel) engages basic (post)modernist concerns including the difficulty of defining, or even experiencing, the self; the fragmentation of public discourse; and the problematic meaning of tradition. [It] engages the question of how to communicate visions of new possibilities . . ." (xvii). Acknowledging that any choice is arbitrary, Werner likens August Wilson's playwriting to Miles Davis's modal jazz improvisation and Wynton Marsalis's neoclassicism (267–77). For me, the aesthetic dimension of Werner's definition illustrates how Wideman's memoir writing signifies on Thelonious Monk's unique composing. In his essay riffing on the silence of Monk, Wideman evokes how the spaces between the sounds define the music (112). In *Hoop Roots* the spaces Wideman leaves in his biography testify to the significance of his basketball career. Again like Monk, Wideman's style transforms all the characters from his biography and history in *Hoop Roots*; they are voiced through his shifting narrative identity. Like Monk's intricate play with a single melody, Wideman exploits simple narratives for their possibilities. Finally, his rhythms are pronounced, again like Monk, playing off beat in a deliberately idiosyncratic manner. Perhaps he has another jazz musician or a composite in mind, but for me Wideman's jazzing story in *Hoop Roots* plays the changes like Monk.

Wideman's writing performs musically like jazz: rhythm is pronounced and diverse, euphony is achieved, repetition is exploited, and voice sounds each character as if he were an instrument. Wideman has always sweetened the challenge of grappling with his themes with "a sensuous, rhythmic experience of language that has a . . . primal appeal" (TuSmith 209). At that level language is a "kind of song" (TuSmith 125). But in *Hoop Roots* Wideman also asserts the primacy of music: "Music carved space . . . usher[ed] in a transcendent reality," most importantly because it integrates body, mind, and spirit. Wideman's prose signifies on African American music: "Transcendent, okay, but better to say music opened me—up and down and all around . . . African people . . . the songs they sang, the rhythms thumped on drums . . . the whole body's bump and glide, lift and fall through air" (15–16). Later Wideman melds music and basketball:

> Great Time your chance to be. To get down. Out. To do it right. Right on time. The game, again like gospel music, propagates rhythm, a flow and go, a back beat you can tune into so time's lonely featureless stretch feels as charged, as sensuous, as accessible a medium as wind or water. You don't really own game time, but the fit feels so close to perfect you can't help believing on occasion it belongs to you. (57)

In the telling—its alliteration, assonance, duple meter, and syncopation—the subject has been jazzed. Finally he gathers up all the basketball players in a ritual: "Performing the ring shout we taught ourselves to shapeshift, conduct our spirits to a region where they could heal themselves, grow strong again, recall and enact their rootedness" (242).

Sometimes Wideman's texts abandon narrative sufficiently to qualify as jazz writing, typically, as Gysin defines it, "free form, automatic performance, or privileging of the musical over narrative" (281). However, no matter how polyvocal and fragmentary, Wideman's stories make meaning. Wideman plays with narrative rules, he has noted, as "the jazz musician interrogates traditional, conventional music" (TuSmith 150).[3] Rather than give voice to all the characters, in *Hoop Roots* Wideman makes them his own.

play with them to be free to learn hoop. Each trip to the playground requires a dance to persuade the watching women that he's obeying their rules (26–32). Note how the circles used to describe his first exposure to basketball reverberate: "I felt comfortably invisible, a ghost who glided into view once or twice, only intruding enough to keep the ball out of the street, guide it back to the circle" (33). Surely he's signifying on Ellison with "ghost" and "invisible." Not recalling whether he made the shot, he recognizes that it changed his life (34). Wideman's account also evokes the neighborhood then and now, juxtaposing urban decay with the significance of the lives of its survivors. Like the quilters described by Thompson, his memoir patterns basketball into his experience as circles.

When he gets into Homewood Court, rhythm is sounded as well as figured by the circle: "Synchronicity. You and time in synch. In touch. Rhythm one name for how the touch feels, how it registers, how you can let go and find yourself part of time's flow. . . . You're not counting but the count's inside you, heard and unheard. . . . Gametime opens like your mouth when you drew your first breath" (57–58). Like music, dancing, and storytelling, playing hoop initiates one into Great Time. Wideman reads the hoop as a door into transcendence: "A small, perfectly round hole guarded by a ring of iron opens in the sky." Wideman connects this circle with that of the beads, the craft of the Diaspora celebrated throughout his epigraphs: ". . . time connects glittering bead to bead, forms them into something tangible, a necklace, and a gift" (59).

IMPROVISATION: THE CHANGING SAME, MAKE IT MINE, MAKE ME OURS

According to many jazz historians and artists, improvisation plays with the motif— as melody, rhythm, and/or intonation—to make it new, to surprise the audience with the unexpected, familiar in new clothes. Inverting, fragmenting, revoicing, and styling the familiar, improvisation explores the possibilities of the material, the instrument, and the musician.[7] Like basketball, writing, or love, such play frees the participants as much as their mastery of the discipline allows them to join the game.

Time in Wideman's writing is circular, linking characters through spirit and identity to every other (L. Baker 271). The circle is a fundamental element in jazz improvisation. The break—when the soloist is given free rein to improvise (Murray 211)—and the cut—where musicians repeat for effect—figure the circle as one returns to the beginning to continue (Snead 71). In the section "Learning to Play," riffs of the twelve-year-old John climbing the stairs to watch over Freed encircle his ascent at Chichén Itzá. Functioning like both cut and break, this form high-lights the connection of memory and significance: the circle is created by human consciousness. In "Learning to Play" Wideman surrounds his near-current affair with a long-lost lover with accounts of his watching over Grandmother Freed. Many long passages noting his own and his grandmother's bodies, the smells, textures, and shapes (69–76, 80, 83–87, 101) dramatize their respective rites of passage: puberty for John and death for his grandmother. Later the narrator will identify his confusion of filial and sexual love emerging from this point (105). Each situation uses the ascent to mark his erotic self: the summer he watched over Freed was the summer he first began to play, and, before his breakup, he and his lover had planned to explore Chichén Itzá, the site of the Mayan ritual basketball court, together. Recounted through a monologue addressed to his estranged lover, the climb at Chichén Itzá makes him wonder "*Am I fleeing from you, from myself, from too much love, no love. . . . When I reach the top of the steps, the pyramid's crown, the edge of the sky, eyes tearing, teeth chattering, buffeted by the wind's siren wail, will I remember how to fly*" (93). The archetypal image of African American freedom, flying brings John home to Great Time.

What threatens community is not mortality, for Great Time transcends this, but racism. Color is the primary marker for race, although it is perceived more subtly by those within a group. Wideman undermines color as a marker with the cover photograph of his grandmother Freed holding his mother as a toddler. Knowing Wideman's biography, we may be puzzled that the mother and child look white, that the building looks like a cabin, so that neither seems emblematic of his childhood in the urban black ghetto of Homewood. However, from the first page we are introduced to the people in this picture as they signify for Wideman, and our connection of race with color has been destabilized, much as it is in Toni Morrison's "Recitatif."

In the final chapter, the jazz riff, "One More Time," Wideman evokes Freed's sepia image with his own hoop self: ". . . with you looking ready to play ball yourself, the coathanger shoulders, long lanky limbs, big hands, we could stroll the long way to Westinghouse Park" (237). This path—the safe way she demanded he take and his boy self did not take on his own— reveals his empathy: he'll meet her halfway. In this circle he has deconstructed race and gender, joining his independent hoop life with his grandmother's steady abiding love.

In the dedication in *Damballah* to his brother, Robby, Wideman recalls [Aunt] Geral's name for a watermelon as a "letter from home" (*Stories* 269–70). Elsewhere he has explained that embracing a stereotype disarms its hostility while claiming its cultural truth (TuSmith 97; L. Baker 271). And so Wideman complicates the stereotypes of the black male—that he's shiftless, a stud, a hustler, and a high flyer— through anecdote, voice, and argument. Wideman is not satisfied to challenge our first impressions. He improvises on stereotypes of the broken ghetto family, the black man as vagrant, the neighborhood as wasteland. Although the men—

especially John French and Eddie Wideman—are gone, their presence and significance is re-created through the storytelling of the women. Although the men
often spend much of their time hanging out, they had struggled to patch together
enough menial jobs to support their families. Although the decaying Homewood
section provides little comfort for its denizens, the playground is a center for recognizing oneself in community. Such improvisation reveals reality.

Even the men testify to community. Wideman renders his meeting with Ed
Fleming at the neighborhood funeral parlor to reflect their respective losses—for
each mourns a young black relative—and triumphs—for each belongs to the
chain of Homewood Court players who mentor and dominate each successive
generation (39–46; 51–56). Part of this chain is imagining how Ed's interaction
with John may have been tempered by Eddie Wideman's treatment of Ed. What
goes around comes around. Like the jazz artist, Wideman has played the changes
on "will the circle be unbroken" into a complex circle, a momentary but ever reforming stay against confusion.[8]

Wideman names two sets of people associated with basketball: the Harlem
Globetrotters during their barnstorming days, and two near-contemporaries whose
hoop connections failed to get them out of the ghetto. Knowing their stories complicates the stereotypes about basketball players and hoodlums. Taking us along
with the Harlem Globetrotters, crowded into an old car on the road to debut at
Hinckley, Illinois, Wideman lets us feel their bodies, their excitement, and their
camaraderie. He had to be there to know there. This is historically accurate and
symbolic of black excellence celebrated and exploited in professional basketball.
But the other story, of Rastas, the brain-damaged orphan who is the only black
allowed to live in Hinckley, mythically figures racist fear, loathing, and lynching.
Rastas's life history is rendered as bitterly damning as the Trueblood episode in
Invisible Man. This fable provides another riff on the African American males'
experience of basketball: it venerates or fears as it exploits his masculinity. And
Wideman uses his own history to place this event, apostrophizing Freed to remind
her that all this happened only a few years after her photo was taken. However, as
Wideman's personal testimony reveals, the history of black basketball is not all
success stories.

In "Naming the Playground," he gives us two crippled bodies, the paralyzed
Maurice Stokes, whose need to continue championship play for the Cincinnati
Royals may have led him to a paralyzing injury, and Eldon, L. D. Lawson, whose
diabetes and drug dealing left him wheelchair-bound. These improvisations put
the street basketball success story into perspective. Each testimony dramatizes
how the ghetto has degenerated since Wideman's youth with exponentially more
crime and violence. Wideman learns of Maurice through a friend he encounters
while attending a wake at the local funeral parlor and of L. D. from his impris-

oned brother, Robby. Each man had been a hero in Homewood, a model, in his own way, to the young John.

This narrative challenges the academic question "Who Invented the Jump Shot?" with personal accounts of the odds against someone from Homewood succeeding. Careful to name whites who helped these men, Wideman condemns systemic racism that arbitrarily limits one's pursuit of happiness. Claiming these representative twentieth-century casualties of double consciousness, Wideman weaves his epigraph of Ismene's lament into his experience of seeing the play *The Gospel at Colonus* with his wife and editor. Thus naturalized, Ismene's words—"How shall I see thee through my tears?"—dramatize their response to the tragedy.

CALL-RESPONSE: IT DON'T MEAN A THING. . . . YOU, TOO, CAN SWING . . . IF YOU PLAY!

While all writing invites the reader's response, Wideman challenges the reader with an "uncomfortable place" he creates with his parody of stereotypes (L. Baker 265). Many scenes of this memoir explore the narrator's intimate fantasies and observations to challenge readers' distance. Wideman's narrative perspective is unstable, shifting from third to second to first person, perhaps in imitation of the shapechanging, or segmenting, that he quotes in an epigraph as a part of the Yoruba aesthetic: "breaking up the surface to create the impression of segmentation, division, and separation" (*Hoop Roots* 161). This art parallels jazz; this complex multivocality of significant others, including the self the narrator has been, dramatizes the human dimensions which are "beyond category."[9]

Although only one phase of jazz musicians, the beboppers, carried the styling of the artist to a paradoxical climax, as exemplified by Miles Davis turning his back on the audience as he expressed his soul, this paradox may be the ultimate irony of the jazz artist: a Duke Ellington, Bill Evans, or Thelonious Monk can never be confused with the other, for each has developed his voice and technique into a unique expression of his soul. And yet this is masked from the audience by his performance style. Such ambiguity makes the reader's position unstable. Like the "Negro" in a racist world, we are put behind the veil, sometimes participating as intimates, at others manipulated by the trickster narrator. Wideman has commented on this paradox: "I write about the most intimate, the most personal events in my life" (TuSmith 209), yet readers can't tell the composed from the biographical. He is constantly exploring his intimate experience in public, protected by the styling creativity fosters.

One particularly vivid fantasy shared with his lover comes teasingly close to the facts of Wideman's life: he did teach at University of Massachusetts; whether the beautiful young woman who has just successfully completed her doctoral defense was an actual student there or not, he gives her a name, an identity, and describes her erotic ambush. This close squeak with his biography also inverts the double stereotype, of black men and of male professors as sexual adventurers and prey. This section reveals that even in his fantasies, the narrator has decided to take a longer view. Although not denying erotic life, the narrator recognizes his responsibility. And the vividness of its detail, down to each playful rationalization as he is trying to dissuade her graciously, engages the reader intimately in his story.

Yet having said this, the segment is also a turn-on; as Wideman cautions/challenges, he often writes "stuff that you can get off on if you're not treating it as a crossword puzzle" (TuSmith 209). And so, he parallels the jazz artist seducing his audience with the erotics of sound. While lamenting and then compensating for his lover's refusal to create a story of her fantasy, Wideman uses it to deconstruct the stereotype of black female sexuality exploited by white males. Each titillates the other with racial crossing in their erotic lives as they celebrate their sadly brief reunion after thirty years. Ingrid Monson's analysis of Coltrane's complex jazz improvisation on the Broadway tune "My Favorite Things" celebrates the authenticity of his musicianship beside whose complexity the original theme seems superficial and predictable. Similarly, here Wideman has played changes on the stereotypes, challenged the reader with genre ambiguity, and shown his virtuosity. While much of the memoir is about losses—including hoop, his wife of more than thirty years, and this rediscovered lover—here Wideman celebrates eros.

And he goes even further, wondering about his sexuality as a perversion of familial relationships. In the next section of *Hoop Roots*, "Learning to Play," Wideman parallels caring for his grandmother to reuniting with this lover to dramatize his struggle to distinguish filial from erotic love.

> Me learning to fear love. I never touched my grandmother, but I did something just as bad. I imagined her to be someone else. A woman I desired. . . . I was scared she'd wake up one morning and tell everybody what a terrible boy I really was. So there I sat, day after day, on my little folding chair. Afraid she's awaken, afraid she wouldn't. Knowing I'd lose her either way. (122)

That a kid who might be dismissed as a ghetto tough was also a gentle caretaker of his grandmother is further complicated by his recognizing in middle age the ambiguity of his motives for this filial watch. As Coltrane and Wideman improvise, neither love nor art is simple although both are "supreme."

In the section titled "The Village," Wideman improvises on the loss that prompted *Hoop Roots*, playing another change on basketball, his being both outside and inside as he watches a street game with his French friend, the "Catherine" to whom he dedicated the memoir. Again set in his biography as a writer in residence in Manhattan, Wideman visits "the Cage"—as this famous court on the corner of Sixth Avenue in Greenwich Village is known by players—the title also evokes the basketball community. This scene works ritually: "Time the thread stringing the beads. Great Time separating yet also connecting the individual and communal experience, the particular and general, high and low, the past, present, and future" (173). He improvises through many perspectives: what Catherine might be imagining about him, about the players; what motivates a short guard in the do-rag "exhibiting *showmanship* . . . or showboating?" (182); whether others even see the playground game. Beneath all is an impulse toward play evoking the dance of hoop.

Wideman riffs on African American culture and history with other African Diaspora writers' stories of their creolization. At last he asks himself: "Has it taken me this long to figure out . . . the subject of this hoop book is pleasure, the freeing, outlaw pleasure of play in a society, a world that's on your case . . ." (179). Like the jazz artist, Wideman improvises in a creative defiance of racism to express the power of the culture: ". . . sport is art and, like any other . . . art form, expresses and preserves, if you teach yourself how to look, the deep structure, both physical (material) and metaphysical (immaterial), of a culture" (185).

Live jazz improvisation is spontaneous and ephemeral, but recordings capture the play of individual creativity and cultural deep structures. Like jazz performance, each reading of *Hoop Roots* is unique, for every reader brings different experiences and beliefs to the stories. Yet Wideman has refined his stories and honed his art, so we must go where he takes us. Among other challenges, for us all, to the question DuBois posed in *Souls*—"Would America have been America without its Negro people?"—our tragic response can be redeemed for a moment, in the circle of improvisation Wideman has wrought.

NOTES

"Will the Circle": Wideman echoes this phrase from the spiritual tradition in "Doc's Story" in *Fever*, reprinted in *The Stories of John Edgar Wideman*. Linda Dittmar uses this allusion to imply an open-ended skepticism in her analysis of Morrison's *The Bluest Eye*. While not using music, her argument emphasizes postmodernist narrative. Epigraph: Ellison 234.

1. I'm referring to these works: *All Stories Are True, Brothers and Keepers, Damballah, Fever, Philadelphia Fire, Sent for You Yesterday, Two Cities,* and *Hoop Roots.*
2. In *The Souls of Black Folk*, W. E. B. DuBois articulates the dilemma of the Negro in America: "It is a peculiar sensation, this double-consciousness, this sense of always looking at one's self through the eyes of others, of measuring one's soul by the tape of a world that looks on in amused contempt and pity. One ever feels his twoness—an American, a Negro; two souls, two thoughts, two unreconciled strivings; two warring ideals in one dark body, whose dogged strength alone keeps it from being torn

asunder" (3). This definition has been used by African American intellectuals, artists, and activists to explain their dilemma. Wideman's narratives thrust readers into this paradoxical perspective.

3. Wideman's reflections on story appear often in his fiction, essays, and interviews. Some representative sources are *All Stories Are True* and the opening of *Damballah*; interviews by Sabatelli (esp. 146–49) and TuSmith (esp. 198–200) in TuSmith *Conversations*; and essays by Wideman: "The Architectonics of Fiction" and "Frame and Dialect: The Evolution of Black Voice in American Literature."

4. Here Wideman illustrates a concept privileged by European and African American aesthetics: T. S. Eliot's 'felt thought,' in "The Metaphysical Poets." And, as Rev. James Cone argues in *The Spirituals and the Blues*, the blues fuses body and soul.

5. Wideman's allusions to African, Meso-, and African American traditions parallels Eliot's use of classic European and Asian traditions in *The Waste Land*.

6. In an interview with Silverblatt, Wideman claims that "art sometimes allows us to enter [Great Time]" (TuSmith 123).

7. Some of the scholars and critics I have found useful in exploring the jazz tradition: Collier; Gabbard; Levine; O'Meally, *Jazz Cadence* and *Seeing Jazz*; Schuller; Stearns; and Williams.

8. Although a structural analysis is beyond the scope of this essay, note how the passages tend to create a pattern typical of jazz improvisation AABA with bridges, vamps, and breaks.

9. This phrase to describe Ellington—his life, his music, and his ambition—is the title of a biography and a CD collection. As Ellington strove for this dimension, it has become the ideal of the jazz musician.

Works Cited

Baker, Houston, Jr. "Belief, Theory, and Blues: Notes for a Post-Structuralist Criticsm of Afro-American Literature." *Belief vs. Theory in Black American Literary Criticism*. Ed. Joel Weixlmann and Chester J. Fontenot. Greenwood, FL: Penkeville Pub. Co., 1986.

Baker, Lisa. "Story Telling and Democracy (in the Radical Sense): A Conversation with John Edgar Wideman." *African American Review* 34 (2000): 263–72.

Balliett, Whitney. "sound of surprise." Quoted in James Clyde Sellman, "Jazz Today." Eds. Kwame Anthony Appiah and Henry Louis Gates Jr. *Africana: The Encyclopedia of the African American Experience*. New York: Civitas, 1999. 1042.

Bennion, John. "The Shape of Memory in Wideman's *Sent for You Yesterday*." *Black American Literature Forum* 20 (1986): 143–50.

Byerman, Keith. "Heart of Darkness: Narrative Voices in *The Souls of Black Folk*." *American Literary Realism* 14 (1981): 43–51.

Collier, James Lincoln. *The Making of Jazz*. New York: Delta, 1979.

Cone, James. *The Spirituals and the Blues*. Maryknoll, NY: Orbis, 1991.

Dittmar, Linda. "Will the Circle Be Unbroken? The Politics of Form in *The Bluest Eye*." *Novel* 23 (Winter 1990): 137–55.

Drewal, Henry John, and John Mason. *Beads, Body, and Soul: Art and Light in the Yoruba Universe*. Los Angeles: UCLA Fowler Museum, 1997.

DuBois, W. E. B. *The Souls of Black Folk*. 1903. New York: Norton, 1999.

Eliot, T. S. "The Metaphysical Poets." *Collected Essays*. New York: Harcourt Brace and World, 1964. 246–50.

Ellison, Ralph. *Invisible Man*. 1952. New York: Vintage, 1990.

———. *Shadow and Act*. 1953. New York: Vintage, 1995.

Gabbard, Krin, ed. *Jazz Among the Discourses*. Durham, NC: Duke UP, 1995.

Gysin, Fritz. "From 'Liberating Voices' to 'Metathetic Ventriloquism': Boundaries in Recent African American Jazz Fiction." *Callaloo* 25.1 (2002): 274–87.

Hasse, John E. *Beyond Category: The Life and Genius of Duke Ellington*. New York: Simon and Schuster, 1997.

Levine, Lawrence. *Black Culture and Black Consciousness*. New York: Oxford UP, 1978.

Monson, Ingrid. "Doubleness and Jazz Improvisation: Irony, Parody, and Ethnomusicology." *Critical Inquiry* 20 (Winter 1994): 283–313.

Munton, Alan. "Misreading Morrison: Mishearing Jazz." *Journal of American Studies* 31.2 (1997): 235–51.

Murray, Albert. "Improvisation and the Creative Process." O'Meally, *Jazz Cadence*, 111–13.

———. *Stomping the Blues*. 1976. New York: Da Capo, 1987.

O'Meally, Robert, ed. *The Jazz Cadence of American Culture*. New York: Columbia UP, 1998.

———. *Seeing Jazz*. Washington, DC: Smithsonian, 1997.

Rushdy, Ashraf. "Fraternal Blues in *The Homewood Trilogy*." *Contemporary Literature* 32 (Fall 1991): 312–45.

Schuller, Gunther. *Early Jazz*. New York: Oxford UP, 1968.

Snead, James A. "Repetition as a Figure in Black Culture." O'Meally, *Jazz Cadence*, 62–71.

Stearns, Marshall. *The Story of Jazz*. 1957. New York: Oxford UP, 1970.

Thompson, Robert Farris. "From the First to the Final Thunder." *Who'd a Thought It: Improvisation of African American Quilts*. Ed. Eli Leon. San Francisco: San Francisco Craft and Folk Art Museum, 1994. 12–25.

TuSmith, Bonnie, ed. *Conversations with John Edgar Wideman*. Jackson: UP of Mississippi, 1998.

Vizenor, Gerald. "Socioacupuncture: Mythic Reversals and the Striptease in Four Scenes." *The American Indian and the Problem of History*. Ed. Calvin Martin. New York: Oxford UP, 1989. 180–91.

Werner, Craig. *Playing the Changes: From Afro-Modernism to the Jazz Impulse.* Urbana: U of Illinois P, 1994.

Wideman, John Edgar. *All Stories Are True.* New York: Vintage, 1992.

———. "The Architectonics of Fiction." *Callaloo* 13 (1990): 42–46.

———. "Black Fiction and Black Speech." *Writers Speak.* Ed. Jules Chametzky. Amherst: U of Massachusetts P, 1984.

———. *Brothers and Keepers.* New York: Holt Rinehart & Winston, 1984.

———. *Damballah.* New York: Avon, 1981.

———. "Dead Black Men and Other Fallout from the American Dream." *Esquire* Sept. 1992: 149+.

———. *Fever.* New York: Henry Holt, 1989.

———. "Frame and Dialect: The Evolution of Black Voice in American Literature." *American Poetry Review* 5 (Sept/Oct): 34–37.

———. *Hoop Roots.* New York: Houghton Mifflin, 2001.

———. "The Killing of Black Boys." *Essence* Nov. 1997: 122+.

———. *Philadelphia Fire.* New York: Henry Holt, 1990.

———. *Sent for You Yesterday.* New York: Avon, 1983.

———. "The Silence of Thelonious Monk." *Esquire* Nov. 1997: 106–12.

———. *The Stories of John Edgar Wideman.* New York: Pantheon, 1992.

———. *Two Cities.* New York: Houghton Mifflin, 1998.

Williams, Martin. *The Jazz Tradition.* New York: Oxford UP, 1970.

Will the Circle Be Unbroken?

"Traveling Here Below"

JOHN EDGAR WIDEMAN'S
THE ISLAND: MARTINIQUE
AND THE STRATEGY OF
MELANCHOLY

GERALD W. BERGEVIN

> WE NEED A STORY, DON'T WE, TO PROP UP
> WHAT FEELS FRAGILE, VULNERABLE. . . . WE'RE
> HAUNTED BY IMAGINED GRIEF, ANTICIPATED
> WOUNDS WE HAVE NO WORDS FOR EITHER,
> EXCEPT "LOST CHILD," WORDS WE CAN'T SAY.
>
> WIDEMAN, *THE ISLAND*

Despite *The Island*'s passionate sex scenes, paradisal setting, and linguistic exuberance, some readers will conclude that it is a pessimistic book. John Wideman says in the introduction that he sought in Martinique the "clarifying distance and difference I desired . . . difficult to achieve at home in the States, even though cultural clash, blending, and incompatibility constitute the bottom-line subjects of my writing" (xxi). The book is a tale of two Martiniques: the pristine island paradise and the former slave colony. The "clash" is between a rich and lively African-based culture and the long shadow of French political and cultural domination. Ostensibly a travelogue (it was published by the National Geographic Society), the book ventures into the minefields of electoral politics, gender, and religion. Most challenging of all, Wideman[1] focuses dead-center on historical slavery and contemporary racism.

Equally prominent clashes or conflicts derive from Wideman's personal life. *The Island*'s main narrative line centers on the romance of the author and Katrine, a French woman, with whom he travels on his three-week tour of the Caribbean island. Always a risk-taker, especially in his use of autobiographical materials, Wideman opens his personal life to the reader's judgment. He writes in the introduction, "[P]arts of this book . . . are attempts to allow myself to be invaded, to live in other skins, to assume risks. Encourage the island to problematize, call into question who I am and who I'm not" (xxvi). Wideman begins his self-critique early in the main text, as in this passage: "So why not me, here on tour, eligible as anyone else to enjoy the island . . . I'm free at last to enjoy the spoils. . . . High John the Conqueroo with his lady, be she black or white or some green-eyed, beige in-betweener" (8). Two disquieting issues surface in this passage: the privileged status he enjoys as a tourist and his being a black man in a relationship with a white woman. Wideman reveals inner conflicts in several later scenes, including one in which he appears flippant after Katrine suffers a miscarriage and another in which he struggles to overcome what he admits is his "embarrassingly macho" sexual jealousy.

Getting older, recovering from divorce, confronting personal fears, dealing with the miscarriage and other difficulties in a late-life interracial romance—these subjects constitute a bittersweet personal tale. However, the personal narrative works in tandem with a trenchant sociopolitical critique occasioned by Wideman's visit to Martinique. In the introduction Wideman says that the personal story presented in *The Island* "arose . . . from the visceral, visual presence of loss and waste, the haunted deadly past alive in Martinique's music, dance, arts, speech, faces—sweet, but always also wistful, fragile, temporary, elusive, *islanded*" (xxviii). There is an interweaving of personal and collective sadness that permeates *The Island* which is best described as "melancholy," in the sense that Anne Anlin Cheng uses the term in *The Melancholy of Race*. Cheng is among many recent scholars who have reconfigured Freud's analysis of melancholy in light of new understandings of personal and social identities. David L. Eng and David Kazanjian, editors of a collection of essays titled *Loss: The Politics of Mourning*, assert that this new scholarship demonstrates the "ways in which loss and its remains are insistently creative and deeply political" (23). Drawing on this scholarship, I argue in this essay that the melancholy in Wideman's *The Island* is a

"Traveling Here Below"

unique composing. In his essay riffing on the silence of Monk, Wideman evokes how the spaces between the sounds define the music (112). In *Hoop Roots* the spaces Wideman leaves in his biography testify to the significance of his basketball career. Again like Monk, Wideman's style transforms all the characters from his biography and history in *Hoop Roots*; they are voiced through his shifting narrative identity. Like Monk's intricate play with a single melody, Wideman exploits simple narratives for their possibilities. Finally, his rhythms are pronounced, again like Monk, playing off beat in a deliberately idiosyncratic manner. Perhaps he has another jazz musician or a composite in mind, but for me Wideman's jazzing story in *Hoop Roots* plays the changes like Monk.

Wideman's writing performs musically like jazz: rhythm is pronounced and diverse, euphony is achieved, repetition is exploited, and voice sounds each character as if he were an instrument. Wideman has always sweetened the challenge of grappling with his themes with "a sensuous, rhythmic experience of language that has a . . . primal appeal" (TuSmith 209). At that level language is a "kind of song" (TuSmith 125). But in *Hoop Roots* Wideman also asserts the primacy of music: "Music carved space . . . usher[ed] in a transcendent reality," most importantly because it integrates body, mind, and spirit. Wideman's prose signifies on African American music: "Transcendent, okay, but better to say music opened me—up and down and all around . . . African people . . . the songs they sang, the rhythms thumped on drums . . . the whole body's bump and glide, lift and fall through air" (15–16). Later Wideman melds music and basketball:

> Great Time your chance to be. To get down. Out. To do it right. Right on time. The game, again like gospel music, propagates rhythm, a flow and go, a back beat you can tune into so time's lonely featureless stretch feels as charged, as sensuous, as accessible a medium as wind or water. You don't really own game time, but the fit feels so close to perfect you can't help believing on occasion it belongs to you. (57)

In the telling—its alliteration, assonance, duple meter, and syncopation—the subject has been jazzed. Finally he gathers up all the basketball players in a ritual: "Performing the ring shout we taught ourselves to shapeshift, conduct our spirits to a region where they could heal themselves, grow strong again, recall and enact their rootedness" (242).

Sometimes Wideman's texts abandon narrative sufficiently to qualify as jazz writing, typically, as Gysin defines it, "free form, automatic performance, or privileging of the musical over narrative" (281). However, no matter how polyvocal and fragmentary, Wideman's stories make meaning. Wideman plays with narrative rules, he has noted, as "the jazz musician interrogates traditional, conventional music" (TuSmith 150).[3] Rather than give voice to all the characters, in *Hoop Roots* Wideman makes them his own.

DOUBLE CONSCIOUSNESS IN *HOOP ROOTS*

With his dedication, epigraphs, themes, and structure, Wideman plays on DuBois's *The Souls of Black Folk* (1903) as a jazz musician plays changes on popular and folk themes. Wideman melds African American, African, and European narrative into a subjective experience of double consciousness.[4] Beyond using the "sorrow songs" to trope the tragic experience of the American Negro through 1903, DuBois created distinctly troubled narrators for two essays in *Souls*. As Keith Byerman has argued, DuBois uses the first-person narrator in "Of the Meaning of Progress" and "Of the Passing of the First Born" to dramatize the psychological stress of double consciousness within the individual, thrusting readers into life "behind the veil" (43–51). *Hoop Roots* improvises a twentieth-century African American subjectivity: readers are both within and outside Wideman's characters, their stories, and the narrator's consciousness. He brings us into the world of Hinkley, the West Village, as well as Grandma Freed's house, challenging the relevant stereotypes with complex human life.

Wideman plays his own changes on the epigraphs in *Souls*, combining his own longings with quotes on rituals of the Diaspora, both personalizing and expanding his world. Epigraphs from *Beads, Body and Soul: Art and Light in the Yoruba Universe* on the African beading ritual and *The Mesoamerican Ballgame* on basketball as a ritual for Mayan peoples bring the Diaspora into Wideman's improvisation. The quote in his frontispiece parallels these arts with his postmodern writing: "beading is thus both a physical as well as a metaphysical experience in which artists become both masters of and mastered by their medium." And so, Wideman responds to DuBois's biblical allusions and prose periods with rituals that signify the deep structure of his culture.

The irony of DuBois's epigraphs, juxtaposing European poetic melancholy with songs of slavery, expresses both the agony and creativity of the enslaved Africans. Similarly, Wideman frames his tales of basketball players with a fictive academic conference on the issue "Who Invented the Jump Shot?" Using story, voice, and the musical dimension of language, Wideman combines European and African American narrative. This, too, accords with the complexity of the jazz artist. As Alan Munton argues, jazz should not be interpreted as solely African American in either its musical or literary manifestations. Added to their mastery of rhythm and voicing from the Diaspora, jazz musicians are also steeped in the European tradition of harmony, structure, and improvisation (235–51). While African American experience is paramount as the subject, theme, and technique in *Hoop Roots*, clearly Wideman's memoir draws on the European and African narrative traditions from the earliest autobiography to the latest postmodern texts.[5]

Wideman also responds to the denial DuBois dramatized: "How does it feel to be a Problem?" Even when it confers an advantage, as in affirmative action, being identified primarily by race subverts the individual and leads to stereotyping. For those who strive to develop their talents, such bias is deflating and frustrating. In previous works, Wideman has challenged readers with the voices of characters caught behind the veil. In *Hoop Roots* we see how their experience of racism has signified for "John." Although Wideman never dramatizes his own explicit suffering from racism in this memoir, he does enter these victims' subjective experience. To DuBois's famous critique of racism, Wideman responds: more than anything else I am me, a complex fictive, biographical being whose self is constantly in flux, but whose ego demands stories to create resonance for his diverse existence(s). Such invention echoes music. While composed of language, the structure and texture of *Hoop Roots* signify like a game, a ritual testifying to basketball and African American culture. As Wideman says: "Multiple consciousness and energy, the fluid situation of freedom that [it] creates, that's what I mean by play" (TuSmith 121–22).

Circle as Meter and Shape

As the fundamental unit of jazz, rhythm provides both the pulse and the overarching structure. In addition to the musical texture of his prose, Wideman's form reflects rhythm in the sense used by Robert Farris Thompson to reveal the African aesthetic in African American quilting. He applies the African term "'blood time' [*kumu mu menga*, literally holding and developing the beat in the blood] . . . a sense of time and patterning emerge, like a spirit, in the fingers to be resolved in finished textiles, or in the tongue, to be resolved as a song or chant" (15). Thompson has returned time to its source, the life of the body and soul, "blood time." And he claims that the resulting patterns in the quilts—asymmetrical, syncopated, in short, highly rhythmic—reflect the "blood time" of the creators. Wideman's prose often reflects these patterns in *Hoop Roots*: he repeats, expands, alliterates to get the point made and evoke its significance. The circle functions as both figure and structure: the hoop, the return, and Great Time. Though not literally rhythm, these circles provide our bearings; wherever we are is connected through meaning to wherever we've been. Great Time reflects the African cosmology which locates each moment simultaneously in circles outside of time.[6]

The hoop, prefiguring and finally melded into the circle of the ring shout, appears in each chapter of the book, signifying his identity as an individual and a part of the community. Wideman encircles his initiation into basketball with his family of women. Through his perspective we appreciate the game he must play with them to be free to learn hoop. Each trip to the playground requires a dance to persuade the watching women that he's obeying their rules (26–32). Note how the circles used to describe his first exposure to basketball reverberate: "I felt comfortably invisible, a ghost who glided into view once or twice, only intruding enough to keep the ball out of the street, guide it back to the circle" (33). Surely he's signifying on Ellison with "ghost" and "invisible." Not recalling whether he made the shot, he recognizes that it changed his life (34). Wideman's account also evokes the neighborhood then and now, juxtaposing urban decay with the significance of the lives of its survivors. Like the quilters described by Thompson, his memoir patterns basketball into his experience as circles.

When he gets into Homewood Court, rhythm is sounded as well as figured by the circle: "Synchronicity. You and time in synch. In touch. Rhythm one name for how the touch feels, how it registers, how you can let go and find yourself part of time's flow. . . . You're not counting but the count's inside you, heard and unheard. . . . Gametime opens like your mouth when you drew your first breath" (57–58). Like music, dancing, and storytelling, playing hoop initiates one into Great Time. Wideman reads the hoop as a door into transcendence: "A small, perfectly round hole guarded by a ring of iron opens in the sky." Wideman connects this circle with that of the beads, the craft of the Diaspora celebrated throughout his epigraphs: ". . . time connects glittering bead to bead, forms them into something tangible, a necklace, and a gift" (59).

IMPROVISATION: THE CHANGING SAME, MAKE IT MINE, MAKE ME OURS

According to many jazz historians and artists, improvisation plays with the motif— as melody, rhythm, and/or intonation—to make it new, to surprise the audience with the unexpected, familiar in new clothes. Inverting, fragmenting, revoicing, and styling the familiar, improvisation explores the possibilities of the material, the instrument, and the musician.[7] Like basketball, writing, or love, such play frees the participants as much as their mastery of the discipline allows them to join the game.

Time in Wideman's writing is circular, linking characters through spirit and identity to every other (L. Baker 271). The circle is a fundamental element in jazz improvisation. The break—when the soloist is given free rein to improvise (Murray 211)—and the cut—where musicians repeat for effect—figure the circle as one returns to the beginning to continue (Snead 71). In the section "Learning to Play," riffs of the twelve-year-old John climbing the stairs to watch over Freed encircle his ascent at Chichén Itzá. Functioning like both cut and break, this form high-lights the connection of memory and significance: the circle is created by human determined refusal to cease mourning, to "get over" one's grief—specifically, grief over the history and legacy of slavery in the Americas. It is my contention that this melancholy operates creatively and politically to keep alive an engagement with the past. Only through such continued engagement does Wideman find it possible to deal with present-day external and internal racial conflicts. Without prescribing actions or predicting outcomes, Wideman's melancholic text clears a space for a hoped-for personal and social renewal.

THE MELANCHOLY TOURIST

The first 100 pages of this 167-page book, constituting its first chapter, are written in the form of a daily journal kept during Wideman's three-week visit. Sober self-assessment and cultural analysis pervade the first journal entry, dated Christmas Day, 2000, that begins *The Island*. In the first paragraph Wideman dismisses the too-easy sentimentality of wishing each other a "Merry Christmas." He admits that Christmas greetings "sound good" and "might redeem (or cushion at least) the daily unavoidable blows of a perilous world" (3). He goes on to explain how the Christianized concept of time has aided the development of racist ideology, including the separate creation of the races. As he declares, "I'm tired of it this morning, the bullshit, the drama, and resolve to shed my own chilly, bone-white garment, awakening in the tropics, the 'sad tropics,' anthropologist Claude Levi-Strauss called this sun and sea and verdant jungle and scouring, caressing, soporific deadly wind" (5). This is not exactly a cheerful attitude toward Christmas at the start of a vacation on a tropical isle. True, he injects a slightly brighter note by calling Christmas a "time of birth for someone somewhere, and who knows what those new eyes will see or disclose" and, finally, wishing the reader "Merry Christmas" (4). Still, it is impossible to ignore the sadness that accompanies the greeting.

Given Wideman's use of autobiography, it is tempting to explain the melancholy of the above entry and other passages in *The Island* in solely personal terms. For example, Wideman begins his nonfiction book *Hoop Roots* with the observation that age is catching up with him. He laments having to give up the lifelong pleasure of playing basketball. On a similar personal note in *The Island*, he describes the time when he first met Katrine as a

> hectic period in my life, the sad aftermath of a thirty-year marriage, remorse, guilt, hassling with lawyers and endless depressing details, little sleep, bumbling around in a kind of fog seeping from scattered pieces of lives no longer fitting together, a sense that I had failed one good woman and thereby disqualified myself for any other, yet still a strong desire to see Katrine again. (15)

This personal revelation provides the background for the scene in which the couple quarrels over whether or not their first encounter was "love at first sight." Wideman admits to changing the subject to end the quarrel, but he claims that he is sincere: "Not a trick, really. Because I'm telling the truth." The truth is that he does not believe in pledging or acting upon absolute faith, as the phrase "love at first sight" implies. Just as he did in the Christmas Day entry, Wideman reveals his skeptical side here. Characteristically, he demolishes hope with one hand while he struggles to rebuild it—on a truer basis—with the other. He refuses to succumb to cliché or conventional thinking at the expense of honesty.

The melancholy of the text deepens as the journal section proceeds and Wideman recounts the couple's experiences on the island. Deeply troubled, and troubling, is the scene in which they quarrel following Katrine's miscarriage (20–22). Wideman thinks to himself, "Why would [Martinique] miss one more lost child." Readers of Wideman's *Philadelphia Fire* and *Two Cities* will recognize the motif of the lost child. Implicit in the motif, and in Wideman's question, is the ultimate test of hope: whether one is willing to bring more children into this world, especially one from an interracial union. Wideman continues: "A portion of each of us dies when the other dies, even if the fallen one is only imagined, fancied, because such an imagined one is truth also, ourselves conceiving ourselves as other. Like the wish to be better we stake in love" (22). Scholars of the politics of loss and mourning often use Freud's essay, "Mourning and Melancholia," as a point of departure. According to Freud, "mourning is regularly the reaction to the loss of a loved person, or to the loss of some abstraction which has taken the place of one, such as one's country, liberty, an ideal, and so on" (243). Freud observed that in many cases the melancholic "knows *whom* he has lost but not *what* he has lost in him." As he states, "In mourning it is the world which has become poor and empty; in melancholia it is the ego itself" (246). In his later book, *The Ego and the Id*, Freud concludes that the ego is *constituted* by objects of loss (18–21). By "a portion of each of us dies" I take Wideman, like Freud, to be asserting that an imagined loss is "truth" because it becomes a part of one's personal identity.

In the journal entry Wideman has a nightmare in which he is a captured African experiencing the horrors of the Middle Passage. As in the Christmas Day journal entry, in this segment the author injects a hopeful note centered on a renewal of the couple's love—"Our old names and colors fading, blending, releasing someone new . . . [W]ill we invent another chance on this island." Starting with the phrase, "I *envision*" (italics mine) and ending with "imagining the sound of a small boat inching through the night sea toward paradise" (22), Wideman encapsulates his hope for the new relationship in the image of the small boat. The couple, like the boat, struggles in a darkened, contentious world. However, the first line of the next journal entry states, "Of course the . . . boat doesn't make it" (22). The text's melancholy is palpable in the phrase, "of course."

Unlike the nightmare the author passively dreamed, the image of the boat is one the author creatively imagined. As an image, the boat might represent our collective journey out of the fog of race. The journey's failure reminds us that such visions are at best ambiguous. As with the concept of "love at first sight," there is a danger of wishful thinking—that one's personal desires become confused with the larger, and more doubtful, enterprise. As in a sentimental romance, imagining a boat or ship braving the stormy seas for distant shores draws on the seductive idea of destiny, a predetermined path to a successful end. For Wideman, the greatest danger is that one's personal hopes might merge with the pernicious notion of Manifest Destiny. As if to subvert all such master narratives, Wideman offers the sad and lonely image of the small boat that fails to reach shore. By denying readers the predetermined successful ending the passage braces them for the difficulties of the journey ahead.

Connecting the personal and the historical in an intimate bedroom scene, Wideman evokes that determined invader of Martinique, Christopher Columbus. He asks his lover, "[T]he two of us, Katrine, will we prove as tough as old, single-minded, vile-smelling, crusty, naughty, greedy, evil-tempered Columbus . . . will we be as lucky/unlucky as blind Columbus and blunder onto the shores of a New World" (19)? He calls Columbus "stupid" and benighted by his own "love-struck" sense of his divine mission (18). He recalls that Columbus heard rumors about an island inhabited exclusively by women. Wideman might be implying here that the conquerors were driven by sexual adventurism—the precursor of contemporary sex tourism—as well as by gold and glory. What is clear is that the rhetoric of romantic love, however one's personal life might play into it, connects in his mind to the ideology and motivation of conquest and enslavement.

Wideman's way of conjoining personal experience and history illuminates our understanding of both. He reminds us that personal desires take place in a social context and are enmeshed in a collective history in which flawed human beings hold sway. At a more cosmic level, he suggests that impersonal and perhaps random forces determine how our lives work out. In any case, it is an illusion to think that God or Providence or Fate is overseeing our personal lives. The romantic notion that "love conquers all" or "all you need is love" is, like Christmas cheer, viewed by Wideman with a jaundiced eye.

Gerald W. Bergevin

RACIAL MELANCHOLY

In Wideman's view, nothing threatens a private vision of individual happiness more than what he calls "the paradigm of race." When Wideman and his companion venture outside their private sphere to encounter Martinique, race is ubiquitous. For example, he and Katrine witness a performance by black dancers staged in a town square for the entertainment of primarily white spectators: "[T]he men [were] costumed in white planter's white suits, the women in turbans matching their ankle-length, colorful, aproned dresses. . . . Pulling Katrine by the arm, I didn't simply leave—I fled . . . feeling sorry [for the dancers], sorry for myself. Sorrow mixed with anger and frustration" (35). This melancholy reflects Wideman's refusal to forget the history of Martinique—specifically, the unspeakable suffering of its enslaved African population. We are reminded that only blissful ignorance makes possible the easy pleasures of the tourist. Later, Wideman laments what is left out of the "minstrel show" performance:

> my ancestors' misery and fortitude and laughing-to-keep-from-crying anguish, my parents' and parents' parents' refusal to be smothered, to be stripped and flayed and disgraced and recycled as grinning clowns. Where in this spectacle am I supposed to find the pursuit of freedom, bloody resistance, any echo of the transcendent, miraculous determination of African people, their choice . . . to be somebody, someday. (38)

Wideman calls the dance a "minstrel parody of old time servants' night off high-stepping and fetching—stepping on me and mine, fetching racist archetypes and stereotypes out of the island's closet . . . gone-with-the-fucking-wind fantasy of the way things were" (38–39). The white crowd reminds him of those in New York City subway stations watching hip-hop performers. The crowd is willing to pay "for all the wrong reasons." Wideman rages against the cultural imperialism that pervades the tourist industry.

The angry rhetoric of this passage is fully justified. Even more telling are the narrator's actions. Wideman says he "fled" the performance because of "sorrow mixed with anger and frustration." His actions should be understood as coming at the end of a long line of previous instances of humiliation and outrage, from the author's distant as well as recent past. His anger and flight are overdetermined, prompted by inchoate forces and not just the travesty on the outdoor stage. Wideman's experience is similar to Cheng's account of a dramatization by Anna Deavere Smith of racial violence in LA, *Twilight: Los Angeles, 1992.* As Cheng puts it, "Watching [Smith's performance] is to be called to occupy a place where you either do not want to be or cannot remain even if you want to. It is impossible, indeed unethical, to try to be 'objective' or immune" (195). Similarly,

Wideman is moved to flee the street scene because to remain is to be implicated, to identify as either spectator or performer, oppressor or oppressed.

Wideman and Katrine came upon the dance by accident. Yet, it was Wideman's choice to come to Martinique, a former slave colony. During the visit, he voluntarily seeks out historical sites of oppression—such as slave plantations—where he knows such intense feelings are likely to arise. His actions and reactions point to what is involved in facing our racial history. As Wideman frequently reminds us, the past is fully immersed in the present. Performers, consciously or unconsciously, are replicating the trauma of slavery. Even with casual observation it is obvious to Wideman that the racial hierarchy continues. For example, he observes that whites and blacks frequent separate restaurants and bars all over Martinique. Many a tourist will remain blissfully ignorant of these realities, or have the experience carefully managed, as part of a tourist "package." But for those who, like Wideman, know better, or seek to know better, to travel physically or imaginatively to these "contact zones" is to open oneself to the likelihood of intense psychic conflict.

In another passage in *The Island*, Wideman describes a visit he made previously to Monticello, Jefferson's Virginia home. He admits that he was "antagonistic and not very patient or discerning" in viewing the site. He observes, "The juice powering Jefferson's home on the range . . . was African slave labor. Slaves invisible as electricity . . . residing in huts cleverly landscaped to be invisible from the master's windows" (69–70). As he does with the dance, Wideman gives a scathing, penetrating critique of the purpose and effect of historical sites like Monticello that recall past splendor, but conveniently ignore the racism that made it possible. Again, his criticism reflects a deeply personal investment that goes beyond objective analysis. There is not a speck of political correctness, or politeness, in this passage in which Wideman describes his urge to set off a bomb at Monticello. Scholars of Jefferson's writings have not given Wideman an answer to his "question about how it felt, what it meant to him, Jefferson's attempt to live simultaneously in domains as separate as Enlightenment Paris and Martinique, a whitened America and one besotted by slavery" (70). When the author admits to an urge to rip open the material culture of Monticello, it is in a sense to expose the ghost in the machine—to discover what drives the nightmare of racism from which humans need to awake.

The Strategy of Melancholy

In analyzing *The Cattle Killing*, one critic finds "an almost evangelical imperative to grapple with and transform history through the power of the imagination"

(Lynch 778). In my view, *The Island* contributes to Wideman's career-long project to reconstruct the historical record while simultaneously providing a personal testimony of survival and renewal. Wideman is a political writer who seeks to transform readers and human society through his writing. Once the political nature of his writing is acknowledged, however, it remains for us to understand how the various elements in his multifaceted texts work to fulfill its purpose.

As stated earlier, *The Island*—filled as it is with pain, sadness, and conflict—is accurately described as a melancholic text. But how can this melancholy serve a political purpose? According to Cheng, multiculturalism often falls short because it restricts itself to calling for recognition of the other and acknowledging past and present grievances. "[G]rievance," she argues, "which has the guise of agency, in fact does not guarantee political action" (173). Instead, what she calls a "*strategy* of melancholia" sets forth a "*project* of culling political insights from a system of pain and grief" (192, italics mine). Transformative politics comes on the other side of grief, not in resting upon grievance. Wideman's ideology and practice confirm Cheng's analysis, as he makes clear in a recent speech titled "The American Dilemma Revisited: Psychoanalysis, Social Policy, and the Socio-Cultural Meaning of Race." His best work lends support to Cheng's assertion that psychic and sociopolitical dynamics are always already interrelated. I believe that a careful reading of *The Island* reveals how inextricably linked are our personal and political lives. Wideman's travel autobiography incorporates deep psychological insights into racial grief that call for political awareness and activism.

Cheng's strategy of melancholy bears a resemblance to creolization, as Wideman uses the term in *The Island*. (I would not collapse the two terms because of the latter's specific roots in the Caribbean.) As responses to racism, both the strategy of melancholy and creolization seek to subvert the paradigm of race. Both constitute a refusal to play the master's game according to his rules. Each is a creative way to confront and transmute immense suffering. Both creolization and the strategy of melancholy can be seen as a kind of dance on top of the grave, a refusal to surrender one's spirit even in the face of total domination.

Further support for seeing a strategy of melancholy operating in *The Island* is the significant presence of Frantz Fanon. Cheng calls Frantz Fanon the "first to gesture toward the conceptualization of race as melancholic" (201, note 24). Both psychologist and revolutionary, Fanon serves as *The Island*'s guiding spirit. Wideman dedicates the book to this famous Martinican, titles chapter 3 "Fanon," and invents an outrageous fiction in which Fanon appears as a main character. What does Fanon mean to Wideman? For one thing, Wideman calls Fanon's writing "often pure Creole" and especially admires its irony. This might lead one to think that he downplays Fanon the activist, the man who fought on behalf of Algerian independence. In assessing current scholarly attention to Fanon, E. San Juan warns against Homi Bhabha's interpretation which mistakenly "converts Fanon into a supreme ironist who purveys 'transgressive and transitional truth' from the 'uncertain interstices of historical change, from the area of ambivalence between race and sexuality'" (318). San Juan argues that this misinterpretation makes Fanon a "supreme ironist" and threatens to leave no stable place from which to launch cultural critique and political action. Instead, he emphasizes Fanon's "overarching purpose [of] attaining 'a new humanism'" (318).

In my view, Wideman and San Juan have the same understanding of Fanon. By identifying Fanon as "a hero in Algeria's war for independence from France" (xxviii), Wideman certainly does not slight Fanon's revolutionary credentials. As a superb stylist himself, perhaps Wideman is in a better position to appreciate Fanon's use of language than San Juan, who is more interested in ideology. However, both Wideman and San Juan understand that Fanon's "irony" is a linguistic strategy with transformative political aims. Here is Wideman's description of Fanon's project:

> Fanon's nascent, decolonized, de-raced individuals, like Nietzsche's ideal artist, must undergo metamorphosis: first a cleansing to become open like a child, then conscious assumption of the burden and lessons of the past, and finally roar and struggle to challenge the past and prepare a better future. The last shall be first, the first last. . . . Creolization begins here, resisting slavery's most evil effect—self-destruction. . . . Creolization works like elegy—lyrically summoning what's absent and desired. . . . Keeps old wounds alive, not because suffering ennobles, but because wounds hurt and creolization wants to insure wounds don't close before healing's complete. (48–49)

Wideman's interpretation of Fanon is an excellent description of the strategy of melancholy. According to Eng and Kazanjian, "[M]elancholia's continued and open relation to the past finally allows us to gain new perspectives on and new understandings of lost objects" (4). What makes it possible to imagine a new world or a new self is exactly this refusal to close the books on the past.

Another way to understand the apparent bleakness of *The Island* is to think of the Existentialists, whose depictions of personal and social despair motivated and expressed their political engagement. For these Western philosophers of the mid-twentieth century, political commitment is an act of will in the face of the absurd, from which, it seems to travelers on this too-solid earth, there is "no exit."

As San Juan reminds us about Fanon, "The influence of Hegel and Sartre cannot be erased" (319). For Fanon and for Wideman, the paradigm of race that informs the present age manifests itself in both the private and public spheres, and there is no understanding one without the other.

Wideman's transformative politics in *The Island* is revealed when he contests the "either/or" options that one scholar presents for Martinique—that is, either to be French *or* West Indian. He argues that the scholar sets forth an essentialist opposition that is at the root of the paradigm of race. Instead, Wideman suggests that creolization offers another possibility:

> The power of an oppressor can be identified, analyzed, fought and overcome. Individual insubordination, imagination, and collective social organizing are the basic ingredients of this resistance. Micro to macro. Our daily choices either support or erode the material conditions condemning us into the half-asleep, half-awake vulnerability of victims. (97)

Individual imagination *and* collective organizing—both are necessary to overcome slavery's legacy of victimization and self-hatred. On both the individual and collective levels, there is the option to refuse to choose the false dichotomies presented as inevitable. Wideman argues that creolization offers a both/and option that is founded upon understanding psychological dynamics.

THE TECHNIQUE OF IMMERSION

So far we have discussed *The Island* mainly as autobiography and cultural criticism. In the latter mode, Wideman editorializes about Nike and globalization, rain forest destruction, and the 2000 U.S. presidential election. History, too, makes its way into the text. Wideman includes a map and brief chronology of Martinican history, and he cites and draws upon reputable historical scholarship. But Wideman, the outspoken public intellectual, *knows* it is not enough to analyze and critique examples of malfeasance and injustice. There is a glut of opinion in our media-saturated society. Wideman makes good use of documentary history, but he is very conscious of its pitfalls and limitations. He argues that, alongside (or in combination with) personal experience, criticism, and history, there must be acts of imagination that create new images, new selves. Such new imaginative acts—"stories" as he understatedly calls them—are essential for the individual, a couple in love, or a culture to survive in the contemporary world.

Wideman goes beyond direct commentary and personal reflection to re-imagine the core meaning of history for our times. He creates new stories in *The*

Island by assuming various voices and perspectives and inventing situations and characters based on history. In chapter 2, titled "Père Labat," he creates a fictional portrait of a historical figure—an administrator of the French colonial slave system. As he states in the introduction, "After discovering the many ways Labat left his imprint—from establishment hero in the economic development of the island to spectral villain in the counterculture of Creole memory—I couldn't resist a brief foray (chapter 2) into the priest's mind." The chapter begins in a tavern in France, and Labat is waiting to sail to Martinique. Later, the scene abruptly shifts to a contemporary mall that packages and sells black urban culture to mainly white suburban youth. The chapter ends with Labat buying several pairs of Nikes. This abrupt transition to a contemporary scene dramatizes Wideman's belief in the intimate connection between past and present. One might say that the writer pours old wine (the facts of historical racism) into a new bottle (the contemporary American scene). The political implications here are left to the reader to discern.

Wideman admits to being intrigued by the psychology of the slave-master Labat, especially by what it must have felt like to have such power over others. In perhaps the most horrifying passage in the book, a slave who is caught trying to flee is brought before Governor Labat. At first Labat says that the slave, who has already been castrated and otherwise mutilated, has been punished enough. On second thought, however, he ponders what he sees as the basis for the vast superiority of whites over blacks, which, of course, he considers God-ordained. By his study of their "savage practices" Labat concludes it comes down to the fact that Africans will not eat parrots, whereas he prides himself on his own parrot recipe which calls for skinning the birds alive. Labat's culinary ruminations must be enacted, so he arbitrarily orders the slave to be flayed, roasted, and displayed as a warning to others. "Let its [*sic*] cries ring out like sweet bells summoning the faithful to worship," Labat says. Painful as it is to read, the passage brings home the psychological and cultural factors involved in white supremacy. The imaginative foray into Labat's mind affects the reader at a more profound level than an appeal to logic or reasoning.

Such a use of fiction to re-imagine the past can be compared to that of other novelists' use of history, to powerful writers such as Toni Morrison. It also bears comparison to what Cheng calls "immersion," as she uses the term to discuss the performance of Anna Deveare Smith. Cheng argues that when a creative artist—especially a writer of color such as Smith—addresses racism in a contemporary American context, the impulse comes from a "hidden grief" shared by individuals and the culture as a whole, and one that is tied inextricably to individual and group identity. This phenomenon arises from a deeper source than is expressed through conscious legal or ethical argument based on "grievance." As Cheng puts it, "[E]thics comes after identification and complicity—that is, after immersion has already taken place" (188). The fictional segments of *The Island* are similar to Smith's theatrical performances in that they perform an ethical and political function that supplements the conscious argumentation presented by the author in his role as cultural critic.

One could say that there is a dramatic impulse—a kind of Shakespearean or Keatsian negative capability—that lies behind Wideman's literary tour de force in chapter 2. Cheng argues that, in her stage performances, Smith uses imitation to subvert authority (180). This is what Wideman does with the figure of Père Labat. By getting inside the head of the slave master, he is following Fanon, who wrote that "whilst blacks must be liberated from their inferiority complex, whites must be liberated from an equally alienating superiority complex" (122). Viewed in this way, Wideman's immersion technique fits into the agenda of critical white studies.

For *Twilight*, Smith conducted extensive interviews with her subjects. Wideman, however, rejected interviewing Martinican "cultural insiders" for his book. Instead, he carefully researched the island's literature and other written records, reflected on his personal experience, and used his fertile imagination to re-create history—most conspicuously by entering into the mind of the slave-master Labat. This is the method he followed in his novel *Philadelphia Fire* when he incorporated the 1985 police bombing of the MOVE community, and again in *The Cattle Killing* when he used the 1793 yellow-fever epidemic to frame what he called a "love story." In these novels, Wideman seeks to portray the spiritual meaning of historical events. Similarly, he states in the introduction to *The Island* that the history of a place draws from two forms of "witness": written documents and the "silent witness we can only imagine" (xxx). It is through immersion in the silent witness of history that Wideman's book performs some of its most powerful psychological, ethical, and political work.

MELANCHOLY, RACE, AND LOVE

In chapter 3 of *The Island* Wideman uses autobiographical materials as he did in the journal entries that constitute chapter 1. In this section, though, "Katrine" has become "Chantal" and "John" is "Paul." In the book's introduction, Wideman invites the reader to speculate about why he felt the need to fictionalize his relationship, but one explanation he offers is that it is a "negative talisman" that might work therapeutically to "ward off my ancient fear of losing what's most precious."

"Traveling Here Below"

A second explanation is that the story of Chantal and Paul "arose . . . from the visceral, visual presence of loss and waste, the haunted deadly past alive in Martinique's music, dance, arts, speech, faces" (xxviii). The fiction is a bittersweet love story prompted by Wideman's perceptions of Martinique, but also dealing with "the real odds against [their love] abounding on any Martinique" (xxviii). The story refers to past events that take place in the Caribbean and elsewhere, but the main setting is Manhattan—a crowded metropolitan island—a setting that serves to emphasize the couple's isolation.

In this story of a black man and a white woman the central conflict is race. This theme explains the chapter title "Fanon" as well as the Fanon quotations that punctuate the text. In his speech, "American Dilemma," Wideman stated, "For Fanon, the problem [of race] is two fold: (a) the external objective force that physically immures colonized or repressed people, and (b) the internal psychological processes dooming human beings to exchange the open-ended becoming of an evolving personality for the fixed, dead-end, either/or identities of 'black' or 'white'" (39). In this fictional chapter, Wideman zeroes in on the interior, subjective experience of being in an interracial relationship. Despite their mutual attraction, Chantal and Paul are not able to escape the racial box in which they have been placed. In trying to articulate their differences, they both revert to type, if not stereotype. Chantal is a liberal white female, attracted to black men partly because they are "forbidden." Paul is a brooding, self-absorbed African American writer—futilely trying to complete his novel about Fanon—who goes into a rage at the thought of Chantal having sex with Antoine, her former boyfriend. Paul says about Antoine, the affluent white Frenchman who was also Chantal's boss, "He bought you. Bought you like they always buy what they want" (135). The narrative bounces back and forth between Chantal's explanations and Paul's recriminations. The overt personal issue that divides them is Paul's sexual jealousy, but the larger issue is whiteness. Chantal describes an incident when she and Antoine, two affluent white people, found themselves walking through a poor black neighborhood late at night. Chantal became frightened, certain that a potential mugger was following them. Some of Paul's most revealing lines come through interior monologue as he considers the meaning of Chantal's story:

> I want to know what you imagined. . . . Two white Europeans parading after dark
> through the grungiest, most unforgiving, most violent quarter of the town . . .
> through the cesspool your bad intentions and good intentions created, a sewer
> where human beings must make lives for themselves swimming in centuries of
> your filth. . . . What gives you the right to rub the privilege of your whiteness, your
> immunity in dying people's faces. (142–43)

Gerald W. Bergevin

83

"I want to know what you *imagined*." Whiteness is a manifestation of the paradigm of race that has become all the more lethal because it is unconscious. What enrages Paul most is that white privilege gives Chantal and her lover a carte blanche of presumed innocence. They feel no sense of responsibility for the entrenched poverty of the black neighborhood, only a primordial sense of danger because of their color. On the other hand, Paul feels on a daily basis the full weight of social injustice and inner conflicts derived from racism. His fury reaches a crescendo when he violently attacks Chantal:

> his scorched fingers digging into her scorched flesh, wanting to hurt, to rip, shaking her till she submits, her head flopping side to side as he looms over her, shaking, shaking, shaking whiteness out and blackness in or blackness out and whiteness out, she remembers thinking some crazy true thought like that just before she stopped thinking and let her body have its way, shaken, sinking. (143–44)

Their inability to negotiate difference causes the couple to separate, although in the aftermath each individually longs for the company of the other. There is no way to resolve a crisis that is defined so starkly as black versus white.

Wideman concludes chapter 3 with another love story, of sorts, that he titles "Revenants," which might be translated as ghosts or dreams. He begins it with a quote from Fanon, this time a more optimistic one: "Today I believe in the possibility of love." The two characters are, again, a black man and a white woman—Frantz Fanon and Marilyn Monroe—icons of blackness and whiteness respectively. As with the depiction of Père Labat, we have figures who are partly historical and partly invented, but the story's dreamlike quality places it outside of time. The vignette begins with Monroe's suicide and Fanon's death from leukemia, both in the glare of intense publicity. The symbolism of white and black extends to Fanon's disease, described as "an overload of leukemia, white corpuscles in the blood that suppress other cells." The fantasy shifts to the scene of a slave ship where the two are forced to dance for the sadistic crew. Fanon and Monroe are projections of our collective unconscious. But, whereas Paul and Chantal fail to connect, Wideman's dream sequence ends on a hopeful note, as the two embrace and Monroe sings, "*Happy birthday, dear Frantz.*"

OUT OF THE RUINS

It is significant that *The Island* sounds its most optimistic note in the dream fantasy just described—optimistic, that is, if you interpret the bizarre scene on a slave ship that ends chapter 3 as a dramatization of racial healing. In chapter 1, the author, writing in his journal, makes only tentative gestures toward a positive way forward. Katrine is, as Wideman puts it, on the "cusp" of menopause, a difficult time to begin a relationship. It is a twilight period in Wideman's life as well. Though re-invigorated physically and emotionally by the romance, he is feeling his age. The couple's sexual passion culminates in a miscarriage and a "lost" child that leads to Wideman's reflections on Martinique's traumatic history and the bleak state of the world. In the nightmarish chapter 2, the author immerses the reader in the sadistic mind of a historical slave master, Père Labat. In chapter 3, Paul and Chantal's relationship is shipwrecked on the rocks of their socially conditioned egos. Though obviously in love, they end up separating—each mourning the loss of the other.

In the fourth and last chapter, *The Island* returns to the autobiographical mode of chapter 1, but with the aim of bringing the personal narrative and the imaginary excursions of chapters 2 and 3 together into something like a conclusion. In the introduction Wideman assures the reader that he and Katrine, in "real life," are doing just fine. Perhaps this authorial comment is needed at the outset because so little that follows seems to offer the reader much hope. In chapter 4, *The Island*'s melancholy tone reaches its culmination. The chapter presents the context, in Martinique's history, for understanding the book's experiments in confronting grief. What also becomes clear is that within the ruins—specifically the ruins of a former slave plantation and of the former capital city that was destroyed by a volcano—there is hope for a personal and collective renewal. This hope resides in what Cheng calls the "potential inhering in 'melancholic subversion' . . . not cure or some complacent satisfaction in 'knowing better,' but subversion in the sense of a *perceptual shift*, of individuals readjusting and realigning their entrenched relationships to one another" (192). As Eng and Kanzanjian put it, there are strategies by which "the past is brought to bear witness to the present—as a flash of emergence, an instant of emergency, and a moment of production" (5). By its mourning of remains, by its fully imagined engagement with loss, Wideman's *The Island* delineates a strategy for personal and social transformation.

The fourth chapter opens with a brief prologue in which the author describes himself sitting in his apartment in New York City some time after his visit to Martinique. He reflects on the volcanic eruption of Mount Pelee on May 8, 1902, comparing the snow falling outside his window to what the Martinicans called *petite neige*, a blanketing of white volcanic ash that presaged that catastrophic event. The rest of the chapter is a single-sentence jazz solo that recaps historical and personal events—for example, going back to his days as a student at Oxford—

and draws together many of the themes and motifs of the book. In this Joycean tour de force, he recounts two epiphanies. The first was when he and Katrine visited Habitation Anse Latouche, a former sugar plantation built in 1643. Here Wideman meditates on the African slaves who built and allowed this enterprise to thrive:

> African slaves . . . all colors, genders, ages, sizes invested here, imprisoned here, buried here . . . Africans whose muteness, tonguelessness overcomes me . . . still so I can listen, interrogate the silence with my own, attend to the muted spirits, summon them, beg them to forgive me for appalling distance, appalling ignorance, forgive me for not avenging their terror, their captivity, their immolation in *beke* ovens whose fires they tended and fed with the fuel of their own dark bodies, my body. . . . (160–61)

Wideman's identification with his "lost brethren" whose burned bodies he calls "my body" has implications that go beyond an acknowledgment of the horrors of slavery. Wideman's response includes a sense of guilt ("[I] beg them to forgive me") not just for not knowing enough about their fate, but for not "avenging their terror." As with Fanon's endorsement of revolutionary violence, this sentiment will not sit well with all readers. However, in his state of righteous grief, Wideman does not repress his angry and violent feelings. He does not endorse the safe (and ultimately hopeless) option of a detached acknowledgment of the past horrors of slavery. Wideman concludes:

> my lost brethren I summon you, beg you to summon me, when our time comes, time to smash and efface, to rest, to find peace, to forgive, Katrine and I the only visitors for the hour or so we spend exploring this lush, intricate killing ground, its rusting machines, its vegetation, its stone ruins, the pervasive melancholy silence of mourning unbroken except for our whispers. . . . (161)

At this moment in the text the pervading melancholic tone of *The Island* achieves its most sublime effect. The remains of the past intrude meaningfully on the present through Wideman's identification with them. The trauma of the past does not recede into futile meaninglessness but is infused with new significance by someone who is willing to absorb that trauma.

The silence of the plantation is broken by a scream that has been a recurring motif in the text: "thick, thick silence until a sudden onslaught of howling startles us . . . maybe . . . the unquiet souls of those kidnapped and raped and tortured and worked to death on the island" (161). Wideman speculates, among other possibilities, that they are the unheard screams of the enslaved Africans for whom Martinique has no commemorative monument (as there is for Josephine,

Napoleon's consort, who prompted the emperor to reinstate slavery). About Edouard Glissant, whom Wideman quotes approvingly earlier in the book, J. Michael Dash writes that "He [Glissant] asks us to look again at the figure of Caliban . . . and restage his barbaric cry not in the organic heartland [of Martinique] but at those frontier spaces of economic interpenetration and cultural interaction" (43). Like Glissant, Wideman alludes to *The Tempest* several times in *The Island* in ways designed to subvert the colonialist ideology of Shakespeare's play. Perhaps it is Caliban who produces "the mysterious bawling, tortured screams" that Wideman hears on Martinique. In any case, the screams fit a melancholic project embodied in the unspeakable, ultimately unknowable grief that derives from our collective traumatic past.

The second epiphany, an imaginative re-creation of history, occurs in *The Island* when the couple spends an hour in the ruins of the cathedral where the inhabitants of St. Pierre, black and white, were immolated by the eruption of Mount Pelee. Wideman uses the technique of immersion by imagining himself as a father seeking refuge for himself and his doomed family on the evening of the catastrophic eruption. He juxtaposes this imagined scene of doom with another in which, before arriving at the cathedral ruins, John and Katrine take time for a swim on an idyllic beach. The nonswimmer Wideman tenderly describes the beauty of the natural scene and of Katrine's body dipping and diving in the waves. Returning to the earlier theme of sexual jealousy, Wideman says, "for a moment I'm free from the need to possess . . . free to stop asking myself *who was she* or *who was I* each time we had let go and dived into pleasure or plunged into love with another, and I think how it ain't nothing but a party, after all" (165). While on the plantation grounds Wideman had specifically mourned the "lost brethren" who suffered and died as slaves, in this final section the sense of loss becomes more general.

In his conclusion Wideman evokes loss as the condition of all natural forms. He muses about "how doggedly, fiercely, hungrily the dance [of life] goes on, chemicals, molecules, bodies attracted to mingle, replenish themselves, the salty brews within and without nearly identical yet also profoundly separate, joining, clashing, sucking, swallowing, braiding, pulling away and joining again, in synch, at risk, at play" (165). Wideman evokes loss as endemic to the human condition, a mournfulness that becomes a condition for continued living. As he suggests, coming to terms with the reality of loss provides the chance for a renewal of spirit that can lead to creative expression:

> the two of us, here, alive at dusk in St.-Pierre wading through the blackened stones of a vanished cathedral at the end of a day so fine and exhilarating I'm

suddenly self-conscious, overwhelmed almost by the need not to possess but to share the plenitude, share my fullness because there's so much, too much to squander or hoard just for myself, just for a day, so I want to share, I'm brimming with the story of the day, the pleasure and need to tell it. (166)

Ultimately, Wideman places readers squarely in that difficult space in which the possibility of love is affirmed but its continuance is not guaranteed. Cheng provides what could be an epilogue: "Love must look away in order not to look away. . . . Thus melancholia, both living with the ghost of the alien other within and living as the ghost in the gaze of another, may be the precondition—and the limit— for the act of imagination that enables the political as such" (194). Wandering in the ruins on Martinique at dusk, Wideman has called forth the ghosts who inhabit the contentious boundary between love—which individuals seek to give meaning to their lives—and politics, the collective effort that is our only hope for a transformed society of the future.

NOTE

1. In this paper I use "Wideman" to refer to both the narrative "I" of this autobiographical text and to the author who constructs it. As he explained in an interview, Wideman feels obligated to clarify when he is giving readers "an accurate, factual, in a sense a documentary picture" of his own life experience (TuSmith 215). In *The Island*, I believe the author makes it clear when he is speaking in his own voice.

WORKS CITED

Cheng, Anne Anlin. *The Melancholy of Race: Psychoanalysis, Assimilation, and Hidden Grief*. Oxford and New York: Oxford UP, 2001.

Dash, J. Michael. "The Madman at the Crossroads: Delirium and Dislocation in Caribbean Literature." *Profession 2002* (2002): 37–43.

Eng, David L., and David Kazanjian. *Loss: The Politics of Mourning*. Berkeley: U of California P, 2003.

Freud, Sigmund, et al. *The Standard Edition of the Complete Psychological Works of Sigmund Freud*. London: Hogarth Press and the Institute of Psycho-Analysis, 1953.

Lynch, Lisa. "The Fever Next Time: The Race of Disease and the Disease of Racism." *American Literary History* 14.4 (2002): 776–804.

San Juan, E., Jr. *Racism and Cultural Studies: Critiques of Multiculturalist Ideology and the Politics of Difference*. Durham and London: Duke UP, 2002.

Smith, Anna Deavere. *Twilight: Los Angeles, 1992. On the Road: A Search for an American Character.* New York: Anchor, 1994.

TuSmith, Bonnie, ed. *Conversations with John Edgar Wideman.* Jackson: UP of Mississippi, 1998.

Wideman, John Edgar. "The American Dilemma Revisited: Psychoanalysis, Social Policy, and the Socio-Cultural Meaning of Race." Keynote Address. *Black Renaissance/ Renaissance Noire* 5.1 (Spring 2003): 32–44.

———. *The Island: Martinique.* Washington, DC: National Geographic, 2003.

Part 2 Fiction

Queering
Blackness
RACE AND SEXUAL
IDENTITY IN
A GLANCE AWAY
AND *HURRY HOME*

KEITH E. BYERMAN

John Edgar Wideman's first two novels, *A Glance Away* (1967) and *Hurry Home* (1970), have received relatively little critical attention, in large part, I would argue, because the overt engagement with high modernism places them outside the conventional model of African American writing.[1] Moreover, another aspect of these texts—the homoerotic—is even more troublesome for black critical discourse. Little room has been found for queer/gay studies in the analysis of black writing.[2] Such a presence in Wideman's early fiction is generally associated with the theme of modernist despair and sterility; in other words, the "queer" is seen as the emblem of a failed modernity, intellectuality, and urban life.[3]

What I propose in this essay is a different reading of these texts in which it is sexuality itself that is the central trope. Through it, Wideman signifies not only on homosexuality but on heterosexuality as well. Moreover, such figuration serves to comment on the relationship between race and sexuality by demonstrating the falsity of all racialized conceptions of gender. Black men, white men, black women, white women all fail to perform their socially determined gender identities in these novels. In effect, all bodies and their physical desires are disparaged.

What meager possibilities remain come through disembodiment, through what might be considered spiritual connections either with others or within the self.

It is worth noting that *A Glance Away* and *Hurry Home* were published at the height of the Black Arts movement and black nationalist discourse on matters of race. The language of poetry, drama, and political rhetoric at the time emphasized the black body—its beauty, its power, and its potential for violence. In many of the same works (by Amiri Baraka, Don L. Lee, Nikki Giovanni, and others), whites (and their "Knee-Grow" allies) were represented as homosexual and cold-blooded. Eldridge Cleaver provides the clearest differentiation in *Soul on Ice*, when he constructs racialized gender categories: the Omnipotent Administrator, the Supermasculine Menial, the Ultrafeminine, and the Amazon. In the same chapter, he describes homosexuality as "the product of the fissures of society into antagonistic classes and a dying culture and civilization alienated from its biology" (177). He also asserts that white men, as expressions of Mind (Omnipotent Administrators) have a strong propensity for homosexuality (180).

During the same time period, and in part as a response to nationalist rhetoric, white discourse embraced the trope of pathology to explain black experience. Whether through the sociological analysis of Daniel Patrick Moynihan or the historical perspective of Stanley Elkins and others, black being came to be depicted in terms of the diseased body.[4] Such figuration can be understood in part as a continuation of the post-Reconstruction imagery of contamination associated with segregation and miscegenation laws.

In this historical context, Wideman's early novels can be understood as efforts to work through and beyond racialized bodies. In both *A Glance Away* and *Hurry Home*, bodies consistently fail as sites of beauty, desire, and even routine sexuality, whether hetero- or homosexual. Instead, they are associated with ugliness, addiction, pain, and self-denial. Every relationship is a failure to the extent that physicality is a factor. So, for example, Eddie Lawson, the protagonist of *A Glance Away*, is viewed with suspicion in the neighborhood bar, in part because he went away to overcome his drug habit. Participation in this community requires a contaminated body; efforts at healing are seen as betrayals of that self-destructiveness, as attempts to go over to the side of "the Man." Despair and escape through drugs are considered part of the meaning of black masculinity.

One striking feature of this first novel is that the only positively represented bodies are those of the dead. DaddyGene and Eugene, seen through the memories of Lawson family members, are strong, life-affirming figures. In fact, their physical presence is often taken as an embarrassment by the women in the family precisely because of their vitality. Appropriately, DaddyGene is first seen at the birth of the grandson named after him:

Freeda, I got me a grandson. Big 'un he's gonna be. Big and bad like his grand-daddy Eugene. A big, bad nigger-Gene, said the tall baldpate man clomping on bunioned feet loudly up the stairs, shrugging off tentative back holding hands and small voice excited of pale receptionist starched white at desk. A bigniggerGene.
   —You can't go up there sir.
   —My little girl's up there lady. You hear me, my little Martha's there and nobody on God's green earth's gonna keep me from my girl. Offshuffling to tune of *Gimme that wine spudie-udie* he went, dedecorumed in glee of life received bearing his name, his flesh and blood redone forever in two bodies precious together under hospital blankets. (3)

Even this forceful being, as we learn elsewhere in the story, needs cheap red wine to keep him going in the face of those who distrust his strength and his blackness and therefore keep him underemployed. He dies drunk in his bathtub.[5]

The grandson Eugene is much like his elder in appearance and demeanor:

He grew fast and rank, a strong hard-handed boy whose shoes had to be left out-side at night. Huge, smelly things Martha [his mother] would carry dangling like fish from their strings, holding her nose but laughing and loving the ritual when he would forget and she would point and shout, making jokes to the others while Eugene cringed and almost cried. It was just to be forgiven and for her to forgive. The tiffs they had. Him standing still, towering a foot over her head listening to her shrill angry voice and cowing from her threatened blows. But when she hit him, it really did hurt her more, his elephant hide and bones and buckles and she would cry. (28)

Each of these giants represents the life force in the family, the focal points of love, anxiety, and hope. Their size and behavior not only serve to energize others, but they also suggest the smallness of life in their absence. In effect, Wideman cre-ates through them a kind of Golden Age of black masculinity, and, when they are gone, the world is greatly diminished. In fact, Martha never recovers from the death of her son in war, though she has two other children:

[T]he postman in an envelope brought all that was left of Eugene, her first born. She was different then. Even after the telegram from the war department she con-tinued those morning vigils [of waiting for notification of Eugene's return]. Clarence [her husband] couldn't stop her, and after her scenes, tears, and a cold, cold anger he feared in himself he stopped trying. (28)

The energy of such male bodies gives strength and vitality to others, but what Wideman emphasizes in presenting them is neither their race nor their sexual potency, but rather their physical presence. Neither DaddyGene nor Eugene is portrayed as sexual or race-conscious. They are simply men who are large, funky, and loud; they are "primitive" in the sense that they cannot be contained within the framework of modern institutions and practices. In fact, modernity in these texts can be said to be the absence of the life force represented by such characters. And for Wideman, the death of funkiness (as both smell and attitude) that is modernity is a cold, bitter, exploitative reality.

In their stead, the novels offer stories of individuals and relationships that are doomed to frustration, exploitation, illusion, and degradation. Bodies, whatever their race, must be made abject; sexuality, even when physically successful, is marked by disgust or anger. Moreover, sexual identities and gender roles—whether male or female, hetero- or homosexual—are complicated and confused; those who attempt to enact conventional roles usually fail. By looking at the dynamics of relationships that Wideman creates in *A Glance Away* and *Hurry Home*, it is possible to see how he uses sexuality as a metaphor of the failures of modernity.

Significantly, the first novel presents those relationships as triangular, often with distinct racial overtones. This arrangement effectively "queers" sexuality, since it transgresses the normative model of heterosexual, intraracial pairings. The presence of the third is not itself the cause of disruption of an assumed norm; rather, that presence merely makes evident the problematic character of the relationships. So, for example, when Eddie returns from his rehabilitation, he goes to see his former girlfriend Alice, the sister of his close friend Brother. They had been lovers before, even when Alice went off to college.

But then Eddie had a brief sexual relationship with one of her white classmates, and she cannot forgive him. In reminding him of his betrayal, she must denigrate Clara, referring to her as "glib, bitch mouth" and to Eddie's desire "for a smell of her white ass" (119). After Alice consents to have sex with him, she returns to that violation of trust as a means of humiliating him: "'Like Clara, Eddie, I gave it to you like Clara. A charity case free of charge on my lunch hour. We're the same now. I can tell her how gentle you are, how understanding. Please leave, Eddie, please get out of here!'" (121). Her words bring all of them into a condition of abjection, since by saying she is now the same as Clara, she is labeling herself a whore. Her language also echoes the liberal hypocrisy of her erstwhile friend, thus politicizing as well as racializing their interrelationships. Clara's white body and Eddie's black one are sites of both desire and shame and thus must be rejected; but this rejection gains Alice nothing. Instead, her body becomes such a site: when Eddie objects that he cannot leave because he loves her, "she hit him once, twice, sharp pummeling blows like a machine thudding on his shoulders and chest" (122). He then responds by carrying her unwillingly into the bedroom. The threat of violence becomes for her the possibility of love and passion:

She sensed his poised, inner stillness, the cold implacability of anything he decided to do. In that moment she loved him, loved the doom in his steel hands cutting into her wrists, the crushing, irresistible weight across her belly. Her lips were
heavy with desire. (122)

But in place of rape, there is sadness and refusal: "he relaxed, the vein disappeared,
the grief, the pain returned" (123). He leaves her on the bed and walks away.
Almost as soon as he is back on the street, "Alice is forgotten" (123). He chooses
to engage only the memories of their childhood together, of Alice as little girl
rather than woman.

In a variation on this situation, Thurley, the central white character, understands his personal failures and his turn to homosexuality in relationship to his
humiliating heterosexual experience. The triangle here involves his friend Al, who
is "othered" in terms of both sexual identity and body. Thurley's wife Eleanor is,
from the beginning of their life together, engaged in acts of humiliation; by the
present time of the narrative, she is said to be insane. From the wedding day on,
she acts to destroy his manhood, by denying him sex or by insulting his performance, while claiming to be insatiable herself. Though he is himself married, Al is
invited by them into a brief ménage à trois, which Thurley agrees to as a way to
save his marriage, but comes to realize is in fact designed by Eleanor to be the
final humiliation. Al's body is the mechanism by which she accomplishes this;
after that experience, the marriage ends, Thurley's relationship with Al is suspended for several years, and Thurley engages only in homosexual sex.

Interestingly, it is Al rather than his friend who is "queered" in all this. When
Thurley goes to visit him after the extended separation, readers are constantly
(through Thurley's perspective) reminded of both Al's effeminacy and his ani-
mality. He is described as small, delicate, and precise, with nervous gestures, yet
covered with "coarse, jet-black hair": "Like a monkey from the back" (78).
Whatever desire Thurley might have for his friend is conditioned by this depre-
cation, whatever consolation and meaning might be drawn from the friendship
is subverted by the focus on flawed, defective, humiliating bodies. The whiteness
of this set of characters serves not so much to make a comment on the dominant
society, as the critics cited at the beginning of this essay suggest; rather, it serves
to indicate both the universality and variety of othering and queering, especially
in matters of the body and desire. Eleanor is a castrating, insane bitch; Al is an
effeminate beast; and Thurley is a self-identified failure as a man, a lover, and a
friend. His present-time sexual activities are primarily with black boys who are
poor and desperate.

As in the two previous examples, the third also involves a woman whose bitter-
ness and frustration lead to attacks on others. In this instance, however, sexuality

functions as an accusation rather than a reality. For Martha, verbal assaults on her daughter and on Brother (Eddie's friend) serve to evade confrontation with the collapse of her own body and her fear of death. Early in the text she has her first sexual experience, and part of her thought process is ambivalence about her body: the beauty of her long, silky hair and the hated freckles and oversized teeth. "How hard it was to be a little ugly girl" (10). When she gets much older and suffers from physical ailments, she turns her animus against Bette, even though the daughter has largely given up her own life to take care of her mother: "A whore. I don't know how many. Even that ape Brother probably, grinning all the time in Eddie's face" (55–56). The comment about Brother is misdirected, since he is albino, bald, and thin. Rather than an implied racial comment, it seems more intended to dehumanize him, which also serves to intensify the attack on Bette. Even Eddie realizes the depth of the mother's spite:

> Mama calls her hussy and a whore. She said Brother snuck around the house, and she could hear them at night like prowling cats from her bed when they thought she was asleep. And said Bette had always been that way, that after her father and DaddyGene had gone there was no keeping boys from her fast womanish ways. Coming at night like cats—Bette cried still, she cried not because it was true, but because it was Mama who said such things, and there was no answer because Mama's words would never change. (104)

Since Martha's accusations appear to be delusional, the explanation for them must lie in her sense of betrayed bodies and desires. *She*, after all, was the daughter who had premarital sex and apparently married because she was pregnant. *Her* men have proved untrustworthy, either because they died unexpectedly or failed to live up to her expectations. *Her* body has betrayed her by becoming crippled, thereby making her dependent on her daughter, who has sacrificed her own life to care for her mother's body. So she projects onto Bette the accumulated guilt and frustration of her own life. Her own desires are linked to death; therefore, desire is an evil. Bette ought to desire something more out of life, but to do so would mean effectively the death of the mother; therefore, Bette must be evil. And because the men in Martha's life betrayed her by dying, the ugly, alien Brother can be the projection of all that male betrayal. She imagines a relationship of promiscuity and bestiality (apes and cats) that embodies all that she has suffered in her life, and thereby evades the self-hatred that is the meaning of her life.

The triangle that brings all this together is the one between Brother, Eddie, and Thurley. The first encounter occurs in a bar in some other city, according to Thurley's memory. What strikes him first about the meeting is the ugliness of Brother:

Thurley noticed all these things, his shabbiness, his lisp, but most of all the pure ugliness of the man's face gutted by pimples and scars like craters in the garish light. His disgust was aroused by this ugliness, by asthmatic sniffling and wheezing between sentences as the albino labored to say something before the catarrh up from his lungs thickened in his throat forcing him to spit down between his legs. The fitful sing-song voice, the human weakness and need that forced the man to serve up his unpalatable being to other men frightened and excited Thurley . . . (46)

This unattractiveness becomes opportunity, as it means that Brother will accept a sexual advance because his features limit his options; in a reversal of the previous scenarios, here the negative view of the body enhances rather than inhibits sex. Having earlier acknowledged the defects of his own appearance, Thurley feels comfortable exploiting those of his would-be partner. In fact, the ugliness is a part of the desire.

But Eddie interferes with the plan, primarily because he rightly sees it as a homosexual encounter with the white man as predator: "Because you're hungry and the price of nigger meat is cheap" (50). His homophobia is tied to race in that he sees black men as willing to submit to such situations out of desperation, not desire, while white men are simply perverse. But race is also tied to the encounter in another way, since the blackness of Eddie and Brother lead a white policeman to assume that they are the predatory figures and to threaten them.[6] Whiteness in this official view automatically means innocence and potential victimization; Thurley is the one presumed to be in danger. Ironically, the officer's appearance frustrates an act of white domination even as it attempts to enforce white power. We learn that Brother, who, in the confrontation, consistently asserts Thurley's basic goodness, finds him again later and lives in his house; their conversations are always about Eddie.

The last section of the novel is completely devoted to the three men, who meet in a bar on the first day of Eddie's return and shortly after his mother Martha had died in a fall. Her death has devastated him, and he and Brother have apparently come to buy drugs to comfort themselves. But this mission is complicated by the community's distrust of Eddie ("I guess I still smell a bit of the Man" [161]) and by the presence of Thurley, who interrupts their expression of grief. As the three of them talk of death, they recall the women in their lives who are each connected for them to the futility of life. This turn, from desire to loss, enables the narrative to move into what can only be called a spiritual conclusion. Out of the dying and grief, out of the physicality and noise of the bar, and out of the trash and smell of the Bum's Forest they go to after the bar comes an experience of transcendence.

But this experience comes by going through rather than outside bodies. Repeatedly the section describes the discomfort that the men endure—the cold, the darkness, the fear of assault from the bums. In addition, much of the narrative comes through the consciousness of Brother, whose mind tends to be very literal and thus attuned to bodies, both those in the present and those from the past. In this way, he offers us a rereading of earlier episodes with Alice, Bette, and Martha. Moreover, when we do hear from the other two men, some of their thoughts follow this more literal pattern. Eddie recalls childhood sexual experiments with Alice and remembers that Bette was the one who had seen so much death in the family. Thurley becomes very attentive to the need to save Eddie by physically keeping him in the bar, if necessary, so he would not go after the drugs that will eventually kill him. The text brings their thoughts together in alternating passages, suggesting that spoken words are not needed for understanding. And all three are sensitive to the fire that Brother has built, to both its warmth and its light. Each one wonders what it would be like to put his hand in the flame. At the end, each simply watches the fire.

The novel is set on Easter Day, so the story can be seen as an ironic commentary on rebirth and resurrection. It is, after all, a holiday devoted to the repudiation of the sacrificed, suffering body in the name of transcendence. Here we have a narrative of the returned son, but that return produces frustration and death, not new life. Yet this conclusion, with its melding of three male minds in a homosocial environment, offers the promise of endurance and community without the distinctions and conflicts of gender and race.

While *A Glance Away* is structured primarily as intersecting and interactive narratives that describe the failures of bodies, *Hurry Home* follows the mental and physical journeys of one character. Nonetheless, its central point is much the same: the body is a site of frustration and anguish. In this work, however, sexual experience occurs with regularity and success; this does not, though, lead to happiness or contentment. In fact, it operates in extremes of either denial or excess, neither of which produces a desired outcome.

The focal character is Cecil Braithwaite, a black law-school student who currently works as janitor for an apartment building in which he and his wife-to-be Esther live in the marginally habitable basement. During the last year of his education, he is required by the terms of his scholarship to live in the dormitory, leaving Esther alone (except for her Aunt Fanny) and forcing her to do much of his work. The novel opens with a series of misunderstandings, secrets, and fantasies having to do with Cecil's relationships. He fantasizes a sexual encounter with one of the women in the building in enough graphic detail to lead readers to question whether the event actually occurs. But each version of this event associates intercourse with death: "As my son died her red hair keeps falling. It is sand through my fingers. Here I lie with this strange white woman and Esther downstairs and Simon dead" (24–25). He suffers a depression every year in November, though Esther does not understand why; he cannot believe that she does not recognize this as his response to the death of their infant son several years earlier. He does not tell her that the scholarship that separates them also pays all his bills; he continues to take money from her and hoards it away. On the day that he graduates, they also get married. That night, she falls asleep quickly, and he takes the opportunity to abandon her for three years. His subsequent travels compose the remainder of the narrative.

In this early section, attitudes toward the body and toward sexuality are established, and they run through the text. Women's bodies are the sites of exploitation, ridicule, and condescension. Fanny is represented as a slightly mad, birdlike creature. The red-haired woman in the apartment is only a sexual body, perhaps desiring him, but always unnamed and unknowable. Esther's physical labor provides for both of them, but this does not prevent Cecil from beating her occasionally or assuming her ignorance and incompetence. When he leaves, he sometimes sends her notes asking for small amounts of money to be sent to a post office box somewhere, but he never stays long enough to get it. Thus, he deprives her of the means of adequately supporting herself and Fanny to no purpose. In addition, he is also subject to readings denying him his humanity. Esther interprets him as a test of her faith sent from God:

> She believed their life together had been preordained by an all powerful force, and since this source was God in heaven, the joining of their lives had to be right no matter how far this rightness might be submerged beneath the troubled surface of their days together. Only after a prolonged battle with herself had she come to realize how God had blessed her. That He blessed her with a trial. Cecil would be her salvation, her road to humility, the means by which she would finally be placed beside her Creator. (9)

That submission, violence, and abjection, as experienced in her relationship with Cecil, would be the way to salvation suggests the extent to which self-abnegation and even self-hatred shape Esther's identity. Her reading denies both of them anything like ordinary humanity; it justifies any behavior by him and any sacrifice from her.

The reverse of this situation occurs in the community. Here Cecil's being is itself the site of ridicule and abuse. His professional ambition, reflected in his carriage and speech, makes him the target of animosity each time he walks down the street. Encounters with his neighbors repeatedly verge on violence and always draw out their sarcasm. Unlike Esther, they see him as absurd and use his arrogance, laziness, and exploitation of Esther against him. Like Eddie in *A Glance Away*, his connection to the white world (in the form of his education) renders him suspect in the black community.

Part 2 finds Cecil in Europe with Charles Webb, a white man who sees the black one as a substitute for his own dark-skinned son. He is willing to pay Cecil's expenses as long as he is content to play this role. Their relationship contains elements of the homoerotic, especially in the context of Webb's memories of sexual encounters with men. But the more important point is his obsession with the lost son that requires the presence of Cecil and that parallels the protagonist's repeated reference to his dead son. Albert, an American living in Spain, warns Cecil of Webb's madness but also suggests the opportunity to manipulate that condition for financial benefit.

Much of this section of the novel focuses on Webb's affair with the black woman Anna, whose race complicated their love—at least in his view. The memory is generated by a letter he receives from her twenty-five years after he left. In it, she talks of her impending death and the son that they had. She explains what she told the child about his father and why. She also comments on a key source of their separation: "Surely your wound healed of itself, and you remembered more of me than the transgression of that stranger to us both, my flesh" (93). Her reference is to an affair she had while he was living in Europe, trying to become an artist. In an older letter, she begs for his forgiveness and proclaims her devotion. But it is clear in the new missive that he was incapable of such compassion:

> You came but you didn't stay. You made love to me as you would to a whore. But it didn't matter. You couldn't stay for long, we couldn't continue looking past each other's eyes each time our bellies were stuck together. And though it was not love, we created what love might create, what only love should be allowed to bring into the world. (92–93)

What is clear in these passages is that both of them have a problem with her body: she, because its urges and needs are beyond her understanding (it is a "stranger" to her), and he, because it (and thus she) betrays his notions of romantic purity and substitutes the physical needs of a flesh-and-blood woman. So Webb seeks the son, out of guilt, though Albert explains to Cecil that he does not want to find the boy, but only to live with the dream of finding him. That dream allows him to evade the truth of his own betrayal and abandonment of Anna, as well as his failure to love her.

Given Cecil's own obsessions and failings, it is not surprising that he acquiesces to Albert's offer of Estrella as a temporary sexual partner. As a prostitute, she bows to his demands without expecting anything other than money in return. There is neither obligation nor emotional commitment. With her, he can achieve any fantasy: "Al did not exaggerate when he sang your skills, five nights waiting for Webb and five different women you were for me" (105). They do not speak a common language, so there is no expectation of communication. He repeatedly refers to her as a beast and emphasizes the "incongruity" of her body:

> Emaciated in shank and back and shoulders, two lumps of rump which jiggle giddily on the bone with each step. Straight rail of body which breaks at the knees and deep waist to kneel as if in supplication but down farther beast on all fours rummaging beneath the red skirt of the bed cover. Surprising the breadth of beam in one who standing has boyish hips but spread they do to matron amplitude. (106–7)

She is both male and female, human and animal, full and empty. Thus, even in this most unrestrained heterosexual scene in the novel, the relationship is "queered" through the representation of Estrella's body. Moreover, the encounter occurs under the symbolic if not literal gaze of Albert, who plays the role of procurer. He is specifically identified with the Dutch traders responsible for the enslavement of Africans, and thus his arrangement of the liaison between Cecil and Estrella can be read as simply one more enslaving transaction. Certainly the thinness of her body suggests deprivation of human sustenance.

The narrative then turns to a journey Cecil takes to Africa. The focus is not on the African experience, however, but on an event on-board ship. During the trip, he meets and has intercourse with Anisse, another woman whose body is almost a man's:

> Anisse looked different with her clothes on. Cecil would have preferred that if she had to dress at all, she dressed like a man rather than try to disguise broad, square shoulders, flat chest and backsides beneath the most outrageously feminine frills and flounces. . . . Freckles for breasts, a squared valley between her jutting hipbones. (111)

In replicating the mannish appearance of Estrella, Wideman overdetermines the association of Cecil with sexual ambiguity. Only masculinized women are sexual partners for him; those who are more overtly female are the subjects of either fantasy or abuse and humiliation. Yet even in the actual sexual experiences, there is no positive outcome: Estrella is simply left behind, and Anisse jumps overboard while Cecil makes no attempt to save her.

But it is important to realize that this treatment of women is not simply misogyny. Rather, desire itself is the target. The narrative turns from Cecil's travels to Esther's journal, which records, among other experiences, a memory of childhood laden with sexuality. The teenaged boys of her community play base-ball on Sundays, but it is also a time of erotic experimentation. They use a box of sanitary napkins as home plate, and the game is always followed by the pairing off of boys and girls. On the only day Esther goes to the game, her father comes to get her and whips her on the way home. Her young body experiences not pleas-ure but the pain of his switch. However, she remembers this event as the begin-ning of her pursuit of salvation. She calls the girls who participate "Hussies," and she thinks of her father as an angry angel. Later, Cecil's abuse of her is seen as part of the means by which she goes through abjection toward greater religiosity.

Like Eddie in the earlier novel, Cecil returns home—but the meaning of that return is not so clear. He comes back to a world of undesired bodies. First, his Uncle Otis tells him the story of a child suffering from progeria. As he unnatu-rally aged, he became hypersensitive to the prospect of dying. The boy's real pain was his awareness of what the disease was doing to his body, his inability to deny the physical destruction of his being.

Returning to his apartment in the middle of the night, Cecil sees Fanny sit-ting at the kitchen table, which she has carefully set for the men in her life—who are now all dead. Like Martha, she has sacrificed the world of the living for that of the dead. She starves herself even as she prepares food for those absent others. And, finally, Cecil enters the bedroom where Esther sleeps, "sprawled naked on her naked bed" (185). He seems to have a moment of insight:

> A moonspot, the moon modeled to the deepened cleft [of her buttocks]. Wherein joy of my desiring. Stirred. Cecil strained his eyes in the darkness. What would there be to see. Perhaps something I had seen before, perhaps I could see more deeply, she would lead me where to look. (185)

Her body would seem to be the means to some perhaps spiritual knowledge. But even in this potentially transcendent moment, the imagery is complicated. It is, for one thing, her buttocks he is watching, the side of the body associated with defecation and anal sex. Further, his language emphasizes looking, not acting. Whatever he may learn, it cannot come through heterosexual desire. Esther's ear-lier abnegation of her body reinforces his male gaze.

In his first two novels, Wideman finds it necessary to reject the body as a site of desire in order to imagine any possibility of deracialized being. Each body and each relationship is a site of pain, exploitation, or sacrifice. They are the means by which the conflicts and struggles of characters are expressed. Modernity, whether black or white, means the failure of desire, the embrace of death. The only faint possibilities lie in accepting the corruption of the body and seeking an awareness outside and beyond it.

Notes

1. The commentators on modernism in Wideman's early career include Coleman, Mbalia, and Ramsey.
2. Other than recent work on James Baldwin and Randall Kenan, there have been few gay readings of black male writers. Among those are Nelson and Nero.
3. See Coleman 11–23 and Ramsey.
4. See Moynihan and Elkins.
5. Wideman makes references to the death in the bathroom of this grandfather figure, often named John French, throughout his writing.
6. By making Brother albino, Wideman can add a further dimension to otherness. Though physically white, Brother is never taken as anything other than white. His condition, marking him as different in the black community, instead makes him the Other of the Other; linked to his willingness to engage in homosexual behavior, his situation makes him multiply "queer."

Works Cited

Cleaver, Eldridge. *Soul on Ice.* New York: Dell, 1968.

Coleman, James W. *Blackness and Modernism: The Literary Career of John Edgar Wideman.* Jackson: UP of Mississippi, 1989.

Elkins, Stanley M. *Slavery.* Chicago: U of Chicago P, 1959.

Mbalia, Doreatha Drummond. *John Edgar Wideman: Reclaiming the African Personality.* Selinsgrove, Pa.: Susquehanna UP, 1995.

Moynihan, Daniel Patrick. *The Negro Family: The Case for National Action.* Washington, DC: U.S. Department of Labor, 1965.

Nelson, Emmanuel. "Towards a Transgressive Aesthetic: Gay Readings of Black Writing." *James White Review* 11.3 (1994): 15–17.

Nero, Charles I. "Toward a Black Gay Aesthetic: Signifying in Contemporary Black Gay Literature." *Brother to Brother: New Writings by Black Gay Men.* Ed. Essex Hemphill. Boston: Alyson, 1991. 229–52.

Ramsey, Priscilla R. "John Edgar Wideman's First Fiction: Voice and the Modernist Narrative." *CLA Journal* 41.1 (1997): 1–23.

Wideman, John Edgar. *A Glance Away.* 1967. New York: Holt, Rinehart and Winston, 1985.

———. *Hurry Home.* 1970. New York: Henry Holt and Co., 1986.

"A Lynching in Blackface"

John Edgar Wideman's Reflections on the Nation Question

Ashraf H. A. Rushdy

John Edgar Wideman's *The Lynchers* has long been considered a crucial text in the evolution of its author's career. As James W. Coleman has noted, it was the first Wideman novel set entirely in the African American community, the first Wideman novel to draw on "black historical tradition, speech, and cultural tradition," a book Coleman and others locate as the "pivotal book" coming at the end of the early novels and beckoning toward the accomplishments of the Homewood books that would follow with their emphasis on family and community (44).[1] Wideman himself notes in an interview that his 1973 novel marks a significant shift in his thinking: "*The Lynchers* is about things coming apart, things destructing. Then the next books are an attempt to reconstruct what came apart" (TuSmith 70). The novel's meditation on destruction and unraveling, I will argue, primarily provides a critical commentary on American ways of thinking about violence as a strategy of nation-building.

The very few critics who have written on *The Lynchers* have focused on the reasons the would-be lynchers of the title fail in accomplishing their purpose. The basic story Wideman tells is of four black men—Willie "Littleman" Hall, Thomas Wilkerson, Graham Rice, and Leonard Sanders—who decide to mobilize the black community by staging a lynching of a white police officer after they kill and mutilate the African American woman who is his lover and prostitute in an effort to enflame community sentiment. The plan comes undone through a series of mishaps and missteps, until, at the end of the novel, Wilkerson has been shot and likely killed by a paranoid Rice, while Sanders sits in a drunken, impotent rage in a bar waiting for Wilkerson to show up, and Littleman is taken to the insane unit at the hospital where he has been kept since his arrest for staging an impromptu protest on the steps of a local school. The only person ultimately killed by the lynchers is one of their own, and the surviving others remain drunk and catatonic, insane and institutionalized, and murderously paranoid and presumably on the run.[2]

In asking why it is that the lynchers fail to live up to the plan, critics have touched on that important point raised in most critical writing on Wideman's early works, the presumed distance that the protagonist-intellectuals of his first three novels feel from the black communities. While noting that *The Lynchers* is the first Wideman novel set entirely in the black community, Coleman also points out that the intellectuals continue to feel alienated from the people in that community and are thereby largely unable to promote "progressive political change in the black community" (44). Coleman argues that *The Lynchers*, like *Glance Away* and *Hurry Home*, is a novel that demonstrates how black intellectuals desire a significant role in salvaging the black communities in which they live and yet end up "isolating themselves from the community to a significant extent because the community is not capable of accepting their contribution" (45, 43). The intellectuals, then, remain isolated, alienated, and ineffectual as they "lose themselves in contemplation of the paradoxes and pitiful conditions of the black community" (58–59). Trudier Harris, who situates her reading of Wideman's novel in a study of the literary representations of lynchings in African American writing, likewise believes that the reason the plan fails has to do with the planners themselves and their relationship to the black community. Harris argues that for the planners the lynching seems an "intellectual exercise" rather than an expression of the kinds of visceral and emotional response that was the "historical motivation" for traditional lynch mobs. Primarily, she notes, this excess of intellect in the planning is a result of the social positions of the intellectuals. Their plan is "theoretical and abstract" because it is the plan of men who are neither married nor propertied— that is, intellectuals without meaningful connections to the community that they hope to liberate by urging them to protect what they already have (135–36).

Another point the critics focus on in diagnosing the failure of the plan is the community that the intellectuals aspire to free from oppression. Coleman argues that the parlous state of the black community itself is a major part of the problem. Wideman, he argues, gives us a bleak picture of the possibility of social change because the lower-class characters who are not alienated from the community are "self-destructive, mean, cruel, simpleminded, or uninventive" (59). The character who embodies these destructive tendencies is Orin Wilkerson (the father of Thomas), who appears in significant scenes at the beginning and the end of the novel. In the opening scene of the novel, he is one of the garbage collectors who swap tales about the freakish sexual appetites of white women; and at the end of the novel, he is visited in prison by his wife after he has murdered his best friend, Childress. According to Coleman, "Orin's carelessness and destructiveness" represent and embody "the external, day-to-day reality of the black community" (56), a state of oppressive social life that is itself "partly responsible for killing the plan conceived to change it" (58). Harris, on the other hand, sees Orin Wilkerson, and the lower-class community residents he represents, as a stark counterpoint to the planners, "men of action rather than men of ideas." Whereas the lynchers spend the whole novel talking about the plan to kill the police officer, Orin murders his friend in the heat of passionate argument. It is, as Harris notes, a "pathetic drama of reality," but the act, destructive as it is, also does stand in parodic mockery of the plotters' "pageantry of a planned symbolic execution" that never does happen (145–46).

The final point on which the critics write concerns the plan itself, the idea of performing an act of symbolic violence as a strategy for social change. Coleman argues that Wideman gives us in the character of Littleman, the architect of the plan, someone to be admired for the "justice, the rightness of his thinking." While some readers may question the practicality of the plan and the idea of "using violent means to attain justice," he contends that many would applaud the plan and see that "Littleman's belief in violence as a means of [liberating the black community] makes him an authentic militant black nationalist" (60–61). For Harris, Wideman does not applaud but rather exposes the deep flaws in Littleman's lynching plan. Positing that Wideman believes that "violence in kind cannot liberate" (142), Harris shows how the idea of lynching as a positive act of liberation is problematic since it draws on a model of terrorism used by white communities, and is therefore both imitative and reactive rather than creative or resistant (134). The moral situation Wideman explores in the novel, Harris contends, is "the desire for revenge on the part of those who lack the depravity necessary to effect that revenge" (141).

Harris, I would argue, provides the more compelling reading of Wideman's politics as it is expressed in *The Lynchers* by more accurately defining the basis of the alienation of the black intellectuals from their community, by carefully assessing the tragic but critical significance of Wideman's representations of community folk who act instead of plan, and by demonstrating the ways that Wideman is more interested in exposing than celebrating the idea of retributive violence. Where I believe Harris is less compelling is in her insistence that Wideman's exposé is motivated by a desire to demonstrate something about a group psychology and to defend a model of black nationalism. Harris comments that though the desire for revenge is fully understandable, the planners are unable to act on it because it goes against their "will" and their "sense of community." They are foiled not only by their sense of class dislocation but primarily because they believe, at some fundamental level, that it is "certainly not permissible to plan to kill a black person," which of course is the first act in their plan—to murder a black prostitute in order to rouse the community to lynch the white police officer who is her pimp and lover. The plan is foiled, Harris concludes, because Wideman wishes to "illustrate how thoroughly antithetical such actions would be to black human nature" and because he believes that the taking of life, "for whatever purpose, goes ultimately against the grain of the concept of nationhood" (141–42).

Two things are worth noting here at the outset. First, I think that in *The Lynchers* Wideman is relatively uninterested in the issue of a group psychology (or anything like a concept such as "black human nature").[3] Second, I think Wideman does not try to make an exculpatory case for the concept of nationhood. *The Lynchers*, I would argue, falls into that loosely defined "school" of African American writing that emerged from and was critical of a discourse of black cultural nationalism that flourished from the mid-1960s to the mid-1970s.[4] Like other writers of that generation of writers—Ishmael Reed, Charles Johnson, and Octavia Butler, to name a few—Wideman raises questions about the complexities of the past and the viability of black nationalism for the present. He sets his novel in the 1970s and has his protagonists interrogate the meaning of resurrecting a historical practice of anti-black violence in order to promote their nationalist agenda. Wideman asks difficult questions about how to understand the past in a meaningful way, how to discern the ways that previous forms of social control continue to exert power over aggrieved communities in sometimes new forms, and, finally, how to counter historical oppression without falling into the same patterns of thinking as the oppressors. In doing so, I would argue that Wideman is exploring the idea of black nationalism in order to expose those unhealthy features that are almost invariably at the heart of strategies of nation-building.

The lynching plan is formulated in a staggered series of scenes throughout the novel. The plan is largely the product of the mind of Littleman, and it is primarily described in his words. In his first and fullest formulation of the plan, Littleman delivers a paean to ritual violence that gives an almost existential spin to the practice of lynching. In his carefully modulated description of what a lynching is and what it is supposed to do, employing a rhetorical delivery meant to inspire and make palpable for the other lynchers the deepest significance of just what they are about to do, Littleman moves through a series of topics that reveal the trajectory of his thinking. He talks first about identity, and how a lynching is a practice that helps create the fundamental divisions that make identity meaningful. Lynching, he begins, is "like going to church" because it helps put "things into their proper perspective," reminding people "of who they are, where they stand," and divides "the world simple and pure." The world so divided—"Good or bad. Oppressors and oppressed. Black or white"—becomes, through the ritual and spectacle of lynching, a world where there is no blurring of boundaries, no complication of identities (60). He then moves on to an appreciation of the "history and tradition" of the practice, making clear distinctions between those "vigilante necktie parties" of the "western model" and the "formal lynching" of the South, which he admires because there "tradition means something" (60–61). Of course, what tradition means in the South is power, and here Littleman hits his stride as he moves from the abstractions of identity and ritual to the materiality of power. Lynching, he concludes, is "about power," particularly the power to "expose the fundamental basis of your relationship to the powerless." Throughout, Littleman describes the exercise of power as an expressive art. Lynching is a "dramatic" medium that must have been invented by a "great artist" because it takes the "raw fantasies" of a people and develops from them a "satisfying, stable form" (61). Only the limitations of imagination—"Imagination which we possess in abundance, fertile, subtle, co-ercive"—act as constraints on what he refers to finally as the "poetry" of "power" (62).

What distinguishes lynching from plain murder, he concludes, is that it is a symbolic and ritual act. Like a "passion play," it sacralizes the coming together of community. Lynching, then, is the strategy of concentrating the various myths that hold a people together into one spectacular act on a specified scapegoat that ritualistically states that "this is the way things really are. Will stay forever" (62). Littleman also discusses the undeniable orgiastic sensibility exposed in lynchings, where white sexual anxieties revealed themselves in charges of rape and acts of castration, but it is interesting to note that he makes a connection between the sexual ("When Rastus burns there is a communal hard-on") and the various levels of communal life: "man to wife, children to families, families to the communities which they have created." What ties the lynchers with the communities is the "open secret" that the action of lynching is performed in the name of the community renewed by this letting of blood. "Complicity. Conspiracy": that is the relationship of those who commit the crime and those who share in it, Littleman concludes (63). Having completed his analysis of the profound significance of lynching for white communities attempting to assert what he calls "White power," Littleman then describes the logic of their plan to generate or assert what presumably he would call Black power. For it to make sense they would have to lynch a white police officer, that primary agent of social control in black communities since lynchings decreased in frequency, and they would have to do it in a way that borrowed from but also transformed the traditional lynching party.

In a later scene, Littleman elaborates on the significance of that transformation, using the discourse of Black Power to describe how the black community's lynching of a white police officer will produce a sensibility meant to contest the "White power" that lynchings had traditionally served to assert. The lynching of the policeman, Littleman maintains, would efface a historical fear and challenge the worldview on which it is based. Since a historical effect of the tradition of lynching in America is that every "black man carries a fear of death in his heart, a fear of death at the hands of white men," Littleman asserts that some act is required to "release our people" from that fear and to provide an example counter to that history (119). The lynching of the policeman would perform that feat: "When we lynch the cop we declare our understanding of the past, our scorn for it, our disregard for any consequences that the past has taught us to fear" (117). The idea behind the lynching, Littleman maintains, is what is important, the lynching itself being a symbolic ritual meant to enhance, to generate, and disseminate that idea, in this case the idea being a resistance to white violence and the claim of finality to white definitions of black reality: "We will lynch one man but in fact we will be denying a total vision of reality" (116). What the lynching does, then, is challenge the worldview that presumed and rearticulated the idea of black inferiority, the belief that black life was expendable and subject to white control, either materially or symbolically. Like the Black Power advocates who defined Black Power itself as "the right to create our own terms through which to define ourselves and our relationship to the society, and to have those terms recognized," Littleman too demands a future "conditioned by new definitions of ourselves as fighters, free, violent men who will determine the nature of the reality in which they exist" (117).[5] The plan of lynching in Littleman's mind, then, is meant to create conditions for African American self-definition; that is the primary transformation lynching undergoes, from a form of white terrorism to a site of black affirmation, from a destructive ritual to a unifying one.

In registering the kinds of unity he believes they will accomplish with their act, Littleman uses two kinds of discourse to describe what the lynching will create: religious and nationalist. In one scene, he talks about how their act will promote a future in which the elements of the lynching (the roles of victim and lynchers) will appear to have been immanent. It "will seem as if he and his lynchers have always existed, patiently waiting to be perceived, a mystery to be worshipped" (172). The lynching is not only a means of creating selfhood, then, but of creating a deity, assisting in the "birth of a God," as Littleman puts it here, a divine being he later calls the "Black God" whom Littleman watches "pass to manhood" (173, 187). It is worth noting that like earlier white-authored lynchings, this black-authored one is meant to create the illusion of permanence, to revise historical imagination so that it seems that this is the way things have always been and will always remain.

The other discourse Littleman employs is that of nationhood. The "total community gives its sanction in a lynching," Littleman notes, either through assertion or through complicity; and actions sanctioned by the total community, then, do not prove the agency of the individuals who perform them but rather become the collective deed of a collective body (117). For Littleman, that collectivity is the nation: "When one man kills it's murder. When a nation kills murder is called war. If we lynch the cop we will be declaring ourselves a nation" (117). If the white community does nothing in response to this declaration, then they will be interpreted as saying "yes you are a nation and we accept the truth of your nationhood, your right to establish your own laws and justice" (118). Even if the white community retaliates by randomly slaughtering members of the black community, it will be interpreted as a "declaration of war, an acknowledgment of the separateness of the community" (118). In either case, the lynching will have promoted a new entity. The Black God who is birthed, it turns out, is the black nation itself.

What, then, is Wideman saying about black nationalism in what is arguably the book in which he most insistently meditates on the positive and negative features of the nation as a meaningful entity? First, it is important to remind ourselves that the strain of black nationalism Wideman takes up in *The Lynchers* emerged in the midst of the Black Power movement, was theorized by Malcolm X and the Nation of Islam, promoted by groups like the Student Nonviolent Coordinating Committee (SNCC), and attempted by cultural nationalist factions like US and the Republic of New Africa.[6] At one point in the novel, when Littleman imagines the scene of the lynching, he speculates that it will be filled with speakers and celebrants who are "Snicks and Muslims and Rams"—that is, members of those black nationalists groups associated with Black Power (65).[7] There are also references to less formal and more insurgent nationalisms associated with Black Power when Littleman mentions the 1965 Watts riots and Jonathan Jackson's attempted kidnapping of Judge Harold Haley from the Marin County Hall of Justice on August 7, 1970 (182). These are moments during the sixties that were "raw, crude sources of energy," according to Littleman, because they exposed the futility of white society and helped imagine the possibility of giving birth to a black nation.

Indeed, one contemporary commentator called the Watts event a series of "revolts born precisely out of a growing alienation from and rejection of many of the basically irrelevant premises and principles of the society," and Jonathan Jackson's brother George reserved the date of his revolutionary action to "reckon all time in the future," a birthday of a nation, as it were.[8] By referencing these formal and informal black nationalist projects, Wideman insistently makes an uneasy connection between what "Snicks, Muslims, and Rams" were theorizing and what Littleman plans to inaugurate with his staged lynching of the white police officer. His novel really is, as he describes it in an interview, "another way of looking at the 60s" primarily because it is a critique of that black nationalism that emerged in the time of Black Power (Coleman, "Interview" 69).

That critique, as Trudier Harris notes, begins with the fact that Littleman's nationalist project requires a vicious act of violence against another black person, which Wideman, according to Harris, eschews as going "against the grain of the concept of nationhood." I would argue, instead, that Wideman is demonstrating precisely the ways that nationalist projects tend to begin with just the kind of intragroup violence that Littleman builds into his plan. The plan to kill and mutilate Sissie, the white policeman's black lover and prostitute, is not just one unsavory aspect in an otherwise sound plan for calling forth a nationalist sensibility in the black community. It is but one instance of the kinds of concerted intraracial violence that haunt the plan from its flawed formulation to its aborted conclusion. Partly, the explanation for the pervasiveness of intraracial violence is to be found in the fact that the plan is intensely violent in its intentions and therefore requires the "lynchers" to accept "the violence that draws them together" (49), and learn to "believe in each other as killers" (50). Given their immersion into a way of thinking that alienates them from any more humane ways of imagining social change, it is a seemingly unavoidable corollary that the violent thoughts they act on will be against those who are closest and mean the most to them.

Moreover, we could say that this is an acting out of their own self-loathing since they would presumably be trying to kill in other African Americans what they find unacceptable in themselves, an exaggerated case of what Rice's mother tells him when she advises him to "cut them no count niggers loose and go about your business" (198). The explanation for the intraracial violence, then, is to be found in that dynamic of "incestuous spite" Littleman fosters among the lynchers —in which each of the lynchers is moved to ruthlessness because each "could see externalized [in the others] that image of himself he struggled to destroy" (229). Littleman himself, the primary architect of this nationalist plan and the one apparently in control of fostering this "incestuous spite," is also a victim of the pervasive violence he installs into the plan. At one point, he fantasizes striking

"A Lynching in Blackface"

and raping an African American woman he meets on the beach (124) and at another of killing the African American orderly who cares for him in the hospital (185). These scenes of imagined ruthlessness reveal both the intensity of violence in Littleman and also his own incapacity to accept culpability.

But, more than simply an aberration, Wideman is showing us that this dynamic of intraracial violence is just what is most dangerous and ever-present in nationalist thinking. One of the first concerns of those putatively organized to create unity in a group is the need to imagine how to deal with those who are deemed insufficiently committed or traitors to the project of the nation. In Wideman's novel, the plotters attempt to "minimize the possibility of individual cop-out by maximizing the certainty that the one who fails cannot hurt the others and will himself be absolutely dealt with" (59). Instead of becoming the kind of cement that unites them in a singular purpose, though, this sensibility that it is acceptable to exert violence against the others in the plan manifests itself in particularly ugly ways. Saunders imagines murdering Rice with impunity: "One more slightly goofy nigger found dead in a locked room" (252). Rice actually murders Wilkerson in a fit of paranoia (240–41). With the exception of the plan of lynching the white police officer, all the other acts of imagined and real violence are against black people. And all of them are rationalized as being necessary to salvaging a plan ultimately meant to unite black people. Here, Wideman was echoing in order to critique some of the key theorists who were "Snicks, Muslims, and Rams" in the sixties. The Chicago Office of SNCC, for example, issued a pamphlet in 1967 in which they claimed their desire for a "oneness with a worldwide black brotherhood" at the same time as they felt that the only way to deal with "black traitors, quisslings, collaborators, sell-outs, white Negroes" was to "ostracize them and if necessary exterminate them" (487, 489). In a 1968 speech delivered at Oakland, California, Stokely Carmichael concluded his expressed desire for individual reformation and black unity ("Every Negro is a potential black man. We *will* not alienate them. . . . We're gonna take time and patience with our people because they're *ours*") with a chilling comment that "we gonna off" whoever does not realize the potential black man within him ("Declaration" 277, 281).

Wideman is also meditating profoundly on this painful tension between a desire for unity, modeled on the idea of the "nation," and the violence exercised against its would-be citizens in the effort to bring it to birth. The moral situation is not simply about revenge, then, but about the problematic issues involved in admittedly more productive strategies for reclaiming and redeeming a people. What has given and continues to give nationalism its appeal is the idea that the emergent nation breaks away from the past and inaugurates a new moment. The rhetoric of "birth" suggests not only that something novel has begun but that the new entity possesses the innocence of the newborn. Nations born from anticolonial struggles conceive of their emergence as a rejection of the corrupt metropole, a leaving of the old world and the birth of the new. Decolonization, Frantz Fanon argued, is itself "the veritable creation of new men" (30),[9] and the black revolution in America, Julius Lester noted, "will give birth to the New Man" (129). This desire for a new beginning, for a state of innocence again, is illusory, however, since those "new men" have up to that point lived their whole lives in a state of colonization and been themselves socialized into that world. And, more frightening, they can imagine their creation only by also imagining the destruction of those who shared with them that earlier colonization which they believe that they (but not others) have transcended. The rationalization for killing Sissie is that she "had lost all power over her life" and was therefore "dead already, a puppet in the hands of those whose whims controlled her" (153). Until they formulated the plan, of course, the lynchers were also caught in the same system that they believe makes Sissie's life less meaningful than theirs.

The desire at the heart of this strain of nationalism is the desire for purity, the source itself of innocence. Contemporary nationalist movements forty years after the sixties, with their grotesque acts of "ethnic cleansing," demonstrate in the very terminology this desire for purity premised on ridding the body politic of whatever is alien. In the sixties, this desire for purity took on the form, first, of the political "blacker than thou" syndrome exemplified in what Addison Gayle mockingly calls "the Professional Black Nationalist," and, then, in the genetic "blacker than thou" attitude which involved painful scrutinizing of genealogy as an indicator of politics (84). At one point in *The Lynchers*, Saunders expresses his suspicion of Wilkerson in just these terms. "In Wilkerson's pale face Saunders was confronted with the image of the raping white devil astride black women. Saunders asked himself how little of the enemy remaining was enough to taint. When the deal went down, when it was kill and be killed would Wilkerson make a clean break, could he shed white man's ways, white man's blood" (156)? Saunders's thinking demonstrates precisely the deep problems encountered when the nation is conceived of as a homogenous body, when race is believed to be a stable quality, and when genetic makeup is conceived of as a marker of political commitment. It exemplifies that desire for an impossible purity, not only of political beliefs, but of biological history. And, of course, that desire for purity inevitably involves that other hallmark of nationalist projects, the desire to control the women of the group.

In an appreciative but critical assessment of Black Power in 1968, Vincent Harding noted that "some female believers in Black Power find it difficult to adjust their western indoctrination of equality to the old-new emphasis on the supremacy of the black man" and accepting the cultural nationalists' models of domestic

"A Lynching in Blackface"

arrangements that are drawn along "almost strictly Pauline lines" (29). Both Angela Davis and Elaine Brown attest to how black nationalists—both in the cultural nationalist United States and in the revolutionary nationalist Black Panther Party—demeaned and exploited women and confused the "birth of the New Man" with the submission of the black woman.[10] In *The Lynchers*, Wideman exposes the premises and problems of this aspect of nationalist thinking—where the idea of woman as property defines the nation, where one can use terms like "their women" with its logical corollary, "our women" (253). The overt form of control over women in Wideman's analysis of the failings of black nationalism involves violence, which, as Davis and Brown show, is usually the covert and implicit threat to women who do not conform or accept the nationalism in question or support the male nationalists who wish to control it and them. It is important to remember, of course, that while the acts of imagined violence against the other men are an effect of the lynchers' plot, the imagined mutilation and murder of Sissie is a planned feature of it. And in showing us the process by which the men become resolved to do unspeakable violence to a woman who is considered doubly traitorous to the black nation—someone who sells her sex instead of using it to birth warriors, someone who sleeps with the enemy—Wideman shows us the ways that nationalist imperatives impel men to need to control women's bodies, their sexual choices, their reproductive rights.

The primary victim of that violence is Sissie, and the putative reason Sissie is chosen is that her known relationship with the white police officer would place suspicion on him when her mangled body is found. But there seems to be an even more intimate connection between the lynchers' fantasies of violence against Sissie and the fact that she has a white lover. Consider that early on, Saunders and Wilkerson both believed that it was possible to modify the plan so as not to kill Sissie. Wilkerson felt that it would be possible to hold her and spread the rumor of her murder and mutilation (218), while Saunders had found "distasteful" the idea of "killing someone [who was] already a pitiable victim" (154). Once both of them become implicated and subsumed in Littleman's nationalist dreams, though, Wilkerson and Saunders devolve into less humane beings.[11] They both stalk Sissie, and they find themselves fascinated by the idea of committing violence against her, Saunders much more than Wilkerson. Consider the very disturbing scene of Saunders creeping outside Sissie's bedroom "to listen through the thin wall" to the sounds of Sissie making love to the "gray boy." Hearing them "grunt and sigh," Saunders had "wanted to punch through the rotten plaster and kill them both in their sweat," making Sissie perform fellatio on him while he made the white policeman beg for his life. "No humiliation would have been enough," he concludes (249). For Saunders, Sissie is not just an instrumental feature in the lynchers' plot, and not just useful because of her relationship with the real target of their plot. His intense rage at her being with her white lover—and his belief that other black women were likewise seduced by promises of being with white men—suggests a far more invidious desire to control the sexual choices of black women, whom he consistently refers to as "bitches." Instead of just killing her, he later fantasizes raping her first, in order, as he revealingly puts it, to "[t]urn her on like no white pig could" (251).

As was the case with southern white lynchers who performed lynchings in order to terrorize black men and women, while at the same time frightening white women into submission to the patriarchal order, Wideman's lynchers also assert control over a population of women by showing them the dangers of their sexual choices. It is certainly noteworthy that Littleman, the person who talks Wilkerson and Saunders out of their sympathy for Sissie's plight, had likewise made the connection between the freedom of black women to express themselves how they wished and the lynching plan he hopes will put an end to that freedom. In a startling scene of recollection and dreaming, Littleman shifts from an imagined conversation with his former lover Angela telling him that she was again dating a "white boy" (170–71) to his immediate preoccupation with his lynching plan. Against the impurity of such interracial liaisons, Littleman proposes the "orderliness, precision, cleanliness, rhythm . . . in an action, a plan such as [he has] conceived" (172). Violence against women—like the acts of Jack the Ripper, who is the subject of a book Saunders reads—is a means of purifying the nation through the control of the sexual options of its women, which, as in Jack the Ripper's case, also came down to "reforming his society through murder" (154).

Littleman is able to persuade Wilkerson and Saunders of the necessity of killing Sissie by noting "how Sissie's life had been stolen, how she could not forfeit what she no longer owned," and by claiming that since "she functioned as a puppet in the oppressor's system, taking her life would be a minor act of sabotage" (154). Neither Wilkerson nor Saunders is fully persuaded by this argument, though, because each of them is aware of the flawed logic. Wilkerson knows that any one of them could equally be said to have had his or her life stolen, that each of them could be designated a puppet in a system that governed their actions. In a society with the awesome power of coercion, all of them are victims. He thinks of his own father and the friend his father murdered. What was the difference between that act of intraracial violence and the one they were planning to commit against Sissie? Why was Sissie chosen instead of one of them? Wilkerson describes it as an "accident"—"How could you form a plan in a world where all that mattered was accidental, a blind jumble of blind forces? Who was Sissie? What accidents had made her the plan's first victim?"—but the situation he is analyzing is not accidental, but purposeful, and not arbitrary but governed by laws of white supremacy (213). Saunders gives the more compelling description of what Wilkerson calls "accident" by dwelling on the ways that the "oppressor's system" in fact co-opted all its victims, and all who lived subject to its power were victims. "Wouldn't all sufferers who submitted, who allowed themselves to be used rather than striking back at the users," Saunders wonders, "wouldn't all of them be guilty, eligible for slaughter, his sick mother if she were still alive, one of the most guilty since she had endured to the breaking point and past" (154)?

Wilkerson's and Saunders's meditations on the complexity of the condition of oppression constitute a good part of Wideman's critique of the kind of nationalism Littleman espouses. Primarily, Wideman demonstrates the numerous complications in the ills of the society that Littleman would cure with what amounts to a panacea. The sort of clarity that Littleman argues lynching will produce— "Good or bad. Oppressors and oppressed. Black or white"—is illusory, and evinces just the kind of desire for purity that almost inevitably leads to mass atrocities. By having the lynching plot be a call for black nationalism, Wideman is showing how that divisiveness, that claim of absolute difference, is impossible and dangerous. In the end, it turns out that Littleman's call is for a form of black nationalism founded on an imitation of an act of white terrorism (lynching), involving violence against the very people the plotters wish to redeem, and premised on the control of a population of women whose choices must be circumscribed in order to give stability and purity to the nation they will birth.

Let me be patently clear that Wideman's critique of black nationalism is not the kind of critique made by liberals in the sixties and seventies—that is, that black nationalism is racially divisive and that we should all gather under a less exclusive banner of a more integrated or multicultural America. His critique of black nationalism is ultimately a critique of nationalism itself. Although he places the idea of black nationalism at the center of his novel, he makes references both to the contemporary colonized nations who are struggling for their independence—notably the allusion to Algiers and the "war cries of the Arabs" (223)—and also to historical national myths of origin: "Fourth of July, Bastille Day, Dien Bien Phu" (104). These references allow Wideman to raise the question so frequently found at the heart of his explorations of the meaning of history, the question of origins. It is telling that Wideman references "Bastille Day," as the occasion associated with the revolutionary creation of the French Republic, immediately before he mentions "Dien Bien Phu," the battleground marking the Vietnamese resistance against French colonization. It could be that he is simply showing how each nation must claim its independence at some point in time, the French citizens from monarchy and the Vietnamese from the French, but it could also be that he is noting that somewhere in the origins of one nation is to be found the source of its later tendencies to exploit another. What the French did to create the republic in storming the Bastille is somehow related to the French colonization of Vietnam and Algeria. This is made more pointedly clear, I think, in the "Matter Prefatory" section of the novel.

While most critics have noted that Wideman uses the "Matter Prefatory" to make the reader aware of the depth and range of historical oppression that demands a plan of retaliation like Littleman's, none seems to have noted how fundamental the idea of white nationalism is to this section of the novel.[12] The first three quotations contain the words of colonial Americans who fear that slavery and the Africans who are its victims will endanger the white American nationalism they are already imagining as their heritage. In the first quotation Governor Alexander Spotswood prays that "Neither The Lust of Dominion, nor The Desire of freedom" may cause African slaves to revolt and cause any harm to the "Strength of Your Country" (3). In the second, Benjamin Franklin advocates the removal of black people who are a blight to what he calls the "Complexion of my Country," and in the third Colonel William Byrd feels that so many Africans are being imported as slaves that the American colony might well lose its white identity and instead "be confirmed by the Name of New Guinea" (4). It is highly telling that the "Matter Prefatory" (and the novel itself) begins not with the descriptions of lynching—such as the list of 116 lynchings in the 1871 petition presented to Congress by Kentucky Negroes (7–13)—but rather with a series of statements on the desired but imperiled whiteness of the nation. Whiteness, Wideman implies, is possible only by the violence imagined or done to black people. In a later book, he will argue that blackness is the "ground against which" whiteness emerges and rises, "the *black* defining, proving, enabling their *white* . . ." (*Fatheralong* 78). In the "Matter Prefatory," he exposes the colonial origins of both this whiteness ("the lovely White," in Franklin's words) and the nationalist setting in which it was rendered possible and which it enabled.

Wideman makes the point, I think, of how the aspirations for freedom and justice that Spotswood, Franklin, and Byrd articulated were made as unavailable to African Americans as were the hopes for equality, fraternity, and liberty to the Vietnamese and Algerians. Later in *The Lynchers*, we encounter more conventional statements excoriating the hypocrisy of American freedom, when, in the Philadelphia setting of the novel, the icons of American independence are mocked by the proximity of American racial immiseration: "Liberty Bell almost close enough to spit on . . . South Street giving the lie to every promise" (111). But even more significant than this exposure of how the American dream of freedom is not available to black Americans is the diagnosis of the fact that America began as and remains a white nation. In its origins lay its future tendencies; in its desire to mark distinctions lay the future divisions.

Wideman, of course, is interested not only in showing the origins but also the manifestations of that nationalist imperative to control and renew power through the exercise of new technologies. Benedict Anderson has shown us the work that newspapers do in creating the sentiments of nationalism, producing "imagined communities" based on a wide and publicly shared act of consumption in which "the imagined world is visibly rooted in everyday life . . . creating that remarkable confidence of community in anonymity which is the hallmark of modern nations (35–36). When Littleman imagines the mass rally at the lynching of the white police officer, he dreams that the local African American newspaper will provide inflammatory coverage that will arouse the community to retributive violence: "A story appears on the front page of the Black Dispatch. Mutilated body found" (65). Partly a critique of the mainstream press' disinterest in covering stories involving black victims—"you haven't read in the white papers" (66)—it is also a reference to the ways that white newspapers historically used to generate mob sentiments and provoke lynchings by their inflammatory reports alleging African American crimes in general and against white women in particular. In an essay on Charles Chesnutt, Wideman dwells profoundly on the pun in a Chesnutt short story in which a character refers to "noosepapers" and thereby evokes the connection between the media and racial violence, between "the lynch rope and the conspiracy of public institutions" ("Chesnutt" 78). The important point Wideman is making in *The Lynchers* is that what was effective in the days of Chesnutt is now no longer so. The dream that the *Black Dispatch* would cover the story, and the "hope" that it might run a picture of the bloody body (237) turn out to be just that, dreams and hopes. In fact, the only newspaper story of a woman's murder and mutilation in the novel is the white media's coverage of the killing of Sharon Tate, "the pregnant movie star" whose death "makes the newspapers full of blood" (45–46). Otherwise, the "imagined community" of black nationalism is only imagined (and never realized) because the infrastructural communications systems are relatively inefficacious, particularly in comparison to the nation-building apparatus of the white mass culture.

Anderson's emphasis on the "mass ceremony" of newspaper readership makes it possible to imagine other forms of "simultaneous consumption" as postmodern rearticulations of nationalism. It is arguable that Wideman is demonstrating the ways contemporary film fulfills the function that newspapers used to do. There is a scene where Saunders watches a movie and notes the ways whites "parade their women butt naked on the screen for anybody to see" (253). White women are seen to be sexually available as well as sexually desirable by the process of their being put on display. Saunders's mistake in his analysis is that he believes that the media used by those in power is a revelation of weakness rather than an assertion of power—they "expose their game in Cinemascope and Technicolor," he claims—and in this way he misses the insidious work that films and other media do in disseminating ideologies, including the valuation of white women and the devaluation of black people (253). The work Franklin had hoped to do by deportation ("excluding all Blacks and Tawneys") is now done by newspapers and movies (4). In *The Lynchers*, Wideman shows us how cultural productions do the work of promoting rather than undermining those nationalist imperatives.

We can see, then, that Wideman critically assesses white American nationalism as much he does black nationalism. In one interview, he revealingly calls *The Lynchers* a "critique of self-reliance," and notes that part of what inspired him to write the novel was his recognition of the connection between white American material success and the lynching of African Americans. Both these "mirror twins" depended on violence, and both revealed the "mechanics, the systemic working of the society." Part of that "working" is the ways that those mechanisms define distinctions amongst populations, the individual self-reliance of those whites who lift themselves up by their bootstraps, the collective degradation of those blacks hanged from their necks (TuSmith 131). As we saw, he points out in the novel that lynching is a ritual of collective violence that is particularly meant to mark differences in stark contrast. This form of thinking (chosen / reprobate) is part and parcel of nationalist discourse everywhere, of course, but in America it took on more stark and enduring forms (the one-drop rule of racial identity, for instance). For Wideman, this American way of violating others on the basis of marking difference is crucially telling. Maybe "it's because Americans have felt so alienated from the land, their past, that the notion of cleavage, the notion of either/or is fundamental," he muses (TuSmith 51). His point, in the end, is that nations require violence, the overt violence of independence struggles, the systemic violence of purifying their population through extermination, the covert violence of creating and deploying definitions and categories, like race.

The Lynchers is a novel that Wideman has, at different times, called "another way of looking at the 60s" and a "critique of self-reliance"—in other words, I think, a novel that takes on the questions of black nationalism and white nationalism. In both cases—and Wideman is not making black and white nationalism equal or equally culpable—he is demonstrating what might well be inherent problems in conceiving of the "nation" as a desirable form of human organization. Indeed, by having Littleman plan to inaugurate the form of black nationalism he advocates through a lynching, Wideman hints that black nationalism, like the plot of lynching itself, is reactive, an imitation of an oppressor's strategy, and that is what weakens it as an effective intervention meant to ameliorate the black community's oppressed position. Consistently, Littleman asserts that their plot depends on, borrows from, and is ultimately bound by the language, history, and precedent of that violent colonizing culture they are attempting to overturn or at the very least separate themselves from. The lynching plot is meant to "say to white people what they have been saying to us for so long" (236). The plotters admit that they are "incorporating their understanding of history and power into our plan. We are saying crystally clear in the language they invented: We are your equals" (118). Accepting rather than rejecting or questioning the dominant culture's language, terms, and understanding of history and power, the plotters' lynching act and the nationalism it is meant to inspire become not a "phoenix rising from the ashes of the old," but rather an entity destined to bear the marks of its birth (232).

Of course, this critique of nationalism does raise some serious problems since it renders difficult the possibility of change, raising the complex question of how one can imagine revolutionary transformation that does not in some way draw on and use those very patterns of behavior that are the cause of oppression. How, in other words, in fact in the words Bob Moses borrowed from Albert Camus to describe the difficult tension of activism in the 1960s, does one cease being a victim without becoming an executioner (Carson 46)? Or, in less individual terms, how does one theorize a collectivity, a body of people joined in a positive and just endeavor, without falling into the problems associated with nationalism? Wideman is more interested in *The Lynchers* in demonstrating the parameters of the problem than in offering satisfying answers, which he would certainly begin to do in his later works that emphasize family and neighborhoods and communities as more flexible forms of social organization that could and should see heterogeneity as a strength, and allow women more voice, agency, and options, without minimizing the continuing importance of resistance to the threats from within and without.

The novel that might profitably be compared to *The Lynchers* for understanding that ambivalence with which it represents the potentials for black nationalism is Ralph Ellison's *Invisible Man*. Both novels end by silencing the advocates of black nationalism (Littleman is placed in an insane asylum, Ras has his mouth pierced by a spear), and both ask powerfully searching questions about what to make of white nationalism, how to accept positive American principles that emerge from a disastrous American history. Ellison asks whether African Americans should "affirm the principle on which the country was built and not the men," or "take responsibility for all of it, for the men as well as the principle," or, the option the invisible man seems to favor, to "affirm the principle because we, through no fault of our own, were linked to all the others, ... *part of them* as well as apart

Ashraf H. A. Rushdy

123

from them" (574–75). Wideman too ponders what it means to be heir of the Liberty Bell and the denizen of South Street, to be "the *black* defining, proving, enabling their *white*." And, like Ellison, he is skeptical whether turning on their head the racial distinctions used to create the American nation at its origin will be a way to undo the damage that was done, since it means accepting and accentuating those terms rather than disputing them.

Like Ellison, Wideman also briefly considers the idealistic and hopeful but problematic conception of connectedness, of being "part of them," in Ellison's terms. In one of Littleman' s more ambiguous but tantalizing meditations, he imagines the connection between past oppression and present immiseration, imagining the rebelliousness of a "slave tossed overboard" reborn in the soul of a baby forced to live in a "vermin infested bureau" on 125th Street. Littleman uses this idea of time collapsing to comment on the unreality of distinctions in the most important collective identities: "As there is no fixed interval between the two conceptions [of slave and baby], neither is there continuity of nation, race, sex" (187). It is admittedly an ambiguous statement, but, in the work of an author who will later state that he does not believe in "the notion of a stable, underpinning personality," preferring a sense of identity based on "what is fragmentary, what is discontinuous," it suggests something about the unease even Littleman has with the nationalism he advocates (TuSmith 76). Finally, what both the authors of *The Lynchers* and *Invisible Man* have in common is that both see the temptation to violence as clearly as they see the dangers of it; and both end on a somewhat melancholic note of waiting, of trying to figure out how to be socially responsible in a complicated world where the options, for those who cannot accept the idea of the others in the self, seem to be destruction of others or destruction of self.

Notes

1. See also Rushdy, untitled review.
2. Cf. Harris 139, 141. Coleman reads the final scene as a representation of Littleman's death, not just his institutionalization (51). Also see Frazier.
3. Although I don't think Wideman uses the phrase "black human nature," there are places in his writing and interviews where he sounds a note similarly essentialist, and at other places where he resolutely maintains that race is wholly a social construction. Throughout his career, he promoted concepts like "racial memories" and "collective experiences that get passed on," which, I think, are at least constitutive features of what Harris refers to as "black human nature." In his interview with John O'Brien, Wideman says: "Racial memories exist in the imagination. I believe that there are certain collective experiences that get passed on. I don't know whether it is through the genes, but there may be other processes that science doesn't have the slightest idea about. Certain

"A Lynching in Blackface"

things have been repeated generation after generation so that there are archetypes" (221). Also see the opening essay of *Fatheralong*, where Wideman begins an essay deeply critical of an essentialist notion of race by noting the cultural "common ground" of people of African descent in the New World (and hints that the "gene pool" is at least still part of the heritage that makes up that common ground) (ix–xxv).

4. I have elsewhere discussed how a group of writers who came of age in the late sixties employed narratives of slavery to discuss some of the nationalist issues of the Black Power movement. Some, like Ishmael Reed, Sherley Anne Williams, and Charles Johnson, employed the form of the slave narrative itself to explore the enabling possibilities and problematic assumptions of that variant of cultural nationalism that rose to prominence in the late sixties. Others, like Gayl Jones, David Bradley, and Octavia Butler, had their narrators live in the 1970s but look back to the period of slavery through the form of a family secret whose exposure helped them understand the fundamental problems of a cultural nationalism that insisted on a kind of ideological and biological purity that their own histories rendered impossible. See Rushdy, *Remembering Generations*.

5. See Carmichael, "Toward Black Liberation" 639.

6. On SNCC, see Carson 133–211. On black nationalism in general, see Van Deburg 129–91 and Draper.

7. "Rams" refers to the Revolutionary Action Movement.

8. See Hamilton 202 and Jackson 329.

9. Fanon also notes the stage of intraracial violence as a necessary feature of decolonization (48).

10. See Davis and Brown on the treatment of women in the Panthers.

11. The scene where Wilkerson makes known his problems with the murder of Sissie and then becomes resolved to it is, in fact, a dialogue with Saunders, but Saunders, we are told, was speaking Littleman's words (219).

12. The "Matter Prefatory" comprises the twenty pages of *Moby Dick*–like quotations revealing anti-black violence in American history that begin the novel (3–23). See Coleman 46 and Harris 130. Cf. Wideman's comments in O'Brien 218.

Works Cited

Anderson, Benedict. *Imagined Communities: Reflections on the Origin and Spread of Nationalism*. 1983. New York: Verso, 1991.

Brown, Elaine. *A Taste of Power: A Black Woman's Story*. New York: Pantheon, 1992.

Carmichael, Stokely. "A Declaration of War." *The New Left: A Documentary History*. Ed. Massimo Teodori. Indianapolis: Bobbs-Merrill, 1969.

———. "Toward Black Liberation." *Massachusetts Review* 7.4 (1966): 639.

Carson, Clayborne. *In Struggle: SNCC and the Black Awakening of the 1960s*. 1981. Cambridge: Harvard UP, 1995.

Chicago Office of SNCC. "We Must Fill Ourselves with Hate for All Things White." *Black Protest in the Twentieth Century.* Ed. August Meier, Elliott Rudwick, and Francis L. Broderick. 2nd ed. Indianapolis: Bobbs-Merrill, 1971.

Coleman, James W. *Blackness and Modernism: The Literary Career of John Edgar Wideman.* Jackson: UP of Mississippi, 1989.

———. "Interview with John Edgar Wideman." *Conversations with John Edgar Wideman.* Ed. TuSmith.

Davis, Angela. *An Autobiography.* New York: International Publs., 1974.

Draper, Theodore. *The Rediscovery of Black Nationalism.* New York: Viking, 1970.

Ellison, Ralph. *Invisible Man.* 1952. New York: Vintage, 1990.

Fanon, Frantz. *The Wretched of the Earth.* 1961. New York: Grove P, 1966.

Frazier, Kermit. "The Novels of John Wideman." *Black World* 24.8 (1975): 21, 36–38.

Gayle, Addison, Jr. *The Black Situation.* New York: Horizon P, 1970.

Hamilton, Charles V. "Riots, Revolts, and Relevant Response." *The Black Power Revolt.* Ed. Floyd B. Harbour. 1968. Toronto: Collier-Macmillan, 1969.

Harding, Vincent. "The Religion of Black Power." *The Religious Situation: 1968.* Ed. Donald R. Cutler. Boston: Beacon, 1968. 3–38.

Harris, Trudier. *Exorcising Blackness: Historical and Literary Lynching and Burning Rituals.* Bloomington: Indiana UP, 1984.

Jackson, George. *Soledad Brother.* 1970. Chicago: Lawrence Hill, 1994.

Lester, Julius. *Revolutionary Notes.* New York: Grove, 1969.

O'Brien, John. *Interviews with Black Writers.* New York: Liveright, 1973.

Rushdy, Ashraf H. A. *Neo-Slave Narratives: Studies in the Social Logic of a Literary Form.* New York: Oxford UP, 1999.

———. *Remembering Generations: Race and Family in Contemporary African American Fiction.* Chapel Hill: U of North Carolina P, 2001.

———. Untitled Review. *African American Review* 34.3 (2000): 544–46.

TuSmith, Bonnie, ed. *Conversations with John Edgar Wideman.* Jackson: UP of Mississippi, 1998.

Van Deburg, William L. *New Day in Babylon: The Black Power Movement and American Culture, 1965–1975.* Chicago: U of Chicago P, 1992.

Wideman, John Edgar. "Charles Chesnutt and the WPA Narratives: The Oral and Literate Roots of Afro-American Literature." *The Slave's Narrative.* Ed. Charles T. Davis and Henry Louis Gates Jr. Oxford, England: Oxford UP, 1985. 59–78.

———. *Fatheralong: A Meditation on Fathers and Sons, Race and Society.* New York: Pantheon, 1994.

———. *The Lynchers.* 1973. New York: Henry Holt, 1986.

"Music Homewood's of Invisibility"

John Edgar Wideman's *Sent for You Yesterday* and the Black Urban Tradition

DENISE RODRIGUEZ

Throughout the *Homewood Trilogy* in general, and in *Sent for You Yesterday* in particular, John Edgar Wideman addresses both the stylistic and sociopolitical underpinnings of the black urban novel through two central, overlapping tropes: music (artistic representation) and invisibility (social ramification). This resulting framework provides Wideman with a means of exploring the historical transformation of urban centers and its specific impact on the African American community. Through his invocation of these interlocking tropes (music and invisibility), Wideman engages touchstones in the African American literary canon, including W. E. B. DuBois's *The Souls of Black Folk*, James Weldon Johnson's *The Autobiography of an Ex-Coloured Man*, Richard Wright's *Native Son*, and, most importantly, Ralph Ellison's *Invisible Man*. Drawing on a tropological theoretical framework, in this essay I explore Wideman's re-inscription of Ellison's 1952 novel, arguing that Wideman's postmodern revision of this seminal text marks a critical departure in the evolving tradition of black urban fiction.

According to Richard Lehan, "the literary text codifies ideas and attitudes about the city and . . . as the city itself changes under historical influence, so do these codes, exhausting traditional modes as they call for new meaning" (230). In other words, historical changes that alter our environment and, by extension, our relationship to and perceptions of that environment, in turn cause us to reevaluate our surroundings through their literary representation. These sociohistorical changes that result in aesthetic developments may be described as "generational shifts." Houston Baker defines such a transformation as "an ideologically motivated movement overseen by young or newly emergent intellectuals dedicated to refuting the work of their intellectual predecessors and to establishing a new framework for intellectual inquiry" (67). The three decades separating the publication of *Invisible Man* and *Sent for You Yesterday* were marked by social and political turmoil that resulted in important changes in the way black artists chose to represent their experiences. An overview of this turbulent period—by way of a brief analysis of *Invisible Man*'s reception history—illustrates the import of Wideman's signifying relationship to Ellison's text and lays bare the historical shift from an integrationist to a postmodernist poetics.[1]

By the early 1940s, Ellison had become disillusioned with the Communist Party, with which he had had close ties for over a decade.[2] This movement away from Marxist politics was marked by a concomitant reconsideration of his artistic objectives. As Robert O'Meally notes, "As early as 1940, Ellison found himself increasingly unwilling to portray the black American as the spirit-broken product of the outside forces set against him" (*Craft* 38). Ellison's departure from the Communist Party had both important creative and social implications, as, in part, it came to mark a turning point in the tradition of black urban fiction.

In *Invisible Man*, Ellison evokes a modernist urban landscape where, as Ihab Hassan notes, "realism and surrealism . . ." are seamless (99). He thus moves away from his former mentor Richard Wright's gritty, naturalistic portrayal of black city life as symbolic prison and, in doing so, depicts a wider range of creative options for his protagonist. For instance, Ellison contrasts Bigger's silence with the Invisible Man's voice (e.g., in his role as a public speaker and jazz aficionado), and he replaces Bigger's prison cell with an autonomous underground of healing. More importantly, while initially both characters are socially marginalized (i.e., "invisible"), they each take a different approach to this condition. While, by hiding, Bigger reinforces his own sense of invisibility and the numerous restrictions that accompany it, Ellison's protagonist ironically adopts a form of self-willed invisibility that thwarts the very forces that contribute to his social erasure in the first place.

Unlike the act of hiding, which represents a type of cowering in the face of authority, the Invisible Man's appropriation of the underground functions as a kind of masking and thus serves a more subversive function. In *Figures in Black*,

Henry Louis Gates Jr. discusses the importance of masking in the African American tradition, noting, for instance, that the use of dialect is a popular form of masking, "a verbal descent underground to the Great Dis" (172). Gates establishes a connection between language (dialect), space (the underground), and the act of masking, noting their combined potential for agency. Similarly, in Ellison's novel, these three aligned elements come into play in the form of music, the underground, and invisibility, and it is the complex utilization of these components that allows Ellison to move beyond the constraints of naturalism toward a more suggestive reading of the trope of invisibility as a source of freedom and potency.

Unfortunately, it was, in part, this movement toward an embraced form of invisibility that led many early critics to reject Ellison's novel, since such a move was either interpreted as a repudiation of communal values or a mockery of limiting social conditions. However, the fact that Ellison both came to favor the experimental techniques of modernists like James Joyce, Fyodor Dostoevsky, and T. S. Eliot and to see a need for a different type of black protagonist willing to step beyond his traditional communal role does not indicate an end to his commitment to the black community. Since the novel was published during the early years of the Cold War, it was quickly associated with the conservative politics of this period by critics who could not see beyond Ellison's rejection of Communism in order to discover his profound sensitivity to and continued interest in issues of race, class, and social justice. Irving Howe, for instance, described both Ellison and James Baldwin as writers who had, in embracing modernist approaches, rejected the political value of social realism and the protest tradition. Using Richard Wright as the image of an ideal black literary figure, Howe criticized what he considered Ellison's failure to use writing as a means of actively protesting American racism. Howe's indictment, published in *Dissent*, and Ellison's rejoinder, which appeared in *New Leader*, together provide a useful glimpse at the social tensions that defined an era of black writing in America.[3]

During the 1960s, Ellison's novel was again rejected—this time by members of the Black Arts movement, an offshoot of the Black Power movement. This period, marked by a radicalism that posited itself as a deliberate response to the passive resistance commonly associated with the Civil Rights movement, was driven by a commitment to African American group consciousness—a quality that many found lacking in Ellison's novel. For many, *Invisible Man* became the quintessential example of the ideological failure of integrationist politics. However, as Larry Neal noted in 1970, "much of the criticism directed against Ellison is personal, oversimplified, and often not based on an analysis of the man's work and ideas" (105). While he treated the novel with suspicion during the sixties, Neal eventually discovered that Ellison's use of the African American folk tradition suggests a much more complex approach to black urban life than he and many of his contemporaries in the Black Arts milieu recognized.

Neal's later perspective is in keeping with a range of more recent scholarly approaches to *Invisible Man* that seek to locate progressive tendencies in the novel, mainly via an examination of Ellison's use of vernacular forms and, in particular, music.[4] Such interpretations indicate that Ellison was not only interested in the crisis of the black community, but that this crisis is an important subtext of the novel. In a 1961 interview, Ellison made the following point on this issue: "When I started writing *Invisible Man* I got to thinking about the ambiguity of Negro leadership during that period. This was the late forties, and I kept trying to account for the fact that when the chips were down, Negro leaders did not represent the Negro community."[5] Furthermore, since, as Robert O'Meally observes, Ellison used jazz music as a model for writing, a brief look at how Ellison defined the role of jazz might underscore the social properties he sees as vital to this musical form and to his own writing.[6] In "The Charlie Christian Story," for instance, Ellison notes that "There is . . . a cruel contradiction implicit in the art form itself, for true jazz is an art of individual assertion within and against the group" and that the jazz musician defines "his identity as individual, as member of the collectivity and as a link in the chain of tradition" (36). Developed in Ellison's assessment is a tension between individual and group objectives in jazz, a strain similar to that depicted in his novel. In other words, while Ellison clearly values communal experience and tradition, he sees the relationship between the self and society as a complex series of negotiations. As a result, like Ellison's jazz musician, the Invisible Man "must lose his identity even as he finds it," and he must lose his community even as he finds one (36).

Thus, understanding that Ellison's novel functions not as a rejection of the African American community, but as an effort to represent communal life in a manner that captures the equivocal nature of the black experience, we are left to examine what Ellison proposes as an alternative and whether or not his distinct vision denotes a sense of agency. Much of the scholarship on *Invisible Man* that argues for the novel's overarching progressive social vision encounters a single problem: the fact that while the novel hints at the Invisible Man's inevitable return to his community, he remains in isolation. For example, Anne Anlin Cheng notes the following: "What is the 'socially responsible role' that the narrator will play by the end of the novel? The narrative has offered us more questions than any final affirmation or particular course of action" (59). In a 1954 letter to Mrs. Henry Dickson Turner, Ellison called the writing of the novel "an act of social responsibility as well as an artistic projection."[7] If the writing itself indicated an act of social commitment, then the fact that the novel never clearly reveals the

Invisible Man's communal function may suggest that perhaps Ellison was unable to fully join social mission to creative expression.

While he rejected Wright's naturalism, Ellison may have encountered a similar crisis of representation or, as Berndt Ostendorf notes, "he may be said to have written himself into a modernist deadlock" (95). Fundamentally, while Ellison challenges the status quo through his introduction of a blues matrix, a complex engagement with African American communal folk traditions, *Invisible Man* closes on a note of isolation. And, while this ending does not necessarily signal despair (since the Invisible Man hints at his return to society) or intentional communal rejection, it certainly does not provide an image of social rejuvenation. By slipping into the hole, Ellison's protagonist escapes social constraints, but he also sacrifices vital ties to members of his community.

In his insightful analysis of *Invisible Man*, Charles Scruggs argues that "Ellison . . . create[s] a character who by the novel's end will be an answer to Bigger [Thomas]" (101). In turn, I would like to argue that in *Sent for You Yesterday* Wideman creates a character who provides an answer to Ellison's Invisible Man. While Ellison points to the resiliency of black culture in America through his incorporation of vernacular and folk traditions, Wideman reclaims these forms in order to more directly depict the challenges black urban communities continue to face—such as the devastating effects of urban renewal programs that have resulted in the displacement of poor, predominantly African American families in cities across the United States.[8] In bringing the Invisible Man out of hibernation, Wideman seeks to reintroduce the isolated artist to his community and thereby explore his social function.

For Wideman, the Invisible Man's journey strikes a personal chord since, like Ellison's protagonist, Wideman also left his community and ultimately sought a way to return to his neighborhood through writing. In *Brothers and Keepers*, for instance, Wideman discusses how his own life's journey took him away from his predominantly black childhood community and into a predominantly white academic world: "To get ahead, to make something of myself, college had seemed a logical, necessary step; my exile, my flight from home began with good grades, with good English, with setting myself apart long before I'd earned a scholarship and a train ticket over the mountains to Philadelphia" (10). *The Homewood Trilogy* represents Wideman's symbolic return to his childhood community. In this journey back, Wideman abandons the "good English" of the college campus in favor of Homewood's rich vernacular.

In a 1972 interview, Wideman noted that "the slave narratives, folklore, and the novels of Richard Wright and Ralph Ellison have been most important to me. And these things are just beginning to become embodied in the things that I write" (TuSmith, *Conversations* 51). The mention of Ellison is crucial, especially since less than a decade later Wideman would begin working on *Sent for You Yesterday*, the novel that most actively incorporates the two central tropes—music and invisibility—in *Invisible Man*. In order to appreciate Wideman's use of vernacular forms and his revoicing of these tropes, it is important to take into account the social-cultural considerations that frame his project. First, like Ellison, Wideman wrote his novel on the fault lines of important sociopolitical changes. He belongs to a group of writers who started publishing during the Black Arts movement but chose not to align themselves with the movement and, instead, examined the fact that neither the pacifist agenda of the Civil Rights movement nor the radicalism of the Black Arts movement has offered decisive solutions to the crisis of black urban communities. Like Ellison, Wideman recognizes that there are no easy answers, no panaceas—just as there are no simple ways of portraying this crisis. However, whereas Ellison turned to a combination of modernist experimentation and black folk traditions as a way of exploring representational alternatives, Wideman engages a postmodern aesthetic that allows him to extend the Invisible Man's dialogue with his community without subscribing to a facile utopian ideal of communal solidarity.[9]

Wideman's aesthetic choices are fueled by a desire to capture the inherent complexity of the black urban condition. For instance, rejecting the reductive notion of a collective black experiential reality popularized during the 1960s, he instead calls attention to the paradoxical nature of the black community by simultaneously depicting its fragility and resilience. In utilizing a range of postmodern tropes such as contingency, polyphony, and fragmentation, he creates a type of "community of resistance."[10] bell hooks defines the concept of a "community of resistance" as an empowering means of rereading marginalized space as a site of agency rather than subjugation and of redressing the exclusion of minority concerns from the broader postmodern debate.[11] At the core of this theoretical premise lies a contradiction similar to the one explored in Ellison's novel—mainly, that between social disenfranchisement (invisibility) and empowerment (music). It is through this conception of a resistant community that Wideman is able to revitalize Ellison's text.

Ellison's "music of invisibility" is personified in the character of Brother in *Sent for You Yesterday*. Brother relates to his literary precursor in two crucial ways: through his invisibility and through his role as neighborhood musician. Wideman parodies Ellison's abstract invisibility by making his character an albino and, thus, the physical embodiment of a genetically determined invisibility. By concretizing invisibility on this level, Wideman moves away from its use as a symbol of both oppression and alienation to a biological fact, a stark reality that can never be elided. However, this use of albinism as invisibility also serves an inherently

Homewood's "Music of Invisibility"

ironic function in the text since it simultaneously produces a type of hyper-visibility. In other words, Brother becomes a dichotomous symbol of absence and presence; he is both the blank page and the written text, and, as Carl tells Doot, his whiteness "made him less nigger and more nigger at the same time" (17). This duality complicates his role in the community. On the one hand, he becomes a point of identification and, on the other, of desired dissociation.

The construction of ironic invisibility permits Wideman to extend his character's social function since, in order for the other characters in the novel to come to terms with their own social invisibility, they must first come to accept Brother's "deformity" and to see it as their own. In turn, the image of invisibility as physical difference functions as an overarching symbol for the Homewood community, a place transformed/deformed by the adverse effects of poverty and racism. Thus, rather than an emblem of social disconnection or rejection, Brother's invisibility articulates collective suffering.

Furthermore, Brother's deformity serves as an apt metaphor for Wideman's narrative strategy, a (de)formative engagement with master tropes in the African American literary tradition. In a different context, Houston Baker describes "deformation of mastery" as an alternative to "a mastery of form."[12] In other words, an artist chooses whether to adopt a tradition in a straightforward manner or to formally challenge the tradition by appropriating and revising aspects of antecedent works in order to push the limits of a creative form in new directions. Wideman's postmodern parody of *Invisible Man* (de)forms or alters the trope of invisibility. According to Linda Hutcheon, "Parody manages to inscribe continuity while permitting critical distance and change" (102). In this sense, parody is crucial to the development of any literary tradition (e.g., the black urban tradition) in that it allows for both connections and ruptures/transformations. Through such an approach, Wideman simultaneously engages *Invisible Man* and moves toward a revision of invisibility that makes it a repository of communal values rather than a sign of isolation.

Wideman further extends his ironic reappraisal of this trope by creating a character who chooses not to speak after his son, Junebug, dies. In abandoning language, Brother ostensibly completes the circle of his own invisibility. However, he never relinquishes his role as Homewood's musician, as Doot notes: "his silence wasn't really silence. Brother made noise all the time" (15–16). By overcoming invisibility—both physical (albinism) and verbal (silence)—through "noise" (i.e., his blues), Brother becomes a symbol of hope to a community searching for a means of transcending its own social erasure.

Yves-Charles Grandjeat calls *Sent for You Yesterday* "Wideman's bluest novel," a comment that echoes Albert Murray's oft-quoted description of *Invisible Man* as "par excellence the literary extension of the blues" (167).[13] Yet, while in *Invisible*

Man music functions as a sensate extension of the protagonist's invisibility, Brother's role as musician actively links him to his community. Ellison's protagonist escapes into the hole and "steps outside of history," renouncing his public speeches and persona for a private world of jazz music and invisibility. For Brother, on the other hand, music carries personal loss—such as the death of his son—directly into the communal sphere where it ultimately functions as a source of healing.

Furthermore, not only does Brother capture the voice of Homewood through music, he also evokes an entire history of African American suffering and survival—as with the story he tells Junebug that refers to the Middle Passage and slavery: "That I had crossed the ocean in a minute. That I had drowned in rivers and dangled like rotten fruit from trees. That my unmourned bones were ground to dust and the dust salted and plowed" (171). It is this ability to merge past with present and the individual with the collective that makes Brother the blues man of the novel, the voice of Homewood. As Carl notes, "Brother could be in both places at once. A Brother in the sky. A Brother humping down Finance Street" (172). Like his invisibility which, as discussed above, paradoxically functions as both a sign of absence and presence, his characteristic flexibility or adaptability carves a unique place for him in the community in the sense that he is both there and not there, *a part* of the community and *apart* from the community. In the end, however, his music, like Albert's, provides his most lasting link to Homewood since it can be recalled even after he dies.

The Invisible Man cannot make the same leap Brother does from silence (individual) to music (communal) or from invisibility (individual) to presence (communal). In *Going to the Territory*, Ellison notes that in vernacular forms one "seek[s] the homeness of home" (143). The image of the vernacular as home is introduced early on in *Invisible Man* and is used to illustrate the transitional quality of the protagonist's liminal retreat. The "homesick" Invisible Man realizes that in his underground refuge he has "found a home—or a hole in the ground, as you will" (Ellison 6). The slippage from "home" to "hole" indicates the flawed nature of the Invisible Man's refuge and points to the fact that it offers only a temporary solution. Vernacular forms are based on shared cultural values and experiences, and the fact that the Invisible Man is left listening to jazz in isolation points to the underlying irony of his condition: he is a blues man without a community.

By contrast, in *The Homewood Trilogy* as a whole, images of isolation and community are counterpoised, while each individual text in the series moves toward a reconciliation between the individual and his/her society. By way of this thematic trajectory, Wideman explores the shift from the hole of isolation to the (w)hole of communal interaction. The distinction drawn here is between Ellison's focus on individual consciousness and Wideman's emphasis on collective or group consciousness. This transition reflects developing sensibilities in the urban novel. In other words, while Ellison, in part, responds to what he felt was a strict and confining focus on group consciousness that suppressed the individual (e.g., in his depiction of the university and the Brotherhood), Wideman reflects upon the fragmentation or dissolution of the black urban community. For instance, in *Hiding Place*, the second book in the trilogy, Tommy rejects his community and withdraws into a space that echoes the Invisible Man's underground chamber, a "deep, dark, warm cave. A cave as black and secret as his blood" (72). Tommy's escape points to the generational discord that plays a central thematic role in the text (and in other Wideman novels such as *Philadelphia Fire* and *Two Cities*) and stresses the need for a collective resolution.

Similarly, *Sent for You Yesterday* contains various images of social disconnection, such as Doot's vision of Cassina Way:

> That's the way it must have been on Cassina Way. Rows of wooden shanties built to hold the flood of black migrants up from the south. Teeming's the word I think of. A narrow, cobbled alley teeming with life. Like a wooden-walled up ship in the middle of the city, like the ark on which Noah packed two of everything and prayed for land. . . . I see islands, arks, life teeming but enclosed or surrounded or exiled to arbitrary boundaries. (21)

Ironically, despite its crowdedness, the depicted landscape connotes a sense of loneliness. Under the reference to Noah's ark lies the more oblique allusion to the Middle Passage, a central symbol of isolation in the African American tradition and one that serves as a painful reminder of the first loss of communal ties (i.e., those to the homeland). Through his juxtaposition of the Middle Passage and Great Migration, Wideman tacitly points to the series of dislocations and fractures that define the black urban experience. Doot also recalls that Freeda and John French's house had a partition that divided it into two parts, one which opened onto Tioga Street and the other onto Cassina Way: "You knew the people across the alley but you seldom went around the block to Tioga. . . . Even if you lived in the end house . . . you seldom had business which carried you around . . ." (20). Like the Invisible Man's hole, the image of the divided house—literally a house divided—captures a sense of social isolation on a spatially delineated level.

Yet perhaps the most graphic example of separation in *Sent for You Yesterday* can be found in Albert Wilkes's description of human dismemberment: "The rack, Albert said. Said he didn't know exactly what ailed him till he saw the picture in his white woman's book, and then he understood exactly. They got us on a rack, John French. They gon keep turning till ain't nothing connected where it's suppose to be" (62). Just as Wideman's depiction of a black albino solidifies Ellison's abstract image by turning it into a physical emblem of difference, his treatment of fragmentation, not merely as an aesthetic device but on a more conspicuous level as a painful historical reality, concretizes the legacy of black oppression. Furthermore, Albert's use of the word "us," rather than "them," indicates a type of historical breakdown and achieves a striking immediacy. The described social atrocities are not safely contained in the past tense. On the contrary, Albert sees himself as an actual victim.

While Albert's explanation of the device used to torture slaves articulates fragmentation on a visceral level, his music carries suggestive undertones of yet another form of disintegration, one that is communal. During his last performance before leaving Homewood, Albert is conscious of an ominous silence lurking between the notes he plays: "Somebody had named the notes, but nobody had named the silence between. . . . The emptiness, the space waiting for him that night seven years ago" (86). Silence is again treated as a counterpart to invisibility. Upon his return, Albert tells John that no one recognizes him after his seven-year absence: "I'm telling you people don't say boo. Like I was invisible" (85). Albert is hiding from the police, so his invisibility is a product of necessity. However, in becoming invisible to the authorities, he compromises his place in the community.

Unlike Brother, Albert is not able to fully mitigate his invisibility, not even through his role as a musician. As Bonnie TuSmith notes, "Although Albert understands and expresses the blues through his music, as an isolated individual he is unable to transcend his self-destructive course of 'acting a fool' . . ." (*All* 92). Albert becomes preoccupied with self-preservation and eventually loses touch not only with his people but with his art—since, after all, the two are integrally related.

According to Wideman, the true artist remains "rooted" in his/her community. He made the following observation in an interview: "I believe that in order for my art . . . to flourish it has to be rooted, it has to be grounded, in that sense, yes, particularly, yes, the very unique ground that you fought for and bled in and created as a people" (TuSmith, *Conversations* 52). For Wideman, the term "rooted" has a double meaning: tradition, in terms of creative and cultural resources, and community, in terms of geographical and social considerations. The artist needs to maintain an active commitment to both.

In this sense, Albert Wilkes's return in the face of danger and his final performance both function as conciliatory gestures or as attempts to reestablish communal ties. The fact that Albert is killed during one of his performances solidifies his place in the community. The blood-stained piano, for instance, functions as an image of sacrifice. Like Brother, it becomes a complex emblem of music and silence, of joy and suffering. Years later, Lucy can still command Albert to play on that very piano: "Albert Wilkes' song so familiar because everything she's ever heard is in it, all the songs and voices she's ever heard, but everything is new and fresh because his music joined things, blended them . . ." (189). This final image of the music connecting things counteracts those foreboding gaps or holes in the music that, like the image of bodily dismemberment discussed above, ultimately foreshadow Albert's final separation from Homewood through death.

Furthermore, Albert Wilkes leaves behind a rich musical and communal legacy, and Brother is its main inheritor. The novel's tri-generational structure allows Wideman to explore a period of roughly forty years (from the 1930s to the 1970s) and various events—both historical and local—that result in the transformation of one specific black urban community. Within this narrative framework, Albert's demise signifies the death of an era, and Brother's role as successor provides a vital link between past, present, and future. While Albert Wilkes falls victim to social impediments, Brother needs to arrive at a way of negotiating and overcoming these strictures. In other words, before Brother in turn dies, leaving Doot in the position of Homewood's next heir, he must restore the community's pride and faith vis-à-vis a return to its musical heritage.

By positing music—the keystone in the African American vernacular tradition—as a source of reconciliation, Wideman locates his character's quest within the larger framework of the evolving black urban literary continuum that can be traced as far back as Paul Laurence Dunbar's *The Sport of the Gods* (1902). In order to fully appreciate Wideman's dialogue with *Invisible Man* specifically and with this aesthetic tradition more generally, we first need to outline the role of a blues idiom as a unifying tropological device in the novel.[14]

In the African American tradition, the blues functions not merely as a creative repository for pain, but as a means of transcending suffering. Leroi Jones argues that "There was always a border beyond which the Negro could not go whether musically or socially. And it was always this boundary, this no man's land, that provided the logic and beauty of his music" (80). In this sense, these performative endeavors serve the subversive function of circumventing social restrictions—at least on a creative/symbolic level—and ultimately of achieving both self and cultural validation. In *Sent for You Yesterday,* this aesthetic orientation—evoked through the novel's tripart generational structure and particularly through the characters of Albert Wilkes, Brother, and finally Doot—paradoxically reveals the sociopolitical fragmentation of Homewood, while simultaneously providing coherence through rhythmic pattern and structure.

I derive the concept of music as an instrument of social cohesion in part from Wideman's own definition of the African American musical tradition in "The Architectonics of Fiction." In this essay, Wideman argues that

Black music is a moveable feast, fluid in time, space, modality, exhibiting in theme and variations multiple relationships with the politically, socially, aesthetically dominant order, the fullest possible range of relationships, including the power and independence to change places, reverse the hierarchy, be the dominant order. (45)

Like Jones, Wideman posits a relationship between music and mobility, noting that this fluidity makes black music a powerful source of cultural transformation. It is through music, for instance, that a character like Brother learns to negotiate social conditions, since, by artistically stepping outside of the parameters of traditional Western culture, Brother is also able to move beyond the dominant culture's imposed hierarchy.

This transition resembles creative maneuverings in a range of African American texts. According to Eric Sundquist, in *The Souls of Black Folks* DuBois weaves African American spirituals to "form a hidden, coded language . . . that recapitulates the original cultural function of the spirituals themselves" (*To Wake* 470). Originally, the purpose of the spirituals was, as Lawrence Levine argues, to produce "the necessary space between the slaves and their owners" and to keep "legal slavery from becoming spiritual slavery" (80). Interestingly, while the entire structure of slavery was built upon a premise of differentiation, it is to this very objective that the spirituals return. By claiming difference on this level, slaves also reclaimed a sense of their individuality and autonomy—aspects repressed in the slave owner's construction of racial polarity. Thus, by reinserting the sorrow songs, DuBois advocates the continued need for an assertion of differentiation that provides agency.

In this sense, the Invisible Man's "music of invisibility" similarly performs a revoicing of DuBois's message in *The Souls*, for, like the spirituals themselves, the "music of invisibility" provides a means of articulating the black experience by drawing on a distinctly African American performative tradition. Like Ellison's hole, this legacy allows the protagonist to step outside the constraints of the dominant culture. However, while in Ellison's text this movement appears in the form of isolation and descent (i.e., the Invisible Man's retreat into the hole), in Wideman's novel this transition is more positively depicted as an ascent in Brother's figurative flight. At the core of this directional distinction lies the fundamental difference separating Wideman's and Ellison's respective projects.

In *Sent for You Yesterday*, images of trains and railroad tracks echoed throughout represent the transformative quality of the blues form. Brother's association with the tracks, for instance, reinforces his position as cultural mediator. As Houston Baker notes, "The 'placeless' . . . are translators of the nontraditional. Rather than the fixed order of cunning Grecian urns, their lineage is fluid, nomadic, transitional. Their appropriate mark is a crossing sign at the junction" (*Blues* 202). Brother's invisibility (i.e., physically, albinism; symbolically, social marginality), music, and, as an orphan, his lack of clear ancestry, exemplify the fluid properties delineated in Baker's study and, in turn, make Brother the quintessential embodiment of a blues poetics.

Brother's death by the train tracks particularly evokes the protean quality of blues music, since the scene redefines death (silence/immobility) as transcendence (voice/mobility): "Homewood spreads out below, a patchwork of tiny streets and houses. But as he rises, as the string gets thinner and thinner . . . his shoulders . . . become skinny and powerful as wings . . ." (*Sent* 178). The image of flight is repeated toward the end of the novel when Lucy discovers a series of drawings Brother made. The drawings depict individual members of the Homewood community with wings on their backs. Upon finding the drawings, Lucy notes that they "Had to be Brother's. Who else but brother would put wings on all the people in his pictures" (*Sent* 193). The paintings unrolled on the family piano perform an intertextual circling back to the first illustration of creative self-expression in the first text of the trilogy, *Damballah*.

In the opening story, Orion, who prefigures the characters of Albert, Brother, and finally Doot, is decapitated by his overseers, and his mutilated body is later discovered by a young slave boy. Orion tells the boy stories about his African heritage and, in the process, he is magically transformed: "Orion's eyes rise up through the back of the severed skull and lips rise up through the skull and the wings of the ghost measure out the rhythm of one last word" (25). The wings in this instance function as musical instruments, connecting art (music and storytelling) to transcendence (flight). Through storytelling, Orion achieves a symbolic coherence that counteracts physical dismemberment.

The use of artistic self-expression as a means of attaining cohesion on both individual and communal levels also appears in *Sent for You Yesterday*. Wideman's portrayal of merging voices establishes a connective framework in the novel. For instance, when Brother plays the piano for the first time, the audience thinks it is listening to Albert Wilkes, and members even address Brother by his predecessor's name. Similarly, as he dies, Brother listens to the voices emanating from a religious tent revival and realizes that they "sounded good to him . . . Almost good enough to make him . . . follow them through the darkness to the shiny tent where . . . all the voices get caught up in the old songs whether they knew the words or not" (97). The intersection of flight and music reveals Brother's social legacy since, through this narrative overlap, the solitary singer comes to be replaced by a communal chorus. In this sense, Brother both *lives* and *dies* with music.[15]

The central image of the rising voices echoes Brother's ascent and further counteracts the role of individual descent depicted in Ellison's novel. The interplay of voices functions as an overarching emblem of social ties and, while Brother never attends the revival, his death awakens a sense of responsibility in Carl, Lucy, and, later, Doot. In the process, their voices similarly merge, and this collaborative arrangement ultimately results in the construction of Doot's multifaceted narrative, the novel's framing chronicle of Homewood life. Thus, a trajectory can be traced from Albert's and Brother's music, which fundamentally has a social function, to the communal voice of the singers that assuages individual pain, to Doot's story that, in encompassing these various strains, draws on and supports both individual and collective experiences.

The novel closes with an image of dancing that further underscores Doot's commitment to Homewood's blues legacy: "I'm on my feet and Lucy says, *Go boy* and Carl says, *Get it on, Doot*. Everybody joining in now. All the voices. I'm reaching for them and letting them go. . . . I'm on my own feet. Learning to stand, to walk, learning to dance" (208). Doot's tentative first steps suggest a willingness to learn the tradition. As James Coleman notes, "Doot has come home to the community and is ready to improvise intellectually while carrying on the community tradition as Albert Wilkes and Brother have done in the past" (114). The image of dancing captures the essence of music on an active, physical level, and Doot's dancing thereby articulates a renewed connection to and engagement with the community.

Like his fictional counterpart, Wideman's own authorial voice "get[s]" caught" up not only with the legacy and voices of his childhood community but, in a broader sense, with those of his literary ancestors. In particular, Wideman's portrayal of Brother's ascent revises the Invisible Man's descent and therefore picks up where Ellison's character leaves off, poised for reentry into society. Furthermore, the image of dancing with which *Sent for You Yesterday* ends indicates a decisive shift away from the passive act of listening to music in solitude (*Invisible Man*) to a dynamic and interactive celebration of this aesthetic tradition.

The Invisible Man's retreat into the bowels of New York City allows him to circumvent rejection by making his marginalization a choice rather than a social imposition. However, this renunciation ultimately signals a kind of solipsism since, in the process, he not only repudiates white culture but also forfeits his position in the black community. Wideman, on the other hand, motivated by a desire to affirm the strength and cultural value of black urban centers, transforms Homewood, a place marred by racism and social disenfranchisement, into a storehouse of meaningful communal interaction. In doing so, he revises the black urban novel and makes more clearly evident the relationship between art and society—between how perceptions about our environment influence the development of creative forms and, conversely, how artistic endeavors may reinforce our commitment to those surroundings.

Notes

1. For an overview of critical responses to Ellison's *Invisible Man*, see Fonteau.
2. For an analysis of Ellison's relationship to the Communist Party, see Mazurek. In his essay, Mazurek provides an insightful overview of Ellison criticism and a response to Barbara Foley's "The Rhetoric of Anticommunism in *Invisible Man*." See also Wolfe's "'Ambivalent Man': Ellison's Rejection of Communism." Wolfe discusses Ellison's novel in relation to the liberal values of the post–World War II anti-Stalinist American Left.
3. For a discussion of the Howe-Ellison debate, see Forman. See also Watts's *Heroism*.
4. It is important to keep in mind that Ellison studied music at the Tuskegee Institute (1933–1936) before he became a writer. His knowledge of the African American musical tradition is evident in *Invisible Man* as well as in numerous essays and interviews. For a discussion of the role of music in Ellison's work, see the following: Dickstein, Harding, and Baker's *Blues*. See also Sundquist's *Cultural Contexts*. Sundquist offers a comprehensive examination of a range of vernacular resources, including folktales and blues lyrics.
5. Quoted in Jackson.
6. See O'Meally's introduction in his book, *Ralph Ellison's Jazz Writings*.
7. See Callahan.
8. For an insightful examination of Wideman's treatment of urban renewal in his novel *Philadelphia Fire*, see Dubey.
9. For an examination of the role of community in Wideman's work, see Page.
10. For a discussion of postmodern techniques in Wideman's fiction, see Hoem. Focusing on Wideman's *Damballah* and *The Cattle Killing*, Hoem argues that Wideman's postmodernism can best be understood in terms of Linda Hutcheon's theory of historiographic metafiction.
11. See hooks, "Postmodern Blackness." See also hooks, *Yearning*.
12. See Baker's *Modernism*.
13. See Grandjeat.
14. Various scholars have noted the important role the blues plays in the novel, including two works cited in the body of this essay: Bonnie TuSmith's chapter on *Sent for You Yesterday* in *All My Relatives*, 84–94; James Coleman's *Blackness and Modernism*. See also Rushdy.
15. See Ellison, "Living with Music."

Works Cited

Baker, Houston. *Blues, Ideology, and Afro-American Literature: A Vernacular Theory*. Chicago: U of Chicago P, 1984.

———. *Modernism and the Harlem Renaissance*. Chicago: U of Chicago P, 1987.

Callahan, John F. "'American Culture is of a Whole': From the Letters of Ralph Ellison." *The New Republic* 220 (1999). Mar. 1999. <http://www.tnr.com/archive/0399/030199/ellison030199.html>.

Cheng, Anne Anlin. "The Melancholy of Race." *Kenyon Review* 19.1 (1997): 49–61.

Coleman, James William. *Blackness and Modernism: The Literary Career of John Edgar Wideman*. Jackson: UP of Mississippi, 1989.

Dickstein, Morris. "Ralph Ellison, Race, and American Culture." *Raritan: A Quarterly Review* 18.4 (1999): 30–50.

Dubey, Madhu. "Literature and Urban Crisis: John Edgar Wideman's *Philadelphia Fire*." *African American Review* 32.4 (1998): 579–96.

Dunbar, Paul Laurence. *The Sport of the Gods*. 1902. New York: Macmillan, 1970.

Ellison, Ralph. "The Charlie Christian Story." In O'Meally, *Ralph Ellison's Jazz Writings* 34–42.

———. *Going to the Territory*. New York: Random House, 1986.

———. *Invisible Man*. 1952. New York: Vintage Books, 1995.

———. "Living with Music." In O'Meally, *Ralph Ellison's Jazz Writings* 3–14.

Foley, Barbara. "The Rhetoric of Anticommunism in *Invisible Man*." *College English* 59 (1997): 530–47.

Fonteau, Yvonne. "Ralph Ellison's *Invisible Man*: A Critical Reevaluation." *World Literature Today* 64.3 (1990): 408–12.

Forman, Seth. "On Howe, Ellison, and the Black Intellectuals." *Partisan Review* 66.4 (1999): 587–95.

Gates, Henry Louis, Jr. *Figures in Black: Words, Signs, and the 'Racial' Self*. New York: Oxford UP 1987.

Grandjeat, Yves-Charles. "Brother Figures: The Rift and Riff in John E. Wideman's Fiction. *Callaloo* 22.3 (1999): 615–22.

Harding, James M. "Adorno, Ellison, and the Critique of Jazz." *Cultural Critique* 31 (1995): 129–58.

Hassan, Ihab. "Cities of Mind, Urban Words: The Dematerialization of Metropolis in Contemporary American Fiction." *Literature and the Urban Experience: Essays on the City and Literature*. Eds. Michael Jaye and Ann Chalmers Watts. New Brunswick, NJ: Rutgers UP, 1981. 93–112.

Hoem, Sheri I. "Shifting Spirits: Ancestral Constructs in the Postmodern Writing of John Edgar Wideman." *African American Review* 34.4 (2000): 249–62.

hooks, bell. "Postmodern Blackness." *A Postmodern Reader*. Ed. Linda Hutcheon and Joseph Natoli. Albany: SUNY P, 1993. 510–18.

———. *Yearning: Race, Gender, and Cultural Politics*. Boston: South End P, 1990.

Hutcheon, Linda. *A Theory of Parody: The Teachings of Twentieth-Century Art Forms*. 1985. Urbana: U of Illinois P, 2000.

Jackson, Lawrence P. "Ralph Ellison, Sharpies, Rinehart, and Politics in *Invisible Man.*" *The Massachusetts Review* 40.1 (1999): 71–85.

Jones, Leroi. *Blues People: Negro Music in White America.* New York: W. Morrow, 1963.

Lehan, Richard. "Urban Signs and Urban Literature: Literary Form and Historical Process." *Studies in Historical Change.* Ed. Ralph Cohen. Charlottesville: UP of Virginia, 1992. 230–45.

Levine, Lawrence. *Black Culture, Black Consciousness: Afro-American Folk Thought from Slavery to Freedom.* New York: Oxford UP, 1977.

Mazurek, Raymond A. "Writers on the Left: Class and Race in Ellison's Early Fiction." *College Literature* 29.4 (2002): 109–35.

Murray, Albert. *The Omni-Americans: New Perspectives on Black Experience and American Culture.* New York: Outerbridge and Dienstfrey, 1970.

Neal, Larry. "Ellison's Zoot Suit." *Speaking for You: The Vision of Ralph Ellison.* Ed. Kimberly W. Benston. Washington DC: Howard UP, 1987. 105–24.

O'Meally, Robert. *The Craft of Ralph Ellison.* Cambridge: Harvard UP, 1980.

———, ed. *Ralph Ellison's Jazz Writings: Living with Music.* New York: Random House, 2002.

Ostendorf, Berndt. "Ralph Waldo Ellison: Anthropology, Modernism, and Jazz." *New Essays on Invisible Man.* Ed. Robert O'Meally. Cambridge: Cambridge UP, 1988. 95–121.

Page, Phillip. *Reclaiming Community in Contemporary African American Fiction.* Oxford: UP of Mississippi, 1999.

Rushdy, Ashraf H. A. "Fraternal Blues: John Edgar Wideman's *Homewood Trilogy.*" *Contemporary Literature* 32 (1991): 312–45.

Scruggs, Charles. *Sweet Home: Invisible Cities in the Afro-American Novel.* Baltimore: The Johns Hopkins UP, 1993.

Sundquist, Eric J. *Cultural Contexts for Ralph Ellison's Invisible Man.* Boston: Bedford Books of Saint Martin's P, 1995.

———. *To Wake the Nations: Race in the Making of American Literature.* Cambridge: Harvard UP, 1993.

TuSmith, Bonnie. *All My Relatives: Community in Contemporary Ethnic American Literatures.* Ann Arbor: U of Michigan P, 1993.

———, ed. *Conversations with John Edgar Wideman.* Jackson: UP of Mississippi, 1998.

Watts, Jerry Gafio. *Heroism and the Black Intellectual.* Chapel Hill: U of North Carolina P, 1994.

Wideman, John Edgar. "The Architectonics of Fiction." *Callaloo: A Journal of African-American and African Arts and Letters* 13.1 (1990): 42–46.

————. *Brothers and Keepers*. New York: Vintage, 1984.

————. *Damballah*. 1981. New York: Mariner, 1998.

————. *Hiding Place*. 1981. New York: Mariner, 1998.

————. *Sent for You Yesterday*. 1983. New York: Vintage, 1988.

Wolfe, Jesse. "'Ambivalent Man': Ellison's Rejection of Communism." *African American Review* 34.4 (2000): 621–68.

Philadelphia *Fire*
and *The Fire Next Time*

WIDEMAN
RESPONDS
TO BALDWIN

LESLIE W. LEWIS

In true call-and-response fashion, John Edgar Wideman's *Philadelphia Fire* presents in striking detail the story of 1980s urban America as "the fire next time" prophesied by James Baldwin in his 1963 nonfiction bestseller of the same title, which itself elaborates on the image "recreated from the Bible in song by a slave": "*God gave Noah the rainbow sign, No more water, the fire next time!*" (141). Wideman responds to Baldwin's warning of a future apocalypse by witnessing for us a city presently on fire, and in doing so he extends the metaphorical connotations and implications of the fire "this time," but also extends Baldwin's voice of concern for black boys, which forms the deep structure of *The Fire Next Time*. Baldwin's fourteen-year-old nephew and namesake, James, whom he addresses in the first essay of *The Fire Next Time*, and all that this young James represents, in his potential and his beauty, brings Baldwin into continued conversation with white America in order to work toward an end to what he terms "the racial nightmare" (141).[1] This nephew's existence, in other words, propels Baldwin to continue to imagine the nation's democratic possibilities, however far removed from present-day circumstances. In *Philadelphia Fire*, John Wideman responds to this focus of

Baldwin's *The Fire Next Time*, predominantly through the structure of the difficult second section of his novel, where plotted story gives way to postmodern metafiction. Reading Wideman in dialogue with Baldwin allows us to understand *Philadelphia Fire*, and particularly its middle section, in its detailed engagement with Baldwin's images, voice, and critique, and to see that the novel digs at issues rooted in contemporary black manhood and recharacterizes the relation between identity, narrative, and the most fundamental existential questions.

Images of the fire "next time"—that is, the way in which Philadelphia is now on fire—begin with the literal fire that brings the writer Cudjoe back to Philadelphia from the Greek island, Mykonos. This fire occurs on May 13, 1985, when police drop a bomb on the row house in West Philadelphia inhabited by members of the organization MOVE, thereby killing eleven people, including five children, and burning out 262 people from fifty-three houses. In part 1, the story of this fire is told by Margaret Jones, who was once a member of MOVE and has an insider's sense of what happened. Here, "the story of the fire" is literally the story of the bombing of MOVE, although the more compelling story that the character Cudjoe wants to tell is the story of the child Simba Muntu's survival of the fire. In part 1, however, Cudjoe also internalizes the fire in ways that set him in motion, in thought and deed. Cudjoe first remembers the children's rhyme: "*Ladybug, Ladybug. Fly away home. Your house is on fire. Your children burning*" (7). However, as he rehearses his interest in the boy who has survived the fire, and reviews his own personal history, including a failed marriage, estranged children, and his ten-year exile on Mykonos, the children's rhyme changes: "*Runagate, runagate, fly away home/ Your house's on fire and your children's burning*" (22).[2] Now more personalized, an answer to Margaret Jones's unasked question of why he is back in West Philly, these lines lead Cudjoe to reflect on himself as writer, and to conclude that, "He will explain to Margaret Jones that he must always write about many places at once. No choice. The splitting apart is inevitable. First step is always out of time, away from responsibility, toward the word or sound or image that is everywhere at once, that connects and destroys" (23). Fire is the image that is here "everywhere at once," that "connects and destroys," and this description from Cudjoe allows us to see two houses simultaneously on fire, one on Osage Avenue and the other within Cudjoe's own psyche.

Written stories move "out of time," according to Cudjoe, as the first step to being "everywhere at once," and this impetus to disregard the time and space constraints of the physical world propels us into the fissures of part 2 of *Philadelphia Fire*, where we are not only in "many places at once," but also with many people. Part 2 opens with the facts of the MOVE bombing, presented in documentary fashion, as if the question of how to tell the story of that particular fire has been answered. Here, it is the story of Cudjoe's metaphorical house on fire that the novel explores, first by introducing a first-person narrator who receives a telephone call from his "lost son," clearly incarcerated, and then by introducing an adult couple watching television in bed only to discover their former neighborhood, Osage Avenue in West Philadelphia, on fire. Cudjoe's metaphorical house on fire is also John Wideman's house. As writer, Wideman introduces us to himself as character, as first-person narrator identified through the naming of this narrator's wife, Judy. And so *Philadelphia Fire* transforms from a story about a fire into a story about writing a story about "fire." One of the quotations included in part 2 reads: "At all times and in all fields the explanation by fire is a rich explanation," and this adds to our sense that a larger explanation of some of life's meaning is in progress (109).[3] In part 2 Wideman's metaphorical house on fire eclipses Cudjoe's own, and Wideman's story of writing the story of fire comes to have a specific and structurally detailed trajectory. Put simply, the narrative structure in part 2 gathers voices together in order to culminate in a letter from the first-person narrator Wideman to his incarcerated son which concludes the section and in a sense recasts the whole section as just such a letter. By finally reaching the point of writing this letter to his son, Wideman successfully takes up the challenge of responding to Baldwin's opening letter to his nephew in *The Fire Next Time*, but also in his response reminds us of the societal changes that have turned the 1960s into the 1980s, thereby also signifying not only the difficulty but the near impossibility of continued cross-generational black male conversation, a point also examined at length in Wideman's meditation, *Fatheralong*.

By following *Philadelphia Fire*'s transformation of one more set of fire images, we can see the complex changes in the times as Wideman mirrors them in urban life. In both parts 1 and 3 of *Philadelphia Fire*, Wideman characterizes the city in terms of a man on fire. In part 1, this city that is a man on fire is written in 1960s language. "If the city is a man sprawled unconscious drunk in an alley, kids might find him, drench him with lighter fluid and drop a match on his chest. He'd flame up like a heap of all the unhappy monks in Asia. Puff the magic dragon. A little bald man topples over, spins as flames spiral up his saffron robe. In the streets of Hue and Saigon it had happened daily. You watched priests on TV burst into fireballs, roll as they combusted, a shadow flapping inside the flaming pyre" (21). This city, characterized through Vietnam War protest images, is on fire as if through self-immolation, and seems to destroys itself in spiritual protest, even while the fire is set by children who act with extreme human cruelty. In part 3, where we also witness a man on fire, he is no longer the unnamed "man sprawled unconscious drunk in an alley," but now J.B., burning alive, who hears "little white boys drenching him in kerosene and throwing a match ha ha ha laughing" (188).[4]

This man on fire is described through a very different set of metaphors: "he's prostrate, flat out, clenching his fists, kicking his toes raw against the cobbled bed of the fountain as wave after wave breaks over him and he riffles like a deck of cards being mixed, like a field of amber grain undulant in the breeze, a snake swallowing a frog, a flag rampant planted in the territory of somebody's chest" (189). This city on fire shows no evidence of protest; instead, it is native land conquered, territory possessed, horror superimposed upon the image of America the beautiful, and it demonstrates, powerfully, a new subaltern reality at the same time it demonstrates new manifestations of power. If J.B. is killed here, he is killed in both body and soul. Burned alive, his body begins to disintegrate, and as it does so he becomes, in image, finally, territory with a flag in his chest. But it is also as if this flag is made a stake and J.B. a vampire, so that with a stake through the heart J.B. is killed and killed again, an overdetermined death, an annihilation that will allow him no future existence in either mortal or immortal realms. With J.B. as the 1980s city on fire, then, we see the enormity of the desperation of these times.

Through his 1980s image of the city on fire, where the fact of children setting a man on fire is carried through and into such a different set of metaphorical meanings, Wideman raises the question: where to find hope now? Cudjoe has explicitly rejected the idea that Timbo, his old friend, now one of the mayor's administrators, proposes, to "forget the fire" and instead "write your sixties novel . . . the story about trying to change the world," the one that Cudjoe drafted twice and then abandoned (87–88). In conversation with Timbo, Cudjoe continues to return to the subject of the MOVE bombing and subsequent fire, an event clearly marked by 1980s, not 1960s, political realities. Yet the 1980s story written of Philadelphia's fire is intertwined with 1960s interests, Cudjoe's and Baldwin's, and incorporates knowledge of those interests even while it shifts time, and thus our point of view. Ultimately, Wideman's letter to his son must encapsulate this shift as it rewrites Baldwin's words of love to his nephew while simultaneously demonstrating changes in the lived dangers for black boys in the 1980s. It is in the context of the political realities of the 1980s, then, which includes Philadelphia's fire and Wideman's incarcerated son, that hope, if it is to mean anything at all, must be rediscovered.

When Wideman declared in an interview that he had *The Fire Next Time* in mind as he wrote *Philadelphia Fire*, he clearly meant to indicate more than a response focused on the repeated fire imagery in both texts (TuSmith 110). *The Fire Next Time* is a work in two parts, both of which are written as letters. As political theorist Lawrie Balfour details, Baldwin's text, taken as a whole, is a "critical meditation on the concepts of freedom and equality" where Baldwin both makes "his own experiences real for those to whom the message of those experiences was inaudible" and re-forms language to accommodate stories not previously given expression (122). In "My Dungeon Shook," the first letter-essay, Baldwin addresses his nephew in order to explain how the conditions in which his nephew lives, the ghetto that surrounds him, do not reflect his own inferiority but rather white society's inhumanity and fear. Integration, he continues, is not about the "impertinent assumption" on the part of white people "that *they* must accept *you*." Rather, the point Baldwin makes to his nephew is that the young man "must accept them [white Americans] and accept them with love. For these innocent people have no other hope. They are, in effect, still trapped in a history which they do not understand; and until they understand it, they cannot be released from it" (19). Baldwin explores this point in detail with his nephew in order to show the way to freedom. On the one hand, freedom is individual and psychological; the lines Baldwin quotes from an African American song are, "*The very time I thought I was lost, My dungeon shook and my chains fell off*" (21). But Baldwin's letter to his nephew is written "on the one hundredth anniversary of the emancipation" and his final point is that "we cannot be free until they are free," meaning, *black* Americans cannot be free until *white* Americans lose their illusions of superiority (22). Young James, Baldwin then implies, has much work to do with his "lost, younger brothers," the white innocents who because they believed others' "imprisonment made them safe are losing their grasp of reality," who consequently now must "see themselves as they are" and "cease fleeing from reality and begin to change it" (21). As we shall see, even in 1980s terms, this is the message that the narrator Wideman finally internalizes well enough to impart it to his son at the conclusion of part 2 of *Philadelphia Fire*, and that Cudjoe also comes to understand by the end of the novel.

In Baldwin's second essay in *The Fire Next Time*, titled "Down at the Cross" and subtitled "Letter from a Region in My Mind," he develops the themes of "My Dungeon Shook" in rhetorically fascinating ways, in order to press the point that black Americans "share the fate of a nation that has never accepted them" and consequently must realize they have no choice "but to do all in [their] power to change that fate" even if this is asking the impossible, for after all, "American Negro history . . . testifies to nothing less than the perpetual achievement of the impossible" (139–40). In other words, while it is still true that black Americans cannot be free until white Americans are free, "the price of the liberation of the white people is the liberation of the blacks—the total liberation, in the cities, in the towns, before the law and in the mind" (130). Only with this liberation, according to Baldwin, can we become a nation and "achieve our identity, our maturity" (131). Baldwin ends "Down at the Cross" with his own version of apocalyptic prophecy: if "the relatively conscious whites and the relatively conscious blacks, who must, like lovers, insist on, or create, the consciousness of the others ... do not dare everything," the "fire next time" is unavoidable. Let us all recommit ourselves, he implores, not only to ending "the racial nightmare" but also to achieving "our country" (141).

Just before Baldwin begins the final argument of "Down at the Cross" that leads him to implore his readers to "achieve our country," he invokes the idea of doing so "for the sake of one's children, in order to minimize the bill that *they must pay*" (139). With this reference he brings his nephew back into his readers' minds, and furthers the image by also remembering the buddies of his own youth. "*What*," he wondered, "*will happen to all that beauty then*?" (140). This, I want to claim, is a touchstone question for John Wideman's *Philadelphia Fire*. Wideman recognizes beauty in the city: in the male form of a basketball player— "Big, black, graceful. Broad shoulders, narrow waist, short, bouncy, almost delicate steps"—and in the form of a basketball game—"Music's inside the game. If you can't hear it, you can see it"—and in the car stereo music that plays from the side of the park basketball court—"Music reigns supreme and there is nothing not listening ... as a high sweet tenor and voices trilling behind it shine like silver, shine like gold" (37, 35, 43). When Cudjoe first hears and then dreams of the children in the park, there is again beauty, and a poetic magic. "Is the language foreign?" he asks himself. "Are these spirit voices? Little folk who emerge from their hiding places at midnight and rule the park" (50). Cudjoe has been out of the country for ten years and a new sound that we now recognize as rap, as hip-hop, has emerged: in the children's conversation "one voice dominates, rapping, scatting till they complete their business" (50). Wideman sees and responds to the beauty of youth that Baldwin names. Wideman also responds, however, to the beauty in the naming. The language of self-expression as employed by Baldwin gives us one answer to the question of what happens to beauty—and demonstrates the way in which beauty lodges within the very words of self-expression to re-form the language (Balfour 134). This is a point that Wideman explores in detail as his narrator in part 2 of *Philadelphia Fire* successfully grapples with how to say anything at all when the pain of living feels unbearable.

Through his use of the techniques of metanarrative in the difficult and densely complex middle section of his novel, Wideman points us to the ways of self-expression and requires that we seriously consider elements of form. This is not to say that his meaning comes to be contained on the surface of his writing, but rather that the meaning within expression and the formal elements of expression become intertwined so that the way they are intertwined is a clear part of his point. In no place is this more obvious than in the Caliban sections of part 2, where *The Tempest* is retold in the style of speech characterized by 1960s-era

Black Arts movement poets. What happens here, we might say, is that the question of youth's beauty combines with Baldwin's own message to his nephew to find freedom and Baldwin's exhortation to his readers to allow freedom, and in this combination becomes the larger metanarrative that is part 2 of Wideman's narrative. Cudjoe, who is explored as some sort of double for Wideman himself ("This airy other floating into the shape of my story . . . Is he mirror or black hole?" [122]), first appears in part 2 wondering "what happened to the kids he taught" (117). He next appears as a character in the narrated story of how he and the children almost produced *The Tempest* as a play in the park. He then becomes the first-person narrator of the continuation of the story of himself as teacher, working with the children to produce *The Tempest*.[5] In the midst of these sections, another narrator, presumably Wideman, tells us: "This is the central event, this production of *The Tempest* staged by Cudjoe in the late late 1960s, outdoors, in a park in West Philly. Though it comes here, wandering like a Flying Dutchman in and out of the narrative, many places at once, *The Tempest* sits dead center, the storm in the eye of the storm, figure within a figure, play within play, it is the bounty and hub of all else written about the fire, though it comes here, where it is, nearer the end than the beginning" (132). This *Tempest* never actually performed, yet "the bounty and hub of all else written about the fire," becomes quite clearly the key, then, to the metanarrative that Wideman here weaves, the story of writing the story of a fire.

There are three significant features to *The Tempest* as it is presented in part 2. The first is that as a production never performed, Cudjoe's *Tempest* is timeless. Wideman's narrator declares about the whole narration that is *Philadelphia Fire* that "this narrative is a sport of time, what it's about is stopping time, catching time" (133; Richard 606). And yet, the point that the narrator makes is that because "Cudjoe did not live to see his play hatched, he did spin from the endless circles of its possibility that second meaning cached in the drama's title: time. Borrowed time, bought time, saved time" (133). The first significant feature about *The Tempest* as it is presented here, then, is that as a production that never happened it remains full of possibility in Cudjoe's mind, remains suspended in an always already present that does not allow it to slip into memory. For Cudjoe, because "the kids were ready" for their performance, knew their lines, the play has come into existence (149); yet because it hasn't been performed, it also hasn't become a past event. This ever-present aspect of the performance, then, allows Cudjoe to continue to imagine the children's Elizabethan English as a living language that has shaped and reshaped itself, ultimately into the poetic rap he hears as children's voices in the park. This has significance for our understanding of Cudjoe's story of the fire, and Wideman's as well. In an interview with Rebekah

Presson, Wideman reminds us that "Simba Muntu, the lion-man-boy, is out there in the street. It's his voice that energizes the raps. It's his voice that's in the background of Philadelphia. It's Simba and his friends who are putting graffiti on the walls. They're the ones who might be responsible for the fire next time unless all that negative energy and anger are somehow transformed to useful purposes— purposes that are useful to them" (TuSmith 110). If somehow the production never performed has unleashed a poetic energy that might engulf the city, might become "the fire next time," then it seems this energy might bear with it also enormous potential for the possible salvation of the city, or at least the salvation of the soul.[6]

While the production never performed is one feature of Wideman's *Tempest*, a significant second feature is that the children were to perform an "original production in the park" (141), a rewritten *Tempest*, but rewritten in ways that are never completely clarified. At one point, Cudjoe implores the children to "stay awhile and help me mount this authentically revised version of Willy's con. We been in the storm too long, chillun, We gon crank up the volume, crank up the volume, to a mighty tempest and blow the blues away" (131), thus suggesting that in the end of this *Tempest*, Caliban comes back into possession of his island. Whether or not this can really happen, even in terms of an original production, is uncertain. In an earlier fragment on this subject the narrator proclaims: "The saddest thing about this story is that Caliban must always love his island and Prospero must always come and steal it. Nature. Each one stuck with his nature. So it ends and never ends" (122). Nevertheless, as a teacher Cudjoe is not comfortable presenting Prospero as the role model for his children; this is why the play is rewritten and presented as an "immortal play about colonialism, imperialism, recidivism, the royal fucking over of weak by strong, colored by white, many by few" (127), and also why Cudjoe names his responsibility "as model and teacher" to unteach and to help "separate the good from the bad from the ugly" (131). Perhaps Miranda becomes the central character in this revisioned play: a young girl, Melissa, is cast as Miranda, and brought forward on the stage of Cudjoe's or Wideman's mind's eye, from a game of jump rope, to deliver the "spurned woman speech" with words usually attributed to Prospero, in order to indicate that a complex relationship between Caliban and Miranda might develop so that Miranda turns on her father and frees Caliban. But no, Timbo objects as the play is taking shape, this revision will not work. Miranda "ain't nothing but a wimp. . . . You got to do better. . . . Everybody knows can't nobody free Caliban but his own damn self" (145). Or perhaps Caliban might become free in the end, Charley suggests, because Prospero has "a change of heart" and "realizes he's fucked up" (145). But this idea, too, is rejected and so the question of what, in the end, happens to Caliban in the revised *Tempest* remains untold.

Finally, this revised and practiced but never performed *Tempest* creates a newly interpreted Caliban. The character Caliban enters part 2 of *Philadelphia Fire* on his own. A fragment begins with a stage direction, parenthetically inserted: "Enter Caliban, heavy, heavy dreadlocks resembling chains drag nearly to the floor" (120). He is characterized as a natural man: naked, but covered by his dreads. When he speaks, we hear "traces of the Bronx, Merry Ole England, rural Georgia, Jamaican calypso, West Coast krio, etc." What he speaks, however, what he names, is that life has been stolen from him. He wants his island back. "Noting make self," he says. "We all somebody's chillren" (121). And then Caliban shape-shifts enough to say words that belong more obviously to Wideman: "Who am so dirty take what him don't belong? Steal from breddar. Steal from son. Break bond. Break word." And for just this moment Wideman's brother Robby and his son Jake enter this text. This Caliban, then, is a powerful figure in terms of his ability to conjure. He also becomes, in part 2, a figure that evokes, from the narrator, a sustained critical meditation, not on the political concepts of freedom and equality, but on the metaphysical idea of self. Here, from Caliban's perspective, the beginning of self-conscious life is considered, and in this consideration Wideman extends the moment of anticipation just prior to Prospero's arrival, enunciates the primal question "*where did I come from?*" that Caliban wonders, and demonstrates the deep, deep desire for language implicit when one human being makes contact with another (146–48).[7]

At one point when Cudjoe is talking with the children about Caliban, he plays with the line, "And thereby hangs a tale" by saying that his job to "unteach" is, "specifically, in this case, to remove de tail. Derail de tale. Disembarrass, disabuse, disburden—demonstrate conclusively that Mr. Caliban's behind is clean and unencumbered, good as anybody else's. That the tail was a tale" (131). By playing with the myth that Africans have tails, Wideman's Cudjoe gets to the heart of this revised *Tempest*: here, the point is to debunk such dehumanizing myths. Caliban has no tail. The children in the ghetto school can learn Shakespeare and perform the King's English. "The play was the thing," our narrator informs us. "To catch a conscience. To prick pride and dignity and say, Hey, we're alive over here. That was Shakespeare youall just saw performed. And we did it" (132). The play was designed, then, to show the larger world the children's humanity and their beauty. In Baldwin's terms from *The Fire Next Time*, the play was designed as a moment that insists on consciousness and so frees white Americans from their illusions of superiority. But then, of course, we are immediately reminded that the play was never performed. Caliban's drama, and the drama of the children's confrontation with the ignorance that stereotypes them, takes place only, continually, within Cudjoe's own consciousness. Ultimately, it is the way that Cudjoe imagines himself or is imagined by Wideman, is imagined *as* himself or *as* Wideman, is remade in the image of his reinterpreted Caliban as a newly formed man of the city who also partakes of the man-child Simba Muntu, survivor of fire, that delivers him or does not.[8]

Cudjoe's drama in part 2, certainly "the central event" and declared so by narrator Wideman, is so because it is "the bounty and hub of all else written about the fire." The story of the fire, and how to write the story of "fire," which now more clearly represents the confrontation that means either destruction or transformation, continues to be *Philadelphia Fire*'s larger concern. In part 2, we are not only involved in Cudjoe's drama of consciousness through the workings of a reinterpreted and ever performing *Tempest*, but are also involved in the drama of consciousness belonging to Cudjoe's double, Wideman. The character Wideman, as introduced in part 2, is experiencing two crises, one involving his relation to his son as a father, and the other involving his relation to himself as a writer. By the end of the section, with the father's letter to his son as the concluding moment, both crises are, at least tentatively, resolved.[9] As noted earlier, Wideman is first introduced as character in part 2 when the phone rings and he begins a conversation with his incarcerated son. From this conversation we infer the difficulties of connection between father and son, difficulties that Wideman comments upon very directly in his later work *Fatheralong*:

> Let me say it again, in the simplest terms. This country, as it presently functions, stands between black fathers and sons, impeding communication, frustrating development, killing or destroying the bodies and minds of young men, short-circuiting the natural process of growth, maturity, the cycle of the generations. This country, as it's constituted now, today, its basic institutions and values, or rather the corrupted version of these institutions and values produced by the paradigm of race, has abandoned its children. (68)

In the fragments of part 2 that represent the developing communication between Wideman and his son, however, it is not just difficulties but possibilities that are explored.

In words, the two "can't move past the initial formulas of greeting" so when the two are again presented in communication, it is their silence as connection that is emphasized. "Say the word *father*," Wideman says. "Now say *son*. Now think of the space between *father* and *son*, as they are words, as they are indications of time and the possibility of salvation, redemption, continuity" (103). The point is that the "nothing" between the words fills the silence. Somehow, "saying nothing is enough to grip the silence" and silence itself, if it is between two people, might also connect them. In this meditation, Wideman realizes, there is an interdependence between father and son, and his own identity as father is not possible without the existence of his son. The consciousness of self that Wideman here explores, his understanding of himself as a father, takes on the weight of Cudjoe's reinterpreted Calibanic quest for identity. The aching loneliness, the question of origins, of generation, and the desire for language in order to communicate, all characteristics of Caliban on his island prior to the moment of contact, become part of Wideman's own existential meditation. With these as the elements of his own understanding of himself as father, he then turns to examine his son's existential state: "How does it feel to be inhabited by more than one self?" Now Wideman wrenchingly places himself in his son's position, imagines what his son "must learn in periods of calm"—"to repeat a story endlessly to himself: there is a good boy, someone who loves and is loved, who can fend off the devils, who can survive in spite of shifting, unstable combinations of good and evil, being and nothingness" (110). When he wonders if this story his son "must never stop singing" can "become a substitute for an integrated sense of self, of oneness, the personality he can never achieve," he reminds himself that, again, it may not be enough but, like the silence, "it's all we have."

Through the extenuating circumstances of his son's life, Wideman questions the relationship between identity and narrative. And while he sees this as his son's question, he also sees it as his own. As writer, he identifies with L. Zasetsky in *The Man with a Shattered World*, who describes the torturous process of trying to find words to tell the story of an illness that prevents him from remembering words (107). Wideman is trying to write in Maine, at the family camp filled with memories that include his son, Jake, and he is having trouble remembering words. He wonders if he will ever try to write his son's story and feels that "not dealing with it may be causing the forgetfulness" he's experiencing, which he compares to Zasetsky's (115). And then he begins to write his son's story in a more direct way, beginning with the lines: "The unmitigated cruelty of the legal system. My son rots in a cell" (115). Here he tells the story of his son, a mentally ill juvenile caught in the adult criminal justice system, held in solitary confinement because the state can literally offer no alternatives, forced, alone, "to suffer and try to make sense of his imprisonment, the chaos of his personality, his terror and guilt" and so "sinking into a profound stupor" like a wounded animal who is instinctually crawling into its den to curl up and die (116). And after a short fragment that introduces Cudjoe and his concern for the children he once taught, Wideman also explores the story of the father of such a son. There is no word that is equivalent to the word *orphan*, used when a child loses a parent, to name a parent who has lost a child, Wideman points out. And yet he nevertheless begins to put into words such a loss, through image piled upon image: in terms of the family photograph representing four generations that is now undone; in terms of an amputated leg and the emptiness where it was and the pain in the emptiness; in terms of confusion as life forms around "absence we've been in the habit of calling one thing, but now it's another without a name" (119–20). By narrating son, and narrating father, Wideman does not make the claim of healing wounds or righting wrongs, but only recognizes that there is an insistence to "speak to it, of it, exist with the pain of its presence and absence speaking to me a hundred times a day, every day" (120). Recognizing this insistence toward expression may also not be enough but, again, for Wideman, "it's all we have."

Part 2 of *Philadelphia Fire* concludes, as we have noted, with a final segment in which Wideman, as father, writes directly to his son. "I will write you soon again," he says, almost indicating that all of part 2 is a very long letter to his son (150). But his point in the end is hope: that his son must "learn to hope in what seems a hopeless situation," and the key, again, is a narrative sense of life. Every day life changes. With each day, one's mind forms a new picture of circumstances. The picture changes, always, if only because one has lived through "one more day of hell" (151). The next day will, necessarily, bring a slightly different outlook. This, as Wideman states, is not intended as consolation. It is the equivalent recognition for his son of his own recognition of the insistence to tell. It is his way "of thinking about some things that are basically unthinkable" and modeling that for his son (151). If his son can narrate the story of himself to himself, then there is hope. This section ends with Wideman's call to his son: "Live your life strongly, fully, moment by moment. Make do. Hold on. . . . We don't know what the future will bring. We do have a chance to unfold our days one by one and piece together a story that shapes us. It's the only life anyone ever has. Hold on" (151). When Caliban, on his island, recognizes his own desire for contact, moves beyond profound stupor, begins to feel the need to distinguish between "words inside or outside" his own mind, to say words aloud if he can, we leave him. Neither Cudjoe nor Wideman say what happens to him next. In some ways, however, this story of Wideman's son extends Caliban into his 1980s self. And here, as in the reinterpreted *Tempest*, exactly who or what he is remains to be seen.

The letter that Wideman writes to his son, when compared to Baldwin's to his nephew, reflects his son's very different set of circumstances occurring in a very different time. Yet much of the basic message remains the same: Wideman's "Hold on" might easily be understood in Baldwin's terms, as invocation to his son that he understand his life in a cell as a reflection of the larger society's inhumanity and fear rather than that society's judgment that he deserves such treatment.

Just as Baldwin's letter to his nephew is presented within the larger structure of *The Fire Next Time*, however, so too is Wideman's communication with his son presented within the larger structure of *Philadelphia Fire*, which finally, in part 3, becomes once again Cudjoe's story. Here, in the final scenes, we see Wideman updating the image of "relatively conscious whites" and "relatively conscious blacks" insisting, like lovers, on the consciousness of others. Do we read the dismal turnout of the crowd for "the memorial service for the dead of Osage Avenue" as failure? Not in Baldwin's terms, nor in Wideman's either, where it is the insistence that counts. When Cudjoe utters the words, "*Never again. Never again*" in the context of Philadelphia's fire, in the context of his own and Wideman's metaphysical "fire," and also in the context of a mob from 1805 "howling his name" and "screaming for blood," because this final passage incorporates an earlier moment in Philadelphia's history when slaves were driven from Independence Square, the words take their meaning from what Cudjoe has learned from Simba: "his ability to survive, and his determination to do things his way" and his "consciousness that it's a very dangerous world indeed," so dangerous that a new world needs to be created because the old one is on fire.[10] The words "*Never again. Never again*" also take on meaning, however, from what Wideman has learned from his son. Words insist. And these words, this phrase "*Never again,*" as Wideman explains in *Fatheralong*, mean that those who speak it say there is hope for a future in which justice will prevail (*Fatheralong* 146).[11] Like Baldwin's, these are righteous and hopeful words. By placing such words before his reader, in the final moment of the novel, Wideman confronts, as Baldwin does, insists, as Baldwin does, that we must all make "our country," over and over again, or burn.

NOTES

I would like to thank the graduate students who were in my Twentieth-Century African American Fiction course during the Spring 2002 semester at The College of Saint Rose. Our discussions inspired this article. Special thanks to Jennifer Filomeno and to Gretchen Ingersoll. This essay is dedicated to the memory of Cathy Selchick.
  1. For details on the publication history of *The Fire Next Time*, see Weatherby 233.
  2. "Runagate," literally a fugitive or runaway, is a word also etymologically associated with "renegade." Used here, it suggests a historical connection between Cudjoe as runaway/renegade father and "runagates" who are fugitive ex-slaves. See Robert Hayden's poem "Runagate Runagate" (in *Collected Poems*) for usage of the term in the latter context.
  3. The quotation is from Gaston Bachelard's *The Psychoanalysis of Fire*.
  4. J.B.'s identity is purposely unclear. He could perhaps be King, leader of MOVE as Wideman names him, who has either survived the bombing or been reincarnated.

Note that King's prior name in the novel seems to have been James Brown. See *Philadelphia Fire* 10. My thanks to student Sarah Oppedisano for pointing to this detail.

5. When Cudjoe's story switches to a first-person narration in this section, there is also the possible implication that Wideman is the speaker of this first-person narrative, and that perhaps Cudjoe and Wideman are merging as characters.

6. There are two rap-influenced children's speeches that suggest movement toward possible salvation. The first, perhaps spoken by Simba Muntu, is a meditation on death that begins, "*If when you die no heaven no place to go where do you go when you die?*" and ends, "*So our blood runs warm and safe inside because there is no place to go after you die*" (50–52). The second, not nearly so innocent as the first, but nevertheless hopeful in its energy and its truth, is perhaps repeated by Timbo as he quotes Simba Muntu (91).

7. James W. Coleman argues that "Calibanic discourse" is a restricting feature of black male discourse that largely defeats "the black male's quest to speak in an empowering voice" (4). Following Coleman's argument, Wideman's attempt to rewrite the trope of Caliban only re-inscribes it. Reading Wideman's novel through the lens of Baldwin, however, shifts our focus to the possibilities inherent in this newly interpreted Caliban. By suggesting the "Abhorrèd slave" speech is not Prospero's but Miranda's, Wideman has shifted the very ground of black self-conscious understanding away from its implicit origin, which always inscribes Caliban's behavior as slavish, and is instead on the cusp of a very new understanding which he attempts to signify by saying of the character Miranda, in his or Cudjoe's version of the play, "we bring her forward to clear the air, to entertain and instruct the next generation" (141).

8. As evidence of deliverance we might also consider the speaker of the fragment that connects Wideman as father meditating on his loss with the dramatic entrance of Caliban. This short paragraph begins, "Who am I? One of you. With you in the ashes of this city we share" (120), and seems to be the composite voice of this remade Cudjoe and/or Wideman, together with Simba Muntu, Ralph Ellison's Invisible Man, and the re-imagined Caliban himself.

9. Jerry Varsava makes the claim that "judicious readers are forced to suspend judgment on the issue of the son's victimization because of the way Wideman presents it"—that is, in a mode "biased by the emotional tug of paternal anxiety and care" (437), in order to claim that Cudjoe's reinterpretation of *The Tempest* is the more effective aspect of part 2. I see both stories as linked. Further, I am not convinced by Varsava's argument that Wideman's point is to show his son's victimization. By my reading, his point is more to demonstrate a father's grief.

10. For Wideman's comment about what Cudjoe has learned from Simba, see TuSmith 109–10.

11. In this text, in reflection upon a reception he attends at the South Carolina Historical Museum, Wideman makes an analogy between this event and a "Reconstruction Ball during the impossible, gilded, *never again* moment when black people mixed socially with the ruling class of whites, controlled the South Carolina legislature, strolled comfortably, freely in the marbled corridors of Justice." It is the context of Wideman's use of the phrase "*never again*" that allows us to define its meaning in this way.

Works Cited

Baldwin, James. *The Fire Next Time.* 1963. New York: Dell, 1988.

Balfour, Lawrie. *The Evidence of Things Not Said: James Baldwin and the Promise of American Democracy.* Ithaca, NY: Cornell UP, 2001.

Coleman, James W. *Black Male Fiction and the Legacy of Caliban.* Lexington: UP of Kentucky, 2001.

Hayden, Robert. *Collected Poems.* Ed. Frederick Glaysher. New York: Liveright, 1985.

Richard, Jean-Pierre. "*Philadelphia Fire,* or the Shape of a City." *Callaloo* 22.3 (1999): 603–13.

TuSmith, Bonnie, ed. "John Edgar Wideman." Rebekah Presson, interviewer. *Conversations with John Edgar Wideman.* Jackson: UP of Mississippi, 1998. 105–12.

Varsava, Jerry. "'Woven of Many Strands': Multiple Subjectivity in John Edgar Wideman's *Philadelphia Fire.*" *Critique* 41.4 (Summer 2000): 425–44.

Weatherby, W. J. *James Baldwin: Artist on Fire.* New York: Dell, 1989.

Wideman, John Edgar. *Fatheralong.* New York: Vintage, 1994.

———. *Philadelphia Fire.* New York: Vintage, 1990.

The Individual and the Collective

THREATENING BLACKNESS
IN WIDEMAN'S
PHILADELPHIA FIRE

STACEY L. BERRY

Individual and communal power have been interconnected themes in the prose works of African American authors since the slave narrative. Novels such as Alice Walker's *The Color Purple* and Toni Morrison's *Beloved* provide examples of these kinds of stories that locate the main character on a journey toward self-awareness that only becomes realized through significant exposure to a healthy black community. The self-awareness, in most cases, stems from the hardships of living as the outsider in a culture dominated by whiteness. The black community generally serves as rehabilitation for the main character, because the group provides strength through common experience. The essence of community in these works also seems to illustrate that the individual's existence is justified through exposure to others similarly situated. In contrast, many authors writing from and about the African American experience provide examples of characters who are unable to find that connection to a healthy community. Nella Larsen's *Quicksand*, for example, follows the main character, Helga, on this type of difficult journey where her disconnection from any racial group sends her on a downward spiral into despair. John Edgar Wideman's 1990 novel, *Philadelphia Fire*, in many ways explores these issues. Through the variety of characters, settings, narrative styles, and numerous other elements, the novel speaks to the complicated nature of blackness, power, and community in contemporary American society. Wideman's investigation reveals a dominant society consisting of various races that embraces and enforces traditionally white cultural codes and standards and exposes the dangerous reality that exists in connection with that power. The result is a novel that presents intertwined messages about the nature of black power stemming from the individual and the community. Wideman's novel serves as a warning to readers about what happens to groups of black people who are viewed as a threat by the dominant society, while simultaneously suggesting that the only true power that black people have is that contained in an individual and therefore less threatening stance.

A comparison of the MOVE organization and the character James Brown (J.B.) illustrates the theme of what is considered threatening black power. Wideman introduces the events of the 1985 bombing of the MOVE organization's house in Philadelphia through Cudjoe's interview with Margaret Jones in part 1 of the novel. Margaret's descriptions of the leader, the members, and the house from the perspective of the outsider represent that held by the dominant society. She makes remarks about the horrible smell and calls the group a "tribe" and its members "savages" (12–13). When she becomes part of the organization, however, she damns any part of herself that she deems to be still outside of the family. After listening to the account, Cudjoe comments that Margaret Jones's love for King, MOVE's leader, "will always be right *and* wrong" (15). This statement suggests that the MOVE group was trying to do something positive that ultimately could not work. The conflict that Wideman posits through this exchange is that the MOVE group represents a return to an African tradition and culture. Rather than capitalizing on earlier conceptions of getting back to the natural, which often suggested a return to Africa, this scene ties into the ideology that African Americans have been subjected to colonialism on American soil and should create a self-defined community there. The reclamation of a more traditional communal lifestyle without removing oneself from the dominant culture does something that other movements had not done. In full view, it rejects the leadership and ways of the dominant society and indicates that new rules and standards are called for. Unlike other less organized or individual acts of subversion, the MOVE group's actions are so threatening because they offer not only a collective nature and force, but also a very public display of resistance. The reaction from the dominant society is to immediately obliterate the threat this new system of order represents. When Cudjoe asks Timbo, the mayor's attaché, why the group was treated in this manner, Timbo replies, "They were embarrassing, man. Embarrassing. Trying to turn back the clock. Didn't want no kind of city, no kind of government" (81). Wideman employs the MOVE organization to represent a collective living outside the accepted social codes of their surroundings. Because their mode of protest involves an ever-increasing group and calls into question the lifestyle and values of the majority, the community is deemed threatening by the power structure and is therefore exterminated.

The element of comparison that clarifies this point is presented in part 3 of the novel through the character J.B. As a homeless man in the streets of Philadelphia, J.B. shares many of the physical characteristics that the city found so deplorable about the MOVE members. He wears dreadlocks and is described as filthy. He roams the streets covered in "sweat, piss, shit" (170). But J.B., as opposed to the members of MOVE, does not live next door. As part of the faceless millions of homeless people in the United States, he is not seen as a threat to the order of society. On this aspect of his character Wideman notes, "No one notices a funky derelict emerging from an almost invisible wedge between two buildings" (180). Invisible to the dominant culture, J.B. is simply ignored.[1] His status as an isolated nonthreatening individual is further emphasized through the suggestion that only a cop with nothing better to do would be interested in stopping him, because "if you stink bad, the cops don't like to touch you" (180). Even though J.B. is part of a "tribe of gypsies," his placement in the novel suggests that as long as he remains invisible, unorganized, and nonthreatening, he will not be attacked by the power structure. Timbo provides an example of the power structure's denial of people like J.B. when he tells Cudjoe, "Back in the good old U.S. of A., we ain't got real poor people" (80). The government does not even recognize this "tribe" as an element of society. The obvious problem with the individual form of protest that J.B. represents is that his station in life does not coincide with any power. Just as the MOVE group was unsuccessful because they posed too much of a visible threat, J.B. lacks the ability to enact any societal change.

Wideman does not leave the readers with these two avenues of black existence in America as the only solutions. Rather, he suggests that the ability to have a voice comes from an intricate balance of these two ideologies. Both Cudjoe, the man searching for the lone survivor of the bombing, and Simba Muntu, the boy who survived the firebombing, provide examples of individuals who have found a voice of power without posing an imminent threat. These characters have been on reverse journeys, which have culminated in a similar way. Simba begins the novel as a child member of the MOVE organization. Immersed in group and tribal culture, he is then violently thrust out of that setting by the firebombing of his home and the murder of his family members. These events leave him homeless and isolated. Much like J.B., Simba is taken in by Margaret Jones's friends and nursed back to health. While J.B. poses as a voiceless war veteran, further emphasizing his powerlessness in society, the reader is told that Simba regains his voice and rides off one day on his bicycle. No one sees him again. Even as a child, Simba seems to recognize the power he holds through all that he has seen and his ability to tell his own story. Because of that power, he must not be too visible in the public eye or he will be eliminated like his family members. Further narrative comments indicate that Simba had been hanging out with his gang, suggesting that the Kids Krusade and the Kaliban's Kiddie Korps groups that emerge later in the novel may be under his leadership. Unlike the highly visible MOVE organization, the Kiddie Korps develops and begins to rise unnoticed. Cudjoe remarks that their graffiti serves as a "ritual mask summoning power; a dream, a revelation as the features of the city change before our eyes" (89). Like J.B., the Kiddie Korps are able to move about the city unnoticed, but they also have a voice through writing which allows their message to be heard. By moving out of an isolated black community that was obliterated, Simba is then able to reenter society in a way that allows him to continue spreading his message.

In contrast, Cudjoe begins in isolation. He attends college, becomes a teacher, and subscribes to the dominant ideas of Western society, which distances him further from his black identity. Timbo tells Cudjoe that their former black student peers are now "[w]alking round like ghosts of they own goddamned selves" (77). Both Timbo and Cudjoe remain influenced by their college years, but through the course of their conversation, Cudjoe shows that he understands the problems associated with those days of casting off blackness. Cudjoe married a white woman and was "ashamed of his skin" (22). He also removed himself from his culture by moving to a Greek island. Through increasingly isolated circumstances, Cudjoe disassociated himself from his identity and from the needs of his community. After the bombing and his subsequent return to Philadelphia, he begins to realize that neither assimilation nor complete isolation will provide him with the answers he seeks. Cudjoe comments on this situation when he decides to tell Margaret Jones that "we're all in this together. That he was lost but now he's found" (22). Part of what Cudjoe has found is that he must capture the stories of others. He tapes Margaret Jones's account of the bombing and searches tirelessly for Simba because he must hear Simba's story. Cudjoe admits that he wants to write a book about the bombing in an attempt to do something about the silence. This desire to document communal events that will raise awareness suggests the kind of individual power that Wideman advocates in the novel. Both characters cycle through group identification and isolation, which results in an understanding that their ability to tell stories holds a valuable currency. Cudjoe and Simba provide examples of individuals who have found voices of power without posing an imminent threat. Their individual, nonthreatening positioning allows them to communicate messages of protest with less chance of being silenced by the power holders.

Wideman, as the author and narrator of the novel, serves as a perfect example of the nonthreatening power of the individual. The writer has the unique role of collector and teller of stories, a role that has been viewed in the black community as tribally based and sacred. Wideman's fiction capitalizes on this traditional perspective, as storytelling or performance has long been a culturally accepted way of presenting countercultural messages or political dissension and is not viewed as a highly threatening force. Since writing is a solitary act, it supports points made throughout the novel that the only safe way to enact change is through individual effort. However, the kind of writing found in Wideman's novel must be community-based and ultimately relies on a community of readers for success. Without the stories from the community, this novel would not exist. The orality of the stories is emphasized through Wideman's choice not to include any of the characters' speeches in quotation marks, a subtle reminder that all of these events are stories being passed on through time. The novel begins with the tale of Zivanias, the captain of a tourist ship who dies in a sea storm. The reliance on the communal aspects of storytelling here is evident through the use of details. We are told that Cudjoe and Zivanias had lunch together once. The presentation of material, however, indicates that Cudjoe knows intimate details about how the sea captain would "hold his boat on course with his foot" and under what conditions he met his demise (4). Even in an isolated setting, such as an island, there are still stories to be told and shared. The novel, then, is a collection of stories recorded through and from various characters. For example, Wideman writes about Zivanias, Cudjoe, and himself, and Cudjoe learns details about the bombing from Margaret Jones, the basketball players, and Timbo—as well as many other characters. Wideman also learns about the bombing by watching CNN. This system of disseminating information to large numbers of people across vast distances mirrors the aim of the novel because it illustrates the importance of preserving, passing on, and interpreting important events. Wideman's reference to the mass media brings attention to these different speakers' voices and points to a place in contemporary society where that power of communication is already in force. His acts of compiling and telling the stories of others in a shared situation relate back to ancient tribal traditions, suggesting the need to retrieve customs that have been lost or suppressed over time. They also encourage comparison with contemporary media. These connections bring the various layers of storytelling together to provide a possible comparison for a place where this kind of communication is already taking place, suggesting that now we must figure out how to use it.

These layers remind the reader of the intricate balance between the individual and the community that Wideman suggests throughout the novel. Wideman points to the power of the word when he says of Cudjoe: "He will explain to Margaret Jones that he must always write about many places at once. No choice. The splitting apart is inevitable. First step is always out of time. Away from responsibility, toward the word or sound or image that is everywhere at once, that connects and destroys" (23). Connecting and destroying seem to be what Wideman is concerned with throughout the novel. He not only wants to draw his readers' attention to the issues at work in terms of race in contemporary American society, but he also attempts to redefine the ways in which black Americans protest their situation. By sharing their experiences with others, writers and artists have a better chance than the MOVE organization of staging a protest that is not only palatable to a wide audience, but also one that is fruitful.

Wideman's mode of writing the novel in a nontraditional format also speaks to the issue of nonthreatening individual power. As the narrator, Wideman casts a traditional narrative voice that runs throughout the novel, but he subverts that voice with the continual interjections of other characters that then become the focus of the novel. This fragmentation of voices mirrors that of the African griot tradition or the voice that speaks the history of many people and many time periods at once. By utilizing this technique while retaining a standard narrator, the narrative rejects some of the stylistic characteristics that dominate much of the Western European literary tradition. It does so, however, in a way that will not necessarily alienate an audience accustomed to that tradition. An example of this mode of balancing the two interests comes in part 2 of the novel when Wideman is discussing Cudjoe's aspirations to produce an all-black production of Shakespeare's *The Tempest*. First, Caliban tells the reader in an African dialect that "Dis island mine. Been mine always. This mother-humping play can't end no oder way" (122). Immediately following these lines, the narrator echoes Caliban's sentiments in more standard English: "The saddest thing about this story is that Caliban must always love his island and Prospero must always come and steal it. Nature. Each one stuck with his nature. So it ends and never ends" (122). This passage serves a dual purpose in the novel by breaking with tradition in form and sentiment, while, at the same time, providing more traditional Western discourse to avoid alienating potential readers.

Similarly, the narrator's voice remains constant throughout the novel, while other characters slip in and out of dialects that are mainly driven by urban slang. This technique provides another way for the writer as individual to reach a larger number of people with his message. When giving her account of the bombing, Margaret Jones's speech is characterized by dialect. Of her experience with the MOVE group's leader, King, she says, "And you know he means them and you understand them better cause he says them black, black like him, black like you, so how the sister gon deny King" (14). As a member of the MOVE organization,

Margaret has accepted her role as an African American and has conceivably come closer to her African roots. Her use of dialect, then, stands as an example of embracing one's heritage. Wideman provides a contrast to this linguistic variety with Timbo's language later in the novel. Upon first greeting Cudjoe, Timbo remarks, "Gimme some skin now. Cudjoe, you scarce mothafucker" (74). Although Timbo uses a street dialect, we later surmise from his attitude that he does not understand the needs of black people in the city. He even tells Cudjoe that their belief that things would get better was a lie, and he actively participates in the system of government that continues to perpetrate violent acts against African Americans. Later in the novel, Wideman uses Caliban's accented voice to show another view from a character who understands the system of power in which he lives. Wideman's presentation of these many different versions of black speech suggests that it is difficult to distinguish between authentic and inauthentic dialect. Margaret and Timbo use a similar dialect to convey their thoughts, but the difference is connected to the concept of reciprocity. Margaret's voice is genuine, because her pronouncements are communally based, while Timbo makes statements and pronouncements that are not necessarily tied to the fostering of community.

Wideman furthers his goal to bridge this relationship between the community and the individual by incorporating elements of the performative. As I noted earlier, performance has been a culturally accepted way of presenting countercultural messages or political dissension and is, therefore, not viewed as such a threatening force. On this topic Wideman comments:

> I know that the only way I'm going to intrigue anybody enough—entice them enough to get at some of those points . . . is to provide a play: a sensuous, rhythmic experience of language that has a first appeal, a primal appeal. Once you're entertaining somebody then you can also instruct them. But you don't begin by scaring them away. At least that's not what I try to do. (TuSmith 209)

One of the ways in which Wideman addresses this issue in *Philadelphia Fire* is through references to music. American music of the 1960s was saturated with political messages from antiwar to pro–civil rights, so this form of protest is easily recognizable to the novel's readers. During his visit with Timbo over lunch, Cudjoe conjures their time together as schoolmates in the sixties. Protest through music is connected to the Kid Krusade when Timbo says, "Of course that rapping music's in it. And the stuff on the walls part of it too" (Wideman 90). Similarly, Wideman peppers the novel with a rapping style in the narrative. These sections remind the reader of the cultural codes contained and associated with rap music which, as a part of hip-hop, was connected to graffiti. Cudjoe makes this connection when he remarks, "Vandalism or tribal art or handwriting on the wall. Whatever the signs meant, they were a transforming presence" (88). This statement corresponds to Wideman's suggestion that individual performance as protest can bring about change; it also suggests how writing is intertwined with community through the incorporation of the word "tribal," and the cultural connection of graffiti with personal and very visible forms of communication. Much like other stylistic devices found in Wideman's writing, the creation and success of the individual act is closely tied to the community through elements such as music and performance.

When the book was released in 1990, a form of hip-hop labeled "gangsta rap" was steadily emerging from the urban ghettos of America. Although this protest music—which confronted the dire need for attention to the problems of drug abuse and police violence against ethnic minorities—was often condemned by the dominant power structure, it took on an overwhelming presence in popular culture and mainstream American music. On this phenomenon the editors of *The Norton Anthology of African American Literature* observed:

> Despite disclaimers, gangsta rappers and others do teach their listeners (in something like the way that realist fiction writers teach their readers) by dealing in rivetingly raw terms the severe, violent nature of life in the no-exit realm of the black urban underclass. Some even tap into the black prophetic tradition by urging listeners to awaken to new levels of political and spiritual consciousness, to read and to prepare to take forthright action in a far-downfallen world. (Gates and McKay 60)

Similarly, in an address to J.B. to "get up off your ass" the novel's narrator comments that "what we need is realism" (157). Much like these rap artists, Wideman knows that the realism he hopes to show to his readers must be presented to them in a consumable fashion. To the extent that the rap artists' aims to reach a widespread audience and spark interest in racial issues have been successful, Wideman has capitalized on their approach to remind his readers of the power of performance to incite change.

Along with popular culture and performance modes involving audience participation, Wideman also makes references to film. Movies provide a context in which the audience sits back and views the images served up to them from filmmakers and, similar to the other modes of communication that Wideman discusses, the individual effort of a film is dependent on the audience to be successful. These subtle references to filmmaking and film style send several different messages to the reader. Wideman reminds his audience that art is a result of the artist's imagination imposing itself on nature or reality and that everything he is conveying through his novel is also interpretation. Upon first hearing of the bombing the narrator contemplates the televised images and his wife's naked body and remarks that both constructions are "leaving me to make something of it" (101). He also suggests that the reader or viewer take a more active role in evaluating and pursuing or rejecting the information provided to them. When first learning of the bombing, Wideman says he and his wife were "impatient for the voice-over to tell us what to think" (100). He further emphasizes the dependence viewers place on other people's images by saying, "What we don't know always carries the potential to harm us, and we know just enough to believe that, so we stay tuned for further developments" (101). Cudjoe's visions of the past evoked by visiting a basketball court in the city take on the mode of a film with Cudjoe as the director, thus suggesting that the individual has the power to interpret and redefine history and culture. Cudjoe exerts control over this memory by trying to recall the nostalgia of the basketball court as a place of reverie and action rather than one of imprisonment and isolation. His attempts to place himself within a created past reveal that he is relying on the "cliché" devices often seen in films in an attempt to reconnect "a then and a now" (31). This reliance on the dominant culture's view of individual identity and change corresponds to a similar message contained in a popular protest piece by artist and civil rights activist Gil Scott-Heron: "You will not be able to stay home, brother. / You will not be able to plug in, turn on and cop out. / [. . .] Because the revolution will not be televised" (61). The power of the performative, in these cases, promotes an element of audience agency in actively pursuing the proliferation of change.

Wideman also incorporates a historical level of the performative cultural protest as well by appropriating Shakespeare. This Western European literary figure wrote plays that critiqued and commented on the political and social situations of the Renaissance period. The novel suggests that the definition of the individual identity and path is largely determined by history. At one point the narrator thinks to himself, "As he drove he considered all the moments of his life that had brought him to this particular moment on a winding, divided street in the year 1987, Amherst, Massachusetts, on his way to do whatever it was he'd set out to do" (105). Wideman's appropriation of Shakespeare's cultural capital provides a reference for the reader who relates to the playwright as a cultural icon. At the same time, Wideman legitimizes his own work as a protest writer by drawing parallels between what Shakespeare was able to do and what he is attempting to do. This kind of stage performance, much like the elements of music, draws the line between the actors and the audience. This separation parallels Wideman's role as author to that of his reader and supports his theme of the power of the individual. His attempt to rewrite Shakespeare's *The Tempest* suggests a way for the individual to reach many people without posing a threat to societal norms. Wideman incorporates elements from Shakespeare's play to call attention to the relevance of words in the contemporary world. He remarks that Shakespeare brings the reader's attention "To the inadequacy of your background, your culture. Its inability, like the inability of a dead sea, to cast up on the beach appropriate role models, creatures whose lives you might imitate. So let's pretend" (128). In proffering the world of make-believe—the world of the play—Wideman removes a certain element of realism from the situation of colonialism in America which might frighten or offend some groups of readers. Yet, his words remind us that even a member of the sacred dead white European male canon discussed issues that can deliver us into a searching analysis of present reality.

Wideman's incorporation of an all-black production of *The Tempest* shares similarities with Haitian writer Aimé Césaire's 1969 rewriting of Shakespeare entitled *A Tempest*, which Césaire adapted for a black theater. Wideman's novel and Césaire's adaptation share the similar project of investigating colonialism and power through the appropriation of Shakespeare. One specific similarity between the two works is the image of the mask. *A Tempest* opens with directions from the Master of Ceremonies: "To each his character, to each character his mask" (1). By allowing the players to choose their masks or roles, the play suggests that the concepts one has about race and identity are social constructions rather than biological ones. This perspective shrouds the individual identity in the context shaped by history and also indicates that putting on these identities is a choice. Wideman's characters, too, are often perceived as if they are masked. Cudjoe sees the basketball players' "faces around him" like "masks" (43). He considered earlier: "Would the players testify, help him tell the story as they cool out after the game" (41). Much like Césaire, Wideman uses the ambiguity that the mask provides to indicate a faceless community ready to act out or tell a story. Further emphasizing the power behind choosing one's own mask as suggested by Césaire's Master of Ceremonies, Wideman utilizes the image of masking during Cudjoe's experience at the bombing memorial: "People rise from the arc of chairs, lift their placards. Wear names like giant masks" (197). While masks evoke a tribal and communal quality that erases the individual identity of the wearer, the symbol also indicates that one has the ability to choose which mask to wear. Wideman's description of the events of the memorial also indicates that the power of the performative can incite passion in the individual audience members. While Césaire focuses on blaming the white colonizers and suggests that the cycle of violence and oppression is endless, Wideman broadens the scope of the argument. Cudjoe comments, for example, that "you could stare forever and the past goes on doing its thing" (5). Wideman's novel continually reminds the reader of the timelessness of the problem, but that the possibility for change exists.

For both Shakespeare and Wideman, the catalyst to a realization of the need for change comes to the audience or reader from an individual. The play offers the enslaved spirit Ariel whose words, in the end, inspire Prospero to reconsider his dominant ways. Prospero derives his power from books, but also from what he can convince Ariel to do for him. Because Prospero's ability to dominate is dependent on this element of compliance, Ariel also possesses a contingent power. Each character relies on the other for his power and freedom. The relationship between the two is complicated in that Prospero cannot free Ariel without also abandoning his access to that level of authority. Ariel reminds Prospero that he would have sympathy for the characters they have imprisoned if he were human. This sentiment causes Prospero to change his previous focus, as he states, "The rarer action is / In virtue than in vengeance" (Shakespeare 5.1.27–28). Through Ariel's reminder of his subjugated role, Prospero understands that he must free those he is holding prisoner. In his final speech, Prospero asks the audience to set him free. He gives up everything and, as an isolated individual, returns the power to the audience. Wideman's novel offers the reader a similar scenario. Ariel, meaning Lion of God in Hebrew, is replaced by Simba Muntu, meaning Lion man (Wideman 17). This connection of names leads the reader to view Simba as a catalyst for change as well. Wideman suggests the play's importance to the workings of the novel when he states, "This is the central event. I assure you. . . . This is the central event, this production of *The Tempest* staged by Cudjoe in the late late 1960s" (132). Cudjoe and his all-Black children's production do not get to perform because of the weather, but there is still hope that Wideman and the story of Simba will make it through to the audience. Simba awakens a need in both Cudjoe and the narrator to think about and investigate their personal histories as well as the MOVE bombing. His story of surviving the bombing also provides Wideman with a framework with which to present an argument for change. Much like Prospero, Wideman the writer is an isolated individual figure asking the reader to take the power and use it for positive change.

    Philadelphia Fire begins with the story of Zivanias, who dies because he ventures out into a dangerous storm at sea. As Shakespeare's Prospero delivers other characters to his island by conjuring up a tempest, Wideman creates a tempest of his own to deliver the reader into the island of his novel where they are confronted with the chaotic and changing world in which he will teach his lessons. This initial sea storm leads to the firestorm that begins to illustrate the need for an individual power structure rather than a visibly threatening community. Although Wideman does not abandon the concept of powerful communities, he emphasizes throughout the novel that an individual like a writer or a performer has the potential to incite change. The novel also indicates that the writer has an individual power that is contingent upon subsequent action from the audience—thus making *Philadelphia Fire*, like Shakespeare's play, a protest and a call to action that is also palatable to a general audience. In contrast to earlier novels, Wideman discards the mode of simply attributing the plight of black people in America to the evils of white or Western society. *Philadelphia Fire* broadens our view of the problem to suggest that a dominant society based on white or Western ideals exists which will not yet embrace the voice of the "other." Wideman's novel suggests that change is possible. In his essay "Everybody's Protest Novel," James Baldwin suggests that "The failure of the protest novel lies in its rejection of life, the human being, the denial of his beauty, dread, power, in its insistence that it is his categorization alone which is real and which cannot be transcended" (1659). Wideman is not interested in categorization as a means of oppression; rather, he presents a mixture of both fictional and nonfictional events through the perspectives of various characters to provide information to his audience so that they, in turn, can make choices. Just as Césaire's Master of Ceremonies actively enlists the audience members to play "the part of the Tempest" and to create "a storm to end all storms," Wideman contends that "[w]e need to perform the stories. They'll inevitably be different because we bring different experiences to them. But we have to feel that we can perform the stories. We have to feel that we have a legitimate right to perform the stories" (TuSmith 122). The novel illustrates that the performative promotes audience agency in the active pursuit of change. Wideman does not dismiss the possibility for future change; in fact, his novel demands a reevaluation of personal and social commitment on the part of the reader.

Note

1. Through the character J.B., Wideman is developing the notion of invisibility presented in Ralph Ellison's watershed novel, *The Invisible Man*. Ellison's character is not invisible to the public eye; rather, he is the center of attention. That attention, however, based on a set of characteristics that are false, renders him invisible. While Ellison develops a more literal sense of invisibility through showing his main character as a societal recluse at the end of the action, Wideman's character represents a chosen public blindness as a form of cultural invisibility.

Works Cited

Baldwin, James. "Everybody's Protest Novel." *The Norton Anthology of African American Literature*. Ed. Henry Louis Gates Jr. and Nellie Y. McKay. New York: Norton, 1997. 1654–59.

Césaire, Aimé. *A Tempest*. Trans. Richard Miller. New York: Theatre Communications Group, 1985.

Ellison, Ralph. *Invisible Man.* New York: Vintage, 1990.

Gates, Henry Louis, Jr., and Nellie Y. McKay, eds. *The Norton Anthology of African American Literature.* New York: Norton, 1997.

"Rap." *The Norton Anthology of African American Literature.* Ed. Henry Louis Gates Jr. and Nellie Y. McKay. New York: Norton, 1997. 60–61.

Scott-Heron, Gil. "The Revolution Will Not Be Televised." *The Norton Anthology of African American Literature.* Ed. Henry Louis Gates Jr. and Nellie Y. McKay. New York: Norton, 1997. 61–62.

Shakespeare, William. *The Tempest. The Complete Signet Shakespeare.* Ed. Sylvan Barnet. San Diego: Harcourt, 1973. 1537-68.

TuSmith, Bonnie. "Benefit of the Doubt: A Conversation with John Edgar Wideman." *Conversations with John Edgar Wideman.* Ed. Bonnie TuSmith. Jackson: UP of Mississippi, 1998. 195–219.

Wideman, John Edgar. *Philadelphia Fire.* New York: Vintage, 1991.

Stacey L. Berry

"All My Father's Texts"

John Edgar Wideman's Historical Vision in *Philadelphia Fire*, *The Cattle Killing*, and *Fatheralong*

Tracie Church Guzzio

All my father's texts and songs, which
I had decided were meaningless, were
arranged before me at his death like
empty bottles, waiting to hold the meaning which life would give me.

JAMES BALDWIN, "NOTES OF A NATIVE SON"

Suddenly, the mist cleared. Below the
people, the earth had changed. It had
grown into the shape of the stories they
told, a shape wondrous and new and real
as the words they'd spoken. But a world
also unfinished because all the stories
had not been told.

JOHN EDGAR WIDEMAN, *FATHERALONG*

In "Notes of a Native Son," James Baldwin seeks reconciliation and understanding with a father already lost to him. As the quote above suggests, Baldwin tries to unravel the mystery of his father's presence and life by examining his stories and sermons, the words that helped this reticent man express his inner self. Baldwin attempts this reading of his father in order to comprehend the legacy of anger and silence that shrouded the man and his relationship with his son. The scene resonates not only as an individual's excursion into the past to find love and redemption but also as a significant trope of African American literature. How can the voices of our fathers save our sons? It is a question posed years ago by Baldwin, and now urgently revisited in numerous works by John Edgar Wideman. It is in the voices of the past, in our "father stories," Wideman writes, that African Americans can creatively confront and re-imagine their painful history in America. These stories, he states, are "about establishing origins and through them legitimacy, claims of ownership, of occupancy, and identity" (*Fatheralong* 63).

Fathers and sons are metaphors here for the past and the present. In Wideman's vision, "father" stories are narratives that connect all of us to the past through literature, through history. The past and the present speak to each other in Wideman's work, sharing a dialogic or contrapuntal relationship. Unfortunately, these created dialogues often serve as the only bridge between fathers and sons, as well as between the past and present in the African American community. Wideman considers this lack of communication one "of the biggest deficits in our culture. It's a space that needs to be filled, and if we don't fill it, all kinds of dangerous stuff gets in there and somebody else gets their evil in there, and each generation is estranged from the next" ("This Man Can Play" 72). The written historical record is a special culprit: the personal stories of African American men and women are buried in the silences of the historical record. It is only by using history as a vehicle for creative revision that these unknown stories can be heard. Or, as Karla Holloway suggests, "in the imaginative act absences in American history as a whole can be filled with African American presence" (10). Wideman's writing is a metafictional, metahistorical return to the past to uncover the father texts, the lost stories, that can fill those gaps in the American historical consciousness. In his assessment of Wideman's work, Charles Johnson praises him as a writer who recovers the past "as an archaeologist might" (75). Though Wideman is clearly invested in revisiting history in his writing, he has warned that history is a "cage, a conundrum we must escape or resolve before our art can go freely about its business" ("The Color of Fiction" 59). How he solves this dilemma is by embracing the Ibo saying, "all stories are true." This oft-repeated phrase in Wideman's work emerges as his aesthetic, the method by which he can address the silences of African American presence in the American historical consciousness.[1] By imbricating fictional narratives with historical accounts, Wideman blurs the lines between genres and discourses, thus dissolving the elevated status we have granted to history and creating new "father" texts.

"All stories are true" can be read as a paradigm for understanding Wideman's historical re-visioning of African American life in the United States. The post-modern version of historiography, if not a direct model, is clearly related to Wideman's project and echoes in the phrase "all stories are true." As Cornel West has declared, the black artist and intellectual must adapt the model of history suggested by Michel Foucault in order to "disrupt and dismantle the prevailing 'regimes of truth'" (143). Wideman's work attempts to destroy the positivistic and monolithic view of history that has often perpetuated the limited "story" of African Americans. While I believe this strategy is ubiquitous in the Wideman canon (found in a nascent form even in his second and third novels, *Hurry Home* and *The Lynchers*), this essay focuses on three works that are most overtly concerned with history: *Fatheralong*, *Philadelphia Fire*, and *The Cattle Killing*. Each work dramatizes a writer's engagement with historiography and its impact on the characterization of African Americans in American history and consciousness. Covering topics such as Africa and colonialism, Prospero and Caliban, slavery, the MOVE bombing, the yellow fever epidemic, and the search for the "Promised Land," these works encapsulate some of the most salient moments in the African American past. And, simultaneously, each of these works specifically comments on the silences and soundings between fathers and sons (unlike many of Wideman's other narratives that focus on the relationships between brothers and/or between mothers and sons).

Wideman's work proposes that our imagined stories of the past are as "true" as the stories that have been recorded by official historians. The history of slavery, lynching, and racism in the United States was written, in many cases, by the very men who had perpetuated the system that created and reinforced these conditions. Wideman illuminates this situation when he expresses unease and anger as he is helped by a historian in North Carolina: "Hadn't the historian's career been one more mode of appropriation and exploitation of my father's bones, the pearls that were his eyes. Didn't mastery of Abbeville's history, the power and privilege to tell my father's story, follow from the original sin of slavery that stole, then silenced my father's voice" (*Fatheralong* 115).

Other writers and postmodernist critics have studied the relationship between history and fiction as well. Influenced by the work of philosophers and post-modernist historiographers such as Michel Foucault and Hayden White, literary scholars and writers have examined the ways fiction has addressed trends in history. Brian McHale, for one, argues that historical fiction in the postmodern era is characterized by the violation of the "seam" between fiction and history, and that postmodern historical fiction visibly contradicts the public record in that it "attempts to redress the balance of the historical record of writing histories of the excluded, those relegated permanently to history's dark areas" (90).

Clearly, Wideman's purpose for the inclusion of public history in his work is to "redress the balance," to ensure that all stories are told. Through the interplay of personal, public, and "fictional" stories, he dismantles an established genre hierarchy that privileges historical writing as accurate, scientific, and truthful—and, therefore, more valid. According to McHale, this too is one of the purposes of postmodern historical fiction: "One of the thrusts of postmodernist revisionist history is to call into question the reliability of official history. The postmodernists fictionalize history, but by doing so they imply that history itself may be a form of fiction" (96). By juxtaposing public history with his autobiography or with his fictions, Wideman equalizes varieties of discourse to suggest that one representation is not more or less valid than another. Part of his mission is to remind us that all experience is, in essence, story; that sociologists, psychologists, and scientists are, after all, primarily storytellers; and that the "uncritical absorption of certain hallowed tenets of Western thought is like participating in your own lynching" ("The Color of Fiction" 64). Wideman suggests that we have the power within us to make and live by our own narratives, and warns that the only way to survive is through the imagination—through stories—by imagining truths of our own making.

Wideman's balance of discourses and voices within his work is reminiscent of Mikhail Bakhtin's theories of heteroglossia and the polyphonic novel. The similarity between Bakhtin's description of the multiple languages embedded in novels and African American literature has been noted by many critics.[2] Wideman's polyphonic narratives include historiography, autobiography, theory, letters, drama, slave narratives, autoethnography, and song lyrics. His blending and layering of "high" and "low" rhetorical styles balance the discourses. This style also resonates in the maxim "all stories are true." When asked to comment on the meaning of the phrase and its expression in his work, Wideman remarked that

> it is profoundly democratic. . . . [W]hen you get right down to it, knowing the fact that all stories are true is as much a place to begin as a conclusion, because it doesn't remove the necessity for sorting through the evidence—of working through the stories. What I like about it in particular is that it decentralizes truth—it fragments the truth. It puts truth in the light of multiplicity, of voices as a kind of construct that you can't arrive at unless you do have a mosaic of voices. (TuSmith 198)

Wideman's description of his work here also suggests the postmodern form known as "historiographic metafiction." As identified by Linda Hutcheon, this

"All My Father's Texts"

form contends that "there are only truths in the plural, and never one Truth; and there is rarely falseness per se, just others' truths. Fiction and history are narratives distinguished by their frames" (109). A work of historiographic metafiction thus embraces plurality by presenting multiple points of view and discourses.

Wideman's method for providing space for these multiple voices is to transgress realistic time and reject linear history; he fractures the narrative line, opening spaces for other voices to be heard. This clearing of space, these silent pauses, are found throughout Wideman's writing. The meaning in many cases can be found in these gaps, or what Bakhtin would call a "chronotope"—a reinvented space where writers or voices usually not accommodated by the dominant discourses can be heard (84-85). These Thelonious Monk–like pauses often alienate readers but also act in Wideman's writing as a "space for infinite possibilities" (Grandjeat 686).

Most of Wideman's work contains some moment out of the public record of history. In some cases, these moments are brief: a name, a date, a place. Even Wideman's earliest novels exhibit this characteristic. It is through story and shared history that Wideman reconnects with his brother, Robby, in *Brothers and Keepers*. He acknowledges that his own path in life would have been easier had he come to this realization sooner: "History could have taught me that I was not alone, my situation was not unique" (*Brothers* 33). While *Brothers and Keepers* investigates personal and genealogical history more fully than it does recorded history, interspersed throughout the text are passages of "public history," including a history of Walnut Street Jail in Philadelphia and a description of the life of the African American community at the turn of the twentieth century. In other cases, Wideman examines the recursive relationship between past and present at length. One could argue that this dialogic relationship is the foundation of the novel *Philadelphia Fire*. Wideman's use of the MOVE bombing in 1985 in Philadelphia and the fictional Cudjoe are the lenses by which he examines his own life and his relationship with his son. The discourses of autobiography, fiction, and history are all simultaneously vocalized in this novel, again highlighting the polyphonic quality of Wideman's writing and the three voices that Wideman himself inhabits in the work.

Most of the more historically conscious works are set in Philadelphia, suggesting that Wideman views the city as a symbolic fountainhead of American history and African American suffering; after all, it was the site of the Constitutional Convention in 1787 where the framers met to ratify the U.S. Constitution *and* to continue the practice of slavery for another eighty years. Wideman revisits the Quaker-inspired Walnut Street Jail in Philadelphia that he mentions in *Brothers and Keepers* in the short story, "Ascent by Balloon from the Walnut Street Jail."

The story is narrated by Charles Williams, an African American prisoner of the jail who, in this fictional account, accompanies Jean Pierre Blanchard in the first hydrogen balloon flight in 1793 as part of a scientific experiment. This event is also reported in a letter in *The Cattle Killing* but here, as in many other Wideman narratives, we see the same story from a different angle. In the novel the story opens with a newspaper account of the flight. The report mentions the duration of the flight and the famous people in attendance, but nowhere is Williams mentioned. Williams's story is silenced by the "accurate" reporting; his presence is also co-opted by the "historical" figures of Dr. Benjamin Rush and Alexis de Tocqueville.

Time is muddled in the short story. Williams rides in the balloon as he sees himself standing in the prison yard below. The slippage of time allows him to imagine his own story free from the constraints of his prison life. What is true about Williams is finally not important: he may not have, in fact, existed at all. But his presence at a verifiable moment in the American past among historical personages poses the necessary question regarding stories of African American life that have been lost to us because of the nature of historiography. The yellow-fever epidemic—which also figures prominently in *The Cattle Killing* and the short story "Fever"—is mentioned here as well. Whether or not the imagined tales Wideman presents within the layers of history are "true" or not is not the issue. Their repetition among different works creates a cumulative effect. The stories feel true because we have heard some version of them before; they confirm one another as if they were factual historical accounts and, thus, carry the weight of veracity.

There is an obvious dialogue between the short story "Fever" and the novel *The Cattle Killing*. Both works relate the yellow-fever epidemic of 1793, and both view the fever as a metaphor for racism and hatred. However, Wideman presents the two works from different points of view. Each work provides new ways of seeing the epidemic beyond the known (or little known) historical accounts. *The Cattle Killing*, especially, provides a multilayered, multivoiced text. The novel is not easily classified by genre given its mixture of history, fiction, and autobiography. Letters, dream visions, even scientific pamphlets are interspersed throughout the text. It is noteworthy that the era in which this novel is set—the late eighteenth century—is also the period in which many Western ideas about scientific and historical writing were established. It is at this time that the treatise and the pamphlet were at their height as written forms, and the novel emerged as a new genre. The split between written discourses has its roots here, as nonfiction and fiction began to be seen as divergent categories. In *The Cattle Killing*, however, Wideman displays many of the written forms popular in the eighteenth century and presents them side-by-side, providing a more complete and accurate view of

"All My Father's Texts"

events and people. At the center of the novel is a picaresque character—a staple of the eighteenth-century novel; there are also epistolary sections, a medical journal, and a conversion narrative. This is clearly an example of a polyphonic novel and, as critic Kathie Birat points out, a "textbook example" of Hutcheon's historiographic metafiction (630).

In an early metafictional moment in the novel's introduction, the "writer" suggests to the reader that this hybridity is what characterizes the work. He cautions that the novel is composed of stories that are "not quite stories. True and not true (check out the facts, dates, murders). Not exactly a novel" (8). The voice challenges us to find out for ourselves, to learn a little history in the process, and to question the validity of such history; it informs us that the point is not to deliver the same story, but to revise what has gone before. Like a jazz musician, Wideman plays with the tradition—improvises around a musical note, echoes it, changes it, and takes it in another direction. It is not about the "song" but about how one plays, what one does with the possibilities of the notes of a piece. In *The Cattle Killing* and elsewhere, Wideman is showing us the possible stories beyond the "true" ones we already know.

The Cattle Killing is populated with verifiable, historical figures such as George Whitefield, Richard Allen, George Stubbs, and Benjamin Rush (renamed here as Thrush). These figures provide the atmosphere of the novel, validating the world that the unnamed protagonist/preacher inhabits. The characters test our notion of what we accept as true. If we believe the stories that have been written about these figures from history, are we not also obligated to acknowledge the veracity of the stories of the "fictional" people of the novel? Certainly, their fictional lives in some way reflect the lives of people unknown to us through the historical record.

The novel begins not in the past, but in the present: a writer is on his way to deliver the manuscript of his new book to his father. The work closes with this same writer's son, a historian, who writes a letter to the writer/father regarding the new novel about the cattle killing. The frames or bookends of the novel signal the balancing act that Wideman is attempting in his aesthetic: the conclusion does not clarify whether the work privileges the literary or historical voice. The voices and their representative discourses are equally valid. The framing also illustrates the sharing of stories between fathers and sons. The writer of *The Cattle Killing* passes on this "father text" to his own father and, later, to the historian/son. The novel stands as a metafictional marker for Wideman's plea to embrace and share father stories.

Wideman includes fictitious narratives in the novel and embeds them in the historical record. The yellow-fever epidemic of 1793 is a "historical" fact; numbers and dates can be verified (Wideman even provides his research materials at the front of the book). The fever hit Philadelphia in July. Within a month it had reached epidemic proportions. Thousands of prominent citizens fled the city, leaving the fever to devour the less fortunate. By the end of October, cooler temperatures brought relief from the disease, but, by then, twenty thousand people, including representatives of the state and federal governments, had left Philadelphia. The fever had claimed more than one-third of the city's population and is still considered one of the worst epidemics in American history.

Richard Allen and Absalom Jones, founders of the A.M.E. Zion Church, were encouraged by Dr. Benjamin Rush, one of the signers of the Declaration of Independence and a prominent physician in Philadelphia, to aid the sick since he believed members of the African race were immune to the disease. Rush's theory proved to be incorrect, and African Americans were the hardest hit among the population. The unnamed protagonist in the novel is one of Allen's volunteers in Wideman's account. Once the epidemic subsided, many white citizens blamed the African Americans who tended the sick for profiting from the disaster and for bringing the disease to Philadelphia in the first place. In the novel, an African American orphanage is burned down. Whether the fire was started by a mob of angry whites, by a tortured African American youth, or by a Philadelphian attempting to purify the diseased air is not entirely clear. It is also not clear if this event is a "historical" fact, but it accurately represents the tenor of the hostilities of the times. That tension, "the fever," Wideman argues in the novel, continues to reverberate today.

The Xhosa cattle killing is also a verifiable historical event. In 1856, a young girl, Nongqawuse, of the Xhosa tribe of South Africa, prophesied that the only way to halt European incursion was to kill the tribe's cattle. This act caused civil dissent, and the social and economic structure of the tribe deteriorated. Essentially, the Xhosa committed cultural suicide by destroying their livelihood. Nongqawuse appears to the protagonist of the novel in a vision to warn him against false prophecies: "Beware. Beware. Do not kill your cattle. Do not speak with your enemy's tongue. Do not fall asleep in your enemy's dream" (147).

The "writer" alludes to this prophecy in the beginning of the work when he cautions that people are listening to new false prophecies, believing new lies meant to destroy them. The prophecy of the cattle killing is a metaphor not only in this novel, but in all of Wideman's works. It is those stories—those accepted as true by the mainstream culture—that must be dismantled, revised, and balanced by new stories and new visions; otherwise, the fate of the Xhosa, the destruction of their lives and culture, will be the fate of African Americans. Wideman layers every event in the novel—including the yellow fever—with the cattle killing, and with the present destructive attitudes and actions embodied in the shooting death of the fifteen-year-old African American boys at the beginning of the novel: "Shoot. Chute. Black boys shoot each other. Murder themselves. Shoot. Chute. Panicked cattle funnel down the killing chute . . ." (7).

Violations of time and linear progression occur throughout the work and are symbolized when the past, present, and future intersect in a vision the preacher has of the crossroads: "in the clearing I witnessed two worlds crossing. One for people like us, who worshiped at St. Matthews. The other a thoroughfare frequented by ancestors, our generations yet to be born" (76). He encounters a mysterious woman here, who could be Dr. Thrush's servant, Kate, who later listens to his stories. The woman may also be the next embodiment of the African woman haunting him. As well, she may be the Xhosa girl, Nongqawuse. As the epigraph at the beginning of the novel tells us, "certain African spirits" inhabit different bodies. Who is this woman, really? The preacher believes all manifestations of her identity because it is his "way of reckoning learned from old African people who said all stories are true" (53). The image of the crossroads also appears in other works by Wideman; it stands as a site where time and space are dislocated in order to observe the past's connection to the present and the future. Yet, it exists outside of history. Time is fluid here, disrupting the linear model of progressive history that denies revisiting the past. At the crossroads, in circular time the past is not only able to be revisited, it can also be re-imagined.

The historian/son at the end of the novel writes to his father, the novelist of *The Cattle Killing*, that he has discovered letters from a man who may have been the brother of the protagonist. These letters violate the boundary between fact and fiction. The letters relate that the brother saw the Xhosa's destruction of their cattle firsthand. This would be a breach of linear time since the preacher witnesses the cattle killing in his vision as a past event, but historically the killing occurred in 1856, more than sixty years after the yellow-fever epidemic and after the time the brother could have possibly been present. The hierarchy that elevates history over fiction has been dismantled, and Wideman's "fictional" creations speak for all those unknown men and women who were real, who did walk the streets of the diseased city in 1793 but whose stories have never been recorded—until now.

The temporal density of the novel is also seen toward the conclusion when the protagonist has a vision of his past, his present, and the country's future. He visualizes the fever, his childhood, the imprisonment of Nelson Mandela and Mumia Abu Jamal, and the memorial for the victims of the MOVE bombing. Wideman will later trace these moments in time to the Xhosa's killing of their cattle, filtered through the African spirit whose description introduces the story of the preacher and the yellow fever. The novel also moves back and forth within its own time, a pattern that the narrator himself notes when he explains to the sick woman listening to his stories that his tales sometimes get ahead of themselves, that they sometimes "jump around." The woman tells him, "I thought all stories go backward," to which the narrator replies, "Backward to go forward. Forward to go back" (54). Wideman often goes "backward" in this work, as well as in other novels, to explain the problems of the present, the "fever" infecting us today. The only thing that soothes the preacher's own "fever" about what happened in Philadelphia and what the future holds is the sharing of stories with the sick woman he attends. Thus, the novel concludes with these lines:

> Tell me, finally, what is a man. What is a woman. Aren't we lovers first, spirits sharing an uncharted space, a space our stories tell, a space chanted written upon again and again, yet one story never quite erased by the next, each story saving the space, saving us. (208)

For Wideman, the only way to combat the past and fight for the future of his community is through creating and sharing stories.

One of the outbreaks of the fever in the preacher's future will be the MOVE bombing. That bombing and its aftermath is at the center of *Philadelphia Fire*. Wideman shifts identities (writer, autobiographer, subject, fictional double) and positions in the text, as well as presents multiple discourses seamlessly (including dramatic monologue, rap lyrics, journalistic reporting, Greek tragedy, and Shakespearean dialogue). The narrative's movement and the author's place within the novel violate our expectations of realism, and, in doing so, question our assumptions about truth and Western discourse. The polyphonic nature of this novel makes it difficult to embrace one narrator as most accurate and reminds us, once again, that all the "stories" here might in some way be true. The multivoiced structure might also reflect the three genres (autobiography, history, and fiction) that we see operating elsewhere in Wideman's work and, once again, it is suggestive of both Bakhtin's and Hutcheon's descriptions of novels.

The text that Wideman argues has one of the most prominent places within Western culture is *The Tempest*, with its characterization of master/slave relationships and descriptions of Caliban. But, juxtaposed with the other stories of the novel, it loses much of its power and position (other stories become just as true). In the novel the protagonist, Cudjoe, attempts to rewrite the Shakespearean play. Then he tells us that it might be a detective story we are reading. Though he attempts to track down the "facts" of the MOVE bombing, he seems more interested in imagining what has happened to the lost boy, Simba. He listens to the eyewitness reports several times in case the story changes. In these reports, readers get very little factual information about the MOVE bombing and the boy. Instead,

"All My Father's Texts"

the event acts as a catalyst for Cudjoe to address the gaps in his own life, his need to do something about "the silence." While the bombing may not seem like a "historical" event—given the amount of time between the bombing and the publication of the novel—in this age of immediate media scrutiny, the moments of that day quickly exist in the texts of American culture in ways that reinforce the negative characterizations of African American life. The depictions of Mayor Goode, John Africa, and MOVE in the local and national press, especially, reflect America's generalizations about African American urban neighborhoods and violence.

The structure of the novel reinforces the silences and gaps that occupy Cudjoe. The novel's fissures are created by fractured narrative, pauses between voices, and the places where unknown stories remain unheard. These intentional gaps do reflect the failure of language, as critic James Coleman has argued, but they are also call-and-response moments for Wideman.[3] In these spaces and breaks, multiple conversations between reader and text take place, and all stories can be heard and told. These silences remind us there are many ways that African Americans have been forced to express themselves beyond the written text. Wideman's own comments about the silence in his work also imply a place where revision occurs: silence is a "dreaming space where what's awaited is imagined and, when it doesn't come, the space where dreams are dismantled, dissolving again into silence. Dreams born and dying and born again in the deep wound of silence, and silence tainted though it is by disappointment and waiting, also a reservoir of hope" ("In Praise of Silence" 548). The moments of silence ask us to fill these spaces with our own stories, as Cudjoe and Wideman have, with stories that will be valid because they exist beside the "factual" ones of the text.

In many ways, the novel is about silence. The multiple voices and discourses create spaces by fracturing the linear progression of the text. In addition, there is the silence of history, the silence about the bombing and about Simba, and the silence that rushes to fill the void that words cannot when Wideman speaks to his son over the phone: "I breathe into the space separating me from my son. I hope the silence will be filled for him as it is for me by hearing the nothing there is to say at this moment" (*Philadelphia Fire* 103). Because the stories of fathers have not been passed on, fathers and sons are often unable to speak—but here even the breathing of the father reaches out to his lost son. Wideman links this section of the novel with the MOVE bombing and with a race riot against African Americans in 1850 as related in *The Annals of Philadelphia*. These events are layered through the imagination, an imagination that has the power to re-envision the painful stories remembered here: "pretend we can imagine events into existence or out of existence. Pretend we have the power to live our lives as we choose. Imagine our fictions imagining us" (97–98).

One of the moments that the novel tries to re-imagine is *The Tempest*, and the history that this Shakespearean drama reflects. As an artifact of colonization and as a literary work, this text is a powerful vision that has, in the eyes of Wideman and Cudjoe, silenced the stories of others. It even infects the conversation between Wideman and his son, Jake. Cudjoe sees *The Tempest* as the "birth of the nation's blues" (127), just as the yellow fever was present in the nation's infancy. Cudjoe tells his students that Caliban is their great-great-grandfather and reminds them that Shakespeare presents the character as violent, weak, vulgar, and illiterate. This play becomes a prominent "story" of African American characterization in American history. Cudjoe informs the students that the past illustrated in the play influences the world they live in now, that Shakespeare

> scoped the whole ugly mess about to happen that day and time which brings us to here, to today. To this very moment in our contemporary world. To the inadequacy of your background, your culture. Its inability like the inability of a dead sea, to cast up on the beach appropriate role models, creatures whose lives you might imitate. So let's pretend. (128)

Cudjoe and his students attempt to rewrite the text. The students never get the chance to perform the play for an audience, but perhaps it is not the success but the process that is important here. While the act of addressing the past may be painful, it is necessary, and, in a sense, there is some hope that the deconstruction of the Caliban story will initiate some change. As Caliban speaks to the audience in Cudjoe's version, the character reclaims his voice and its power to transform and re-imagine his story because "everybody knows can't nobody free Caliban but his own damn self" (145). Only by reaching beyond the stories of the masters, of the guardians of American history, can one create one's own stories. The play is meant to empower the children, but we are not certain what impact the process had on them in the present time of the novel. The act of writing their story and believing that it could be as true as the ones they are told, however, is the essence of Wideman's desire to create spaces in our narratives for new stories to be heard.

The narrator implies further that *The Tempest* is an important key to understanding his work; that as the "fabulator," he is telling us the play is central to the novel, to the bombing, to everything. For all the possible associations between Caliban and Wideman/Cudjoe in the novel, we cannot fail to realize that Wideman/Cudjoe are also reminiscent of Prospero. As fabulators, Wideman/Cudjoe imagine their worlds and create their own stories and identities. This, in itself, is a revision of historical assumptions.

The connection between past, present, and future is dramatized in the closing section of the novel. Cudjoe is waiting at Independence Square for the bomb-

"All My Father's Texts"

ing victims' memorial service to begin. Looking around, he is reminded of a riot that took place in the square on July 4, 1850, against African Americans. He feels the ghosts from that incident brush past him and fill the square. The past and the present meet when Cudjoe "hears footsteps behind him. A mob howling his name. Screaming his blood. Words come to him, cool him, stop him in his tracks. He'd known them all his life. Never again. Never again. He turns to face whatever it is rumbling over the stones of Independence Square" (199). The "fever" that caused the incident, the racism and hatred that spurred it on, has followed Cudjoe all his life. The burden of that history has always been the "footsteps behind him," but now Cudjoe is ready to confront history no matter how painful. "Never again" will he run away from who he is or from his past.

In Wideman's canon, the work that most clearly celebrates the idea that father stories must be known and passed on is *Fatheralong*. More obviously a memoir than the other works discussed here, *Fatheralong* stems from a journey that Wideman takes with his father to Promised Land, South Carolina, the seat of the Wideman clan. This movement is an inverted historical trope, tracing these men as they leave the "promised land" of the North to travel South. It is a voyage of self-discovery and familial reconnection. It is also a redemptive quest for Wideman, who, as a young boy, had not wanted to visit his father's family in the South, the place where they "lynched black boys like Emmett Till" (*Fatheralong* 16). Wideman now sees an opportunity to learn about his past—the history of his people—and to repair his relationship with his father. He discovers in the course of this journey the importance of "father stories"—stories that strengthen ties to the past and establish identity and manhood in the wake of racism; stories that have been historically denied the African American father and son.

Throughout the work, Wideman struggles to understand ways to connect to his father and to his own sons. What will sustain them? What will save them? In one of these sections, he associates father stories with the notion that all stories are true. Reading Chinua Achebe's *Things Fall Apart*, he muses on an oral fable recounted in Achebe's novel. It is a story passed down from generation to generation regarding the interconnections of the past, present, and future: "in each recounting the fabled bout happens again, not in the past, but alive and present in Great Time, the always present tense of narrative where every alternative is possible, where the quick and the dead meet, where all stories are true" (62). This battle happens at the crossroads, the site of memory and history that we saw in *The Cattle Killing*. Wideman presents this "fabled bout" as a father story, a fundamental tale that reveals its own necessity: "how they are about blood and roots and earth, how they must be repeated each generation or they are lost forever" (63). This idea resurfaces when Wideman sees before him a path that leads to the land owned by his ancestors, and then sees the same path as the one that leads to the prison holding his youngest son in Arizona. The past, present, and future are all connected here, and the connection embodies the hope that Wideman must sustain for his son.

Fatheralong also stresses the need to revise the past and create one's own definitions. When Wideman cannot locate Promised Land on any map he muses that "Promised Land lies where it does to teach us the inadequacy of maps we don't make ourselves, teach us the necessity of making new maps, teach us how to create them, re-imagine connections others have forgotten or hidden" (94–95). Fatheralong is haunted by failure, but it also slowly embraces hope, and, like many of Wideman's works, mourns for the lost children: his son Jake, the orphans in The Cattle Killing, and Simba in Philadelphia Fire. The urgency of Wideman's writing reminds us that if the past cannot be re-imagined, if new maps cannot be drawn, if new stories cannot be told, the children and the future are in peril. Wideman believes, unflinchingly, in the power of "the story" to save us, himself, his family, his people—to gather each tale in a world broken by the paradigms of race and devastating loss. His work is marked not only by his stylistic virtuosity and his "dismantling of the 'regimes of truth,'" but also by his blues spirit which, despite its own painful awareness of self and history, continues to transcend.

NOTES

1. "All Stories Are True" is the title of both a short story and a collection of stories. Wideman also uses the phrase in The Cattle Killing and Fatheralong. The phrase can be found in interviews with James Coleman, Bonnie TuSmith, and Ishmael Reed (see TuSmith, Conversations.)
2. See Andrews, Stone, Jablon, and Henderson.
3. See Coleman.

WORKS CITED

Andrews, William. To Tell a Free Story. Urbana and Chicago: U of Illinois P, 1988.

Bakhtin, Mikhail. The Dialogic Imagination. Ed. and Trans. Michael Holquist. Austin: U of Texas P, 1981.

Birat, Kathie. "'All Stories Are True': Prophecy, History, and Story in The Cattle Killing." Callaloo 22.3 (1999): 629–43.

Coleman, James. Black Male Fiction and the Legacy of Caliban. Lexington: UP of Kentucky, 2001.

Grandjeat, Yves-Charles. "'These strange dizzying pauses': Silence as Common Ground in J. E. Wideman's Texts." Callaloo 22.3 (1999): 685–94.

Henderson, Mae Gwendolyn. "Speaking in Tongues: Dialogics, Dialectics, and the Black Woman Writer's Literary Tradition." *Reading Black, Reading Feminist*. Ed. Henry Louis Gates Jr. New York: Meridian, 1990. 116–42.

Holloway, Karla. *Moorings and Metaphors: Figures of Culture and Gender in Black Women's Literature*. New Brunswick, NJ: Rutgers UP, 1992.

Hutcheon, Linda. *The Poetics of Postmodernism*. New York: Routledge, 1988.

Jablon, Madelyn. *Black Metafiction*. Iowa City: U of Iowa P, 1997.

Johnson, Charles. *Being and Race: Black Writing since 1970*. Bloomington: Indiana UP, 1988.

McHale, Brian. *Postmodernist Fiction*. New York: Metheun, 1987.

Stone, Albert. "After *Black Boy* and *Dusk of Dawn*: Patterns in Recent Black Autobiography." *African American Autobiography*. Ed. William Andrews. Englewood Cliffs, NJ: Prentice Hall, 1993. 171–95.

TuSmith, Bonnie, ed. *Conversations with John Edgar Wideman*. Jackson: UP of Mississippi, 1998.

West, Cornel. "The Dilemma of the Black Intellectual." *Breaking Bread*. Ed. bell hooks and Cornel West. Boston: South End P, 1991.

Wideman, John Edgar. *Brothers and Keepers*. New York: Henry Holt, 1984.

———. *The Cattle Killing*. Boston: Houghton Mifflin, 1996.

———. "The Color of Fiction." *Mother Jones* Nov./Dec. 1990: 59–63.

———. *Fatheralong*. New York: Random House, 1994.

———. "In Praise of Silence." *Callaloo* 22.3 (1999): 547–49.

———. *Philadelphia Fire*. New York: Henry Holt, 1990.

———. "This Man Can Play." *Esquire* May 1998: 70–74.

The Funky Novels of John Edgar Wideman

ODOR AND IDEOLOGY IN *REUBEN*, *PHILADELPHIA FIRE*, AND *THE CATTLE KILLING*

STEPHEN CASMIER

"Shave excess hair from the body and wear cologne. Shower." So reads the second line of the infamous "Atta Document," the "rule book" found in the luggage of the "suspected ringleader" of the September 11 attacks on the World Trade Center ("Focus Special"). Clearly, the attackers feared that somehow the wrong smell could telegraph their intentions or unmask their beliefs. They seemed aware that odors exude ideology. Smells render an object attractive or repulsive, telling people whether to come closer or to flee. They mark boundaries, determine proximity, denote social position, promote mating, manifest kinship, and expose enemies. Odors bear traces of bodies. They are tainted by the mysterious, the primal, the unknown, and the unstable—the inchoate. In all, they produce a foundation for discrimination and moral judgments, revealing what a society accepts, rejects, and fears.

Understanding, worrying, figuring, invoking, and deploying the awesome power of what one critic calls "the politics of perception" (Oksiloff 40) is a major element of John Edgar Wideman's *fin-de-siècle* fiction. Indeed, through their use of smell, three of these works—*Reuben* (1987), *Philadelphia Fire* (1990), and *The Cattle Killing* (1996)—respond to what Susan Buck-Morss describes as Walter

Benjamin's call for a "politicization of art." Such an art would "*undo the alienation of the corporeal sensorium, to restore the instinctual power of the human bodily senses for the sake of humanity's self preservation*" (5). This is the role of the funky text. It is the synesthetic antidote to the anesthetized senses that takes us beyond the facile duality between seeing and hearing represented by a supposed conflict between oral and literate cultures. It is the smelling salts for a somnambulant, alienated, and self-destructive society. *Reuben*, *Philadelphia Fire*, and *The Cattle Killing* represent Wideman's wafting towards the funky text.

Each sense perception has a powerful effect on our understanding of ourselves and the world. Since at least Descartes, sight has dominated the other senses in the West in ways that have altered our perception of the world. Indeed, one theorist describes the modern era as one of "ocularcentrism," where knowledge is modeled on "specularity" (Jay 316). This has had extraordinary benefits, says Karsten Harries. "[M]odern philosophy . . . our science and technology, even our common sense . . . owe much to Descartes" and what she calls his concept of the disembodied, "Angelic Eye" (28). Because it privileges the most abstract and alienating of senses, "speculation" gives rise to the modern conception of the subject, says Martin Jay: "Speculation is closely identified with . . . dialectical thought, for it both acknowledges the difference between subject and image and sublates it into a grand unity, an identity of identity and non-identity" (316).

Specularity also enables an illusion of expropriation that underpins various forms of exploitation. A naked sense of power awakens once the "fleeting word" (and later products of technology, such as photographs and moving pictures) gets pressed onto a space where it can be controlled and manipulated.[1] Through its disembodied reflections, representations, and reproductions such speculation produces the illusion, for example, that labor may be separated from the laborer. So, as it produces the transcendent, disembodied eye, and the modern, reflexive subject, it also enables the exploitation of the body left behind. While it provides a giddy sense of immortality, the body's abstraction and projection onto flat, visible, and reproducible surfaces enable it to be dissected, dismembered, pieced together, and re-imagined.

Meanwhile, ocularcentrism deadens the other senses (in an era that would otherwise provide sensory overload). As a remedy (and exploitation of this deficit), contemporary culture has replaced experience with synesthetic illusions that anesthetize our awareness of sensory deprivation. These illusions present the various sense perceptions as functions of sight. Such illusions render satisfactory, for instance, the experience of going to a trendy bakery where each loaf of bread looks different but really smells and tastes like all the others. They are buttressed by classical Hollywood cinema, which can, for example, present war in all of its attractiveness—as mere surface and symbol—while neglecting, in the words of one scholar, the actual, "faint, sweetish, slightly faecal smell" of death (Watson 114). Although these illusions of experience purport to stimulate the senses, they actually put them to sleep. "These simulated sensoria alter consciousness, much like a drug," says Buck-Morss, who designates such illusions "phantasmagoria."[2] She adds: "It has the effect of anaesthetizing the organism" (22). The result is deadly. Here, Buck-Morss summarizes the outcome witnessed by Walter Benjamin who lamented "the crises in cognitive experience caused by the alienation of the senses that makes it possible for humanity to view its own destruction with enjoyment" (37).

Wideman responds to such a crisis in contemporary society with the emergent, funky text that is the synesthetic counter-illusion to sight's phantasmagoria. In this case, synesthesia refers to the combining and mixture of sense perceptions that disrupts the eye's illusions. Funk, a Black Atlantic phenomenon, embodies such recombinations. Indeed, it begins as an African American description of a smell that also describes a sound.[3] In his *Flash of the Spirit* (1984), Robert Farris Thompson discusses the roots of this concept:

> The slang term "funky" in black communities originally referred to strong body odor, and not to "funk," meaning fear or panic. The black nuance seems to derive from the Ki-Kongo lu-fuki, "bad body odor," and is perhaps reinforced by contact with fumet, "aroma of food and wine," in French Louisiana. But the Ki-Kongo word is closer to the jazz word "funky" in form and meaning, as both jazzmen and Bakongo use "funky" and lu-fuki to praise persons for the integrity of their art, for having "worked out" to achieve their aims. In Kongo today it is possible to hear an elder lauded in this way: "like, there is a really funky person! — my soul advances toward him to receive his blessing" [. . .] Fu-Kiau Bunseki, a leading native authority on Kongo culture, explains: "Someone who is very old, I go to sit with him, in order to feel his lu-fuki, meaning, I would like to be blessed by him." For in Kongo the smell of a hardworking elder carries luck. This Kongo sign of exertion is identified with the positive energy of a person. Hence "funk" in black American jazz parlance can mean earthiness, a return to fundamentals. (104–5)

This is what it meant at the dawn of the Civil Rights era when African American jazz musicians attempted to democratize their music and bring it back to the people. By the end of the Black Power era, it was a genuinely popular music bursting with synesthetic force. The music of George Clinton, for example, emanated a funky synesthesia that seemed in direct opposition to the disembodied, odorless world of specularity—the world of a character that he dubbed 'Sir Nose d'Voidoffunk.' During this period, musicians and audience fanned their legs and danced the "funky chicken" while singing: "Make my funk the P-Funk/I want my funk uncut/Make my funk the P-Funk/I wants to get funked up/I want the bomb,

I want the P-Funk/Don't want my funk stepped on" (Friedman). Unlike the products of specularity, these words are charged with synesthetic confusion—smells and sounds that should not be cut or stepped on. Yet, the result is anything but anesthesia. Instead, it is a stirring of consciousness designed to awaken our instincts for survival. Funk, says George Clinton, is "whatever it needs to be in order to survive" (qtd. in Friedman).

Indeed, smell, like no other sense, awakens the instinct for survival in addition to being a truly synesthetic and inherently subversive, upsetting sense. Of all the senses, smell is the best equipped to resist the confusion of the synesthetic illusions produced for sight. Smell receptors bypass sight's confusions and impositions as they go directly to another part of the brain (Keverne 282).

So, when Wideman invokes smell, he invokes the subversive, stimulating, and awakening power of odor, which gives us access to other worlds and other ways of being. *Reuben, Philadelphia Fire*, and *The Cattle Killing* reveal that Wideman shares Benjamin's misgivings about the status of the senses and society's ability to survive. As a response, these works exude funk and work to undermine the synesthetic illusions of ocularity, which has hijacked our senses, our imaginations, our experiences, and our memories. They awaken us, prompting us to feel and to remember.

REUBEN

The novel *Reuben* presents the story of Reuben and his efforts to reunite a mother, Kwansa, with her lost son, Cudjoe, who was spirited away by his estranged father. As a funky text, *Reuben* mostly attempts to counter sight's hegemony through an emphasis on a certain notion of African American orality. Yet, the novel also represents some of Wideman's first steps away from the binary opposition between literacy and orality that his earlier works engaged. "Contrary to *The Homewood Trilogy*," says Klaus Schmidt in an article on *Reuben*, "the voices constructed in *Reuben* rarely find common ground" (95).

Sense perceptions other than sight intrude upon the novel. They do this through acts of memory. In fact, *Reuben* constantly toys with culture and the mechanism of memory. At first this occurs through the invocation of orality and cultural memory as a response to official history. The novel begins as if it were an oral history transcription. The narrator responds to questions in the style of the slave narratives or perhaps Wideman's own interviews of family members for the stories that make up the works of *The Homewood Trilogy* (*Damballah* [1981], *Hiding Place* [1981], *Sent for You Yesterday* [1983]) and *Brothers and Keepers* (1984). "Don't ax me," says the narrator while describing Reuben's trailer. "And who needs to know stuff like that about color or shape" (5). These are juxtaposed against the presentation of the quintessentially visual efforts of Eadweard Muybridge to arrest time in a series of photographs, an effort that also resonates with Wideman's own decision to pin down his family's stories through writing. The pictures, the oral histories, and the written stories work to extend memory as they equally depend upon it in their reconstructions of life and movement. In this case, storytelling becomes an archetypal act of memory. Memory is also an essential part of the act of reading or of watching a film, an act evoked by Muybridge who developed the zoopraxiscope, a progenitor of the motion picture projector. As these devices depend on memory, they also model it, presenting it as an act of hearing or seeing that takes on the structure of early novels or motion picture flashbacks. Such memories underpin hegemony as they create controllable, collective memories and thus experiences. This is an element of phantasmagoria, where, according to Buck-Morss, "everyone sees the same altered world, experiences the same total environment" (23).

Smell, however, offers an alternative model of memory. Smell memory is not a flashback; it is much more powerful. Odor memory, says Lyall Watson, "is apparently simple, direct, unconscious, even 'primitive,' and very resistant to decay or later interference" (180). It cannot be controlled. *Reuben* uses smell to invoke a type of memory unbound by the sequential and ephemeral sense of time marked by sight and hearing. As smell accesses memories, it also provides an alternate sense of identity, an identity that does not rely on seen external differences or the threatening, authenticating myths of official documents.

So, after Waddell steals Cudjoe, Kwansa partly relies upon smell as a defense against community and official judgments that depend upon appearances and only *see* her the way she has always *seen* herself: "a nappy-head, ashy-legged little girl." Kwansa crafts her response through a description of her mother, whom she remembers as a voice, a touch, and a smell, not an appearance:

> Because her mother loved her so much, held her in her arms and whispered secrets, fed her the world in easy, soft pieces. It comes and wraps round her. Feathers, wool, tickly almost [. . .] Like I used to hold a corner of a rag and rub my nose and suck my thumb. That comes back, too. The taste of it. But I don't remember how she looked . . . but I smell her and feel a kind of cuddly warm thing wrap round me and it's her sure nuff from those years before she died. . . . (57)

Smell unlocks memory as a force that can counter the visual illusions of the present. It presents Kwansa with her own, radical identity that connects her to another, caring body. Such a body lies outside visual representation. As it tells its story of love and security, smell also provides Kwansa with her own, distinct history, one that lies inaccessible to the myths, stereotypes, and official accounts that delimit black lives in the inner city.

Stephen Casmier

A more ambiguous treatment of funk occurs with the character of Wally, Reuben's friend and client. Wally has no problem with appearances. In fact, he has learned to take advantage of the sense of alienation that comes with a vision-addicted world: "Wally'd taught himself to profit from detachment" (99). On the surface, Wally is a respectable basketball recruiter for a major university. Beneath the surface, he is a liar, a con man, a thief, and perhaps a murderer. Wally can lead such a double life because he embraces the type of memory provided by ocularity: "Wally treats his life like a memory so he won't have to worry about what's happening to him" (102). He likens this memory to a videotape machine: "playing it fast-forward or reverse, stopping or starting in the middle or end" (102).

Nevertheless, funk threatens to disrupt Wally's illusions and reconnect him to other bodies, displacing the disembodied, controllable memories and identities with inalienable bodies and their smells. This occurs as he remembers his upbringing in his grandmother's house:

> In his grandmother's kitchen. Food smells, the reek of burnt grease baked into blackened burners of the stove. And above the kitchen odors, blending with them, partaking of them, the smell of his grandmother, the scent of her presence as strong in the little kitchen as it was in her bedroom, the bathroom. She was an old woman so her smell was compounded of things he didn't want to name, things an old woman wore next to her body, the body itself, whatever it became . . . He was bothered by her odor no more than he was bothered by his own funk, that envelope of body wrapping the idea of Wally. His grandmother's house didn't stink. It was as if she'd taken a blanket she'd slept under for years . . . and stretched it over roof, doors, windows, shutting their three rooms away from the treacherous streets. (105–6)

It is amazing to apprehend that Wally's memories of his grandmother are much like Kwansa's memories of her mother. They come without external pictures as they also associate security with a smell. It is also interesting to note that such memories, because they exist outside an ocular regime, connect Wally to Kwansa in ways that dismiss simplistic notions of gender that rely on that which can be seen. Although Wally is resistant to it, the feminine smell of his grandmother identifies him. He later says that "the love smell of that blanket trapped and embarrassed him." Still, the smell not only forms the foundation for his own identity, it also enables him to recognize a community of others who diffuse similar smells. "Each house he'd visit had a blanket of its own . . . the funk of their strange lives accumulating, betraying them, as he was betrayed by his own cave full of shadows. . . . These are your people, Wally" (106). Thus, despite Wally's investment in the alienation of ocularity, this evocation of funk enables the novel to gesture toward something that exists outside the mirror of infinite regress within which Wally (and contemporary readers) feels trapped. Wally feels. So do readers who experience descriptions of smell that are too vivid not to stir up their own recollections of other bodies, kitchens, and communities.

PHILADELPHIA FIRE

The same tension between and mixture of oral and literate cultures, which characterizes Wideman's earlier writing, also pervades *Philadelphia Fire*. Indeed, *Philadelphia Fire* is largely a story of the struggle between spoken testimony and official histories. Nevertheless, it is also a profoundly sensuous novel that uses smell to express indeterminacy and confusion while overturning and reversing accepted values. Smell allows the novel to introduce the threatening, the unknown, and the inchoate—the feelings awakened by the group described by the novel and annihilated by Philadelphia police in 1985.[4] This enables the novel to teach readers how to savor the funk that is more redeeming than threatening.

Philadelphia Fire begins with the story of a character named Cudjoe, a somewhat frustrated African American writer living in self-imposed exile on a Greek island. In his exile, he becomes haunted by accounts of a young child (Simba Muntu) who is the only survivor of a fiery police raid on his home in Philadelphia (much of the story has direct connections to the actual bombing of the MOVE group in Philadelphia in 1985). The boy lives in a house with ten other people who reject many of the trappings of contemporary society. The neighbors complain. The mayor reacts, and the police attempt to oust the group from their home by bombing it. Everyone is killed except the little boy, whose fleeing image haunts Cudjoe. Cudjoe returns to America, to Philadelphia, to recover the lost child and the lost dreams the child represents.

Philadelphia Fire is Wideman's most outwardly funky novel. Darryl Pinckney grudgingly acknowledges this in an early review of the book. However, he believes this is a negative aspect of the novel and is incompatible with its seemingly postmodernist orientation. According to Pinckney, Wideman suffers from a wish to prove that he can be both poetic and funky: "'Claim the turf, wear it like a badge, yet keep my distance, be of the street but not in it.' Not one to overlook a single odor in the 'stink of spring,' Wideman frequently enjoys unsavory images" (19). In *Philadelphia Fire*, the unsavory is the inchoate. And, the principle aim of this magical bundle in the guise of a novel is to teach readers the joys of embracing— of deeply inhaling, tasting, and touching—unknown odors, tastes, and sensations.

As noted earlier, odors render an object attractive or repulsive. The sense of smell therefore tells people whether to come closer or to run. In this way, odors signal dogma and ideologies. They reveal what a society accepts and what it rejects. *Philadelphia Fire* uses smell to repel the reader before transforming its funk into an attractive quality.

Stephen Casmier

In the story of Margaret Jones and the Family, for example, smells express indeterminacy and confusion as they overturn and reverse accepted values. In her narrative, Margaret Jones excites a sense of repugnance as she describes her first meeting with King, the founder of the Family: "He's the dirtiest man I ever seen. Smell him a mile off . . . Smelled him long before I seen him. Matter of fact when I stepped down off the bus something nasty in the air. My nose curls and I wonder what stinks, what's dead and where's it hiding" (11).

Yet, Margaret Jones braces herself against the odor and approaches King. She begins to listen to his message and finds him unsettlingly attractive. Then she realizes that his message and his smell are the same:

> Held my breath walking past him and wasn't more than a couple of months later I'm holding my breath and praying I can get past the stink when he's raising the covers off his mattress and telling me lie down with him. By then stink wasn't really stink no more. Just confusion. A confused idea. An idea from outside the family, outside the teachings cause me to turn my nose up at my own natural self. Felt real ashamed when I realized all of me wasn't inside the family yet. I damned the outside part. Left it standing in the dark and crawled up under the covers with King cause he's right even if he did things wrong sometimes, he's still right cause ain't nothing, nowhere any better. (15)

Thus, King's odor is both wrong and right; it is both revolting and attractive. This forms the foundation of an important inversion and social critique. For Margaret, feeling revolted by the natural odor of the human body becomes wrong. She equates the "funky" natural smell of the human body with health and the sterile lack of smell with sickness. She then offers her own gloss on Benjamin's diagnosis: "Society hates health" (10).

This transformation of values through the sense of smell is reminiscent of another group of discredited, dreadlocks-wearing radicals—the Mau-Mau of Kenya. Ian Henderson lards his book, *Man Hunt in Kenya* (1958), with descriptions of the disagreeable smell that infused the air surrounding Mau-Mau fighters:

> My first impression of them was their nauseating smell. It was so strong that I found I could not stand near them. The feeling was evidently mutual, for one of them instantly vomited on smelling a bar of soap taken from Gathieya's pocket. In the days to come I saw many terrorists sickened by the smell of soap on our bodies. Nothing seemed to revolt them more than cleanliness. (75)

Henderson heightens the reader's sense of repugnance (and superiority) with this image of terrorists who reject cleanliness. Yet, at one juncture in the book, Henderson's disdain for the fighters in civilization becomes latent admiration for them in the forest. For when a rhinoceros decides to attack Henderson as he

The Funky Novels of John Edgar Wideman

tracks the fighters, the animal ignores his aides—former Mau-Mau fighters that "smell of the forest"—and chases after the "clean" Europeans (108–9). Thus, in the forest, the "nauseating smell" and rejection of cleanliness serve as a means of protection for the fighters.

Similarly, James Brown in *Philadelphia Fire* wears his smell as a shield of protection from a society that preys on the weak. A homeless man, J.B. is vulnerable. He sleeps on the street where anyone can harass him, including roving gangs of children and malevolent police officers. Funk is his only protection: "If you stink bad, the cops don't like to touch you. Won't frisk you. Except with their nightsticks and boots. Less personal. Hurts but you like it better than the pawing, slapping, shoving, their fingers pinching through your skin" (180). Finally, the novel abounds with instances where Cudjoe also enjoys his own body odor, "relaxing in his own funk" (40).

As with Wally and Kwansa, Cudjoe's sense of taste and smell reminds him of his responsibilities and connections to other souls, other beings, other bodies. For example, while Cudjoe stands in "his funky bathroom" one morning, the smell triggers a powerful, counter-synesthetic experience that awakens deadened memories (68). Cudjoe suddenly remembers a trip to the art studio of his former mentor's wife. The atelier sits atop a barn.[5] The odors and atmosphere overwhelm Cudjoe's senses. They remind him of what society urges us to forget—that is, our place in the food chain and the chain of life:

> Large, moist-breathed beasts had inhabited this space. Their blood was on his hands, in his belly. Their presence like a hood settling over him. He could feel the texture of their rough hides. He was wearing them. He was inside the steady churning of their guts. He tasted liver, heart, lungs, the sour salty mash they'd brew into piss. (69)

His tongue and his nose thus allow him to experience and remember things he can neither see nor hear. They connect him to the past and to others. This is morbidly evident in Cudjoe's description of the fauna of Clark Park. Although the park is two miles away from where "the fire had burned," Cudjoe observes that the sense of taste and smell could cross the divide of time and space:

> If the wind right, smoke would have drifted here, settled on leaves, grass, bushes. Things that eat leaves and buds must have tasted smoke. Dark clouds drifting this way carried the ashy taste of incinerated children's flesh. Could you still smell it? Was the taste still part of what grew in the park? Would it ever go away? (28)

Although the eyes and ears may forget, the tongue and nose still remember. And in *Philadelphia Fire*, such a memory is a radical act as it undermines the forgetfulness and illusions of memory provided by contemporary society.

Stephen Casmier

Toward the end of the novel, Cudjoe appears as a person without a discrete identity. Loss and grief in the novel define and undo him. His body seems to lack integrity as it turns to smoke and blends with the smoke from the burned house and children. But this is also how smell works as our bodies dislodge and emanate airborne chemicals that directly enter and excite the brains of others. Thus Cudjoe does not lack identity so much as he has accepted an alternate sense of self that is not imagined as a reflection on a mirrored plane. Instead, as he takes in his own funk and the funk of others, he accepts his body as something concretely, inseparably bound to others.

THE CATTLE KILLING

Curiously, *The Cattle Killing* at first appears to regress from the funky synesthesia of *Reuben* and *Philadelphia Fire*. It actually appears to directly evoke the transcendent, disembodied, "angelic 'I'" (Eye) of Descartes through a narrator named Isaiah who cavalierly switches between the nickname "Eye" and the first-person pronoun "I": "Eye is a convenience, a sort of in-person once upon-a-time convenience when I write his name" (11). This is then supported by the deliberately nonfunky, eighteenth-century diction of the narrator, a devolution from the African American orality Wideman worked so hard to represent in his earlier writing. Still, the novel embraces funk in other ways as it savors a synesthesia that works to maintain the integrity and power of each sense perception instead of allowing one sense to make the others over in its own image.

Like *Reuben* and *Philadelphia Fire*, *The Cattle Killing* consists of numerous fragmented stories. Most of these stories center around the experiences of a young, anonymous preacher who traverses the city of Philadelphia and its environs during the yellow fever epidemic at the end of the eighteenth century. The reveries and memories of this preacher give rise to other stories that ultimately transgress the limits of place, time, race, and gender. *The Cattle Killing* develops the message of the other novels as it deals explicitly with the notions of myths, dreams, sleep, false prophecies, and self-destruction. Gene Seymour terms the anesthesia depicted in *The Cattle Killing*, "imagination sickness." Says Seymour: "Through style and content, Wideman has made it his calling—really his burden —to chart deficiencies in imagination, both collective and individual" (58). Such deficiencies lead to the type of self-destruction described earlier by Susan Buck-Morss in her analysis of Walter Benjamin's "Artwork essay" jeremiad. According to Buck-Morss, this essay laments the joy evinced by a people witnessing its own destruction. In *The Cattle Killing*, the narrator warns that "there are prophecies in the air, prophecies deadlier than machines" (7–8). The novel overflows with instances of self-destruction: A young prophetess, moved by a vision, prompts the Xhosa people to participate in their own genocide through the slaughtering of their cattle. African American boys gun each other down as they are melded into images of cattle moving blindly through slaughterhouse killing chutes. And a small, abused, orphaned boy satisfies his rage by setting fire to an orphanage of children.

Thus, the novel also exhorts against the self-destructive anesthesia of contemporary society. It responds to this state through its funk, its emphasis on smell as a counter-synesthetic illusion that challenges the current, conceptual order. Within *The Cattle Killing*, smell questions the rational as it provides access to the mysterious, the magical, and the unknown. Smell has this ability, says Watson in *Jacobson's Organ*, because:

> Smell is the witch's sense, sniffing out the spirit of what has been, detecting an essence after the fact of its existence. It is the formula for time travel, lingering on for decades as the scent of cedar in an old sea-chest. It lies at the heart of premonition and clairvoyance, carrying our consciousness well outside the confines of the body. (147)

Smell senses the possibilities of what cannot be foreseen, offering access to a yet-to-be imagined order produced by an alternate sense of memory, time, space, consciousness, and identity.

The sense of smell is constantly emphasized throughout *The Cattle Killing*. It offers a reorientation of Western consciousness that treats time—past, present, and future—as something other than a series of cinematic flashbacks. Instead, smell produces a nonsequential state of being that is embodied by the young preacher whose consciousness spans continents and centuries. Though the preacher may be a man of the word, he is often depicted using his other senses—particularly those of smell and touch—to appraise a situation and break through walls and exterior obstacles that hinder what one can see. He is thus different from contemporary Westerners who overrely on sight and hearing to perceive the world. The preacher, instead, uses his sharply tuned senses to go beneath and beyond surfaces. For example, when he dips his fingers into a jar of salve, he uses his nose to tell the story of some lotion—the people that made it and the woman that gave it to him:

> An odor rises from the jar, almost harsh, many odors compounded into one, more pleasant than unpleasant when, rather than shying away, he lets himself breathe it, search it. He coats his fingertips, brings them closer to his nose. Mud in it and meat frying, honey, wet pine needles flooring the forest, sage, black leaves moldering at the bottom of a pile returning to soil, mint, blue sleeves, applerot, this woman's scents collecting at the cavemouths and hollows of her body while she sleeps, the bread smell of her skin warmed all night beneath the bedclothes. (140)

Stephen Casmier

Through his alert senses, the preacher breaks down one odor into many. Each ingredient invades him, bringing with it traces of its origin. It transforms him into a being lodged in different times and different places.

In *The Cattle Killing*, smells are portals to alternate realities and other ways of knowing. The novel begins with the writer character eager to get out of the stifling atmosphere of a writers' conference. This conference represents a boring, banal, confining, hypocritical, and unimaginative present. The repugnance of this atmosphere is captured through the description of the breath of a participant at the conference: "somebody's garlic breath sitting next to you at breakfast saying he's always admired your work" (3). This passage reveals one aspect of the sense of smell. "Smell," Walter Ong says, "is a come or go signal" (117). And in this case, smell signals the writer's decision and ability to leave one world of repugnant smells and be drawn toward another, better, yet-to-be imagined world that he only knows by its scent.

The novel presents the banal, limited world of ocularity as a place of mostly repugnant odors and smells that should be avoided or covered up. When Liam first enters London, he recoils from the "city's assault on my senses, the stench and tumult of a tannery" (110). As he assists in the delivery of a child, he senses the perfume of the English noble woman—a "French essence, no doubt, to disguise the raw Anglo-Saxon odors of birth" (118). Meanwhile, at the outset of his journeys the preacher encounters the "stink" of death (mingled with self-destructive bigotry) in a cabin in the Pennsylvania wilderness (24). Yet, he is also driven toward the odors of the elusive woman that he seeks throughout the text. Indeed, at many junctures, the woman seems to be more of an odor than a body. For example, when he awakes from his dream about the cattle killing, he can only remember the smell of the prophetess, which melds with that of another "her": "When I awakened I was covered in sweat. Naked on the grass under the starry African sky. The scents of her body mixed with mine. A smell I recognized and have never forgotten" (148).

And on many other occasions he refers to the "scent of her" (30, 39, 52, 76) as one of her most salient and enduring characteristics. This is because, as a scent, she points toward unimagined possibilities. Such possibilities, unbound by time and space, present notions of consciousness and identity that cannot be described or seen. Instead, they must be sensed. This enables the narrator to blend together locations, events, and people—Ramona Africa, Mandela, Philadelphia, Capetown, and Pittsburgh (206). It enables him to blend the ailing father with Liam's wife, Kate, the Xhosa prophetess, and other characters that sight and conventional notions of time, space, and identity would keep separate. As a scent, they easily blend together. "Tell me finally," says the narrator towards the end of the novel, "what is a man. What is a woman" (208).

Through such invocations of funk, Wideman has produced three novels that go against the anesthetizing illusions of contemporary society. Through their funk—their efforts to make us feel and remember—these novels work to awaken us. They recall stories that society wants us to forget and reveal the unbreakable bonds that we have with one another. In all, they remind us of what it means to be, what it means to smell, human.

NOTES

1. This discussion of seeing, hearing, consciousness, and alienation owes a major debt to Walter J. Ong and ideas presented in *Interfaces of the Word: Studies in the Evolution of Consciousness and Culture* and *The Presence of the Word: Some Prolegomena for Cultural and Religious History*.

2. I offer, here, an interpretation of Benjamin's and Buck-Morss's ideas. By phantasmagoria, she means the principle that produces the staged, "simulated total environments in miniature" of "shopping malls, theme parks, and video arcades [. . .] the goal is the manipulation of the synaesthetic system by control of environmental stimuli" (22). In light of the work of Walter Ong, Marshall McLuhan, and Martin Jay, I distill this notion so that it refers to transforming all sense perceptions into a product of seeing.

3. This is not supposed to happen, says Lyall Watson. Watson paraphrases Joseph Williams who observes that: "Almost every adjective from touch and taste moves up to attach itself finally to smell, but no known primary olfactory word in English has ever shifted to any other sense" (189).

4. In *Discourse and Destruction: The City of Philadelphia Versus MOVE*, Robin Wagner-Pacifici asserts that a terror of the inchoate lay beneath the city's attempt to destroy MOVE, the group a police helicopter bombed in 1985 (148).

5. The barn as workplace reappears in *The Cattle Killing* as the place where Liam paints. Wideman himself worked over a barn at his home in Massachusetts.

WORKS CITED

Buck-Morss, Susan. "Aesthetics and Anaesthetics: Walter Benjamin's Artwork Essay Reconsidered." *October* 62 (Fall 1992): 3–41.

"Focus Special: The Atta Document in Full: Last Words of a Terrorist." *The Observer* 30 Sept. 2001: 17.

Friedman, Ted. "Making It Funky: The Signifyin(g) Politics of George Clinton's Parliafunkadelicment Thang." 1993. Accessed 12 Mar. 2002. <http://eserver.org/music/text/Friedman-Making.it.Funky.html>

"George Clinton." D. Fricke and F. Ockenfels. *Rolling Stone* 587 (1990): 74.

Harries, Karsten. "Descartes, Perspective, and the Angelic Eye." *Yale French Studies* (1973): 28–42.

Henderson, Ian, with Philip Goodhart. *Man Hunt in Kenya*. New York: Doubleday, 1958.

Jay, Martin. "The Rise of Hermeneutics and the Crisis of Ocularcentrism." *Poetics Today* 9 (1988): 307–26.

Keverne, Eric B. "The Nature of Smell," *Perspectives in Biology and Medicine* 45 (Spring 2002): 281–86.

McLuhan, Marshall, and Quentin Fiore. *The Medium is the Massage* (1967). Corte Madra, CA: Ginko Press, 2001.

———. *Understanding Media : The Extensions of Man*. 1964. Corte Madra, CA: Ginko Press, 2003.

Oksiloff, Assenka. "Eden Is Burning: Wim Wenders's Techniques of Synaesthesia." *The German Quarterly* 69 (Winter 1996): 32–47.

Ong, Walter J. *Interfaces of the Word: Studies in the Evolution of Consciousness and Culture*. Ithaca: Cornell UP, 1977.

———. *The Presence of the Word: Some Prolegomena for Cultural and Religious History*. 1967. Minneapolis: U of Minnesota P, 1981.

Pinckney, Darryl. "'Cos I'm a So-o-oul Man: The Back-country Blues of John Edgar Wideman." *Times Literary Supplement* 23 Aug. 1991: 19–20.

Schmidt, Klaus. "Reading Black Postmodernism: John Edgar Wideman's *Reuben*." *Flip Sides: New Critical Essays in American Literature*. Frankfurt: Peter Lang, 1995. 81–102.

Seymour, Gene. "Dream Surgeon." *The Nation* 263.13 (1996): 58–60.

Thompson, Robert Farris. *Flash of the Spirit: African and Afro-American Art and Philosophy*. New York: Vintage, 1984.

Wagner-Pacifici, Robin. *Discourse and Destruction: The City of Philadelphia Versus MOVE*. Chicago: U of Chicago P, 1993.

Watson, Lyall. *Jacobson's Organ and the Remarkable Nature of Smell*. New York: W. W. Norton, 2000.

Wideman, John Edgar. *The Cattle Killing*. Boston: Houghton Mifflin, 1996.

———. *Philadelphia Fire*. New York: Henry Holt, 1990.

———. *Reuben*. New York: Henry Holt, 1987.

Williams, Joseph. "Synesthetic Adjectives." *Language* 52 (1976): 461–78.

"Ill Seen Ill Said

Tropes of Vision and the Articulation of Race Relations in *The Cattle Killing*

Jennifer D. Douglas

> Look? Too weak a word. Too wrong. Its absence? No better. Unspeakable globe. Unbearable.
>
> Samuel Beckett, *Ill Seen Ill Said*

Beckett's words highlight the relation between sight and speech by positing vision or the lack thereof as a metaphor for verbal expression. He remains skeptical about the efficacy of language to convey ideas or describe images, to articulate and enunciate that which is seen, and even to see clearly in the first place. As his title indicates, imperfect vision accompanies imperfect articulation, and the placement of sight before speech suggests a process whereby seeing precedes and influences verbal expression. Sensory information acquired through the eyes translates to images which the brain interprets, categorizes, and stores so that a person can verbalize a past experience or image. Putting optical experience into words involves a process of translating, in a way, from sensory data to verbal expression, and, as Walter

Benjamin posits, translation actually becomes a transformation as the brain processes, synthesizes, and verbalizes (73). This transformation between sight and speech forms a crucial link in the process of storytelling—that of conveying an image from memory or imagination to another person.

In *The Cattle Killing*, tropes of vision embedded in this storytelling process tell their own tale of the strained race relations in the novel. The transformation of images from sight to speech, and the inadequacy of words to convey the intensity and impact of these images, places the ruptures involved in communication alongside the racial disjunctions in the novel—beginning with the central image of the Xhosa cattle killing. Vision, for Wideman, transcends physical sight to enter the realms of dream, prophecy, and leadership within the black community of eighteenth-century Philadelphia, but all of these areas merely highlight the chasm, the impaired vision, that exists between members of the black and white communities. In this essay I will explore the connection between vision, articulation, and race relations to show that tropes of vision point to the difficulty of telling one's own story and bridging the racial gaps that appear when vision fails to produce clarity of interracial understanding.[1]

In order to discuss the relation between vision and verbalizing, I want to draw on Stuart Hall's definition of the term *articulation*. In addition to the standard sense of speaking or uttering, *articulation* also points to, in Hall's words, "the form of a connection that *can* make a unity of two different elements, under certain conditions. It is a linkage which is not necessary, determined, absolute and essential for all time" ("On Postmodernism" 141).[2] By defining *articulation* in this manner, I argue that tropes of vision in the novel lead to a literal articulation in the storytelling sense, but they are also linked to the portrayal of race relations. In this second sense, Wideman brings together two disparate concepts and creates a connection between them that may not exist in other contexts. My reading of the novel depends on accepting this joining of concepts and viewing the descriptions of sight through this interpretive lens.

The Cattle Killing abounds with visual references, emphasizing by their very plenitude the necessity of seeing, both literal and metaphorical, for storytelling. In the prelude chapter, the present-day narrator reminisces about his youth in Pittsburgh and quickly recalls his nickname—"Eye"—short for Isaiah. This immediate visual reference points to the role of storytellers as witnesses, observers, possessors of sensory acuity. Storytellers require clarity of vision, and Wideman demonstrates the difficulty of maintaining that clarity amidst bewildering and oppressive circumstances. Indeed, the central image of the novel, the Xhosa people's slaughtering of their cattle, presents a paradigm for the rupture of vision that occurs between races in the book. As Wideman writes in this first chapter:

The image haunts [the writer]. Xhosa killing their cattle, killing themselves, a world coming apart. A brave, elegant African people who had resisted European invaders until an evil prophecy convinced them to kill their cattle, butcher the animals that fleshed the Xhosa's intricate dreaming of themselves. (7)

This quote elucidates the central paradox of the visual tropes: the fact that seeing, whether in the literal sense or in the metaphorical construction of prophecy as "second sight," can deceive as well as illuminate, and sometimes accuracy of vision actually heightens the painfulness of a situation. By placing this image as a backdrop in the novel, Wideman sets up the articulation (in both senses) of vision and race relations and particularly the layers of misunderstanding in interracial communication.

II

While it may seem obvious that vision, in the physiological sense, creates a rupture between the races because of physical differences, prophecy and religion also serve as paradigms for sight and ways in which black and white people fail to connect in the novel. Faith, by biblical definition, requires "being sure of what we hope for and certain of what we do not see" (Hebrews 11:1). Christianity, the dominant mode of faith presented in the novel, thus relies on belief in the unseen, or rather a spiritual vision that may or may not correspond to visible events. Prophecy, by extension, consists of "second sight" that allows the believer to receive a message from God and convey it authoritatively to the people—a process that can be abused, as the novel shows. In line with Kathie Birat's argument, I posit that Wideman deconstructs the language of prophecy by utilizing the same light and dark terminology to describe both religious liberation and racial stereotypes of black people as evil (Birat 634).

The central image of the Xhosa's cattle killing underlies the race struggles that permeate these stories, and Wideman couches this image in the idea of false prophecy—that the Xhosa are deceived by a vision of liberation that actually causes their destruction. Wideman's account of this event occurs in the context of a dream given to the preacher by Nongqawuse, the Xhosa girl whose vision prompts the people's action and leads to their downfall. In this dream, itself a kind of sight and a vehicle for prophecy, Nongqawuse relates the coming of the whites, the plagues that they bring to people and cattle, and the stranger who tells her that killing the cattle will save the people. Despite the elders' initial disbelief, the Xhosa eventually follow the edict in desperation, only to lose their livelihood and tribal identity. Nongqawuse warns the preacher not to succumb to the same temptation: "Beware, she said. Beware. Beware. Do not kill your cattle. Do not speak with your enemy's tongue. Do not fall asleep in your enemy's dream" (Wideman 147). Her words coalesce all the racial experiences in the novel into a paradigm of distrust and watchfulness. The injunction not to "fall asleep in your enemy's dream" supposes that losing one's sight and consciousness means taking on those of another person, the white person, the enemy. Fritz Gysin, also writing about prophecy in the novel, agrees that Wideman "focuses primarily on Nongqawuse and her vision which he interprets as a central case of false prophecy and then transforms it into a warning directed at African Americans across the centuries" (624). As this story illustrates, relations between whites and blacks have been characterized by false prophecies, visions put forth by one race at the expense of the other. Growing outward from this central story, the other stories in this book form concentric circles that register the cultural and historical repercussions of black subjugation by a white colonial power, representing ruptures in vision that continue to plague our cultural consciousness.

From the Xhosa cattle killing, the notion of false prophecy crosses into the realm of religion in general and to the ways in which black people work for an equality of church long before they achieve any equality of state. Religion continues the vision paradigm by its emphasis on inner light and the distrust of appearances. The novel's itinerant preacher, converted by a follower of the English Reverend George Whitefield,[3] preaches vehemently against trusting appearances: "Men are blinded by the light. Seduced by appearances" (Wideman 20). Instead, he encourages his congregation to "Feed the light" of God within themselves and eschew what they see with their physical eyes. Placing the weight of discernment on spiritual growth rather than physical sight agrees with the Christian doctrine of salvation as the beginning of a spiritual journey of inner transformation and a death to unholy physical desires; it also offers a way for a black congregation to maintain dignity in the context of systemic prejudice against them. White Christians, although professing to worship the same God, refuse to allow their black brethren equal access to the church's resources, which prompts black people to seek out separate communion to meet their spiritual needs. The preacher's message to distrust appearances, then, offers a coping mechanism or method of transcending their circumstances. For the black people at St. Matthew's, choosing to hold additional meetings in an arbor after the traditional church service frees them to worship in their own manner. More importantly, though, it actually accentuates the racial segregation so prevalent in society. The apparent agency that they exert merely confirms Wideman's view, as stated in an interview, that segregation doesn't answer the problem of racial friction.

Although the white people tolerate the blacks' presence, their barely concealed hostility comes to the surface when the preacher has a seizure during a service and

"Ill Seen Ill Said"

falls to the floor. These fainting fits, in themselves, illustrate the distortions of vision that occur between the races. As the preacher describes them, an unnatural calm precedes the frenzy of darkness and "rioting devils" that accompany a fit. For a time he writhes, mouth foaming and limbs shuddering, until another calm quells the fit and produces, for a short time, an extraordinary clarity of vision: "Words can't describe the clarity. Suffice to say I *see*. For a brief, blessed interval a glorious seeing restores the world to me. Restores me to the world" (Wideman 58). After one of these seizures occurs in church, his congregation takes him to their arbor and believes that the fit is a manifestation of prophecy because his first words come from the prophet Jeremiah, "*Behold, I am making my words in your mouth a fire . . .*" (Wideman 72). This amazing clarity that the preacher experiences, growing out of the darkness of the fit, once again juxtaposes physical vision that occurs in the normal light of day with a kind of hyper-vision that grows out of an internal experience. With the clarity of vision comes a sense of the world reassembled from its fragmented parts into a cohesive whole—seeing the world without the boundaries that people impose on it and the invisible lines, including race, that divide it into uncrossable territories. As the clarity fades to the ordinary (and ironic) blindness of sunlight, the preacher wishes that he could share his vision with another and gain the communion of understanding. Wideman's description is worth quoting at length because of the explicit connection between vision and the sense of unity and harmony that occurs during this intense clarity:

> I wish someone else, one of my friends in the clearing, anyone, could read the glad tidings in my eyes. See how each separate, lonely thing connects for an instance [sic] with its lost brethren. As in a mirror my eye finds my eye. Or as in another's gaze I find my self. The play back and forth. A simple fellowship, each freeing the other, making the other real. (Wideman 74)

As we see here, vision leads to a validation of identity and existence that frees the other person to find and act authentically him- or herself. This clarity of vision and dialogic visual communication represent the goal of racial harmony that quickly fades in the realities of the sun's harsh light. The preacher's fits, in which he enters a period of darkness, parallel the threshing-floor descriptions of James Baldwin in *Go Tell It on the Mountain*, but these fits more explicitly pertain to interracial frustration rather than the refining of one person's character.[4] The preacher, who has accepted a spiritual leadership role, functions as a sort of visionary for his congregation, so his fits are symptomatic not only of a physical ailment but also of a societal evil that he wants to mend but cannot. His wish to share his vision with others speaks to a desire for fellowship both within the community of blacks and across racial boundaries.

In part 2 of the book, Wideman introduces Bishop Allen as another visionary preacher who begins a separate black church in Philadelphia. Allen's journey away from the white church begins with a visual transformation: "[The elders] changed shape before his eyes, transformed by the evil clouding their hearts as they laid hands on him and his brethren at prayer" (Wideman 154). Realizing that the white elders of the church will never tolerate black parishioners, Allen decides that he must work to provide black people with their own church. This segregation of the races results from Allen's accurate assessment of the racism in the white church and prompts him to take a "step into darkness," the leap of faith that allows him to leave the church in dignity. Despite his reputation in the city and the novel's description of him as a "pilgrim, as witness, pioneer, and point man," Allen doubts the efficacy of his work and even struggles with the desire to be white so that his life will not consist of a continual battle for freedom. Like Noah, Allen "begs for a vision of the new world at the far end of this threatening path— the earth restored, flood receded, peace" (Wideman 159). His clarity of vision gives him courage to act, but forming a separate church certainly does not resolve the tension between races; it gives the blacks a place to worship in freedom but separates them even further from the white power locus of society. Bishop Allen's story, though indicative of the impact that one person can make, emphasizes the continued impairment of vision that characterizes race relations in the novel. Even Dr. Thrush, who outwardly supports the project of the black church, calls it his "hobbyhorse," thus diminishing its importance as a way to humor the "other" and keep black people on the margins of society (Wideman 161).

The preacher's eventual rejection of both the faith and his call to preaching mark a final disjunction between his vision of a restored world and the dark truth of real life. His stutter at the end represents a literal loss of articulation, in the sense of utterance, but it also dis-articulates—according to Hall's definition—his societal vision and its fulfillment. As he confesses, "Between what I want to say and the saying of it, a shadow passes" (Wideman 205). This shadow literally clouds the enunciative process, thus questioning the effectiveness of both preaching and storytelling as modes of personal and racial healing. By intentionally describing the stutter as a visual defect, Wideman completes the circle of vision as a prerequisite to storytelling and a metaphor for prophetic vision that attempts and fails to effect a final reconciliation. Although the struggle for clarity between the races doesn't wholly succeed within this novel, part of Wideman's motivation in writing it may be the continued impact that these stories have on the state of race relations today.

III

In a dark wood, in a bramble,
On the edge of a grimpen, where is no
secure foothold,
And menaced by monsters, fancy lights,
Risking enchantment.

T. S. Eliot, "East Coker"

So the unreasoning goes. While the eye
digests its pittance. In its private dark.
In the general dark.

Samuel Beckett, *Ill Seen Ill Said*

Wideman foregrounds the idea of sight at the beginning of the novel by presenting the preacher at dawn, watching the light illuminate the world around him. Light reveals, in this description, the objects and shapes obscured in darkness, but it also increases vulnerability: the preacher "fears the light" because "You see out now, now anyone can see in" (Wideman 18).[5] Rather than comforting the preacher by dispelling the darkness, it "deceives" in its "meaningless play upon surfaces," acting as a medium of deception and an illusion that darkness won't allow. Light has also lost the ability to articulate, "struck dumb since the moment it witnessed sin," and darkness has acquired the truth that the light can't express (Wideman 19). This discussion of light and dark, especially at the beginning of the novel, establishes a tension between clear vision, deceptive vision, and lack of vision; ironically, the narrator seems to posit that the greatest clarity of mental vision, for black characters, occurs when literal vision has failed. Throughout the novel, darkness serves as the site of revelation, while the light of day often presents a veneer of stability or justice that the night will shatter. Often, the apparent interracial harmony, or at least tolerance, that exists during the day erupts into a painful cacophony in the dark, illuminating at night what the daylight attempts to obscure.

Fredric Jameson's discussion of postmodernism also figures here because he highlights the idea of depthlessness as particular to postmodern textuality. His statement that "depth is replaced by surface, or by multiple surfaces" seems apropos to my discussion of vision because of Wideman's focus on the deceptiveness and glare of light reflecting and refracting off objects (Jameson 70). As a postmodern novel, *The Cattle Killing* highlights its own status as created text through the repeated interventions of the preacher describing the storytelling process in terms of the inadequacy of words to convey the full intent of his thought.[6] The preacher concurs with this analysis by admitting, "My tales are poor, untidy things. No beginnings nor ends. Orphan tales whose sole virtue is you listen" (Wideman 29). The palimpsest quality of these stories, being layered over one another, interlacing and overlapping, points, in one sense, to a narrative depth resulting from multiple stories being superimposed. Vis-à-vis Jameson, however, this very intertextuality exposes the contradictions inherent in sight: namely, that the apparently civil relations between races can shift or evaporate in the same way that language allows for textual play and multiple interpretations. Seeing does not necessarily lead to understanding, or at least any permanent reconciliation. In a sense, this analogy *articulates* or connects the idea of African American with the postmodern by relating the slippage inherent in a postmodern reading of texts with the slippery quality of identity. In the same way that textual decentering accompanies a postmodern reading of texts, the visual shifts—alternating between the physical and the prophetic—and the deceptiveness of light accompany the shifting identities of black people intra- and interracially.[7]

The preacher's stay with Liam and Mrs. Stubbs affords more examples of darkness illuminating the truth better than light. Most obviously, the killing night illustrates the hidden hostility that the whites in the town have harbored toward Liam and Mrs. Stubbs for being an interracial couple. Although they maintain civility when Liam goes to town, their seething discontent becomes a killing rampage in the wake of the plague in Philadelphia. This act of cowardice, murdering innocent blacks under cover of night, actually reveals the truth of stubbornly embedded racism far more than the outward courtesy that they display in daily interactions. Liam's account of his work with George Stubbs also reveals a secret trade in cadavers, especially in the corpse of a pregnant black woman. Liam's description of the ghoulish scene of bidding over this woman's body paints the room as a "cavelike . . . subterranean chamber," flickering with candles in the darkness and away from the prying eyes of the general public (Wideman 133). In this womblike enclosure, insulated and mostly dark, the truth of body trafficking becomes apparent, and Liam shrinks from the animalistic descriptions of the black woman. His reaction to seeing her as a commodity, useful for the purposes of art or dissection, provokes an intense identification with her: "The African woman on the table was my sister, mother, daughter. I slept inside her dark stomach. . . . They'd find me cowering in the black cave of her womb again, dead and alive, alive and dead" (Wideman 137). In this context, the cover of night and the secrecy of the meeting reveal truth that could never be shared legally and that the participants attempt to hide.

The orphans' story also polarizes the deceptiveness of light with the gruesome truth of darkness by relating the horrendous conditions that abandoned children endure locked in the cellar at night, only to be brought into the schoolhouse during the day and taught by a naïve Mrs. Thrush. As the orphan on trial describes it, the journey from cellar to daylight does not release the orphans from their oppressive circumstances, but only prolongs their suffering until they enter the cellar again:

> [T]he light you yearned for all night in the cellar's darkness does not free you. Its chore when it blazes is to separate you from the others so you can each climb the ladder, go about your duties, receive the punishments due you, the lessons, cleaning other people's filth, the hateful slop you steal and gobble so you don't starve. The light changes none of it. (Wideman 193)

Light does not, and perhaps cannot, liberate here; it merely marks the time between periods of darkness that are the reality of the orphans' existence. They may have survived the plague, but their lives have become a cycle of torture that the blind Mrs. Thrush cannot see, literally or conceptually. The orphan's anger toward Mrs. Thrush for representing his oppressors and his greater anger toward Kathryn for adapting to the white people's world lead him to fantasize about the violence that he finally brings to fruition in murdering the other children. Although his crime kills a large number of people, it only speeds the work of the starvation and disease that white people had already allowed. The orphan's just anger leads to his own killing night, but his subsequent guilty verdict only emphasizes that the whites never face repercussions for their crimes.

Although the orphan hates Kathryn for her role in the white people's society, her life also reflects an apparent truth during the day and another reality at night. Dr. Thrush, who appears to be a respectable Philadelphia doctor in support of the independent black church, uses her body for his own sexual pleasure to exploit the master/slave relationship that he pretends to eschew. Kathryn, who becomes Mrs. Thrush's literal eyes and recorder, places herself in the margins of the other's story, interjecting her own moans into the spaces of the text. She pities Mrs. Thrush for being "doubly blind," lacking both literal sight and knowledge of her husband's hypocrisy. To use Beckett's words from the epigraph, this "private dark" of blindness, although innocent on Mrs. Thrush's part, extends into the "general dark" of Kathryn's and the orphans' abuse. After Kathryn and the preacher forge a friendship, Kathryn relates her story openly, safe in the communion of another black person to voice her anger and frustration. In her description, darkness can't mask the heinous violation of her body and Mrs. Thrush's fidelity: "As if the darkness of night is a cover for his wicked trespass" (Wideman 201).

Kathryn's pregnancy allows her to tell Mrs. Thrush her shameful secret, finally exposing the truth that she couldn't express before. Mrs. Thrush's lack of sight connects vision to the process of articulation again, demonstrating a metaphorical blindness between the races that prevents communication. Darkness may reveal the truth of pervasive racism and allow the two women to empathize through their betrayal, but it also emphasizes the disjunction between them and the fact that black people seem to gain communion only with one another.

IV

> Some mornings I'm frustrated by the pause [in my writing process], disquieted by a foreboding that no words exist, that even if there are words, they will always fail. . . .
>
> John Edgar Wideman,
> "In Praise of Silence"

Storytelling also serves the purpose of preservation in the sense of witnessing and recording people's stories. The process of seeing an event, remembering it, and re-creating that event in words *articulates* vision with the work of cultural recovery, which occurs, according to Hall, "partly through memory, partly through narrative" ("Eternity" 19). Seeing becomes instrumental in constructing a historical record and in preventing the oppressive power, in this case the white colonizer, from denying responsibility for acts of racist violence. In thinking about his relation to the preacher, the novel's anonymous narrator describes his stories as "*testimony witnessing what surrounds them both this very moment, an encompassing silence forgetting them both, silence untouched by their passing. . . . The terror of its forgetfulness . . . would be unbearable unless he imagined . . . someone else, passing like him . . .*" (Wideman 13).[8] As Lisa Baker posits, the writer acts as witness and recorder, collaborating with the audience in creating a narrative space and simultaneously deconstructing previous notions of reality. The writer's role thus requires the keen vision to see, the discernment to understand, and the intellect to express. In French, the connection between these three activities becomes apparent since the verbs *savoir* and *pouvoir*, "to know" and "to be able to," respectively, both contain the verb *voir*, to see (Hebdige 200). For the purpose of discussing race relations, storytelling prevents the erasure of black stories by white narratives and metanarratives, thus giving voice to the marginalized black population in eighteenth-century America. These stories also represent countless oth-

"Ill Seen Ill Said"

ers, "leaking, bleeding" into each other (Wideman 13). Stories themselves act as witnesses, thus extending the literal sight into a historical and cultural necessity for documenting the experiences of the underrepresented.[9] Although Wideman's stories record the cruelty whites inflict on blacks and allow the reader to identify with black characters, vision generally becomes linked to verbalizing racial tensions, in effect "seeing" and telling about the *lack* of sight between people of different colors.

Wideman first engages the issue of racial strife through the episode of the preacher and the old man in the secluded cabin. With typically visual language, he relates the old man watching the preacher's approach through an "eye" in the side of the cabin, fostering unease in the preacher immediately. The weight of these observing eyes prompts a question of existence, the preacher wondering whether "he need[ed] someone else's eyes to make him real" (Wideman 23). Compounding the preacher's discomfort, the shriveled white man in the cabin immediately asks him if he is the devil and flinches when the preacher lifts the ax to chop wood for the man's fire. This surreal scene, ending with the ax handle breaking and the preacher imagining himself tearing the man to shreds, helps to establish the disjunction of sight that will continue throughout the novel. White man and black man meet, watch each other warily, and fail to communicate. The splintering ax and the preacher's subsequent pondering—"Does he need someone to tell him what's happened. Was there a witness. Who. Where."—questions whether the white man's gaze even constitutes a witness, much less an empathetic witness (Wideman 25). The preacher can hardly acknowledge this man's vision after the white man mistook him for the devil; skewed vision from the start cannot lead to an empathetic witness later. Despite the preacher's polite words and actions, he and the white man never achieve understanding. Each sees the other within the paradigm of his past experience, and, despite the peacefulness of their encounter (the preacher does not obey his impulse to kill the man), they move no closer to seeing beyond the superficial boundary of skin color.

However, sight can also create an affinity among black people. In the drowning of the African woman with the white baby, the preacher's offer to help and witnessing of her watery disappearance prompts him to research her history and keep the story of her bravery alive. His claim as he tells the story to the mysterious addressee—"[I]t happened and I was there and now I'm here telling you"—foregrounds the importance of telling stories for the creation and preservation of personal and racial identity (Wideman 47). The preacher's self-conscious interruptions during the story, questioning his ability to convey what he saw and the listener's role in reconstructing the scene, create a dual sense of the storytelling process as transforming memory into words that may preserve or destroy what they describe. His sharing of her intensely personal moments—undressing, urinating in the sand, the gaze they exchange, and her determined stride into the water—make him a part of her story rather than a detached observer. Her disappearance, though seemingly the end of her life, prompts him to research her past, an act that extends the mystery of her story and renders their encounter only one act of a play that must continue.

The preacher's relationship to Liam and Mrs. Stubbs also shows how racial affinity, identifying with someone of the same color, leads Liam to break his self-imposed silence and tell the stories he has held within himself for so long. Mrs. Stubbs relates his transformation from loquacious storyteller to practically mute man, and Liam admits that the light in himself began to "dim, flicker, expire" as shame and anger drove him into silence (Wideman 126). When the preacher joins their family of two, his blackness allows Liam to speak freely about his journey from Africa to England, his transformation from healer to indentured servant and artist.[10] As Liam admits, "I didn't know how deeply I missed another like myself beside me until you arrived. So many stories to tell" (Wideman 131). His opportunity to articulate his past to the preacher, both in its literal telling and in creating a bond between them, revitalizes his relationship with his wife as well—from their resumption of marital relations to his painting her in the barn. During the preacher's stay with the couple, the relationships also acquire a strange dynamic through the covert observation of each other. After Liam and Mrs. Stubbs rescue the preacher from the storm, for example, only Mrs. Stubbs knows about the erection she gives the preacher while he is unconscious; conversely, only the preacher knows how long he observes her bathing in the morning. When Mrs. Stubbs asks the preacher to massage her back, he engages in this intimate activity without the knowledge or observation of Liam. This circle closes when the preacher sees Liam painting Mrs. Stubbs in the hay mound of the barn, depicting her in a rainbow of colors that mirrors the way he saw her bare back the day he rubbed salve into it. These incidents ironically reveal the limited way in which we know other people, and that even people in the most intimate of relationships may fall short of comprehensive sight. On the other hand, the myriad of shades in Liam's painting, and his agency in changing them, present one of the most optimistic pictures of reconciliation in the novel. Of course, the story ends in the killing night, the blindness of racial hatred squelching the clarity of sight they had achieved.

After nearly two years at the Stubbs's house, the preacher ventures to Philadelphia and quickly becomes involved in Bishop Allen's movement. He and Kathryn become friends after their initial meeting at Dr. Thrush's house, at first each wary of trusting the other too much. The narrator relates their thought processes upon seeing each other for the first time, emphasizing the discomfort in "undressing, sounding out the other." Each thinks, "*Will I see nothing or see my own face in the mirror of this other whose eyes search mine for confirmation or dismissal or love"* (Wideman 200). This searching for empathy and acceptance parallels the preacher's earlier wish that another could experience the clarity of vision that accompanies his seizures, wanting someone else to share in the hope that floods him at that moment. The freedom that their relationship affords for Kathryn to express the agony of Dr. Thrush's abuse typifies the ways in which intraracial relationships in the novel can soothe but not heal the wounds inflicted by interracial relationships. The perceptiveness and empathy that flows from the racism that each has experienced provide the foundation for their friendship.

Wideman couches all these stories in the preacher's relating them to a mysterious listener, a woman whom he visits in an effort to heal her with the stories. This "speaking into the dark," in his words, recalls Bishop Allen's leap of faith and the visionary quality inherent in using words to encourage faith or change (Wideman 78). By creating a listener within the text, Wideman emphasizes the dialogic quality of storytelling and the way in which speaker and listener must work together to complete the stories, often going backward to go forward, reworking their shared vision. When the preacher questions his ability to articulate, using words to build a bridge to the listener, he asks himself, "Will [the listener] share the story with me, dream it all again in [her] own words. The parts I say, the parts I don't or can't" (Wideman 40). The listener participates in the storytelling by completing the images herself, by stitching together the seams in the story, making her own "hideous progeny," to borrow Mary Shelley's term. At the end of the novel, the preacher's stuttering makes the reader question whether the stories have healed anyone, or whether he has simply lost his facility for language in the process of trying to tell them. As he laments to the listener, "I talk, maybe you listen, but you're not better, not stronger. . . . You cannot live in this fallen place. Love can't live here" (Wideman 205). In a society fraught with so much racial tension, the preacher questions whether words can heal anyone. His vision, once idealistic and enthusiastic, has become jaded and weary of conveying the pain he sees.

The return of the present-day narrator at the end of the novel offers hope that the sojourn can continue, that stories can produce relief or freedom. The process of articulation, transforming images into words, effects some healing even if it cannot cure systemic evil. Perhaps over time, the accumulation of stories is what prompts change by denying the possibility of forgetting. In *The Location of Culture*, Homi Bhabha recognizes the importance of the witness in the formation of cultural identity, especially in postcolonial discourse. Wideman's narrative technique of couching the novel within layers of stories makes the witness in turn a storyteller who hopes that his words will *enlighten* the listener. As Bhabha states:

Jennifer D. Douglas

In the figure of the witness of a postcolonial modernity we have another wisdom: it comes from those who have seen the nightmare of racism and oppression in the banal light of the everyday. They represent an idea of action and agency more complex than either the nihilism of despair or the utopia of progress. (254–55)

In *The Cattle Killing*, the writer tells these stories "so my dead are not strangers," thus identifying him with the task of remembrance and even the reformation of language itself (Wideman 207). If, as Mikhail Bakhtin claims, language is "ideologically saturated," then the storyteller's impetus toward articulation and enunciation must contend with already-tainted language (271). Bhabha also notes the time and space between vision and verbalization, what he calls "the *signifying lag* between event and enunciation" (244). In accord with Henry Louis Gates Jr.'s explanation of *signifying* in black vernacular, Wideman's novel is a prime example of the black subject speaking from the margins of society and, in Kathryn's case, literally in the margins of her white mistress's diary. The preacher's stories serve both as a literal enunciation of events he witnessed (and participated in) and a signifying on white culture's ignorance of and refusal to meet the needs of both the preacher and other black people. *The Cattle Killing*, then, exposes the impaired vision existing between black and white people, the role of prophecy as warning or cultural warfare, and the possibility of keen insight among black people. Vision becomes the basis for a storytelling that both enunciates the pain of racism and preserves these wrenching experiences as a witness for those who come after. Despite the awkwardness of putting images into words and the fallibility of these words to *articulate* experiences, I hope, like Beckett at the end of *Ill Seen Ill Said*, that words give us "Grace to breathe that void. Know happiness" (86).

NOTES

1. "Race" is, in itself, an issue of contestation, since theorists like Anthony Appiah have pointed out that biologically speaking races don't exist as we know them. Like Lucius Outlaw, however, I see race as a social construction based, from a visual standpoint, on the grosser physical characteristics of skin color, hair, and bone structure as well as the obvious separation that white people have imposed on people of non-European descent.
2. In the rest of the essay, the word *articulate* will be italicized when used in Hall's sense.
3. As Rimas J. Orentas describes him, Whitefield was associated with the holiness movement of John and Charles Wesley, played a large role in the Great Awakening in the United States, and made seven trips to speak in America during the mid-1700s.
4. In Baldwin's description of John's threshing-floor experience, John moves from a terrifying darkness full of fear and the certainty of judgment to a reconciliation with God: "For his drifting soul was anchored in the love of God; in the rock that endured

forever. The light and the darkness had kissed each other, and were married now, forever, in the life and the vision of John's soul" (266–67). Wideman's description of the
preacher's fits mirror the terror and lack of control that John experiences, even though
Wideman explains the fits as a physical ailment rather than a manifestation of God's
power.

5. Thomas Keenan expresses the same sense of vulnerability in his essay "Windows of
Vulnerability": "The window can breach, tear open, the 'protection' that is the human
subject, overcome it with a violence that proves remarkably resistant to knowledge
(especially that of vision) or representation" (127).

6. Similar to Wahneema Lubiano's discussion of the narrative technique in James
McPherson's "Elbow Room," *The Cattle Killing* also "consistently draws attention to
itself as a narrative in its metacommentary on the structure, demands, expectations,
and failures of storytelling" (Lubiano 162).

7. While I eschew a monolithic conception of black identity, I have chosen to focus on
the elusiveness of black/white relations as a breakdown of sight in this novel.

8. Like Robert Frost's description of his poetry, storytelling for this writer acts as a
"momentary stay against confusion," or at least the erasure created by the inexorable
passing of time (Frost 777).

9. This novel parallels Eudora Welty's description of her writing as a means of creating
clear vision, or "part[ing] . . . the veil of indifference to each other's presence, each
other's wonder, each other's human plight" (355).

10. While I recognize that gender may also play a role in the affinity between Liam and the
preacher, race seems to be the most prominent factor in Liam's decision to share his
stories.

WORKS CITED

Appiah, Anthony. "The Uncompleted Argument: DuBois and the Illusion of Race." *"Race,"
Writing, and Difference*. Ed. Henry Louis Gates Jr. Chicago: U of Chicago P, 1986. 21–37.

Baldwin, James. *Go Tell It on the Mountain*. 1952. New York: The Modern Library, 1995.

Baker, Lisa. "Storytelling and Democracy (in the Radical Sense): A Conversation with John
Edgar Wideman." *African American Review* 34 (2000): 263–72. *Proquest* 20 Feb. 2002.

Bakhtin, M. M. *The Dialogic Imagination*. Ed. Michael Holquist. Trans. Caryl Emerson
and Michael Holquist. Austin: U of Texas P, 1981.

Beckett, Samuel. *Nohow On*. New York: Grove Press, 1980.

Benjamin, Walter. *Illuminations*. Ed. Hannah Arendt. Trans. Harry Zohn. New York:
Schocken Books, 1968.

Bhabha, Homi K. *The Location of Culture*. London, New York: Routledge, 1994.

Birat, Kathie. "'All Stories Are True': Prophecy, History, and Story in *The Cattle Killing*."
Callaloo. 22.3 (1999): 629–43. *Project Muse* 20 Feb. 2002. < http:// Muse.jhu.edu/
journals/callaloo/v022/22.3birat.html>.

Frost, Robert. "The Figure a Poem Makes." *Collected Poems, Prose, & Plays.* New York: The Library of America, 1995. 776–78.

Gysin, Fritz. "'Do Not Fall Asleep in Your Enemy's Dream': John Edgar Wideman and the Predicaments of Prophecy." *Callaloo.* 22.3 (1999): 623–28. *Project Muse* 20 Feb. 2002. <http:// Muse.jhu.edu/journals/callaloo/v022/22.3gysin01.html>.

Hall, Stuart. "Ethnicity: Identity and Difference." *Radical America.* 23.4 (1989): 9–20.

————. "On Postmodernism and Articulation: An Interview with Stuart Hall." Ed. Lawrence Grossberg. *Critical Dialogues in Cultural Studies.* New York: Routledge, 1996. 131–50.

Hebdige, Dick. *Hiding in the Light.* New York: Routledge, 1988.

Jameson, Fredric. "Postmodernism, or the Cultural Logic of Late Capitalism." *Postmodernism: A Reader.* Ed. Thomas Docherty. New York: Columbia UP, 1993. 62–92.

Keenan, Thomas. "Windows: of Vulnerability." *The Phantom Public Sphere.* Ed. Bruce Robbins. Minneapolis: U of Minnesota P, 1993. 121–41.

Lubiano, Wahneema. "Shuckin' Off the African-American Native Other: What's 'Po-Mo' Got to Do with It?" *Cultural Critique* 18 (Spring 1991): 149–86.

Orentas, Rimas J. "George Whitefield: Lightning Rod of the Great Awakening." 24 Apr. 2002. <http://dylee.keel.econ.ship.edu/UBF/leaders/whitfild.htm>.

Outlaw, Lucius. "Toward a Critical Theory of 'Race.'" *Anatomy of Racism.* Ed. David Theo Goldberg. Minneapolis: U of Minnesota P, 1990. 58–79.

Welty, Eudora. *The Eye of the Story: Selected Essays and Reviews.* London: Virago, 1987.

Wideman, John Edgar. *The Cattle Killing.* Boston: Houghton Mifflin, 1996.

"Ill Seen Ill Said"

"And the Arc of His Witness Explained Nothing"

BLACK FLANERIE AND TRAUMATIC PHOTOREALISM IN WIDEMAN'S *TWO CITIES*

TYRONE R. SIMPSON II

> VISIBILITY [IS] A COMPLEX SYSTEM OF PERMISSION AND PROHIBITION PUNCTUATED ALTERNATELY BY APPARITIONS AND HYSTERICAL BLINDNESS.
>
> AVERY GORDON, *GHOSTLY MATTERS: HAUNTING AND THE SOCIOLOGICAL IMAGINATION*

> WHY DID EVIL PROSPER ROUND HERE AND CHILDREN DIE.
>
> JOHN EDGAR WIDEMAN, *TWO CITIES*

An elderly black photographer's decadent revel in words as accurate carriers of meaning inaugurates John Edgar Wideman's *Two Cities*. Dictionary in hand, Martin Mallory, one of the novel's traumatized protagonists, confirms that the definition of the word "zoo" resonates with the images and ideas about urban ghettoization that he harbors in his head. The anonymous narrator tells us, "The words tell him what he supposed they would.... He liked it like that. When words led him into a familiar place" (1). Mallory's peculiar meditation on the term "zoo" begs questions. What set of circumstances could have occasioned this private relish in the English language? Why would momentary proof that language provides a reliable technology of meaning grant Mallory such comfort? The narrative later demonstrates that its protagonist is a perspicacious one, uniquely hip to the philosophical challenges that the era of postmodernism presents peoples of the West. According to cultural theorists, this is an epoch in which we have found our grand metanarratives wanting—particularly in how these universalizing concepts disciplined people of color and women—and the epistemological fragmentation that has seemingly ensued as a result suggests that there never was a common cultural code through which we could manufacture a consensus about reality.[1] As well, if we rely on the observations of Fredric Jameson, we languish in a schizophrenic condition. Advances in communication technology and the needs of Capital to bombard subjects with images that may motivate them to consume have instilled a fetishistic preoccupation with signifiers and surfaces which obscure all processes that enable their existence. This same schizophrenia destabilizes our sense of history and cultural memory. Though contemporary cultural production acknowledges the archive and sometimes pillages it in moments of creative desperation, its use of the past is a disemboweling one, a habit that violently decontextualizes artifacts out of historical significance and legibility. That signs are ruptured, that signifiers seem so profoundly alienated from their signifieds in the cultural arena, may explain Mallory's appreciation of a small, discrete moment in which a word possessed a more harmonious relationship with its referent.

The efficient transport to the familiar that "zoo" provides elates Mallory because of his need to represent the complex material processes that have contributed to urban ghettoization—a task that serves as both his mission and challenge. Concomitant with the philosophical crisis that postmodernism has ushered forth are the geopolitical ravages affected by postmodernity. We may characterize the attitudinal shift among modern and postmodern urban planners as one in which utopic pretension has given way to brazen pragmatism. Though the utilitarian aspirations of modern urban design brought us vast development tracts of housing projects, they could still claim that good intentions constituted the character of their architectural motivations. Modern designers did not seek to isolate, marginalize, and squeeze the residential spaces of the metropolitan poor with the racist and agoraphobic aggression that motivates city planning today. Structural apartheid in Western metropolises has become so acute that Los Angeles historian Mike Davis criticizes present discourse regarding the city for being "strangely

"And the Arc of His Witness Explained Nothing"

silent about the militarization of city life so grimly visible at the street level" (223). In an attempt to "get things right" (13), to understand why metropolitan power has waged cold war on the urban poor, and to capture its traumatizing effects on ghetto inhabitants, Mallory's small celebration of "zoo" reads as the equivalent of a soldier savoring a sumptuous feast before marching into battle.

Indeed, his gratitude toward the word's accuracy underscores how important the issue of representation will be to the project of the novel and anticipates the euphoria he will experience if fortunate enough to achieve his representational goals. But it is also a final salutation, a mournful concession that words are incapable of accurately representing the realities with which he is concerned. His pessimistic view leads him later in the novel to muse over "the way words fooled you into believing you could say the very thing you mean" (189). Mallory leaves the novel's exposition convinced that no serendipitous encounters with language await him in the future and that some other medium must meet his representational ambitions in its stead.

Taking Mallory's attitude of futility toward language as a cue, this essay meditates on the three existential challenges that *Two Cities* proposes, confronts, and hopes to overcome. First, since epidermal blackness has been an invitation for racialized injury and oppression throughout the history of the United States, what incident may count as *the* defining trauma in the life of a particular black male subject? Second, how does a traumatized black male subject testify to the trauma he and other ghetto residents have sustained when the structure of trauma itself frustrates its own representability? Third, how does this black male subject represent trauma—despite its resistance to representation—amidst a philosophical climate that he feels is rightly circumspect towards technologies of representation, memory, and reference? In exploring these issues, I demonstrate how the mobility of the black body through metropolitan space—the very movement that contemporary U.S. urban structures seek to impair—serves as a prerequisite for any testament to black urban trauma that Mallory may offer. By peregrinating through Philadelphia and Pittsburgh and taking pictures of all that he sees, the protagonist breaks with a Western tradition of urban walking, observing, and representing known as *flanerie*. In addition, I show that among the myriad traumatic experiences Mallory has had to overcome, his witnessing the murder of a fellow black soldier, Gus, during World War II functions as the foundational trauma the protagonist feels compelled to symbolize for himself and for other black urban Pennsylvanians. The compulsion to witness Gus's death moves Mallory to abandon language in favor of the more realist representational technology of photography, whereby his stylized form of picture taking—a style that scholars have called "traumatic realism"—constitutes only a partially referential representational practice. Through this traumatic photorealism, Mallory not only draws a parallel between his injury and those of other black urban Pennsylvanians who subsist in ghettoized conditions, but he also creates a visual memorial that engenders communal self-reflection. Not unlike the photographs of a tortured and murdered Emmett Till and the enraged African American protest that emerged in response to them, Mallory's photographic enterprise hopes to break the cycle of trauma that is often bequeathed to ghetto youth and inculcate an emboldened sense of responsibility among its viewers to resist race-based oppression.

●●●
●●●

My attention to Martin Mallory and his representational exploits departs from what the novel's subtitle—"A Love Story"—suggests its primary concern to be. The subtitle has encouraged writer Walter Mosley to observe, "the story is simple enough: boy meets girl, boy loses girl, etc." (12). This claim arises from the novel's troubled romance between Robert Jones, a fifty-year-old divorcee, and Kassima, a thirty-five-year-old widow who has lost two sons to gang violence and a husband to prison and AIDS. In the middle of the tale, Kassima leaves Robert, hoping to avoid the trauma of losing another black man to the horror of the streets. However, evidence of the subtitle's subterfuge or polysemy lies in how Mallory's struggle with the issue of representation starts and ends the novel. In addition to Mallory's private celebration of accurate signifiers, we learn in the introductory chapter that Mallory is haunted by the death of John Africa, a character named for and based on the very real leader of a predominantly black "back-to-nature" militant group known as MOVE (short for "the movement"). Mallory mourns the murder of John Africa which, inside and outside the fictional universe of the novel, occurred at the hands of the police, and wrestles with the meaning of this assassination as it relates to him and to the black neighborhood in Philadelphia where it took place. The novel's closing chapter finds Kassima and Robert burdened with the charge of holding a funeral for Mallory, who was a boarder in Kassima's house, and determining whether to burn or publicly reveal the late tenant's pictures of the community. In addition to framing the narrative's content, Mallory appears several times throughout the novel: to lament his abandonment of his wife and children, to listen to the tales of Kassima's woeful past, to narrate his stint of military service in Italy during World War II, to correspond with the Swiss Surrealist sculptor Alberto Giacometti about representational theory, to listen to a restaurant owner tell the story of his son's imprisonment, and to discuss MOVE's resistant tactics against the police with his friend, John Africa. In short, if love and romance constitute the thematic center of *Two Cities*, the most ardent affection lies between Mallory and the aggrieved black residents of Pennsylvania's

"And the Arc of His Witness Explained Nothing"

largest urban regions. To look at Mallory as marginal to the diegesis of the novel would be a significant misrecognition.

Though the matter of which character assumes primacy within the novel may spark hefty debate, most observers would agree that these personages exist for the grander purpose of limning ghettoization under the spatial regime of post-modernity. As sociologist William Goldsmith observes, "the standard, one must say approved, condition for African Americans in US cities is to live in racially homogeneous neighborhoods" (40). Not lost on Mallory, Kassima, or Robert is the understanding that the ghetto is a racial phenomenon—an urban socio-structural feature that many in the United States see as part of the natural geographic order. Robert comments on this matter when registering his observations about the black boys enlisted in local gang warfare: "they die for the color of their skin, the color that is [Robert's] color. . . . Color keeping them here, passing each other on the streets" (223). If blackness, as Robert suggests, renders urban bodies inert and makes them susceptible to the ritualistic carnage of ghetto violence, then physical mobility becomes the crucial commodity by which black subjects can pursue their own social safety and political viability.

It is indisputable that John Africa's MOVE organization sees mobility as a weapon of political resistance. For the outspoken leader, the ghetto simply extends the immobilizing logic of racial identity. Africa complains that the "mostly white" urban power structure that runs Philadelphia has "a picture of African people locked up in their minds and nothing's gon change it" (229). The immutable logic that phenotypic blackness signals certain subterranean truths about the human body encased within it has shaped oppressive social policies that harm black life. In response, John Africa demonstrates that the organization's name is not simply an abbreviation of its full name. He criticizes local blacks for "staying put where they put us" and insists that "Move's about not standing still. Move's about biting the damned hand that calls itself feeding us" (229).

That the MOVE leader would befriend the protagonist is not surprising because, despite his less communal sensibilities, Mallory's behavior shows that he shares Africa's commitment to movement. Evidence of the war veteran's investment in mobility lies in the final word Mallory seeks in his forage through the diction-ary during the novel's exposition. "Zugunruhe," a German word that means "the migratory drive," identifies the principle that organizes the ex-soldier's entire life. The protagonist remarks regretfully on this during a conversation with Kassima in which he rationalizes abandoning his wife and children in favor of the army. He states, "No choice. Believed I had to leave if I wanted a life. Stole myself. Like a runaway slave. Stole myself and the price was leaving my family behind, my people behind" (107).

Invoking all the imagery of African fugitives stealing away from enslavement in the antebellum South, Mallory indicts the very behavior he repeats to forestall the depredations of the urban ghetto and its resulting nihilism. We later learn that Mallory's mobility enables the war veteran to negotiate the ghetto psychically while dwelling in its clutches. By the end of the novel, there is no doubt that due to "a lot of walking alone," Mr. Mallory has "trekked all over the city" (227). This aggressive ambulation, despite suffering a war injury that left him with a "leg he [wouldn't] ever be able to depend on again" (196), is quite an accomplishment and bespeaks the extent of Mallory's resistance to the racialization of urban space. In familiarizing himself with the urban maze, he fulfills Michel De Certeau's vision of resistant perambulatory practices by which to craft a critical hermeneutic about metropolitan power.

According to geographer Steve Pile, a specific type of urban walking and observing—the perceptive stroll of the *flaneur* rather than the surveillant march of the constable—inspired De Certeau's famous essay, "Walking in the City," because of their potential transgressiveness (Pile 228). The French critic would have been quite enthused about the model of *flanerie* that Mallory offers because the protagonist does not acquiesce to commodity culture as did his nineteenth-century predecessor. Critics agree that the emergence of the *flaneur* coincided with the birth of the modern metropolis in the mid-1800s. Specifically, Charles Baudelaire's collection of poems, *Paris Spleen* (1859)—and later Walter Benjamin's critical assessment of the poet's movements and writings—brought the habits of *flanerie* into scholarly purview (Tester 1).

A composite sketch of the *flaneur* reveals an anonymous, near-disembodied, leisurely male observer-journalist traversing the city streets in the interest of identifying what features and behaviors constituted the urban. In performing and evaluating Parisian *flanerie*, Baudelaire and Benjamin both sought, according to Keith Tester, "the meaning of modernity" for the various Western peoples experiencing it (1). This is the very puzzle Mallory wishes to solve, since virtually every stage of modernity has meant misery for black life. In a lamentable reflection on a moment when Mallory watched his former wife from afar without being detected, the narrator comments on an optic obsession that marks him as the essential *flaneur*:

> And what might he see in her brown eyes. Himself dead too. Why was he drawn to the secrets behind other people's eyes, other people's windows. . . . See them without being seen. Hovering, floating outside in the empty dark, did he spy on people's private lives because he couldn't imagine such a life for himself, a body and feelings anchored, touching, being touched. (85)

Despite the poignant manner in which the narrator accounts for Mallory's flanerie, Benjamin would have been the first to argue that such a passage could not exist in postmodern literature. Benjamin predicted that, because of the total penetration of capital, the lording of the rational over all material culture, and the predominance of the commodity form in the West, "there would be no spaces of mystery for the flaneur to observe" (Tester 13). With everything rationalized under capital, the meaning-making endeavors of the urban walker would be unnecessary. Benjamin's oracle was incapable of anticipating how capital would restructure itself in the era of globalization and the myriad ways uneven development would become manifest on the urban landscape. With the divestment from and deindustrialization of several U.S. cities, there are certain urban pockets that capital has abandoned or treats with indifference. Both Mallory's black Pittsburgh and Philadelphia are results of such economic marginalization. Thus, the acute spatial otherness of these ghettoes extends the life of the *flaneur* in the figure of Mallory.

But the extension of the *flaneur* into the era of postmodernity is not mimetic. Mallory possesses a class sensibility that starkly rivals that of Baudelaire. Scholarship on the *flaneur* demonstrates that he labored in the service of the bourgeois class with which he identified. First, as Tester observes, idleness and strolling are two key ingredients for successful *flanerie*. The *flaneur* sustained his leisure by commodifying his ethnographies as tales for sale. Thus, his accounts of the city sought an audience capable of purchasing such writings—the middle class—and were very sensitive to the needs of such an audience. Second, Susan Buck-Morss notes that the *flaneur*'s reportage aimed at domesticating the unpredictable social arena of public space and assuring middle-class readers that only passive observation was necessary to understand urban life (103). According to David Frisby, the *feuilleton* pieces (newspaper sketches) used caricature to eviscerate the seeming threat of "the dangerous classes" to make the city appear friendlier to bourgeois adventure. Though Baudelaire appeared "capable of grasping concrete historical experience," the poet would depict the tribulations of laborers without offering any "knowledge that could change the situation" (Frisby 96; Buck-Morss 110). These critical observations paint the picture of a *litterateur* bent on buoying the social esteem of the bourgeoisie while profiting from the organic spectacles that emerged from the travails of the urban working class.

Mallory is literally a *flaneur* of a different color. The U.S. government, through the pension promised him as a former military serviceman, furnishes the photographer's leisure. As well, Mallory's reportage—the photographic image—is not a commodified enterprise or a product of passive inspection. The medium, as I elaborate upon later, enables him to pursue a personal as well as a public crusade.

A remark in one of his epistles to the sculptor Giacometti makes clear the war veteran's desire to wield the camera as a weapon of meaning: "My pictures are pretty postcards with the world arranged nice and neat. But I don't want to hide the damage. I want to enter the wound, cut through layer by layer like a surgeon, expose what lies beneath the skin" (119). Mallory pursues ghetto images to develop what Wideman calls the vitally necessary "seventh sense" of urban African Americans (Wideman, *Brothers and Keepers* 221). Mallory walks the streets so he can learn "to see the invisible prison" (146) of the two "inner cities" he has called home. He becomes pessimistic about his representational project not because of the pictures' modest market value but because he deems it inadequate. After his death, Kassima confesses to Robert, "[Mr. Mallory] made me promise. And promise not to look. Nothing to see he said. Negatives, he said. Just burn them" (111).

Beyond being reluctant about his photographs' display, Mallory does not intend his aesthetic labor to sate the consumptive desires of bourgeois viewers who more than likely reside well beyond the boundaries of the ghetto. When the photographer says that he wants to "free others to free themselves" (119), he is not merely referencing the surrealistic interplay of images he hopes a viewer would encounter in his photographs. He is also alluding to the emancipatory effect these pictures would have on a black urban audience. Mallory wants to visually set loose the people and events of this marginal space in a way that would disrupt their sojourn on the social margin.

• • •
• • •

The progression of the narrative, if one can call it such, demonstrates that a close reading of *Two Cities* is not necessary to identify psychic trauma as the organizing dynamic of the story. Similar to other instances of U.S. postmodern fiction, *Two Cities* is a universe in temporal chaos—a condition clinicians and theorists understand as a traumatic symptom. Mallory dies halfway through the novel, only to reign triumphant as a corpse in the denouement. Moreover, one can argue that the novel's temporal development perishes at the behest of this scarred and disoriented hero, Mallory, who is the story's primary preoccupation. In their meditation on how traumatic memories are engraved upon the human psyche, two psychologists observe that the traumatized subject "live[s] out [its existence] in two different stages of the life cycle, the traumatic past, and the bleached present" (Van Der Kolk 177). The novel's exposition points to physical symptoms of the hero that should cause any observer some concern:

> They're coming more often. These strange, dizzy pauses in the middle of what
> he's supposed to be doing, brushing his teeth, strolling across a bridge. . . . You're

"And the Arc of His Witness Explained Nothing"

dizzy because you're in two places at once or too many places. . . . The map in your head, your hands, the million pictures your eyes snap to guide your feet and ears and lungs are blurred. Ten maps at once or no map. (12)

Clearly, Mallory has lost touch with his internal compass and has become incapable of competently shepherding his body through time and space. His condition is serious and made more ominous because he seems to possess no resources to discern the temporal and spatial differences among the events of his life or explain why they confuse him. The narrator expands on Mallory's dilemma later in the exposition:

Everything connects and nothing connects. Two simple truths and each made perfect sense on its own but together they mystified him. Once upon a time he'd stood on the Spring Garden Street Bridge with John Africa. Today he's in another city, alone in a room on Cassina Way. . . . And the arc of his witness explained nothing, brought him no closer to solving the puzzle, the truth of a moment lived then, the truth of another moment lived now, and him always muddling somewhere in between, becoming a stranger to himself. . . . (7)

Here, the indiscernibility between one's past and one's present, the sense of subsisting in between time, the paralyzing aphasia, the difficulty of organizing the events of one's life into a coherent progressive narrative, the compulsion to witness—these are classic symptoms of traumatized subjectivity. As Cathy Caruth observes in her definitive work, *Unclaimed Experience*, trauma is "a break in the mind's experience of time" (61). That Mallory continually confuses the narrative of his life evinces some psychic wound from which the protagonist is unable to heal.

Though there are several experiences that make Mallory's life a painful one, *Two Cities* suggests that the protagonist's most profound emotional injury occurred as an American soldier in Italy during World War II. His tour of duty is initially bearable because a fellow black urban Pennsylvanian, Gus, is a member of his company. Unfortunately for the two soldiers, they learn that the crusade against Hitler has done little to improve flesh politics within the American army. The men plot a sexual rendezvous with two local women, only to become the doomed quarry of their fellow soldiers who seek to penalize the duo's miscegenating practices with the ultimate discipline. The gunfire kills Gus and the two women, but Mallory's luck allows him to escape with only a mangled leg. The narrator recounts his arrival to the safety of his platoon:

Not his night to die. Somehow he hobbles and crawls back to the road where his gang is working and his home boys truck him to base and blame a sneaky fucking

Nazi sniper. Neat enough lie to get everybody off the hook he tells John Africa. You know. Something like enemy activity reported at blah blah hour in sector blah-blah. In separate incidents one U.S. soldier KIA, one wounded, two civilians dead from enemy fire blah, blah, blah. . . . Same dying. Same lies to cover it up. Same clean slate. So true it's past true. . . . (197)

According to Caruth, what makes an experience traumatic is "the way it was precisely not known in the first instance" (4). An event injures a person because it is so shocking, sudden, and unexpected that the subject is incapable of understanding what is happening to her/him at the time that it occurs. The immediate incomprehensibility of the event often results in the past interrupting the present through flashbacks and nightmares as the psyche attempts to assimilate what has transpired. Moreover, mental relief can only come at a point where the victim is able to locate what Caruth figures as a "wound that cries out," a material symbol that gives testament to the traumatic occurrence.

Under these conditions, Mallory should have long ago thrown this incident into the dustbin of his own personal history. He was aware when the ambusher's bullet penetrated his leg. Additionally, the resulting gimp serves as a symbolic reminder of the horror of that event. However, critical traumatic material that accompanies his physical injury evades symbolization. For instance, without the privilege of his letter to Giacometti or the testimony of the omniscient narrator, the violent policing of racial apartheid as figured in the murders of Gus and the Italian women and the reality that this sociosexual boundary extends beyond American borders would remain unrepresented. Moreover, the mendacious narrative that the American army concocts about this racist assault seeks to forestall such a discrediting narrative about the military from becoming public. Quite simply, the essence of his trauma lies not in the crippling bullet wound to his leg but in witnessing the lynching of a black man and two European women who engage in cross-racial, consensual sex. Thus, well before the postmodern epoch, Mallory experiences a crisis in representation—one that emerges from the military's treacherous manipulation of words in accounting for his injury. It is not surprising, then, that Mallory comes to repudiate language as an imprecise medium later in life; nor is it surprising that knowledge of the attack in Italy cannot transcend the boundaries of his own psyche. The army veteran refers to the incident in a confessional footnote of a letter he writes to a dead man—a modest testimonial gesture that seems more the equivalent of a journal entry or a traumatic remembrance recounted to himself.[2] Readers learn of the assault through the narrator's enigmatic report in the latter portion of the novel. Thus, Mallory's body and mind fail to give evidence to the decidedly racial trauma that he experienced—a trauma that proceeds throughout the novel unsymbolized, warranting psychic literalization.

• • •
• • •

The material and psychic obstacles that work to prevent Mallory from witnessing the trauma by no means lessens his compulsion to narrate the traumatic event. Clinician Dori Laub asserts that "there is, in each [trauma] survivor, an imperative need to *tell* and thus to come to *know* one's story" (63). Unfortunately, the protagonist must overcome a formidable handicap to fulfill the responsibility trauma has bequeathed him. His circumspection toward the representational capacity of language, partly prompted by the army's subterfuge, leaves him with one less medium upon which he could rely to tell his tale. The desperation that comes with being dispossessed of this communicative tool may explain Mallory's epistolary remark to Giacometti that "[i]n the hills of Italy I decided to become a photographer" (178). That the war can make a photographer out of Mallory suggests that he has found a substitute for the untrustworthy linguistic forms of communication.

Yet, Mallory's embrace of photography may have as much to do with issues of reception as they do with matters of presentation. According to Jacqueline Goldsby, Americans were becoming inured to the hypnotic power of representational media and the images it circulated even before World War II. As far back as 1937, Goldsby notes, John Dos Passos, a novelist for whom the merits and demerits of mass media took on a peculiar fascination, declared Americans "an eye-minded people" (254). The long tradition of photography and its subsequent culmination in the form of television in the mid-twentieth century changed the perceptual and, thus, the epistemological propensities of peoples in the United States. More recently, critic Susan Sontag suggested that American eye-mindedness has enabled the photograph to arrogate full hegemony over how people process their interface with reality. Sontag ventured, "Ultimately having an experience becomes identical to taking a photograph of it, and participating in a public event comes more and more to be equivalent to looking at it in photograph form" (24). Mallory may be anxiously aware of the risks of traumatic testimony in postwar America. We may see Mallory's new allegiance to the photograph, then, as a strategic representational ploy to maximize the audience that can receive and believe his testimony about his traumatic encounter with American racism.

Unfortunately, the imaginary correspondence Mallory has with Giacometti occurs not merely for the hero to reveal repressed memories, but for him to air the lack of certainty he (as well as the author) holds towards photography's mimetic potential. Alberto Giacometti (1901–1966), a Swiss-born sculptor and painter, aligned himself firmly with the Parisian Surrealist movement in the early 1920s. In the process of developing his craft, he arrived at the insight that it was impossible for art in any way to correspond to sight. He believed that the moment the artist turned his eyes away from his object, he was relying on memory rather than vision. This "practical phenomenology of perception" that critic Willy Rotzler suggests Giacometti strove to develop has a profound impact on Mallory's representational philosophy (16). In short, the protagonist concedes that he cannot pin his mimetic hopes on his photographic practice. He capitulates to this idea in his first letter to the artist:

> When my photos were developed, I found little or no trace of what I thought I'd seen before I snapped the shutter. I learned from you to expect disappointment. You admitted failure, even welcomed it. Said it's impossible to copy a world that never stops changing. Seeing is Freedom, you said. Art fakes and freezes seeing. Artists can't copy what they see, you said. . . . Should I stop asking my pictures to be mirrors. (82)

According to both Mallory and Giacometti, representation effaces some of what was present in the object before mediation. This limitation poses a unique challenge for witnesses like Mallory who hope to represent their own trauma. Marianne Hirsch offers such a caveat in her work on Holocaust photographs. She stipulates that such horrific pictures "cannot in any way claim to represent, in the sense be commensurate with, the crime it purportedly depicts" (Hirsch 14). The alleged antidote to language's representational volatility proves to be another unstable medium. Mallory becomes a friend of the camera while aware that his new accomplice will make his traumatic testimony only slightly easier to effect.

Another factor that threatens to undermine Mallory's testimony is the problem of what precisely should be the content of his photographs. If the war veteran relied on language to narrativize his trauma, then the object would be clear: he would strive to write or verbalize the tale of the army's murderous assault on him and his friends. But through the visual register, a photographer can only *show* existential damage, not *tell* it. Since time has abducted the tangible materials that could serve as testimonial images (i.e., decaying corpses) to Mallory's pain, the hero has nothing to put on display. What then could be the content of his photographs? What images would aptly correspond to the exploits of a military lynch mob?

I want to argue that Mallory fills in the blanks of his photographic mise-en-scène with the logical extension of the lynching ritual: the postmodern urban ghetto and the discipline it exerts on black life and mobility. If the objective of white supremacy as manifested in the lynching ritual is to maintain a prophylactic border between whiteness and blackness, then one of its primary charges must be to keep white women out of the carnal clutches of black men. This directive costs Gus, Gina, and Francesca (the two Italian women) their lives. Additionally, if law and moral opinion anathematize such white vigilantism, then the proxemic requirements of racial hierarchy necessitate spatial structures to consummate the deeds that violence cannot. Thus, urban segregation is a sublimation of the desire to keep black men and white women separated.

This is certainly the opinion of geographer Heidi Nast, who uses psychoanalysis to demonstrate how the security of the white Western nuclear family has always depended on the control of black male bodies. Nast submits that the West has organized its social spaces to meet the unconscious demands of "racist oedipalization," in which the incest taboo requires the white patriarch to prevent the coupling of his wife and his black "son" (the latter became a ward of the white father by colonial/slave laws that deprived black men of their rights to property and citizenship). Using the city of Chicago as a test case, Nast finds that "racist imaginary-symbolic renderings of black men as rapists were critical to urban renewal in the U.S." (231). It stands to reason that if the ghetto is the spatial sublimation of lynch logic, Mallory's photographic representation of the ghetto would capture vestiges of the trauma that he endured and give some account of the long historical trajectory by which American racism has evolved. He would be aligning his injury with the grander, less visible structures of racial oppression that daily beset urban African Americans. The hero's commentary after another dizzying flashback to the moments immediately after the MOVE assassination demonstrates that he senses the resonance between his past victimization and that of other contemporary metropolitan blacks:

> Would all the young men he saw nowadays in the city streets, the ones whose stories he'd tried to take pictures of, *whose stories were his and his story theirs,* so thick, so thin, piled one atop the other, would they all wind up sooner or later . . . in prison if they didn't wind up dead. Young men yet there seemed to be more than one generation of them tangled up in this misery. (174, italics mine)

In Mallory's mind, the misery that mires him and these black boys is too austere for the abstraction language and numbers perform upon it. Photography seems to be a final, desperate resort to produce a form of testimony that translates his own personal healing into a communal affirmation of the unacknowledged suffering through which urban black Pennsylvanians are surviving.

That Mallory seeks his own healing through that of the community reveals the organizing unconscious of the novel and another reason that photographs become the crucial medium through which he pursues his redemptive ends. Consistent with his temporal dizziness, Mallory wishes to deeply imbricate the past with the present of black urban Pennsylvanians. The protagonist hopes to revisit a moment in which pictures engendered nationalistic cohesion and political activity: namely, the Emmett Till murder. Wideman has admitted that the murder of Emmett Till has a lingering impact on his psychic life. He begins his 1997 essay, "The Killing of Black Boys," with the pronouncement that "A dead black boy named Emmett Till continues to bear witness to a society that murders its children of color again and again" (Wideman, "Killing" 1). He then proceeds to detail a nightmare he himself continues to have about a monster, in the form of Emmett Till, chasing him through his old Homewood neighborhood in Pittsburgh. The opening moments of this essay reterritorializes a southern rural act of traumatizing terror to the urban North, connects Till's mid-century death to contemporary black male victimization, and underscores the importance of witnessing this past event.

Through Till's recurring, near-ghostly appearance in *Two Cities*, the novel accomplishes the three very same gestures as the essay. In fact, one can argue that Till's appearance cleaves the story into quarters.[3] The significance of Till's (un)timely sightings throughout the story is that the circumstances and results of his slaughter mirror the trajectory of events through which Mallory hopes to process his own originary trauma. Till met his demise through a lynching—an act of violence aimed at disciplining cross-racial sexual desire. Mallory's friend, Gus, is guilty of the same crime and meets the same fate. Moreover, Till's gruesome death generates horrific photographs that subsequently galvanize and nationalize the struggle for black equality in the United States. Mallory seeks to have Gus's death do the same for black Pennsylvanians. It is also the photograph of Till's open casket in the September 1955 issue of *Jet* magazine that tilted African Americans into indignation and dauntless protest. Quoting David Halberstam, Jacqueline Goldsby notes that the murder of Till and the trial of his attackers "became the first great media event of the civil rights movement" (254). Goldsby also observes that the NAACP posted records in collected donations and registered members that year (254). Thus, when Mallory states his hope that his "pictures will remind people to keep a world alive around them, to keep themselves alive at the center of a storm of swirling emptiness" (91), he expresses a desire for his photographic memorial to positively influence blacks as the *Jet* magazine photo did. He wishes his pictures to parry away the inevitable nihilism that consumes the inhabitants of an environment so burdened with death and misery. He produces the photographs to provide a witness to his own suffering; to account for a particular national, postwar history of black male trauma (that connects

Gus, Till, John Africa, and urban gangbanging) and the pain it has caused the community; and to legislate against the political amnesia that would allow these acts and their resulting emotions to go unaddressed.

• • •
• • •

Mallory's desire to create a coherent photographic narrative of postwar black male victimization cannot be fulfilled without his finding a resolution between his trauma's demand for representation and representation's alienation from mimetic reference. If our eyes, as Mallory submits, take evanescent snapshots of reality that "disappear instantly, leaving no trace behind" (91), how do we document our world? How do we capture—and most importantly, reproduce—the full essence of a moment that only presents itself to us in that millisecond in which it is manifest? Moreover, how does Mallory record a traumatic moment for which he provided inadequate witness shortly after it happened? How does he visually resurrect a moment that is profoundly lost, a moment that time and psychic damage has rendered unrecoverable, regardless of the form of mediation he uses? Taking Giacometti's tutelage and his own circumspection about perception to heart, Mallory creates a photographic method that desperately pursues the ever-absconding referent. He describes his practice in a second letter to his adopted surrealist mentor:

> I want people to see my pictures from various angles, see the image I offer as many images, one among countless ways of seeing, so the more they look, the more there is to see. A density of appearances my goal, Mr. Giacometti. So I snap, snap, snap. Pile on layer after layer. A hundred doses of light without moving the film. No single, special, secret view sought or revealed. One in many. Many in one. (91)

His closest friend, Kassima, compliments Mallory on his photographs of people in the community, noting, "Not just anybody could take pictures of how people feel inside. He was a special man" (210). But neither Kassima nor Mallory recognize the extent to which his photographic method of "shooting and not allowing the film to advance" (175) evinces his traumatized condition and provides a means of representation that partially solves the conundrum of reference. According to Hirsch, the obsessive repetition that characterizes Mallory's photographic approach is a "traumatic fixation," a form of artistic behavior that resembles how traumatic episodes revisit the consciousness of its victims (29). But as surrealism aficionado Hal Foster theorizes, this proclivity is precisely what enables Mallory's art to approximate a reference to the trauma he hopes his photographs represent. Foster argues that the traumatic material addresses its audience "less through content than through technique" (132). While Mallory's repetition screens the traumatic objects from view, it simultaneously reveals the effects of trauma. Providing evidence that a trauma has occurred, his pictures create an opportunity to narrativize his past injury and thus heal from its effects (Hirsch 8). Through this "traumatic realism," as Michael Rothberg calls it, Mallory submits his past "as an object of knowledge" that allows him and his neighbors in Pittsburgh to analyze, process, and possibly understand the violence of lynching and its spatial reincarnation, the postmodern ghetto (140).

Unfortunately for the audacious cameraman, time proves itself uncooperative again. Mallory dies before he heals. More lamentably, even though he does print a set of photographs that he has taken of others, he buckles under the same nihilism that he seemed sworn to resist. In instructing Kassima to burn the photographs, Mallory threatens to undermine his photographic project and turn his *flanerie* into a monologue of the eternally mute. This is surprising because Mallory himself likened his craft to that of a blues musician. In a conversation he had with John Africa, Mallory admits that fears about his photographs' lack of reference moves the cameraman to keep his pictures secret. He fails to realize that his traumatic realism should put his anxiety about reference to rest and that his testimony, like any other bluesman, needs a listener. Hirsch observes that critical to the phenomenon of trauma and its healing is the "intersubjective relation" they engender, or, as Caruth states, their capacity to lead one to "an encounter with another" (Hirsch 12; Caruth 8). Fortunately for Mallory, he acquires Kassima, the final intimate friend of his life. Kassima's friendship with Mallory and the intimacy they achieved by "talk, talk, talk[ing] about everything" (115) creates a connection that prevents her from destroying his work as he requested. Ironically, then, by defying Mallory's last will, Kassima preserves his only testament. Since the pictures survive, the possibility of the community's healing and redemption remains intact.

The culmination of Mallory's representational endeavors occurs at the end of the novel. This episode marks the one moment in which the time of the novel and the stage of the story seem commensurate—thus suggesting a potential healing. Robert and Kassima arrange a modest funeral for Mallory on the same day that a local teenage gang holds a service for one of their fallen comrades. This coincidence does not become significant until the rival gang decides that the murdered boy is not dead enough. Intent on disrespecting their opponents, the rioting gang rushes the funeral home and steals two caskets—one with the body of the opposing gang member, the other with that of the deceased Mallory. As the gang defaces both corpses in the streets, Kassima deploys her own voice and Mallory's art to quell the madness. She dumps the pictures at the feet of Mallory's lifeless body and exclaims, "Look. Look what you've done to him. Look what you done to yourselves. Look. Look" (238). Apparently, the private conversations she had with the deceased photographer before he died equipped her with insight into his artistic intent. In addition, she reports having "talked, [and] preached" (238) to the assembly, providing the pictures with an interpretative, sermonic score to give voice to the otherwise inarticulate images. This spontaneous hardscrabble picture gallery has a mesmerizing effect on the belligerents. Kassima notes, "Then some of them started . . . picking up pictures, looking at them, looking at each other, handing them around, talking, walking off with the pictures in their hands. . . . And that was the beginning of the end of the worst part of that day" (239).

Defying the aesthetic infertility that characterizes ghettoized space, Mallory's photographs create a sacred environment out of the otherwise infernal urban blacktop. The postmortem pictorial supplies the stained-glass imagery to the urban church that his art has spontaneously erected in the streets. Yet the pictures' ability to stimulate serious contemplation is not only made by the moment or Kassima's impassioned soliloquy, but by the particular objects Mallory tried to capture through this form.

As opposed to most photographs of, say, a family album, the pictures do not hearken back to a distant past or feature distant beings. The photographs capture in plastic the very people who constitute its audience, not those ancestors (like Till, Africa, Gus) whom racism and violence destroy. Thus, these viewers cannot echo Sontag's postulation that "photographs . . . haunt us" with the same ardor as the theorist because Mallory's pictures allow them to be their own ghosts (89). By making refractive mirrors rather than phantoms out of his photographs, Mallory disrupts the hauntings and traumatic cycles that enthrall the entire community. The young audience will not dwell on lost souls of the past, but on salvageable souls of the present. The pictures sacralize ghetto life and insist that the community members, especially the youth, reckon with their conditions and seek mutual healing. We are led to believe that the photographs begin a new chapter in the life of black Pittsburgh.

Wideman's imagined redemption of black urban life through traumatic representation compels us to reflect upon how and to what effect images of the Black Atlantic circulate within insatiable economies of mass consumption. The means by which we come to know racialized urban ghettoes of contemporary American cities provide ample evidence that the real has abandoned us for good. Corporate media provide the most perverse forms of postmodern flanerie; they grant us access to the spatial Other through journalistic photography, nightly news programs, Hollywood film, and rap music. This formidable panoply of ghetto representation frustrates sober attempts to approximate the real challenges that urban growth coalitions, deindustrialization, underemployment, joblessness, and disenfranchisement have brought to bear on inner-city residents. The image production of the ghetto ascribes to it a certain historical depthlessness that stultifies any interest in identifying the causes of ghettoization. *Two Cities* petitions, possibly naively, for a racial politic that seeks progressive control over the black image. Popular culture's persistent pimping of the most sensational forms of black personality suggests that to acquire such power—as Martin Mallory hoped—might require that we die for it.

NOTES

1. For accounts of the epistemological crises of postmodernism, see Harvey, Jameson, and Lyotard.
2. Mallory's reference to his lingering resentment toward Gus's lynching and the global expanse of racism in his letter to Giacometti is featured in the text as: "This footnote (confession?) as good a way as any, perhaps, to close a conversation that never had a chance to begin" (179).
3. Brief references to Till occur on pages 11, 118, 194, and 223.

WORKS CITED

Buck-Morss, Susan. "The Flaneur, the Sandwichman and the Whore: The Politics of Loitering." *New German Critique* 39 (1986): 99–140.

Caruth, Cathy. *Unclaimed Experience: Trauma, Narrative, and History*. Baltimore: The Johns Hopkins UP, 1996.

Davis, Mike. *City of Quartz: Excavating the Future of Los Angeles*. New York: Vintage, 1992.

Foster, Hal. *The Return of the Real: The Avant-Garde at the End of the Century*. Boston: MIT P, 1996.

Frisby, David. "The Flaneur in Social Theory." *The Flaneur*. Ed. Keith Tester. London: New York: Routledge, 1994. 81–110.

Goldsby, Jacqueline. "The High and Low Tech of It: The Meaning of Lynching and the Death of Emmett Till." *The Yale Journal of Criticism* 9.2 (1996): 245–82.

Goldsmith, William W. "From the Metropolis to Globalization: The Dialectics of Race and Urban Form." *Globalizing Cities: A New Spatial Order?* Eds. Peter Marcuse and Ronald van Kempen. Oxford: Blackwell, 2000. 39–53.

Harvey, David. *The Condition of Postmodernity: An Enquiry into the Origins of Cultural Change* Cambridge: Blackwell, 1990.

Hirsch, Marianne. "Surviving Images: Holocaust Photographs and the Work of Postmemory." *The Yale Journal of Criticism* 14.1 (2001): 5–37.

Jameson, Frederick. *Postmodernism or the Cultural Logic of Late Capitalism.* Durham: Duke UP, 1991.

Laub, Dori. "Truth and Testimony: The Process and the Struggle." *Trauma: Explorations in Memory.* Ed. Cathy Caruth. Baltimore: The Johns Hopkins UP, 1995. 61–75.

Lyotard, Jean Francois. *The Postmodern Explained.* Minneapolis: U of Minnesota P, 1992.

Mosley, Walter. "Love among the Ruins." Rev. of *Two Cities*, John Edgar Wideman. *New York Times Book Review* 4 Oct. 1998: 12.

Nast, Heidi. "Mapping the "Unconscious": Racism and the Oedipal Family." *Annals of the Association of American Geographers* 90.2 (2000): 215–55.

Pile, Steve. *The Body and the City: Psychoanalysis, Space, and Subjectivity.* London: Routledge, 1996.

Rothberg, Michael. *Traumatic Realism: The Demands of Holocaust Representation.* Minneapolis: U of Minnesota P, 2000.

Rotzler, Willy. "Alberto Giacometti and His Times." *Alberto Giacometti and America.* Ed. Tamara S. Evans. New York: CUNY, 1984. 9–19.

Sontag, Susan. *On Photography.* New York: Farrar, 1977.

Tester, Keith, ed. *The Flaneur.* London: Routledge, 1994.

Van Der Kolk, Bessel, and Onno Van De Hart. "The Instructive Past: The Flexibility of Memory and The Engraving of Trauma." *Trauma: Explorations in Memory.* Ed. Cathy Caruth. Baltimore: The Johns Hopkins UP, 1995. 158–82.

Wideman, John Edgar. *Brothers and Keepers.* New York: Vintage, 1984.

———. "The Killing of Black Boys." *Essence* Nov. 1997: 122+.

———. *Two Cities: A Love Story.* Boston: Mariner, 1999.

Retrospective

Optical Tricksterism

Dissolving and Shapeshifting in the Works of John Edgar Wideman

Bonnie TuSmith

As in those quirky Escher drawings or the geometric designs of dyed African gourds, figure and ground cavort promiscuously, exchange places, bird becomes fish becomes bird, different pictures, different spaces represented, near and far not fixed, everything shapeshifting, changing position and meaning depending on when, where, how I look, how the design looks at me. Which questions we ask each other.

John Wideman, *Hoop Roots*

In the final pages of *Hoop Roots*, the terms "dissolving" and "shapeshifting" appear in Wideman's meditation on the photograph of his grandmother, Freed, holding her child (Wideman's mother) on her hip. This "sepia study of urban poverty . . .

a portrait of forms bred by the lives of poor folk in the city's margins . . . forms simultaneously ephemeral and monumental" (233–34), as the narrator describes the image, aptly encapsulates the writer's perspective on life and art. We often peruse old family photographs out of nostalgia or for purposes of identification. The faces of loved ones are what we see. What Wideman the writer seems to notice, however, are the edges and borders—how a dress hemline "dissolve[s] into glare," how background becomes foreground from a certain angle, how shapes shift and change places.

What lies beneath the surface? A Wideman story can always be counted on to pose this question. Take photography or basketball, the narrator says in *Hoop Roots*. We assume both to be simple, straightforward activities. Beneath the surface, though, "Like the best naturalistic paintings, the photo, the game are layered." Beneath the apparent scene or action, "countless other scenes glide and shimmer" (232). The individual *and* the collective, the obvious *and* the hidden, feelings and emotions on the verge of coalescing—these are Wideman trademarks, themes that he frets over and picks at like scabs. All the while a barely audible voice intones: be brave, be fearless; you can't do any good if you're afraid to go there, if shame holds you back.

Blunt confession can backfire. Middle-class Americans love to pry into other people's lives, vicariously experiencing their misfortunes from the comfort of our living rooms. Witness the popularity of based-on-a-true-story TV dramas and "reality TV." If a serious writer delves into aspects of the human psyche that most of us would prefer to keep hidden, however, we may very well turn against him to retain a "safe" distance. But for a writer with the formidable artistic range and intellectual depth of John Wideman, the challenge is to tell stories through his particular lens or vision—with all the necessary complexities, the beautiful *and* the ugly, intact. Over the years, in his various permutations as an artist of the written word, Wideman has approached the multilayered nature of human experience with a commitment worthy of his craft. No matter how unreliable or easily distorted the medium of language might be, words are potentially transformative. Getting the story right is important because, since "all stories are true"—an enigmatic proverb Wideman learned from African storytellers—then the *right* story can save lives.

Thus, Wideman maintains a precarious balance in his writing. Knowing full well that "Gray areas don't sell" (TuSmith, *Conversations* 142), as he acknowledged in an interview, he nevertheless taps into this murky, liminal space every chance he gets. One thing that has struck me about Wideman's writing is how frequently an object being observed transforms, shapeshifts, or even undergoes a "melt-down." Fluidity, liminality, fragmentation—these concepts are au courant

Optical Tricksterism

in theorizing postmodern writing, with perhaps an added edge for contemporary writers identified with the margins of American society. Whenever an object under scrutiny refuses to remain stagnant—thus, evading easy categorization or identification—the reader might justly suspect the presence of Trickster. The study of mythic tricksters in various indigenous and contemporary cultures has provided significant insight in recent years. In Gerald Vizenor's works, for example, the Chippewa trickster Nanabozho often plays a significant role. According to Vizenor, a formidable cultural theorist and writer, "trickster discourse" requires, above all, a sense of play. The trickster figure in tribal cultures is a "brilliant act of the imagination"; it offers "intellectual liberation from representation" and, thus, frees us from the deadly adherence to "terminal creeds."[1] Vizenor's articulation of trickster discourse, including how linguistic play enables liberation, is central to Wideman's art.

In a previous publication I used the term "literary trickster" to describe another contemporary American writer.[2] As I am aware that labels are inherently reductive, I confine my analysis here to narrative strategies in Wideman's texts where this designation seems apropos: namely, the palimpsest, the dissolve, and the shapeshifting antics of Legba the Trickster.[3] In the short story collection *Damballah* (1981) and in the novels *Sent for You Yesterday* (1983), *The Cattle Killing* (1996), and *Two Cities* (1998), such strategies play a significant role. In these and other Wideman texts, it takes at least two media—the medium of human sight to actively observe, and the medium of language to name and describe—to get at what we see. By taking a close look at specific passages in these texts, I show how Wideman utilizes trickster strategies to convey an important message. At a basic level this includes, as the author once noted from his African American ancestors, how to "change the joke and slip the yoke."[4]

In the United States, the legacy of black slavery renders skin color the primary marker of a person's "race." According to the color theorist Patricia Sloane, "Color is a visual phenomenon. As a society, we need to sharpen our skills at visual thinking, at reasoning about what we see in an intelligent manner. Artists are trained to think in visual terms, but the skill is too important to be taught just to artists. In this post-humanist age, we need to become seriously interested in understanding what we see, an endeavor more noble, necessary, and interesting than understanding who we are" (viii). What makes Sloane's statement especially relevant to Wideman is the vexing issue of race. Sloane's position is an ethical one. As humans, we see color and interpret what we see through our cultural biases. If a society is preconditioned to make value judgments based on visual markers such as human skin tone, then each citizen is responsible for recognizing this and "becom[ing] seriously interested in understanding what we see." In the following discussion on Wideman's optical tricksterism, I suggest that the writer means to deconstruct assumptions about visual perception and teach us a different way of seeing.

Scholars seem to agree that Wideman's artistic goal is to imagine a viable world beyond the lie of race. As one literary critic puts it, in Wideman's works, "Storytelling has the potential of erasing the slavers' shuttle" (Richard 656). Another critic claims that in *Two Cities*, the author attempts to get beneath surface representation in order to offer African Americans a new lease on life beyond the confines of race (Simpson 224-25). I agree with both formulations. Assuming that Wideman's lifelong project is to help extricate us from the paradigm of race, how has the writer been working toward this goal? As readers we might note that, from his first published book to *Hoop Roots* and beyond, Wideman has been experimenting with the phenomenology of visual perception. This is already apparent in his first novel, *A Glance Away*.

Eddie Lawson, one of two protagonists in the novel, returns home after a yearlong stay in a drug rehabilitation center. The title of the novel actually appears halfway through the book: "He hoped so badly Alice would be home, that like Brother she would be waiting unchanged, even in the same clothes, as if time were never more than the space between a glance away and back" (105). Eddie's wish that his one-year absence were only "the space between a glance away and back" seeks to collapse time into space, with the comforting notion that if human experience can be squeezed into this minuscule space, change can be avoided. The desire for a frozen, Edenic past reflects Eddie's need for personal agency. Does Eddie have control over his life? If the closest thing that he has to feeling empowered is a wistful desire to have someone he loves remain stagnant, then he has very little power. The contrary-to-fact phrase "as if" makes the point that Eddie, like all humans, has no control over the passing of time. Even as we wish for immutability and certainty in life, experience teaches us that nothing stays the same. The anxiety that this knowledge induces is reflected in several Wideman characters.

In *Sent for You Yesterday*, Carl agonizes over the notion that if he did not wake up one morning, his hometown would disappear (26). This anxiety requires him to be vigilant, a burden that proves too heavy over the years. Carl's mother, Freeda French—a recurring character in Wideman's fiction and memoirs—is also credited with such thoughts in her youth. The narrator tells us that as a girl, one day Freeda was washing dishes and caught a soap bubble. She daydreamed that she would make a wish and then release the "rainbow." Before she could do this, however, something distracted her: "Something had broken the spell, made her look away and the strange bubble had burst. . . . Gone before she could whisper her wish, set it free. . . . Since that day, whenever she looked away from something, she was never sure it would be there when she looked back" (31–32). Human existence is fragile. The lesson that a split second of inattention can result in devastating loss instills fear in Carl and Freeda. As exhibited in these and other Wideman characters, taking the safe route is a likely response to such fear. Toward the end of the novel Carl's lover, Lucy, observes that Carl—and, by extension, an entire generation of Homewood residents—had given up on life too easily and, thus, lost what counted (197–98).

So far, the concept of "a glance away" seems straightforward. Where Wideman's tricksterism comes into play is to include a word here and an image there that inevitably complicate the story. Take Freeda's epiphany, for example. The soap-bubble reverie could have been simply a young person's first realization of loss. The opportunity to say something more is too good to pass up for the trickster writer, though. Immediately preceding the passage quoted above is this curious description: "Tilted in a certain way the colors disappeared and the glistening skin reflected the kitchen, the kitchen made tiny and funny-shaped like a face in a spoon. With one puff she could set the room and the rainbow free" (31). Viewing the kitchen through the bubble yields visual distortion. Like seeing one's funny-faced reflection in a spoon, the room appears trapped in the bubble and the bubble is trapped between Freeda's fingers. Freeda fantasizes that she has the power to free both hostages, but then quickly loses the opportunity. So, at an early age, she learns that her "power" is ephemeral.

Two clues in the passage should be noted. First, the rainbow-colored bubble actually loses its colors and, after "the colors disappeared," the entire room is entrapped in this colorless bubble. Second, the warped-looking room is likened to the distorted image of "a face in a spoon." Tracking references to the Middle Passage in Wideman's writings, the critic Jean-Pierre Richard poses the rhetorical question, "Will the craft of fiction eventually displace the 'narrow ship' of racial history?" (656). Richard argues that, from the 1970 novel *Hurry Home* in which Arthur Rimbaud's metaphor of the "drunken boat" is thematized to evoke the slave shuttle, to the Homewood Trilogy (1981–83) where the shuttle *idea* transforms into the narrative *technique* of "'back and forth' storytelling" and, in Wideman's subsequent works, becomes "full-fledged narrative," Wideman's art has made significant progress toward eradicating racial history. It would be difficult to overstate the significance of this feat by the ethically and politically committed Wideman.

We might recall that, in the story "Damballah," the slave-boy narrator meditates on his own reflection in a spoon while polishing silverware in the "root cellar." The cellar evokes a slave ship's hold where abducted Africans were forced to lie "spoon fashion."[5] Used in a postbellum story, "spoon" is emblematic of a people's collective history and Freeda's reverie conjures this past. The spoon, similar to the back-and-forth rhythm idea, serves as a narrative shortcut for invoking the history of race in America. Both the slave boy and young Freeda have seemingly innocent, even playful thoughts about spoons. In the latter case, Freeda is not credited with thoughts about African ancestors lying "spoon fashion," so the Middle Passage connection has to be attributed to the implied author in the text. Behind this textual echo is the writer Wideman signifying on his own texts.[6]

And what about the rainbow bubble that is now colorless? We are told that prior to catching the bubble Freeda was thinking of color: "She had been thinking of all the new people arriving in Homewood. Colored people, they said. Ignorant, countrified niggers, they said, from the South. Downhome niggers they said so black and brown sounded nasty and she was thinking about color when she pulled her hand up out of the water" (31). Freeda herself is light-complexioned, the color of "a cup of milk mixed with a tablespoon of coffee." Because color bias is attributed to a collective "they"—ostensibly, the earlier black settlers of Homewood who, over time, had lightened considerably—the passage indicates that the daydreaming girl is processing what she had heard in her community. If she adopts this bias, she joins the ranks of "high yellow" African Americans who look down on darker-complexioned neighbors. By having the bubble first lose color and *then* reflect a distorted image of the kitchen, the trickster writer evokes the historical white appropriation of (black) space. So what we have is a light-skinned black girl holding a colorless (suggestive of white people) soap bubble that, however fragile itself, visually imprisons the small kitchen, "the warmest, brightest room in the house [of black people]." Freeda's instinctive desire to free both the bubble and the imprisoned room is thus symbolically connected to race relations in the United States. That the bubble bursts before Freeda can act suggests the limits of individual agency. A collective wrong—the wholesale oppression of a people—requires more than a young girl's wishful thinking to rectify. The lesson Freeda learns from the experience is that she is ineffectual. She then wonders whether "living is learning to forget" so that she should "settle for whatever came next" (32–33).

Of course, this interpretation is still too pat for Wideman. The double-consciousness inherent in being visibly nonwhite in America requires constant vigilance. This awareness reminds the writer, and the rest of us, not to pass judgment on others prematurely. After gaining insight into Freeda's psyche, the reader is presented with a profile of Freeda as an adult: "But she held on to her God, and held on to her family and swore to herself she would cling as long as there was breath in her body. And the oath was strong, and her arms grew strong but never stronger than the voice tearing her away" (33). This description tells us that there is heroism in someone who, in spite of knowing the risks, "cling[s]" ferociously to life and ceaselessly battles with "the voice tearing her away." Freeda French, the fictionalized version of Wideman's maternal grandmother, is thus presented as a whole person with the weight of her people behind her. She is both weak and strong: a "racist" in that she harbors color prejudice, and a courageous, "good" person in spite of such limitations.[7] In other words, she is fully human.

At one point in the narrative the first-person narrator steps in to tell us: "My grandmother Freeda had been just a girl then. In that other room, that other world, enchanted by a soap bubble. She remembered its exact shape now. A long watermelon blister of soap . . ." (31). In the dedication "To Robby" in *Damballah*, the author reminisces over watermelons—how John himself was afraid to eat them, how Robby was not, and how their aunt had called the fruit "a letter from home." By describing the bubble as watermelon-shaped, the narrator here associates it with African Americans' collective history of enslavement and the racial stereotype of "pickaninnies." The bubble is colored, but colorless when it shape-shifts; the bubble is rainbow-colored and watermelon-shaped; these alternative truths can be viewed as an experimental version of what Wideman does with visual perception, with racial history, and, though seldom acknowledged, with ethnic humor. The author's fear of being associated with a watermelon-eating black boy runs deep and encapsulates a part of his racial psyche. In the book's dedication he gives his brother Robby full credit for not being "afraid of becoming instant nigger, of sitting barefoot and goggle-eyed and Day-Glo black and drippy-lipped on massa's fence . . ." (*Damballah* 5). In this comic description, an oppressed people's source of pain is simultaneously named and defanged by the word artist. John praises Robby and laughs at himself—thus thrashing his demon and "slipping the yoke" one more time. This is Trickster as his most charming and cunning self.

In response to his own question as quoted earlier ("Will the craft of fiction eventually displace the 'narrow ship' of racial history?"), Richard makes a key observation regarding Wideman's body of works: "But memories of the Africans lying spoon-fashion in the hold keep resurfacing. The Trade resists erasure. It will take long years and many stories before such narrative shuttling, as emerged out of initial themes and metaphors, can function as palimpsest and subvert the slaver's passage" (659). This contention, especially in relation to Wideman's earlier works, has merit. However, given the ugly truth of slavery in the United States—a history that implicates all Americans and continues to prove a heavy burden on those of African ancestry—"erasure" may be an unrealistic, even undesirable, goal. Wideman is aware of this, I believe, and has devised strategic moves to counteract the psychic power that the legacy of slavery has had on African Americans. By playing with language, the trickster writer specifies for us the value of human life. I will trace through a few textual instances of what might be called the Wideman counterpunch.

If we start with the premise that humans have little power in life, where do we go from there? Beyond unethical, quick-fix solutions such as exploiting others to fulfill one's desires, is there another path to self-fulfillment? Teaching oneself to *see* things in a different way would be one possibility, and this is certainly within the purview of creative writers today. The popularization of photography and cinematography in the early twentieth century taught writers filmic techniques that transformed the way stories were narrated. When applied to literary narration, techniques such as close-ups, jump-shots, fade-outs, splices, frozen images, and panoramic views gave stories a sense of dramatic engagement and immediacy well beyond the formal realism of the nineteenth-century novel. Through the medium of the written word, such techniques have contributed to narratives that capture the metaphoric potential of the visual. The dissolve, for one, is a cinematic technique that has made a healthy transition from modernist to postmodernist works of literature. Put simply, the dissolve is when one scene disintegrates while another emerges beneath it, with an overlapping moment when both scenes are blurred. In mid-twentieth-century cinematography, this technique lost popularity as more advanced means of making visual transitions were developed.[8] Incorporating such cinematic techniques into literature, however, is another matter.

Arguably, a narrative strategy that became outdated due to technological advances is, in the different medium of literary art, still viable today. In the essay "*The Moviegoer* as Dissolve," Martin Luschei analyzes the use of cinematic technique in Walker Percy's 1960 novel. According to Luschei, Percy effectively utilizes the dissolve throughout the novel to portray self-deluded characters living inauthentic lives. An example is when the narrator/protagonist visits his aunt and makes this observation about the aunt's servant: "Mercer has dissolved somewhat in recent years. . . . I hate it when his vision of himself dissolves. . . . Then his eyes get muddy and his face runs together behind his mustache" (26). The various ways in which, in Luschei's words, individuals "have dissolved themselves into roles" (26) or are on the verge of dissolution render Percy's existentialist novel an apt character study. As a literary trope, the dissolve captures the mood, tone, and other intricacies of human consciousness that elude the camera lens.

While Percy's novel effectively utilizes the dissolve as social commentary, Wideman's works play with the dissolve, the palimpsest, and other special effects of layering and unlayering to explore more complex notions of identity and human experience. In *Damballah*, the story "Across the Wide Missouri" presents a larger-than-life image of the 1950s film icon Clark Gable. A self-assured man stands in front of the mirror brushing his teeth with Scotch. In recalling the special afternoon he once spent at the movies with his father, the narrator unabashedly declares, "The white man at the mirror is my father." What he means is that the movie hero epitomizes every child's fantasy of the perfect dad, "doing good and being brave and handsome and thundering like a god across the screen" (140). In thus evoking his feelings for his father, the narrator reminds us that the image is symbolic—a way to tap the purity of an experience and its concomitant feelings without conscious distortion. As the narrator puts it, "It's a blurring of reality the way certain shots in a film blur or distort in order to focus" (140). Attaining clarity of vision, especially in the psychic realm, through a conscious blurring of external reality is a Wideman forté. The writer has utilized this basic concept to great advantage in his subsequent works.

The Cattle Killing, Wideman's 1996 novel on the late-eighteenth-century fever epidemic in Philadelphia, applies the principle of the dissolve to broaden how and what we see. Halfway through the novel the young black preacher, awakening in bed and coming back to life after having nearly frozen to death in a snowstorm, secretly observes the woman who had saved him: "An old woman undressing by the fire and I almost turned my head, but this time I wanted to see exactly what time costs. What it steals, what it leaves . . . Then you began to change. Turning, twisting, leaning, bending. Arms over your head. A woman's motions, gestures old as time. Time evaporating like bathwater from your skin as you dry in front of the fire" (95). In this passage, age recedes in the eyes of the beholder until an old woman performing her toilette transforms—or dissolves—into her former youthful self: "Perhaps I turned away an instant. Perhaps in that brief, brief absence, another woman, no, girl, took your place. A supple, smooth-fleshed girl toweling her freckled back . . . As she hurries into her clothes, the black redness of her hair reflects fire. Fire catches color from her hair" (95). The observer now perceives a young girl whose vibrantly colored hair interacts with the fire she is standing next to. That her hair lends color to the fire is intriguing. There is no suggestion of danger, of getting burned by the flames. Instead, two different elements—hair and fire—borrow from each other to their mutual benefit. If the borders between old age and youth, between a physically tangible element such as human hair and an intangible element such as fire, can be crossed through visualization and evocative wordplay, then why stop at a single woman? So we find in the next paragraph: "Was the room full of women. Women stepping into the cask, out of the cask. Each one different. Or changing. Different women, Different ages. Magically transformed by water, fire, air" (96).

When the old woman directly addresses the young preacher, her "patient," in the next scene, the narrative point of view remains with the preacher. The woman serves hot tea while the patient thinks: "Her hands thick-veined, big-knuckled, bony . . . Hands attached to wrists attached to one of the women he'd been watching. Which one had stepped out of the tub into this skin, these hands, these shapeless layers of wool and linen" (97). Since there is only one woman in the room, is the patient delusional and his perspective unreliable? Such a conclusion misses the point, I would argue.

Appearing as it does halfway through the novel, the preacher's careful scrutiny of Mrs. Stubbs in this scene serves to connect other female characters in the text. In terms of time sequence, the present action in the novel is the preacher telling stories to an ailing white woman who is sleeping in a loft. His storytelling is a means of keeping the listener alive. At one point in his ongoing narration, the preacher cites his stay with the Stubbses as an uplifting experience from his past. Prior to this point in his daily storytelling and appearing earlier in the novel, he tells of having followed an African woman carrying a dead baby. The woman walks into a lake and disappears. The listener reproaches the preacher for not having attempted to save the African woman. The preacher explains that he waited for the woman to come out of the lake and, even though he waited all night, he should have waited longer: "I didn't wait long enough. I lost faith. Deserted her. She trusted me, asked me to help, but I didn't wait long enough" (48). The notion that the African woman would have emerged out of the lake eventually if the eyewitness had kept faith reflects a different view of life and death. Given the fantastic situation already established between the storyteller and the listener, the preacher's contention does not seem outrageous. With the dreamlike tone and sincerity of the narration, verisimilitude is beside the point. The storyteller's next move reveals what Wideman is doing with the women in this novel. "She returned," the preacher insists. "I know she did. If I'd waited, I might have found you sooner. Before it was too late." The shift from "she" to "you" suggests that the preacher views the women, both black and white, who have crossed his path as embodiments of a single spirit. The author's dedication in the novel supports this reading. "To Jamila [Wideman's daughter]," it states, "who arrived with one of those tough, beautiful old souls that's been here before." The recurring-spirit motif introduced by the preacher offers hope, as this section of the text ends with an italicized refrain: "*Perhaps it's not too late. Perhaps it never is*" (48).

In a city plagued by disease, violence, and death—the historical setting of Philadelphia in the 1790s—Wideman manages to stare down all the horror and pronounce his novel "a love story."[9] The final lines of the novel are central to this understanding:

> Tell me, finally, what is a man. What is a woman. Aren't we lovers first, spirits sharing an uncharted space, a space our stories tell, a space chanted, written upon again and again, yet one story never quite erased by the next, each story saving the space, saving itself, saving us. If someone is listening. (208)

Optical Tricksterism

As a story structured on mutual caring between a man and a woman, *The Cattle Killing* offers a way of viewing the world that cuts through our preconditioned expectations. A black man tells stories, a white woman listens. Each person finds his or her role crucial to survival. The idea of forging human connection through storytelling grounds the novel in mythic or, as Wideman is fond of observing, Great Time as understood in African folk cultures.[10] In accord with this line of thinking, by tracking the novel's artistic treatment of female characters—including Mrs. Stubbs, the African woman, the listening white woman, the "blue" woman who appears when the preacher has an epileptic fit, and Mrs. Thrush's servant Kathryn—the reader comes to realize that the spirit lives on and, thus, "perhaps it's not too late."

Wideman's subsequent novel, *Two Cities* (1998), is actually identified as a love story on its dust jacket. The theme of love and loss between two main characters, Robert and Kassima, is an obvious candidate for this claim. However, readers looking for standard stories of romantic love would be hard-pressed to find one here. In *Two Cities*, Wideman's ongoing meditation on love revolves around individual acts of courage. That is, *knowing* that there's nothing out there, the individual acts out of faith that his or her effort would still make a difference. This stance seems in accord with the primary assertion of twentieth-century existentialism that existence precedes essence and, therefore, it is a person's actions that generate the meaning, or essence, of his or her life.[11]

One major story line in this "tale of two cities" is the affinity Mr. Mallory, amateur photographer and elderly boarder in Kassima's house, has for the renowned Surrealist Swiss sculptor Alberto Giacometti.[12] In his letters to the sculptor (which were never mailed), Mallory seeks to articulate an aesthetics of art and, by extension, his view of the world. What Mallory has learned from Giacometti is the idea that art cannot be mimetic, since "it's impossible to copy a world that never stops changing." Mallory describes the lesson thus: "Even with a live model sitting in your studio, you said, you can't copy what you see. Your eyes must choose. Study either model or copy. Lose sight of one or the other. *When you turn from the model to shape a portrait or clay figure, it's memory and habit, not sight, that guide your hand*" (82, emphasis mine). This is an invaluable lesson for Mallory. If what the artist sees cannot be captured in a chosen medium—such as clay or film—then the art that is produced is a product of human memory and imagination. This phenomenon actually frees the artist as well as the viewer to see different things when viewing a work of art. Mallory draws from this understanding when explaining his artistic aim:

> I want people to see my pictures from various angles, see the image I offer as many images, one among countless ways of seeing, so the more they look, the more there is to see. A density of appearances my goal, Mr. Giacometti. So I snap, snap, snap.

> Pile on layer after layer. A hundred doses of light without moving the film. No single, special, secret view sought or revealed. One in many. Many in one. (91)

This description aptly reflects what the writer Wideman himself does when he takes a close look at something or someone: for example, Mrs. Stubbs taking a bath (in *The Cattle Killing*). The question remains, why is this "One in many. Many in one" artistic aim desirable, and what does it accomplish? To some contemporary readers, the slipperiness of such representation is simply hard work with no immediate reward. Why go through the trouble? one might ask. For the remainder of this essay, I trace through Mallory's thoughts to ascertain what makes his artistic approach and, as the author's stand-in, what makes the Wideman approach worthwhile.

In James Joyce's epic novel *Ulysses*, the protagonist Stephen Dedalus frets over what he terms the "ineluctable modality of the visible."[13] Put simply, he worries that human sight cannot avoid patterns, that we see only external form or type rather than internal content or substance. The tension between surface typology and core spirit is especially of interest to a writer who struggles with the paradigm of race. If human form, including skin color and body type, is "ineluctable" to the viewer, then we cannot stop at this first line of vision. After the photographer's death, Kassima tells Robert that Mallory's photographs of the people in the neighborhood are beautiful, and declares passionately, "Not just anybody could take pictures of how people feel inside." Robert concurs and says, "he caught us dead to rights, no doubt about it. No hiding from his camera. Snap. Mr. Mallory got the goods on you. Caught you red-handed" (210). This dialogue indicates that, from Kassima's and Robert's perspective, Mallory succeeded in his art. However, this assessment does not account for the gray pictures that Mallory intentionally made by snapping again and again without advancing the film. While his one staunch supporter, Kassima, is completely baffled by these blank, "ruined" photos —and Mallory apparently takes his intentions to his grave—we readers have more insight into the matter. After all, Mallory's letters to Giacometti include the following statement:

> My pictures are pretty postcards with the world arranged nice and neat. But I don't want to hide the damage. I want to enter the wound, cut through layer by layer like a surgeon, expose what lies beneath the skin. Go where there is no skin, no outside or inside, no body. Only traffic always moving in many directions at once. Snapshots one inside the other, notes played so they can dance away, make room for others. Free others to free themselves. (118)

From this statement we recognize that Mallory had more lofty goals than playing "candid camera." In connecting Giacometti with Romare Bearden and Thelonious

Monk, African American painter and pianist, respectively, Mallory concludes that all three artists share the virtue of "turn[ing] things loose" (118). Mallory's success as an artist is not just catching his subject in an unguarded moment. Yes, because he is "of the people" and not above them, through his chosen medium he is able to show how "people feel inside." (In one letter he confesses, "Many years ago . . . I decided to live alone. Suffered the loneliness and pain of cutting myself off from other people only to discover when I started taking pictures, others still lived inside me" [82].) However, Mallory's real success—and "failure"—lies in the gray pictures. His understanding of life, of human worth, of love enabled him to take these photographs. He died, however, before he could find a way to "free" these piled-on images captured on film. It is thus significant that, even though Kassima doesn't understand the significance of these gray photos, she does salvage the negatives in the final scene of the novel. This leaves open the possibility that someday, someone will come along to print out the hundreds of images on each negative for others to see.

But, why do we need such pictures? Here's what Mallory explains to Giacometti:

> Invisible views. They are what attract me to your art. You force me to see something not there. See missing ingredients I must supply, if I dare. . . . What I mean when I say invisible views is this: our eyes take snapshots. Like a camera. A million, million frames day in and day out. Too quick to keep track of. Each one disappears instantly, leaving no trace behind. Except from these snapshots we build a world of things with weight, shape, things that move and last. We believe in them. Depend on them. . . . We forget how spirit and mind piece the world together glimpse by glimpse. We forget our power. Forget that one naked, sideways stare, one glance away changes everything. (91)

This passage is revealing. Thirty-odd years after publishing a novel titled *A Glance Away*, the writer's angst over the devastation of human loss—as expressed through references to "a glance away" in various subsequent works—has metamorphosed into a message of hope. The human spirit, the human mind—these are our true sources of power. The observer fills in the blank, utilizes human imagination to create meaning. When Mallory says, "You force me to see something not there. See missing ingredients I must supply, if I dare," he is referring to the spaces and gaps that each snapshot frame generates and leaves behind, each blink of our eyelids that, as in glancing away for a split second, "changes everything." Whereas in Wideman's earlier works the glance away is to be feared, the more mature understanding finds opportunity in loss. As Mallory puts it, "If I ever get good, my pictures will remind people to keep a world alive around them, to keep themselves alive at the center of a storm of swirling emptiness" (91). Ultimately, Mallory pays homage to Giacometti for the sculptor's courage and humanity. "Again, thank you for your example," he writes. "Thank you for staring hard at the world, for losing it and not looking away, for piecing something together out of nothing, for remembering what's lost" (83).

Kassima recalls that, shortly before his death, Mallory had praised her for not being a bitter person after having lost a husband and two sons to violence and disease. Finding Mallory's dictionary after his death, Kassima notices that the entry for the word "bitter" had been marked for her to find. Mallory had written and erased the words "love," "bitter," and "sweet" at the bottom of the page, "in a scribble-scrabble thicket of what might be those words repeated again and again, darkly scoring, nearly scratching a hole in the paper, the three words over and over, one atop the other." This palimpsest reminds Kassima of African American trickster tales: "a briarpatch, tarbaby pit of jagged strokes and swirls like the trap the foolish, flop-eared rabbit she'd read stories about to her boys got tricked into and couldn't escape from until he tricked the trickster" (204). The parallel between Mallory's gray photos and this "scribble-scrabble . . . briarpatch, tarbaby pit" cannot be overlooked. In identifying Mallory as a trickster figure—however surreptitiously—the novel offers a way out for those who can take Trickster's shapeshifting, multilayered identity to heart.

In a flashback toward the end of the novel, Mallory's friend John Africa makes the following observation: "The whites got an idea about us and won't let the idea go. Can't let it go. Scared to let it go" (228). In declaring that "Move's about not standing still," John Africa reminds us that individual and collective action are necessary to transcend the paradigm of race. In picking at scabs, blurring physical forms, and superimposing one human image on top of another, John Wideman manages to tell tales that ultimately "slip the yoke."

NOTES

1. See Vizenor, *Native American Novelists* and *Narrative Chance*. See also Reesman, Hyde, and Smith.
2. See *All My Relatives* 46–60.
3. See Gates's *Signifying Monkey* 21.
4. See Wideman, "Playing."
5. See Richard's fascinating account of this image in "From Slavers" 661.
6. See Gates's definition of "signifying" in *The Signifying Monkey*.
7. In my 1997 interview with Wideman, the author explained that his grandmother was "'color struck,' and that meant that she didn't like dark people—she didn't think they were good looking." See TuSmith, *Conversations* 202.
8. See "Dissolve" in *A Dictionary of Literary, Dramatic, and Cinematic Terms*.

9. "In a way, it's a love story," Wideman explains in a 1996 interview. See TuSmith, *Conversations* 188. Also, the novel includes the following dialogue:

> Philadelphia. Love is buried in its name, you know.
> Love. Love, sir. Surely not during the season of plague. A most unlovely time, by your word.
> Very little love. Yes. Yes. But love was there. The city would not have survived without it. (49)

10. See Mbiti's *African Religions and Philosophies*.
11. See Macey, "Existentialism," in *The Penguin Dictionary of Critical Theory*.
12. Alberto Giacometti (1901–1966), Swiss-born sculptor known for his abstract bronze sculptures of the "thin man." *Chambers Biographical Dictionary* describes these as "long spidery statuettes, rigid in posture yet trembling on the verge of movement, suggesting transcience, change and decay."
13. See Joyce, *Ulysses* 37.

WORKS CITED

"Dissolve." *A Dictionary of Literary, Dramatic, and Cinematic Terms.* Eds. Sylvan Barnet et al. 2nd ed. Boston: Little, Brown and Co., 1971.

Gates, Henry Louis, Jr. *The Signifying Monkey: A Theory of Afro-American Literary Criticism.* New York: Oxford UP, 1988.

"Giacometti, Alberto." *Chambers Biographical Dictionary.* General Ed. Magnus Magnusson, KBE. 5th ed. Edinburgh: Chambers, 1990. 582–83.

Hyde, Lewis. *Trickster Makes This World: Mischief, Myth, and Art.* New York: Farrar, 1998.

Joyce, James. *Ulysses.* 1914. New York: Random House, 1961.

Luschei, Martin. "*The Moviegoer* as Dissolve." *The Art of Walker Percy: Stratagems for Being.* Ed. Panthea Reid Broughton. Baton Rouge: Louisiana State UP, 1979. 24–36.

Macey, David. "Existentialism." *The Penguin Dictionary of Critical Theory.* New York: Penguin, 2000.

Mbiti, John. *African Religions and Philosophies.* Oxford: Heinemann, 1990.

Reesman, Jeanne Campbell, ed. *Trickster Lives: Culture and Myth in American Fiction.* Athens: U of Georgia P, 2001.

Richard, Jean-Pierre. "From Slavers to Drunken Boats: A Thirty-Year Palimpsest in John Edgar Wideman's Fiction." *Callaloo* 22.3 (Summer 1999): 656–64.

Simpson, Tyron R. "'And the Arc of His Witness Explained Nothing': Black *Flanerie* and Traumatic Photorealism In Wideman's *Two Cities.*" *Critical Essays on John Edgar Wideman.* Knoxville; U Tennessee P, 2006. 221–39.

Sloane, Patricia. Preface. *The Visual Nature of Color.* New York: Design Press, 1989.

Smith, Jeanne Rosier. *Writing Tricksters: Mythic Gambols in American Ethnic Literature.* Berkeley: U of California P, 1997.

TuSmith, Bonnie. *All My Relatives: Community in Contemporary Ethnic American Literatures.* Ann Arbor: U of Michigan P, 1993.

———, ed. *Conversations with John Edgar Wideman.* Jackson: UP of Mississippi, 1998.

Vizenor, Gerald, ed. *Narrative Chance: Postmodern Discourse on Native American Indian Literatures.* Norman & London: U of Oklahoma P, 1989.

Vizenor, Gerald. *Native American Novelists.* Videocassette. *Films for the Humanities and Sciences.* 1995.

Wideman, John. *A Glance Away.* New York: Holt, Rinehart and Winston, 1985.

———. "Benefit of the Doubt: A Conversation with John Edgar Wideman." Interview with Bonnie TuSmith. In TuSmith, *Conversations* 195–219.

———. *Damballah.* New York: Avon, 1981.

———. *Hoop Roots.* Boston: Houghton, 2001.

———. "Playing, Not Joking, with Language." Rev. of *The Signifying Monkey* by Henry Louis Gates Jr. *New York Times Book Review* 14 Aug. 1988: 3.

———. *Sent for You Yesterday.* New York: Avon, 1983.

———. *The Cattle Killing.* Boston: Houghton, 1996.

———. *Two Cities.* Boston: Houghton, 1998.

Optical Tricksterism

Bibliography

MARK J. MADIGAN

Primary sources are U.S. editions of books written and edited by John Edgar Wideman, along with forewords, introductions, prefaces, and afterwords written by him, and interviews with the author. The secondary sources are journal articles, book chapters, dissertations, and books on Wideman published in English, not including book reviews. The aim is to list all of the most important and readily accessible works by and about Wideman.

PRIMARY SOURCES
Books

A Glance Away. New York: Harcourt, Brace and World, 1967. Chatham, NJ: Chatham Bookseller, 1975. New York: Holt, Rinehart and Winston, 1985.

Hurry Home. New York: Harcourt, Brace and World, 1970. New York: Henry Holt, 1986.

The Lynchers. New York: Harcourt Brace Jovanovich, 1973. New York: Dell, 1974. New York: Holt, 1986.

Damballah. New York: Avon, 1981. New York: Vintage, 1988. Boston: Houghton, 1998.

Hiding Place. New York: Avon, 1981. New York: Vintage, 1988. Boston: Houghton, 1998.

Sent for You Yesterday. New York: Avon, 1983. New York: Vintage, 1988. Boston: Houghton, 1997.

Brothers and Keepers. New York: Holt, Rinehart and Winston, 1984. New York: Penguin, 1985. New York: Vintage, 1995.

Reuben. New York: Henry Holt, 1987. New York: Penguin, 1988.

Fever: Twelve Stories. New York: Henry Holt, 1989. New York: Penguin, 1990, 1991.

Philadelphia Fire. New York: Henry Holt, 1990. New York: Vintage, 1991. New York: Penguin, 1992.

The Stories of John Edgar Wideman. New York: Pantheon, 1992.

All Stories Are True. New York: Vintage, 1993.

Fatheralong: A Meditation on Fathers and Sons, Race and Society. New York: Pantheon, 1994. New York: Vintage, 1995.

The Cattle Killing. Boston: Houghton, 1996. Boston: Mariner, 1996.

Two Cities. Boston: Houghton, 1998. Boston: Mariner, 1999.

Hoop Roots. Boston: Houghton, 2001. Boston: Mariner, 2003.

The Island: Martinique. Washington, DC: National Geographic, 2003.

God's Gym: Stories. Boston: Houghton, 2005.

Anthologies

The Homewood Trilogy. [*Damballah, Hiding Place, Sent for You Yesterday*]. New York: Avon, 1985.

The Homewood Books. Pittsburgh: U Pittsburgh P, 1992.

Identities: Three Novels. [*A Glance Away, Hurry Home, The Lynchers*]. New York: Henry Holt, 1994.

Edited Books

The Best American Short Stories, 1996 (with Katrina Kenison). Boston: Houghton, 1996.

My Soul Has Grown Deep: Classics of Early African-American Literature. Philadelphia: Running Press, 2001. New York: Ballantine, 2002.

20: The Best of the Drue Heinz Prize. Pittsburgh: U Pittsburgh P, 2001.

Forewords, Introductions, Prefaces, and Afterwords

Abu Jamal, Mumia. *Live from Death Row.* New York: Addison-Wesley, 1995.

Blaustein, Noah, ed. *Motion: American Sports Poems.* Iowa City: U Iowa P, 2001.

DuBois, W. E. B. *The Souls of Black Folk.* New York: Library of America, 1990.

Hurston, Zora Neale. *Every Tongue Got to Confess.* Ed. and introd. Carla Kaplan. New York: HarperCollins, 2001.

McMillan, Terry, ed. *Breaking Ice.* New York: Penguin, 1990.

Plumpp, Sterling D. *Blues Narratives.* Chicago: Tia Chucha P, 1999.

Thelwell, Ekwueme Michael. *Ready for Revolution: The Life and Struggles of Stokely Carmichael (Kwame Ture).* New York: Scribner's, 2003.

Interviews

Interview. By Laura Miller. *Salon Magazine* 11 Nov. 1996. *Salon Interview Archive* <http://salonmagazine.com/nov96/interview961111.html>.

Conversations with John Edgar Wideman. Ed. Bonnie TuSmith. Jackson: UP Mississippi, 1988. Interviews by Gene Shalit (1963), John O'Brien (1972), Wilfred D. Samuels (1983), Philip G. Howlett (1983), Sheri Hoem (1984), Kay Bonetti (1985), James W. Coleman (1988), Judith Rosen (1989), Charles H. Rowell (1989), Rebekah Presson (1991), Jessica Lustig (1992), Michael Silverblatt (1993), Ishmael Reed (1994), Patricia Smith (1995), Arnold E. Sabatelli (1995), Michael Silverblatt (1995), Renee Olander (1996), Derek McGinty (1996), Bonnie TuSmith (1997).

"Body Language." By Lisa Baker. *Atlantic Unbound* 7 Oct. 1998 <http://www.theatlantic.com/unbound/bookauth/ba981007.htm>.

"From *Brothers and Keepers* to *Two Cities*: Social and Cultural Consciousness, Art and Imagination: An Interview with John Edgar Wideman." By Jacqueline Berben-Masi. *Callaloo* 22.3 (1999): 568–84.

"Storytelling and Democracy (in the Radical Sense): A Conversation with John Edgar Wideman." By Lisa Baker. *African American Review* 34.2 (2000): 263–72.

"10 Burning Questions for John Edgar Wideman." 9 Nov. 2001 <http://espn.go.com/page2/s/questions/johnwideman.html>.

Interview. By Steven Beeber. *Paris Review* 44.161 (2002): 136–60.

"Basketball, Race, and Love." By Christopher Weber. *ColorLines: Race, Culture, Action* 6.1 (Spring 2003): 36–39.

SECONDARY SOURCES

Anderson, Crystal Suzette. "Far from 'Everybody's Everything': Literary Tricksters in African American and Chinese American Fiction." Diss. College of William and Mary, 2000. *DAI* 61.12 (2000): 4827.

Andrade, Heather. "'Mosaic Memory': Auto/Biographical Context(s) in John Edgar Wideman's *Brothers and Keepers.*" *Massachusetts Review* 40.3 (1999): 342–66.

Ashe, Bertram Duane. "From within the Frame: Storytelling in African-American Fiction." Diss. College of William and Mary, 1998. *DAI* 59.8 (1998): 2975.

Auger, Philip George. *Native Sons in No Man's Land: Rewriting Afro-American Manhood in the Novels of Baldwin, Walker, Wideman, and Gaines.* New York: Garland, 2000.

———. "ReWrighting Afro-American Manhood: Negotiations of Discursive Space in the Fiction of James Baldwin, Alice Walker, John Edgar Wideman, and Ernest Gaines." Diss. U Rhode Island, 1995. *DAI* 56.9 (1996): 3576A–77A.

Bennion, John. "The Shape of Memory in John Edgar Wideman's *Sent for You Yesterday.*" *Black American Literature Forum* 20.1–2 (1986): 143–50.

Benthien, Claudia. "'The Whiteness Underneath the Nigger': Albinism and Blackness in John Edgar Wideman's *Sent for You Yesterday*." *Utah Foreign Language Review* (1997): 3–13.

Berben, Jacqueline. "Beyond Discourse: The Unspoken versus Words in the Fiction of John Edgar Wideman." *Callaloo* 8.3 (1985): 525–34.

———. "Promised Land and Wasteland in John Wideman's Recent Fiction." *Revue Francaise d'Etudes Americaines* 19.48–49 (1991): 259–70.

———. "Voice as Persona in John Wideman's Current Fiction." *Voix ethniques/Ethnic Voices, G.R.A.A.T.* 8 (1992): 97–106.

Berben, Jacquie. "Towards a Black Realization of the Hegelian Ideal: John Edgar Wideman's 'Homewood.'" *Cycnos* 4 (1988): 43-48.

Berben-Masi, Jacqueline. "Mother Goose and Brother Loon: The Fairy-Tale-in-the-Tale as Vehicle of Displacement." *Callaloo* 22.3 (1999): 594–602.

———. "Prodigal and Prodigy: Fathers and Sons in Wideman's Work." *Callaloo* 22.3 (1999): 677–84.

Birat, Kathie. "'All Stories': Prophecy, History and Story in *The Cattle Killing*." *Callaloo* 22.3 (1999): 629–43.

Byerman, Keith. *John Edgar Wideman: A Study of the Short Fiction*. New York: Twayne, 1998.

———. "Vernacular Modernism in the Novels of John Edgar Wideman and Leon Forrest." *The Cambridge Companion to the African American Novel*. Ed. and introd. Maryemma Graham. Cambridge, England: Cambridge UP; 2004. 253–67.

Carden, Mary Paniccia. "'If the City Is a Man': Founders and Fathers, Cities and Sons in John Edgar Wideman's *Philadelphia Fire*." *Contemporary Literature* 44.3 (2003): 472–500.

Casmier, Stephen. "Resisting the Frame Up: *Philadelphia Fire* and the Liberated Voices of Ramona Africa and Margaret Jones." *Cycnos* 19.2 (2002): 225–40.

Challener, Daniel D. "The Autobiographies of Resilient Children: *Brothers and Keepers, Hunger of Memory, I Know Why the Caged Bird Sings, This Boy's Life*, and *The Woman Warrior*." Diss. Brown U, 1993. *DAI* 54.10 (1993): 3747.

Clausen, Jan. "Native Fathers." *Kenyon Review* 14.2 (1992): 44–55.

Coleman, James W. *Blackness and Modernism: The Literary Career of John Edgar Wideman*. Jackson: UP Mississippi, 1989.

———. "Going Back Home: The Literary Development of John Edgar Wideman." *College Language Association Journal* 28.3 (1985): 326–43.

Crawford, Margo Natalie. "Transcendence versus the Embodiment of Racial Abstraction in Novels by William Faulkner, Toni Morrison, and John Edgar Wideman." Diss. Yale U, 1999. *DAI* 60.12 (2000): 4426.

Dubey, Madhu. "Literature and Urban Crisis: John Edgar Wideman's *Philadelphia Fire*." *African American Review* 32.4 (1998): 579–95.

———. "Photography and Voyeurism in *Reuben*." "Pornography and Voyeurism in *Philadelphia Fire*." *Signs and Cities: Black Literary Postmodernism*. Chicago: U Chicago P, 2003. 109–31.

Espinosa-Aguilar, Amanda L. "Interpreting the Rhetoric of Anger in the Autobiographical Writing of Ethnic Americans." Diss. U Nevada-Reno, 1998. *DAI* 60.1 (1998): 0129.

Fabre, Michel. "Opening of the Symposium in Tours." *Callaloo* 22.3 (1999): 587–93.

Feith, Michel. "'The Benefit of the Doubt': Openness and Closure in *Brothers and Keepers*." *Callaloo* 22.3 (1999): 665–75.

Frazier, Kermit. "The Novels of John Edgar Wideman." *Black World* 24 (1975): 18–35.

Grandjeat, Yves-Charles. "Brother Figures: The Rift and Riff in John E. Wideman's Fiction." *Callaloo* 22.3 (1999): 615–22.

———. "'These Strange Dizzy Pauses': Silence as Common Ground in J. E. Wideman's Texts." *Callaloo* 22.3 (1999): 685–94.

Grant, Nathan. "Promised Lands: The New Jerusalem's Inner City and John Edgar Wideman's Philadelphia Story." *Masculinist Impulses: Toomer, Hurston, Black Writing, and Modernity*. Columbia: U Missouri P, 2004. 145–81.

Guzzio, Tracie Church. "'All Stories Are True': John Edgar Wideman's Responses to History." Diss. Ohio U, 1999. *DAI* 60.4 (1999): 1132.

Gysin, Fritz. "'Do Not Fall Asleep in Your Enemy's Dream': John Edgar Wideman and the Predicaments of Prophecy." *Callaloo* 22.3 (1999): 623–28.

———. "John Edgar Wideman's 'Fever.'" *Callaloo* 22.3 (1999): 715–26.

Hennessy, Margot C. "Listening to the Secret Mother: Reading John Edgar Wideman's *Brothers and Keepers*." *American Women's Autobiography: Fea(s)ts of Memory*. Ed. Margo Culley. Madison: U Wisconsin P, 1992. 295–321.

Hoem, Sheri I. "Disabling Postmodernism: Wideman, Morrison and Prosthetic Critique." *Novel: A Forum on Fiction*. 35.2–3 (2002): 193–210.

———. "Recontextualizing Fathers: Wideman, Foucault, and African American Genealogy." *Textual Practice* 14.2 (2000): 235–51.

———. "'Shifting Spirits': Ancestral Constructs in the Postmodern Writing of John Edgar Wideman." *African American Review* 34.2 (2000): 249–62.

Howley, Colin. "'Ball and Chain': The Basketball Court and the Trope of the Prison Yard in Contemporary African American Narratives." *Aethlon: The Journal of Sport Literature* 21.1 (2003): 79–91.

Hume, Kathryn. "Black Urban Utopia in Wideman's Later Fiction." *Race and Class* 45.3 (2004): 19–34.

————. "'Dimensions' and John Edgar Wideman's Mental Cosmology." *Contemporary Literature* 45.3 (2004): 19–34.

Janifer, Raymond E. "The Black Nationalist Aesthetic and the Early Fiction of John Edgar Wideman." Diss. Ohio State U, 1996. *DAI* 58.2 (1997): 456.

————. "Looking Homewood: The Evolution of John Edgar Wideman's Folk Imagination." *Contemporary Black Men's Fiction and Drama*. Ed. and introd. Keith Clark. Urbana: U of Illinois P, 2001. 54–70.

Jimoh, A. Yemisi. "John Edgar Wideman: *Sent for You Yesterday*." *Spiritual, Blues, and Jazz People in African American Fiction*. Knoxville: U Tennessee P, 2002. 191–201.

Julien, Claude. "Introduction." *Callaloo* 22.3 (1999): 537–46.

————. "The Silent Man's Voice in 'The Statue of Liberty.'" *Callaloo* 22.3 (1999): 740–49.

Lee, James Kyung-Jin. "Multicultural Dreams, Racial Awakenings: The Anxieties of Racial Realignment in American Literary Works of the 1980s." Diss. UCLA, 2000. *DAI* 61.6 (2000): 2302.

————. "Where the Talented Tenth Meets the Model Minority: The Price of Privilege in Wideman's *Philadelphia Fire* and Lee's *Native Speaker*." *Novel: A Forum on Fiction* 35.2–3 (2002): 231–57.

Lucy, Robin. "John Edgar Wideman." *Contemporary African American Novelists: A Bio-Bibliographical Critical Sourcebook*. Ed. Emmanuel S. Nelson. Introd. Deborah G. Plant. Westport, CT: Greenwood, 1999. 482–90.

Lynch, Lisa. "The Race of Disease and the Disease of Racism in John Edgar Wideman." *American Literary History* 14.4 (2002): 776–804.

Mbalia, Doreatha Drummond. *John Edgar Wideman: Reclaiming the African Personality*. Selinsgrove, Pa.: Susquehanna UP, 1995.

Morace, Robert A. "The Facts in Black and White: Cheever's *Falconer*, Wideman's *Philadelphia Fire*." *Powerless Fictions? Ethics, Cultural Critique, and American Fiction in the Age of Postmodernism*. Ed. Ricardo Miguel-Alfonso. Amsterdam: Rodopi, 1996. 85–112.

Murray, Rolland Dante. "Beyond Macho: Literature, Masculinity, and Black Power." Diss. U Chicago, 2001. *DAI* 61.7 (Jan. 2001): 2718–19.

Muyumba, Walton M. "Trouble No More: Blues Philosophy and Twentieth-Century African-American Experience." Diss. Indiana U, 2001. *DAI* 63.1 (2001): 189.

Neumann, Christopher Jay. "Metahistorical Fiction: Writing History into Being." Diss. U North Carolina-Chapel Hill, 2002. *DAI* 63.3 (2002): 947.

Palleau-Papin, Francoise. "Of Balloons in John Wideman's Fiction." *Callaloo* 22.3 (1999): 645–55.

Pearsall, Susan. "'Narratives of Self' and the Abdication of Authority in Wideman's *Philadelphia Fire*." *MELUS* 26.2 (2001): 15–46.

Phelan, James. "Reading across Identity Borders: A Rhetorical Analysis of John Edgar Wideman's 'Doc's Story.'" *Reading Sites: Social Difference and Reader Response.* Ed. and introd. Patrocinio P. Schweickart. New York: MLA, 2004. 39–59.

Ramsey, Priscilla R. "John Edgar Wideman's First Fiction: Voice and Modernist Narrative." *College Language Association Journal* 41.1 (1997): 1–23.

Raynaud, Claudine. "Mask to Mask. 'The Real Joke': Surfiction/Autofiction, or the Tale of the Purloined Watermelon." *Callaloo* 22.3 (1999): 695–712.

Richard, Jean-Pierre. "From Slavers to Drunken Boats: A Thirty-Year Palimpsest in John Edgar Wideman's Fiction." *Callaloo* 22.3 (1999): 656–64.

———. "John Edgar Wideman: A Bibliography of Primary and Secondary Sources." *Callaloo* 22.3 (1999): 750–57.

———. "*Philadelphia Fire*, or the Shape of a City." *Callaloo* 22.3 (1999): 603–13.

Roark, Chris. "John Edgar Wideman." *African American Autobiographers: A Sourcebook.* Ed. Emmanuel S. Nelson. Westport, CT: Greenwood, 2002. 379–85.

Rodriguez, Denise Gema. "Space, Form, and Tradition: Recontextualizing the Contemporary Ethnic-American Novel." Diss. City U of New York, 2001. *DAI* 62.9 (Mar. 2002): 3049.

Rushdy, Ashraf H. A. "Fraternal Blues: John Edgar Wideman's Homewood Trilogy." *Contemporary Literature* 32.3 (1991): 312–45.

Samuels, Wilfred D. "John Edgar Wideman." *Dictionary of Literary Biography* (33): 271–78. Detroit: Gale, 1978.

Saunders, James Robert. "Exorcizing the Demons: John Edgar Wideman's Literary Response." *Twayne Companion to Contemporary Literature in English.* Eds. R. H. W. Dillard et al. New York: Thomson Gale, 2002. 477–86.

Schmidt, Klaus H. "Reading Black Postmodernism: John Edgar Wideman's *Reuben*." *Flip Sides: New Critical Essays in American Literature.* Ed. Klaus H. Schmidt. Frankfurt: Peter Lang, 1995. 81–102.

Trussler, Michael. "Literary Artifacts: Ekphrasis in the Short Fiction of Donald Barthleme, Salman Rushdie, and John Edgar Wideman." *Contemporary Literature* 41.2 (2000): 252–90.

Tucker, Linda Gail. "Lockstep and Dance: Containment and Resistance in African American Men's Lives and Representations of Them." Diss. U Alberta (Canada), 2001. *DAI* 63.6 (2001): 2286.

TuSmith, Bonnie. "'One More Time': John Edgar Wideman's *Sent for You Yesterday*." *All My Relatives: Community in Contemporary Ethnic American Literatures.* Ann Arbor: U Michigan P, 1993. 84–94.

———. "The 'Inscrutable Albino' in Contemporary Ethnic Literature." *Amerasia Journal* 19.3 (1993): 85–102.

Varsava, Jerry. "'Woven of Many Strands': Multiple Subjectivity in John Edgar Wideman's *Philadelphia Fire.*" *Contemporary Fiction* 41.4 (2000): 425–44.

Waligora-Davis, Nicole A. "The Ghetto: Illness and the Formation of the 'Suspect' in American Polity." *Forum for Modern Language Studies* 40.2 (2004): 182–203.

Weets, Tatiana. "The Negotiation of Remembrance in 'Across the Wide Missouri.'" *Callaloo* 22.3 (1999): 727–39.

Wilson, Matthew. "The Circles of History in John Edgar Wideman's *The Homewood Trilogy.*" *College Language Association Journal* 33.3 (1990): 239–59.

Contributors

HEATHER RUSSELL ANDRADE, Florida International University.

JACQUELINE BERBEN-MASI, University of Nice, Sophia Antipolis.

GERALD W. BERGEVIN, Northeastern University.

STACEY L. BERRY, University of Nebraska-Lincoln.

KEITH E. BYERMAN, Indiana State University.

STEPHEN CASMIER, St. Louis University.

JENNIFER D. DOUGLAS, University of Rochester.

TRACIE CHURCH GUZZIO, State University of New York–Plattsburgh.

KAREN F. JAHN, Assumption College.

CLAUDE FERNAND YVON JULIEN, Université de Tours, France.

LESLIE W. LEWIS, The College of Saint Rose.

MARK J. MADIGAN, Nazareth College of Rochester.

EUGENE PHILIP PAGE, California State University, San Bernardino.

DENISE RODRIGUEZ, The College of Mount Saint Vincent.

ASHRAF H. A. RUSHDY, Wesleyan University.

TYRONE R. SIMPSON II, Vassar College.

BONNIE TUSMITH, Northeastern University.

Index

black speech, 167. *See also* black English; vernacular

black subjectivity, 47–48, 51

black urban fiction. *See* urban fiction

blackness, 95, 99, 120, 162, 164, 216, 223, 225, 233

blood time, 61

blues, 57–58, 68n4, 131, 133–34, 136–40, 141n4, 141n14, 152, 186, 188, 236

blurring of reality, 251

body, xiv, 46, 84, 86–87, 94, 96–104. *See also* black body

borders, 50, 54, 244, 251

Braithwaite, Cecil (character). *See* Cecil

Brother: character in *A Glance Away,* 96, 98–100, 105n6; character in *Sent for You Yesterday,* 10, 26, 58, 132–34, 136–40, 246

Brothers and Keepers, xii–xiv, 3–14, 27n5, 28n9, 28n12, 35, 37, 45, 49, 52–54, 55n4, 55n6, 61, 67, 131, 179, 194, 228

bubble, soap, 246–49

C

Caliban, 44, 87, 150, 152–56, 158nn7–8, 166–67, 177, 184, 186

Carl (character), 26, 133–34, 140, 246–47

Catherine (character), 32, 39, 66–67

Cattle Killing, The, ix, xiv, 10, 50, 77, 82, 141n10, 175–89, 191–204, 205–20, 245, 251, 253–54

Cecil (character), 100–104

"change the joke and slip the yoke" (African American saying), 245, 256

Chichèn Itza, 34, 52, 62–63

Christianity, 73, 207–8

cinema, 192, 201, 250. *See also* film

circularity, ix, 20, 61–64, 67, 133, 139, 151, 183, 208, 210, 216

city, xv, 127–28, 135, 147, 150, 152, 154, 158n8, 162–64, 167, 169, 179, 182–83, 195, 222–23, 226–27; on fire, 145, 148

civil rights movement, 129, 132, 193

collective: consciousness, 134; history, 75, 248–49; identities, 124; journey, 75; loss, 50; memories, 195; organizing, 80; performance, 50; sadness, 72; suffering, 133; the, and the individual, 161–73, 244

Clinton, George, 193–94

colonialism, 152, 162, 170, 177

color: prejudice, 249, 254; skin, 63, 84, 215–16, 218n1, 225, 227, 245, 248, 254; struck, 256n7

Coltrane, John, 66

Columbus, Christopher, 22, 75

common ground, 13, 18, 46, 125n3, 194

community. *See* black community

creativity, xv, 60, 65, 67

creolization, 67, 78–80

criminal justice, viii, 155

critical realist writers, x

critical reception of Wideman, x–xii

Cudjoe (character), 146, 148–58, 162–71, 179, 184–87, 194–95, 197, 199–200

D

"Daddy Garbage," vii

"Damballah," 57, 247

Damballah, xi, 24, 63, 67n1, 68n3, 139, 141n10, 245

dancing, 62, 140

desire, failure of, 104

deterritorialization, 26

dialect, 129, 166–67

dialogism, 8, 14n6, 176, 179, 209, 217

Diaspora, Black, 60, 62, 67

dissolve, xv, 250–51

Doot (character), 27n5, 58, 133, 135, 137, 139–40

double-consciousness, xiv, 58, 67n2, 248

Douglass, Frederick, 45–46, 55nn5–6, 55n8

dream, 27, 34, 54, 75, 84, 118, 121, 150, 164, 180, 182, 185, 200, 202, 206–8, 217; daydream, 246, 248; dreamlike tone, 252

drunken boat, 247
DuBois, W. E. B., 67n2, 138

E

Ellison, Ralph, xiv, 57, 62, 67, 123–24,
   127–44, 158n8, 172n1
Eliot, T. S., xi, 23, 68nn4–5, 129
Esu-Elegbara, 52. *See also* Legba
essentialism, 46, 80, 124n3
existentialism, 79, 253
experimentation, 48, 52, 132
Eye (character), 200

F

fabulator, 186
faith, viii, 47, 74, 101, 137, 207, 210,
   217, 252–53
family, individual and, 3–15
Fanon, Frantz, 78–80, 82–84, 86, 116,
   125n9
father and son, 35, 154, 187
Fatheralong, 17–29, 35–38, 46–54, 120,
   125n3, 154, 157, 175–77, 187–88,
   188n1
Fever, xii, 67, 67n1
"Fever," 180
film, 251, 253–55. *See also* cinema
flanerie, 223, 226–27, 236, 253
flaneur, xv, 226–27
fluidity, 138
folk traditions, x, 131–32
fragmentation, 44, 52, 58, 132, 135–37,
   166, 222, 244
free association, 44
Freed or Freeda (character), 26, 32,
   38, 60, 62–64, 95, 135, 244,
   246–49
Freud, Sigmund, 72, 74
funk, 95–96, 163, 191–204

G

Gable, Clark, 23, 250
genres, blurring of, 9, 25, 27, 36, 54, 66,
   177–78, 180, 184
ghettoization, xv, 222, 225, 238
Giacometti, Alberto, 224, 228, 230–32,
   235, 238–39, 253–56, 257n12
"glance away, a" (phrase), 246–47, 255
Glance Away, A, 9, 26, 47, 93–105, 246, 255
Glissant, Edouard, 87
Great Migration, 135
Great Time (African concept), xiii, 21, 32,
   34, 37, 39, 45, 48–52, 54–55, 59, 61–63,
   67–68, 187, 253
grief, xiii, 22, 71, 73, 78, 81, 85–87, 97, 99,
   158n9, 200

H

Hall, Willie "Littleman" (character), 107–24
Harlem Globetrotters, 39, 64
healing, xiv, 8, 50, 84, 94, 128, 134, 156, 217,
   233, 236–37
Hiding Place, xi, 8, 40n4, 40n6, 135, 194
historical re-visioning, 177
historiographic metafiction, 141n10,
   178–79, 181. *See also* metafiction
history, public, xiv, 178–79
*Homewood Trilogy, The (Damballah, Hiding
   Place, Sent for You Yesterday)*, x–xi, 27,
   127, 131, 134, 194, 247
Hoop Roots, vii, xiii–xiv, 18–19, 25, 28nn8–9,
   31–41, 44, 51, 53–54, 57–70, 73, 243–44,
   246
Hurry Home, 28n8, 93–105, 108, 177, 247
hope, xi, 28n12, 35, 47, 51, 54, 74–75, 85,
   88, 95, 133, 148, 156–57, 185–86, 188,
   217, 234, 252, 255
humor, ethnic, 249
hybridity, 181

politics, 45, 53, 72, 78, 80, 88, 109, 116, 128–29; of perception, 191

polyphonic: narratives, 178; novel, 181, 184; quality, 179; space, 14n6; texts, 44

postmodernism, 44, 50, 58, 141n10, 211, 222, 238n1, 225 , 227

"Praise of Silence, In," 40n5, 185, 214

preacher (character), 181, 183–84, 200–202, 207–18, 219n4, 219n10, 251–53

prison. *See* imprisonment; incarceration

Promised Land, 19–22, 177, 187–88

prophecy, 182, 206–9, 218

Q

queer theory, xiii, 93–105

quilting, xiii, 44–55, 55n3, 61–62

R

race relations, 206–7, 210, 214, 248

racial healing, 84, 210

racial hierarchy, 77, 233

racism, x, xiv, 21, 39, 46–47, 61, 63, 65, 67, 72, 77–78, 81, 84, 129, 133, 140, 177, 180, 187, 210, 212, 214, 217–18, 231, 233, 237, 238n2

racist oedipalization, 233

rainbow, 21, 145, 216, 246–49

realism, 128–29, 168, 170, 184, 250; traumatic, 223, 236

reality: collective black experiential, 132

reconciliation, 134, 137, 176, 210, 212, 216, 218n4

redemptive quest, 187, 234

religion, 72, 207–8

renewal, personal and collective, 85

representation, 43–56, 223–24, 230, 232–33, 235, 237, 245–46; visual, 195, 219n5

Reuben, xii, 9, 10n10, 191–204

revolutionary potential, 45, 51, 53

rhythm, 59–62, 118, 139, 248

river, 45

Robby (brother), xiv, 7–13, 14n4, 14n7, 14n9, 18, 35, 46, 52, 57, 63, 65, 179, 249

runagate, 146

Rush, Benjamin, 180–82

S

salvation, 48, 101, 104, 152, 154, 158n6, 208

schizophrenia, 222

self-reflexivity, x, 6, 52

self-reliance, critique of, 122

senses, the, xiv, 192–94, 199, 201–2, 207

Sent for You Yesterday, xi, xiv, 10, 14n10, 26, 27n5, 58, 67n1, 127–44, 194, 245–46

sexual ambiguity, 103

sexuality, viii, xii, xiii, 66, 79, 93–105

Shakespeare, 22, 153, 169–71, 186

shapechanging, 65

shapeshifting, xv, 59, 153, 243, 245, 249, 256

sight, 192; and photography, 221–39; and smell, 191–204; and speech, 205–20; and tricksterism, 243–58. *See also* visual perception; photograph(y).

signifier, 222, 224

signifying, 25, 55, 62, 128, 218, 248, 256n6

silence, 13, 38–39, 40n5, 59, 86, 133–34, 136, 139, 154–55, 164, 176, 185, 214, 216

slave shuttle, 247

slave-master, 81

slavery, xiii, 45, 53, 60, 72–73, 77, 86–87, 120, 125n4, 134, 138, 177, 179, 245, 249–50

sociopolitical agency, 46

sound, erotics of, 66

specularity, 192–94

spirit, 59, 61–62, 78, 87, 150, 171, 183, 252–55; Nigerian, xiii, 54 sport, xiii, 31, 34, 67, 151

storytelling, xi, xiv, 25, 48, 50–51, 53, 62, 64, 139, 165, 195, 206, 210, 212, 214–15, 217–18, 219n6, 219n8, 247, 252–53; back and forth, 247

Student Nonviolent Coordinating Committee (SNCC), 113, 115, 125n6

Surrealism, 224, 228, 232, 235, 253

survival, viii, xiii, 5, 7, 9, 12, 34, 47–48, 51–52, 78, 134, 146, 194, 253

synesthetic sense, 192–94, 199, 201

T

tactile sense, x

tarbaby, 28n13, 256

Tate, Sharon, 121

terminal creeds, 245

Till, Emmett, 187, 224, 234–35, 237, 238n3

tourist, 72–73, 76–77, 165

transcendence, 25, 44, 62, 99–100, 139

trauma, viii, ix, 9, 22, 77, 85–87, 221–39; psychic, viii, 228

trickster discourse, 245

tricksterism, xv, 53, 65, 243–58

Two Cities, xv, 28n8, 28n13, 57, 67n1, 74, 135, 221–39, 245–46, 253

U

unreliable narration, xiv, 244, 252

urban fiction, xv, 127–28

urban walker, 227

V

vernacular, ix, 130–32, 134, 137, 141n4, 218. *See also* black English; black speech

violence, x, xi, xv, 46, 57, 64, 76, 86, 94, 96, 101, 107–26, 168, 170, 185, 213–14, 224–25, 233–34, 236–37, 252, 256; collective, 122; intraracial, 114–15, 118, 125n9

visual perception, x, xiv–xv, 46, 72, 83. *See also* sight; and photography

voice, narrative, 7, 45, 166

W

Wally (character), 196–97

watermelon, 63, 249

web, 5, 8–12, 19

Western discourse, 55, 166, 184

white supremacy, 81, 119, 233

whiteness, 83–84, 97, 120, 133, 161, 233

Wilkes, Albert (character), 58, 137, 139–40

witness, viii, xii, 12, 53, 82, 85, 210, 214–15, 217–18, 221–39

words. *See* inadequacy of words

World Trade Center, 191

X

Xhosa cattle killing, 181–83, 202, 206–8

Y

yellow fever epidemic, 82, 177, 180–83, 186, 200

Yoruba, 32, 60, 65

Z

zoo, 221–23

zoopraxiscope, 195

Zugunruhe, 225